Children's Well-Being: Indicators and Research

Volume 27

Series Editor

This series focuses on measurements and indicators of children's well-being and their usage, within multiple domains and in diverse cultures. It presents measures and data resources, analysis of data, exploration of theoretical issues, and information about the status of children, as well as the implementation of this information in policy and practice. By doing so it explores how child indicators can be used to improve the development and the well-being of children.

The series provides an international and applied perspective by bringing in a variety of analytical models, varied methodologies, and discussions on wide-ranging social policy regimes. This is a companion to the journal *Child Indicators Research* and is an exclusive channel for book publication in the field of measures and indicators of children's lives. The diverse and international advisory board of experts in the field ensures a thorough review of proposals and manuscripts in this series.

The series accepts high-quality, high-impact, and academically sound scientific monographs and contributed volumes. Volumes that add novel insights into the child indicators field are especially encouraged.

Dagmar Kutsar • Mai Beilmann • Oliver Nahkur
Editors

Child Vulnerability and Vulnerable Subjectivity

Interdisciplinary and Comparative Perspectives

Springer

Editors
Dagmar Kutsar
Institute of Social Studies
University of Tartu
Tartu, Estonia

Mai Beilmann
Institute of Social Studies
University of Tartu
Tartu, Estonia

Oliver Nahkur
Institution of Social Studies
University of Tartu
Tartu, Estonia

ISSN 1879-5196 ISSN 1879-520X (electronic)
Children's Well-Being: Indicators and Research
ISBN 978-3-031-61332-6 ISBN 978-3-031-61333-3 (eBook)
https://doi.org/10.1007/978-3-031-61333-3

Estonian Research Council PRG700

This Springer imprint is published by the registered company Springer Nature Switzerland AG
The registered company address is: Gewerbestrasse 11, 6330 Cham, Switzerland

Preface

This book has been prepared within the framework of the project "Vulnerability in Childhood and Vulnerable Subjectivity: Interdisciplinary Comparative Perspective", funded by the Estonian Research Council (Grant No. PRG700 for 2020–2023), but its roots go back to a previous grant by the Estonian Research Council (PUT1513 for 2017–2019) and the close cooperation with colleagues from the International Society for Child Indicators (ISCI) and the Children's Rights Academic Network (CREAN), to whom we are all grateful. The Children's Worlds International Study and its supplement, documenting children's subjective well-being during the COVID-19 pandemic, and the qualitative study, Children's Understanding of Well-Being, have been a collaborative effort to provide new theoretical and methodological explorations of children's lifeworlds and evidence for improving their lives. We are grateful to the Jacobs Foundation for its support of the international collaboration on the Children's Worlds data collection. We owe thanks to our international colleague from the ISCI network, Professor Graciela Tonon (Research Centre in Social Sciences, Universidad de Palermo, Argentina), for her contribution to the concluding chapter of this book.

From this book readers can find a conceptual model for looking at childhood vulnerability and how it is reflected in different life domains of children, such as family, school, the legal system, and healthcare. There is one domain—the children's vulnerability in the digital world—that our research had not covered, and we invited colleagues from the EU Kids Online network (Veronika Kalmus, Signe Opermann, Susana Batista, Natalie Tercova, and Marie Jaron Bedrosova) to fill this gap. The preparation of their chapter received funding from the European Union's Horizon 2020 Research & Innovation programme under Grant Agreement No. 870612. Veronika Kalmus' work was supported by a grant from the Estonian Research Council (PRG1761). Natalie Tercova's and Marie Jaron Bedrosova's work has received funding from the Czech Science Foundation, project No. 19-27828X. We would like to thank you all for your excellent contribution. We would also like to express our admiration for the innovative ideas presented by Triin Noorkõiv and Laura Palling—a small team from Clanbeat—and thank you for your contribution to this book. Our thanks also go to Anna Markina and Beata Žarkovski (School of Law, University of Tartu, Estonia) for their expertise and co-authoring efforts.

We are grateful to the parents and other responsible adults who allowed the researchers to have a glimpse inside the lives of the children. However, our most heartfelt thanks go to all the children who participated in the research and shared their perspectives, joys, and worries, as well as lived experiences. Without their contribution, our worldview and academic understanding would be limited, and this book would never have been written.

We hope that this book will find readers who are intrigued by the research and issues we discuss and who share our commitment to finding ways to improve children's lives.

Tartu, Estonia Dagmar Kutsar
Tartu, Estonia Judit Strömpl
Tartu, Estonia Kadri Soo
Tartu, Estonia Katre Luhamaa
Tartu, Estonia Kristi Paron
Tartu, Estonia Mai Beilmann
Tartu, Estonia Oliver Nahkur

Contents

List of Figures

List of Tables

Chapter 1
Introduction

Dagmar Kutsar, Mai Beilmann, and Oliver Nahkur

"Human vulnerability arises from our embodiment which carries with it the immanent or ever-present possibility of harm, injury or misfortune" (Fineman, 2010, p. 267). Vulnerability is a human condition as it is universal and relational, referring to relationships between individuals and between individuals and society (Fineman, 2010; Herring, 2016). *Vulnerable* thus means "able to be damaged" (Virokannas et al., 2018) and it can be seated not only inside the individual (related with low self-efficacy), personified (attached to a particular person or group) but also relational; that is, determined and cumulated in relationships between individuals in diverse life situations and environments. In sum, all people can be vulnerable in some situations (Nussbaum, 2004)—while some people and groups accumulate more vulnerabilities than others do. Children are by nature vulnerable, determined by their position among generations in society as minors with a dependent status. They stay out of the decision-making over and distribution of social wealth as adults cover their needs (e.g., Qvortrup, 1994; Wintersberger, 1994; Finkelhor, 2008). Moreover, vulnerability grows out of subjectivities (perceptions, cognitions, opinions about lived experiences) and converge in inter-subjectivity as "…the variety of relations between perspectives that can belong to individuals, groups, or traditions and discourses, and they can manifest as both implicit (or taken for granted) and explicit (or reflected upon)" (Gillespie & Cornish, 2010, p. 19). Inter-subjectivity is a reservoir of emerging, mutually generated vulnerability; for example, in the child's relationship with child protection workers, lawyers and medical professionals, when power is imbalanced, the child is disempowered, or the professionals are incompetent or unethical. The latter often happens when the child's agency is disregarded, their rights are not trusted or are misinterpreted or abused.

D. Kutsar (✉) · M. Beilmann · O. Nahkur
Institute of Social Studies, University of Tartu, Tartu, Estonia
e-mail: dagmar.kutsar@ut.ee; mai.beilmann@ut.ee; oliver.nahkur@ut.ee

D. Kutsar et al. (eds.), *Child Vulnerability and Vulnerable Subjectivity*, Children's Well-Being: Indicators and Research 27,
https://doi.org/10.1007/978-3-031-61333-3_1

Research with children (e.g., Kutsar et al., 2019; Nahkur & Kutsar, 2019) refers to the importance of the child's close environment; for example, the child's basic need to be cared for (have good relationships in the family and with friends) and to feel safe both at home and school as crucial preconditions to enjoy a good childhood. This research evidence goes in line with several authors confirming the importance of following children's rights in their close environments and decreasing their vulnerabilities (e.g., Casas et al., 2013; Kosher & Ben-Arieh, 2016; Kosher et al., 2014; Lansdown, 2005; Navarro et al., 2015; Strózik et al., 2016). However, awareness of children's rights among adults across countries is still low and often misinterpreted, especially from the perspective of power vs. rights, responsibilities, and generational order (e.g., Desmet, et al., 2015; Duncan, 2019).

Today's children live their "ordinary lives in extraordinary times" (Millei et al., 2022), characterised by increasing family complexity, environmental anxieties, rapid development of artificial intelligence and information technologies, the Covid-19 pandemic, outbreaks of war in various places in the world and the refugee crisis. During extraordinary times, the accumulation of vulnerabilities endangers children's mental health and subjective well-being. At the same time, there are expectations placed on the children—today's children should have knowledge and skills to navigate the uncertainties that the rapidly changing environments around them offer, and to build a better future for all by acquiring high resilience and employability potential (OECD, 2018). Agency implies a sense of responsibility to participate in the world and, in so doing, to influence people, events and circumstances for the better. Child agency should contain self-confidence, purposefulness, self-regulation, and respect for the well-being of others—existential intelligence (term from Hildebrandt, 2009). Although the OECD (2018) stresses the importance of child agency, unfortunately it drops the need to monitor children's rights in everyday practices. Research with children has shown that both child agency and well-being are relational, children are agentic partners in the co-creation of well-being, and among other factors, the acceptance of children's rights by adults and other children is a precondition for this (Fattore & Mason, 2017). Exercising agency depends on the functioning of co-agency—the interactive, mutually supportive relationships that help a child to take responsibility and participate in the world, and progress towards valued goals (OECD, 2018, p. 4). Children's well-being is created and preserved in interactions between peers and adults as agentic parties in different relational environments and related structures (e.g., diverse family structures; (in)flexible social support systems; (dys)functional policies).

Child vulnerability and its foundations in children's perceptions and interpretations of their lived lives as expressed in their opinions need special attention. The authors of the present book aim to enhance dialogue between childhood and children's rights studies. The role of children's agency and autonomy, including their right to participate in decision-making processes related to their own life, has a special emphasis in this book. Among others, the book discusses ethical considerations and challenges connected to the participation of vulnerable children by researching sensitive topics. Although the law requires their involvement, studies about the social practices of children's participation in decision-making are scarce.

This book explores how vulnerability in childhood develops within subjects in relationships with other people (other children, parents, and specialists, such as teachers, social workers, and judges), how it is created through welfare, health care, education, and justice systems, and last not least, empowered by multiple crises, such as the Covid-19 pandemic and the Russian war in Ukraine.

This book addresses children's vulnerability theoretically, methodologically, and empirically, including from the perspective of cross-country comparisons. Besides the comparative overview, it also discusses domain-based child vulnerability in the case of Estonia. The book is research-driven but also practice and policy oriented, aimed to raise awareness of child vulnerabilities and increase children's well-being. Among others, it describes the results of participatory action research with extremely vulnerable children with traumatic pasts in Estonian substitute care, and Ukrainian children with refugee status in Estonia. The book supplies an overview of how to increase child well-being by decreasing vulnerabilities and building resilience. It combines approaches from different disciplines, such as Psychology, Sociology, Law, Educational Science, Social Work and Media Studies.

Part I provides theoretical, ethical, and methodological insights into studying child vulnerability. Oliver Nahkur proposes a conceptual framework for understanding child vulnerability as the risk of harm to the child's well-being. He makes a step forward from pre-existing risk-centric conceptualisations and conceptualisations linking child vulnerability and resilience, as in his proposed framework these are dealt with as a continuum. This conceptual framework has been empirically tested in the process of the development of a new child vulnerability measure, presented in the next section of this book also by Nahkur. Mai Beilmann and Judit Strömpl address the ethical and methodological considerations of involving children in social research, with special attention to the participation of children in vulnerable life situations. They discuss whether ethical committees scrupulously following formal requirements; that is, demanding active parental consent to children's participation in research, regardless of the child's age and will, to protect children from potential harm, may indeed make it impossible to exercise the children's right to express their views on critical issues affecting their lives. However, many ethical issues can be resolved by adopting the child-friendly methodology as demonstrated in this book.

In Part II, child vulnerability from different angles is explored. This section starts with a chapter authored by Oliver Nahkur. He proceeds from the conceptual model created in the beginning of the book and introduces a new composite indicator ICSVRI, the International Child Subjective Vulnerability-Resilience Index. The ISCVRI aims to be an international cross-country comparable measure of child subjective vulnerability. Next in this section, Dagmar Kutsar focuses on the closest environment in children's lives—the family—and explores children's opinions concerning different family arrangements. By drawing data from a variety of small-scale quantitative and qualitative studies conducted with children in Estonia, she concludes that acknowledging children's rights, developing effective conflict resolution and parenting skills are the first steps towards better family life for children. Kadri Soo focuses on the next important environment for children—school—and explores the sources of vulnerability in the school environment. The topic is intriguing because children in Estonia collect high scores in the PISA test while their satisfaction with school is low compared to many other countries. Based on data from the National School Satisfaction Survey, she demonstrates that the qualities of relationships, such as support, caring, respect and trust, in student-student and particularly in student-teacher relationships reduce or prevent children's vulnerability and contribute to enjoying well-being in the learning environment. Kristi Paron develops an understanding of the child-patient's right to autonomy and explores how children's autonomy emerges as an effect of reciprocal actions reiterated by social actors involved in a healthcare relationship. She also addresses one of the most complicated aspects of child autonomy—assessing the child's maturity to give due weight to the child's view. This is done by way of the example of Estonian health professionals' perceptions about how they involve child-patients in decision-making. Veronika Kalmus, Susana Batista, Signe Opermann, Natalie Tercova and Marie Jaron Bedrosova propose an operational definition of online vulnerability and explore its relationships with subjective vulnerability. Moreover, they demonstrate the role of digital skills in reducing the unintentional experience of online risks and harms in the case of adolescents and conclude that researching children's subjective and online vulnerabilities is a methodological challenge, yet a much-needed endeavour to provide new cross-disciplinary knowledge in the field. The next angle of child vulnerability is the legal system, focused on by Katre Luhamaa, Anna Markina, and Kristi Paron in their chapter. The authors explore child agency and the exercise of rights within the legal system and examine whether the system is sufficiently attuned to children's needs. They use Estonian legal proceedings as a case study to provide empirical insights into how the legal processes address the child's position as a vulnerable yet agentic, and to an extent, autonomous actor. Judit Strömpl concludes this section by broadening the understanding of trauma as a major source of vulnerability and develops ideas for developing trauma awareness as a general principle for preventing traumatising situations for children.

Part III of this book is devoted to child vulnerability in times of crisis, more specifically the health crisis related to the Covid-19 pandemic and the Russian war in Ukraine. It starts with a chapter co-authored by Kadri Soo and Oliver Nahkur. Using data from "Children Worlds" (ISCWeB) and enriching these with evidence from qualitative studies conducted among children in Estonia; the focus is on the aspects related to home and school and children's emotional state during the Covid-19 pandemic. The authors demonstrate the differential effects of the pandemic on children, including both the rise and decline in overall subjective well-being, depending on individual, relational and situational factors that mitigate or exacerbate their vulnerability. The authors also highlight how the situation of the pandemic adversely affected the emotional state of many children, increasing the risk of mental health problems. Yuliia Kravchenko and Judit Strömpl address the vulnerability of Ukrainian refugee children in the Estonian education system during the Russian war in Ukraine. They discuss the experiences of Ukrainian refugee schoolchildren in Estonian basic schools and their Estonian peers in adapting to the new situation, and bring the children's voices and suggestions to the reader. They indicate the need to develop a trauma sensitive school where the teachers and other staff members are aware of signs of traumatic experiences and can deal with them.

Part IV demonstrates ways of reducing vulnerability and building resilience in children. Judit Strömpl begins this section by introducing Life Story Work as a new method to reduce child vulnerability in Estonian substitute care. With the help of participatory action research, she reveals helpful aspects of this method in supporting the development of the child's positive identity. In the next chapter, Laura Palling and Triin Noorkõiv introduce a children's mental well-being assessment experiment in Estonia, which aims to create prompt and direct value for the children—promoting their agency and building their resilience. It enables children to become more aware of their mental well-being and the steps they themselves could take to strengthen it, and to provide input for the relevant decisions of stakeholders: schools, local governments, the state, parents, and mental well-being service providers. Graciela H. Tonon concludes the book with a theoretical reflection on the need for and the importance of generating public policies to overcome the vulnerability of children.

Acknowledgement Work on this chapter was supported by a grant from the Estonian Research Council (PRG700).

References

Casas, F., Bello, A., Gonzalez, M., & Aligue, M. (2013). Children's subjective Well-being measured using a composite index: What impacts Spanish first-year secondary education students' subjective well-being? *Child Indicators Research, 6*(3), 433–460.

Desmet, E., Lembrechts, S., Reynaert, D., & Vandenhole, W. (2015). Conclusions: Towards a field of critical children's rights studies. In W. Vandenhole, E. Desmet, D. Reynaert, & S. Lembrechts (Eds.), *Routledge international handbook of children's rights studies* (pp. 412–429). Routledge.

Duncan, M. (2019). *Participation in child protection. Theorizing children's perspectives*. Palgrave Macmillan.

Fattore, T., & Mason, J. (2017). The significance of the social for child well-being. *Children & Society, 31*, 276–289. https://doi.org/10.1111/chso.12205

Fineman, M. A. (2010). The vulnerable subject and the responsive state. *Emory Law Journal, 60*(2), 251–275.

Finkelhor, D. (2008). *Childhood victimization*. Violence, crime and abuse in the living of young people.

Gillespie, A., & Cornish, F. (2010). Intersubjectivity: Towards a dialogical analysis. *Journal for the Theory of Social Behaviour, 40*(1), 19–46.

Herring, J. (2016). *Vulnerable adults and the law*. Oxford University Press.

Hildebrandt, S. (2009). Multiple intelligences in the knowledge-based society. In C. Clouder, B. Heys, & M. Matthes (Eds.), *Improving the quality of childhood in the European Union. Current perspectives* (pp. 142–151). Alliance for Childhood European Network Foundation.

Kosher, H., & Ben-Arieh, A. (2016). What children think about their rights and their well-being: A crossnational comparison. *American Journal of Orthopsychiatry, 87*, 256–273. https://doi.org/10.1037/ort0000222

Kosher, H., Jiang, X., Ben-Arieh, A., & Huebner, E. S. (2014). Advances in children's rights and children's wellbeing measurement: Implications for school psychologists. *School Psychology Quarterly, 29*(1), 7–20. https://doi.org/10.1037/spq0000051

Kutsar, D., Soo, K., Strózik, T., Strózik, D., Grigora, B., & Bălătescu, S. (2019). Does the realisation of children's rights determine a good life in eight-year-olds' perspectives? A comparison of eight European countries. *Child Indicators Research, 12*(1), 161–183. https://doi.org/10.1007/s12187-017-9499-y

Lansdown, G. (2005). *The evolving capacities of the child.* Innocenti Insight. UNICEF Innocenti Research Centre.

Millei, Z., Silova, I., & Gannon, S. (2022). Thinking through memories of childhood in (post) socialist spaces: Ordinary lives in extraordinary times. *Children's Geographies, 20*(3), 324–337. https://doi.org/10.1080/14733285.2019.1648759

Nahkur, O., & Kutsar, D. (2019). Social ecological measures of interpersonal destructiveness impacting child subjective mental well-being: Perceptions of 12-year-old children in 14 countries. *Child Indicators Research, 12*(1), 353–378. https://doi.org/10.1007/s12187-018-9542-7

Navarro, D., Montserrat, C., Malo, S., González, M., Casas, F., & Crous, G. (2015). Subjective well-being: What do adolescents say? *Child & Family Social Work, 22*(1), 175–184. https://doi.org/10.1111/cfs.12215

Nussbaum, M. (2004). *Hiding from humanity: Disgust, shame and the law.* Princeton University Press.

OECD. (2018). *The future of education and skills 2030. Education 2030. The future we want.* Available online: http://www.oecd.org/education/2030/E2030%20Position%20Paper%20.pdf

Qvortrup, J. (1994). Childhood matters: An introduction. In J. Qvortrup, M. Bardy, G. Sgritta, & H. Wintersberger (Eds.), *Childhood matters. Social theory, practice and politics* (pp. 1–23). Avebury.

Strózik, D., Strózik, T., & Szwarc, K. (2016). The subjective well-being of school children. The first findings from the Children's Worlds study in Poland. *Child Indicators Research, 9*(1), 39–55. https://doi.org/10.1007/s12187-015-9312-8

Virokannas, E., Liuski, S., & Kuronen, M. (2018). The contested concept of vulnerability—A literature review. *European Journal of Social Work, 23*, 327–339. https://doi.org/10.1080/13691457.2018.1508001

Wintersberger, H. (1994). Costs and benefits – The economics of childhood. In J. Qvortrup, M. Bardy, G. Sgritta, & H. Wintersberger (Eds.), *Childhood matters. Social theory, practice, and politics* (pp. 1–23).

Dagmar Kutsar is an Associate Professor of Social Policy at the University of Tartu, Estonia. Her research interests are family, childhood, and welfare research and policies. She is a former board member of the International Society for Child Indicators (ISCI) and a principal researcher for the International Survey of Children's Worlds. She is also a board member of the Children's Rights Academic Network (CREAN) and the International Commission on Couple and Family Relations (ICCFR). She has partnered in several international research projects (e.g., EU 6FP PROFIT, IPROSEC, NoE EQUALSOC and EU FP7 FLOWS). She has been a member of the Standing Committee of Social Sciences of the European Science Foundation, the Executive Committee and Chair of the National Associations Council of the European Sociological Association, and an expert for the EU FP7 Youth Social Inclusion Cluster at the European Commission. She was a member of the Advisory Group for the Widening Programme at the EU Horizon 2020 and an Advisory Group member for the UNICEF Report Card Nr 16.

Mai Beilmann is an Associate Professor of Empirical Sociology at the Institute of Social Studies, University of Tartu, Estonia, and a former youth worker. Her research focuses mainly on children and youth studies, particularly child/adolescent vulnerability in the education system, NEET youth and youth work, youth civic and political participation, values, and social capital. After working for seven years for the European Social Survey, she joined the Estonian team of the International Survey of Children's Well-Being (ISCWeB) in 2019. She is a member of the Estonian Young Academy of Sciences and since 2018, she has served as the president of the Estonian Association of Sociologists.

Oliver Nahkur is a research fellow of Research of Social Wellbeing at the University of Tartu, Institute of Social Studies, Estonia. He is a member of the International Society for Child Indicators (ISCI) and the Estonian team of the International Survey of Children's Well-Being (ISCWeB); secretary-treasurer of the International Sociological Association, Research Committee No 55 – Social Indicators. He actively contributes to the development of child well-being data in Estonia. His research interests include child well-being and vulnerability research and social indicators research, including from a cross-national comparative studies perspective. In one of his latest research publications, he studied the change in children's subjective relational social cohesion with family and friends during the Covid-19 pandemic in 18 countries across the globe.

Part I
Theoretical and Ethical Insights into Studying Child Vulnerability

Chapter 2
Conceptual Framework for Understanding Child Vulnerability

Oliver Nahkur

2.1 Introduction

Vulnerability is universal (Fineman, 2010; Herring, 2016) but also particularly relevant for certain population groups. Children have been associated with vulnerability for centuries (Brown et al., 2017). Although all children are vulnerable, some are more vulnerable than others. For the latter, the term *children at risk* (Andresen, 2014) is also used.

It is important to reduce risk in the lives of children. By adopting the United Nation's Convention on the Rights of the Child, almost all countries in the world have taken responsibility to decrease vulnerability among their children. However, what do we mean by child vulnerability? In conceptualisations of vulnerability used in research, practice and policy, the focus has long been solely on risks and their reduction. According to Newman and Blackburn (2002), we have previously been pre-occupied with risk and its avoidance, to the extent that it has reduced the opportunities for children to intentionally take risks and learn important competencies. Moreover, as vulnerability implies weakness, paying attention to weaknesses rather than strengths predisposes children's dependency and passivity and erodes their autonomy (Virokannas et al., 2020). Children should not be seen as an *object of concern* (Daniel, 2010), but as active agents capable of preventing and managing risks in their lives themselves. Focusing only on minimising danger inhibits the promotion of children's well-being (Daniel, 2010). All in all, there is a need for conceptualisations of vulnerability (Virokannas et al., 2020) that simultaneously focus on weaknesses and strengths.

O. Nahkur (✉)
Institute of Social Studies, University of Tartu, Tartu, Estonia
e-mail: oliver.nahkur@ut.ee

D. Kutsar et al. (eds.), *Child Vulnerability and Vulnerable Subjectivity*, Children's Well-Being: Indicators and Research 27,
https://doi.org/10.1007/978-3-031-61333-3_2

There are some positive developments in research, practice, and policy in that regard. In research in the 1980s, emphasis shifted from risks to the concept of resilience (Howard et al., 1999). Resilience refers to exposure to risk or adversity and the manifestation of successful adaptation or better than expected outcomes in the face of that risk or adversity. With the development of studies of resilience in children and families, a shift from deficit models toward more positive and inclusive models that focus on strengths has occurred also in multiple domains of practice, including psychology, psychiatry, paediatrics, nursing, school counselling, family therapy, social work, and interdisciplinary prevention (Masten, 2021). The OECD (2019) has recently introduced a framework applying the concept of building resilience to policy design to overcome child vulnerability. Building resilience requires reducing the number of risks and increasing the number of factors contributing to resilience in a child's world (OECD, 2019).

In line with these developments, the aim of this chapter is to introduce a conceptual framework for understanding child vulnerability as the risk of harm to a child's well-being in relation to his/her resilience. It stems from the ecological model of child development by Bronfenbrenner (1979), the social-ecological model of resilience by Ungar et al. (2013) and previous multidisciplinary knowledge on the most common vulnerability and resilience factors. Although some scholars (e.g., Sugland et al., 1993; Hall et al., 2022) have proposed conceptualisations linking child vulnerability and resilience, this framework goes further, as they are considered a continuum. This conceptual framework has been empirically tested in the process of the development of a new child vulnerability measure presented in Chap. 4 and can potentially contribute to the understanding of the remaining chapters.

First, child vulnerability and resilience as concepts are introduced. Second, the most common factors contributing to child vulnerability and/or resilience are introduced, and third, an overall conceptual framework for understanding child vulnerability is presented.

2.2 Child Vulnerability and Resilience as Concepts

2.2.1 Child Vulnerability

Although the concept of *child vulnerability* is frequently referred to in children's rights literature and even incorporated as a key concept in child developmental studies, it is not well defined (Brown, 2011; Brown et al., 2017; Jopling & Vincent, 2016; Schweiger, 2019). For example, according to Arora et al. (2015), child vulnerability implies those children who are more exposed to risks than their peers. According to Schweiger (2019), vulnerability can be considered the channel for harm as risks can translate into harming the well-being of the child. Therefore, vulnerability is not in itself necessarily harmful, and it is about whether risks translate into harm to the child's well-being. Child vulnerability is a probabilistic concept; for example, "one child is more vulnerable than others" means that his/her well-being is more likely to be harmed. In this chapter, child vulnerability refers to the high(er) risk of harm to a child's well-being—how children are doing in their lives (Soffia & Turner, 2021), including their subjective feelings and experiences as well as their living conditions (Ben-Arieh et al., 2014)—and factors contributing to this are called vulnerability factors or risks.

Types of Child Vulnerability

Child vulnerability can be objective or subjective. Objective child vulnerability is primarily related to the child's living conditions; for example, can a child eat dinner at home regularly or is (s)he going to school with a black eye several times a year. In addition to objective vulnerability circumstances, child vulnerability depends on how the child perceives the risks (subjective vulnerability; see also Chap. 4). Moreover, whether risks translate into harming their well-being depends more on a child's perceptions about the risks than the objective circumstances. For example, living in a materially deprived home (objective vulnerability) may not translate into harm if the child does not perceive it as such.

Vulnerability can be distinguished based on the source of vulnerability. Vulnerability can have internal and external sources (Andresen, 2014; Giesinger, 2019; OECD, 2019; Rogers et al., 2012; Schweiger, 2019), or in other words vulnerability involves risks with an internal and external side (Chambers, 1989) in children's physical and digital lives. Vulnerability related to internal risks can be called *inherent vulnerability* (Schweiger, 2019), but in this chapter it is called *individual vulnerability*. Examples of child individual vulnerability (or *internal risks*) are the lack of certain cognitive, physical and emotional abilities (Schweiger, 2019).

Vulnerability related to external risks is referred to in this chapter as *environmental vulnerability* (or situational vulnerability according to Schweiger, 2019). For example, environmental vulnerability may arise from children's relationships, physical living conditions, the security situation in the country etc. However, environmental vulnerability should be further classified, as some environmental risks are more important for child vulnerability than others. According to Bronfenbrenner's (1979) ecological model of child development, a child, with all his or her personal characteristics, interacts first and foremost with the family, but also with friends and school. These direct interactions compose the child's *microsystem*, and this is the level with the strongest direct influence on children. Therefore, risks related to family, friends and school can be classified as *direct environmental vulnerability*. Examples of direct environmental vulnerability include parental domestic violence or abuse, mental health problems and drug and alcohol misuse [also known as the Toxic Trio by Brandon (2009, p. 1109), which is known to present a very high risk to children], and low parenting skills. In addition, risks related to the child's *mesosystem*, interactions between the different structures within the microsystem; for example, between parents and school, are related to direct environmental vulnerability. The wider community; for example, parents' social networks, the conditions in the local community, and access to and quality of services are elements of the *exosystem*, which primarily affects the child indirectly by influencing the different structures within the microsystem. The *macrosystem* refers to the wider societal context of cultural norms and values, policies, economic conditions and global developments. Therefore, risks related to the local area or community, the wider society and global developments can be classified as *indirect environmental vulnerability*. Examples of indirect environmental vulnerability for children are poor employment opportunities, the Covid-19 pandemic (see Chap. 11), and the Russian invasion of Ukrainian territories (see Chap. 12).

A sub-type of environmental vulnerability is *structural vulnerability*, as structural processes and institutions can be sources of vulnerability (Virokannas et al., 2020). For example, family, and education, healthcare, justice and welfare systems, can be structural sources of child vulnerability.

2.2.2 Child Resilience

Closely linked with the idea of child agency, the vulnerable child can simultaneously be a strong child (Andresen, 2014), as children cope with vulnerability in many different ways and with very different outcomes. For example, growing up in poverty is not necessarily harmful for all children as child poverty is further mediated by several other factors, like strong social networks, well established social services, or innate psychological resilience factors as vulnerability diminishers. Consequently, some children act more adaptively than expected, whereas others with comparable risks suffer severe delays and maladjustment (Masten & Garmezy, 1985; Rutter, 1987). At first, this phenomenon was described as *invulnerability*, but eventually leading scholars settled on the term *resilience* (Masten, 2018). In this chapter, child resilience refers to the low(er) risk of harm to a child's well-being, and factors contributing to this are called resilience factors or resources.

Types of Child Resilience

Resilience can be distinguished based on the source of resilience. According to the social-ecological model of resilience by Ungar et al. (2013) and Bronfenbrenner's (1979) ecological model of child development, it is possible to distinguish individual, direct and indirect environmental resilience. One example of child individual resilience is having good mental health, direct environmental resilience is the existence of at least one family member the child can talk when necessary, and indirect environmental resilience is living in a safe neighbourhood.

2.3 What Makes a Child Vulnerable or Resilient? Overview of Common Risks and Resources

There are factors more frequently associated with child vulnerability and resilience. To get a general overview of these most common (but not all possible) factors, a literature search was conducted in two waves in September 2020 and April 2021.

More specifically, the focus was on child (1) vulnerability or (2) resilience or (3) vulnerability and resilience factors commonly reported in publications offering an overview of different factors contributing to child vulnerability and/or resilience as a central and broad concept. Therefore, the following papers were excluded: review publications providing information about problem-specific (e.g., child maltreatment, drug abuse) vulnerability/resilience factors; original empirical articles exploring the impact of specific factors on problem-specific child vulnerability/resilience (e.g., family related factors to child maltreatment); empirical articles exploring the impact of factors on child vulnerability/resilience based on specific samples (children of alcohol abusers, depressed parents etc.); and papers in languages other than English. Overall, 25 papers (11 from Google Scholar, 5 from Google search as grey literature, 0 from Scopus and 9 by screening the reference lists of selected papers) were selected and these are marked with an asterisk in the reference list. If there were newer versions of selected publications in April 2023, the latest version was used.

Factors presented in the 25 papers selected were classified as individual (see Tables 2.1) and direct (Table 2.2) or indirect (Table 2.3) environmental vulnerability and/or resilience factors. Direct environments are those involving important relationships—with parents/caregivers, teachers, schoolmates, peers and friends—in the lives of children, and family and school as the locations where they are living their everyday lives. Indirect environments include the local area, country/society and the rest of the world.

The most reported factors are introduced below. In the case of individual factors, parental or caregiver and family factors, at least five, and in the case of other factors, at least three publications refer to them as vulnerability and/or resilience factors.

2.3.1 Individual Vulnerability/Resilience Factors

Individual vulnerability/resilience factors are related to the child's health, personality, cognitive, psychological, and social skills, outlook, identity, talents and interests (see Table 2.1, also for references). Having bad mental or physical health, difficult temperament, low academic and cognitive abilities, negative self-esteem, low sense of control over one's life, poor self-regulation, low social competences, including social problem-solving skills, lack of a sense of humour, and having a minority status can increase a child's vulnerability. However, having good mental or physical health, easy temperament, including being sociable, high academic and cognitive abilities, positive self-esteem, high sense of competence and self-efficacy, high sense of control over one's life, good self-regulation, high social competences, including social problem-solving skills, having a sense of humour, high empathy and capacity to understand others, high hope, faith, optimism, having goals and aspirations, sense of direction and meaning in life, having a strong, positive cultural/religious/spiritual identity, and having hobbies, extracurricular activities, recognised talents and accomplishments can increase a child's resilience.

Table 2.1 Most common individual level factors contributing to child resilience (R), vulnerability (V) or both (RV)

	Resilient	Factors	Vulnerable	Source
Individual				
… health	Good (low stress)	Mental health	Bad (disability/ illness; problems)	RV: Hall et al. (2022) V: Arora et al. (2015), Arafat et al. (2019), OECD (2019), Smith and Carlson (1997), Vision (2019)
	Good/No physical limitations	Physical health	Bad (disability/ chronic illness; problems)	RV: Sugland et al. (1993) R: Kumpfer (1999) V: Arora et al. (2015), OECD (2019), Hall et al. (2022), Smith and Carlson (1997), Vision (2019), Arafat et al. (2019)
… personality	Easy-going/ Flexible and optimistic	Temperament	Difficult	RV: Hall et al. (2022), Smith and Carlson (1997), Sugland et al. (1993) R: Newman and Blackburn (2002), Ferenczi et al. (2015), Franke (2014), Gutman (2020), Zolkoski and Bullock (2012), Waller (2001), Arafat et al. (2019)
	Yes	Sociable		R: Arafat et al. (2019), Daniel and Wassell (2002), Gutman (2020), Smith and Carlson (1997), Zolkoski and Bullock (2012)
… cognitive skills	High	Academic and cognitive ability, intelligence	Low	RV: Hall et al. (2022), Franke (2014), Sugland et al. (1993), Smith and Carlson (1997) R: Newman and Blackburn (2002), Ferenczi et al. (2015), Masten et al. (2023), Kumpfer (1999), Gutman (2020), Zolkoski and Bullock (2012), Arafat et al. (2019), Hornor (2017), Noltemeyer and Bush (2013) V: Vision (2019), Waller (2001), Arora et al. (2015)

… psychological skills	Positive	Self-esteem	Negative	RV: Sugland et al. (1993) R: Howard et al. (1999), Gutman (2020), Zolkoski and Bullock (2012), Arafat et al. (2019), Hornor (2017), Smith and Carlson (1997) V: Arora et al. (2015)
	High	Sense of competence and self-efficacy		R: Daniel and Wassell (2002), Smith and Carlson, 1997, Ungar and Liebenberg (2005), Waller (2001), Howard et al. (1999), Masten et al. (2023), Cutuli et al. (2020), Newman (2002), Franke (2014), Arafat et al. (2019)
	High/internal	Sense of control over life/Locus of control	Low/external	RV: Sugland et al. (1993) R: Newman and Blackburn (2002), Newman (2002), Gutman (2020), Hornor (2017), Daniel and Wassell (2002), Noltemeyer and Bush (2013)
	Good	Self-regulation	Poor	RV: Hall et al. 2022 R: Masten et al. (2023), Cutuli et al. (2020), Gutman (2020), Zolkoski and Bullock (2012), Waller (2001), Noltemeyer and Bush (2013), Masten (2018)
… social skills	Good	Interpersonal and communication skills/ social competence	Bad	RV: Sugland et al. (1993) R: Hall et al. (2022), Newman and Blackburn (2002), Howard et al. (1999), Ferenczi et al. (2015), Masten et al. (2023), Kumpfer (1999) Daniel and Wassell (2002), Ungar and Liebenberg (2005), Hornor (2017), Waller (2001)
	Good	Social problem-solving skills	Bad	RV: Hall et al. (2022), Sugland et al. (1993), R: Howard et al. (1999), Masten et al. (2023), Cutuli et al. (2020), Kumpfer (1999), Franke (2014), Waller (2001), Arafat et al. (2019), Smith and Carlson (1997), Masten (2018), Daniel and Wassell (2002), Ungar and Liebenberg (2005)
	Present	Sense of humor	Lack	RV: Sugland et al. (1993) R: Newman and Blackburn (2002), Masten et al. (2023), Kumpfer (1999) Daniel and Wassell (2002), Ungar and Liebenberg (2005), Noltemeyer and Bush (2013), Waller (2001), Smith and Carlson (1997)
	High	Empathy for others and capacity to understand others		R: Newman and Blackburn (2002), Franke (2014), Daniel and Wassell (2002), Ungar and Liebenberg (2005), Waller (2001), Kumpfer (1999), Arafat et al. (2019)

(continued)

Table 2.1 (continued)

	Resilient	Factors	Vulnerable	Source
… outlook	High	Hope, faith, optimism		R: Masten et al. (2023), Cutuli et al. (2020), Waller (2001), Masten (2018), Ungar and Liebenberg (2005), Hornor (2017), Smith and Carlson (1997)
	Yes	Having goals and aspirations, sense of direction and meaning in life		R: Ungar and Liebenberg (2005), Waller (2001), Howard et al. (1999), Masten et al. (2023), Cutuli et al. (2020), Kumpfer (1999)
… identity		Minority status/ Immigrant background/ Ethnic minority status	Yes	V: Vision (2019), Zolkoski and Bullock (2012), Sugland et al. (1993), OECD (2019)
	Yes, strong, positive identity	Cultural and/or spiritual/religious identification		R: Newman and Blackburn 2002, Ungar and Liebenberg (2005), Noltemeyer and Bush (2013), Waller (2001), Smith and Carlson (1997)
… talents and interests	Yes	Hobbies, extracurricular activities, recognized talents/ accomplishments		R: Masten et al. (2023), Cutuli et al. (2020), Kumpfer (1999), Newman (2002), Waller (2001), Hornor (2017), Daniel and Wassell (2002)

Table 2.2 Most common direct environmental factors contributing to child resilience (R), vulnerability (V) or both (RV)

	Resilient	Factors	Vulnerable	Source
Direct environmental				
Parental/caregiver				
… health	Good	Mental health of the parent(s)	Poor	RV: Terrisse (2000) V: Hall et al. (2022), Vision (2019), Ferenczi et al. (2015), Gutman (2020), Arora et al. (2015), Hornor (2017), Sugland et al. (1993) R: Franke (2014), Arafat et al. (2019), Daniel and Wassell (2002)
	Good	Physical health of the parent(s)	Poor	RV: Terrisse (2000) V: Vision (2019), Gutman (2020), Arora et al. (2015) R: Franke (2014), Arafat et al. (2019)
… health behavior	No	Alcohol/drug abuse	Yes	R: Daniel and Wassell (2002) V: Hall et al. (2022), Ferenczi et al. (2015), Kumpfer (1999), Gutman (2020), Arora et al. (2015), Hornor (2017)
… relationship quality with the child	Good	Parent-child relationship quality	Poor	RV: Hall et al. (2022) R: Newman and Blackburn (2002), Masten et al. (2023), Luthar (2015), Cutuli et al. (2020), Kumpfer (1999), Franke (2014), Gutman (2020), Waller (2001), Arafat et al. (2019) V: Arora et al. (2015)
	Secure/at least to one	Attachment with parent/caregiver	Insecure	RV: Hall et al. (2022), Luthar (2015) R: Ferenczi et al. (2015), Cutuli et al. (2020), Kumpfer (1999), Gutman (2020), Arafat et al. (2019), Smith and Carlson (1997), Masten (2018)

(continued)

Table 2.2 (continued)

	Resilient	Factors	Vulnerable	Source
… safety/violence	No/Low	Child maltreatment	Yes/High	V: Hall et al. (2022), Vision (2019), Ferenczi et al. (2015), Franke (2014), Gutman (2020), Zolkoski and Bullock (2012), Arora et al. (2015), Hornor (2017), Smith and Carlson (1997), Luthar (2015) R: Ungar and Liebenberg (2005)
… care	Authoritative: positive and consistent/encouragement; skilful	Parenting	Harsh: negative and inconsistent/lack of parental guidance and direction; encouragement/skills	RV: Hall et al. (2022), Luthar (2015), Gutman (2020), Sugland et al. (1993) R: Howard et al. (1999), Masten et al. (2023), Cutuli et al. (2020), Waller (2001), Masten (2018), Ungar and Liebenberg (2005) V: Arora et al. (2015)
	Appropriate and consistent discipline: use of appropriate rules and expectations, clearly define limits and consistently enforce rules, consistent parental monitoring	Parental discipline: limit setting and monitoring	Inappropriate and inconsistent discipline: harsh, power-assertive discipline, inconsistent parental monitoring	RV: Luthar (2015), Sugland et al. (1993) R: Howard et al. (1999), Masten et al. (2023), Cutuli et al. (2020), Kumpfer (1999), Noltemeyer and Bush (2013) V: Smith and Carlson (1997)
… support	High	Perceived social support	Low	RV: Ferenczi et al. (2015) R: Newman and Blackburn (2002), Masten et al. (2023), Luthar (2015), Cutuli et al. (2020), Newman (2002), Zolkoski and Bullock (2012), Noltemeyer and Bush (2013), Smith and Carlson (1997), Ungar and Liebenberg (2005) V: Arafat et al. (2019)
	Yes	Developmental support, provide access to knowledge, ability to provide support and guidance		R: Howard et al. (1999), Waller (2001), Smith and Carlson (1997), Masten et al. (2023), Cutuli et al. (2020), Kumpfer (1999)

… education and cognitive abilities	High	Parents' level of education	Low	RV: Ferenczi et al. (2015) R: Waller (2001) V: Gutman (2020), Zolkoski and Bullock (2012), Arora et al. (2015), OECD (2019), Sugland et al. (1993)
… relationship quality with each other	No	Parental separation/ divorce	Yes	R: Daniel and Wassell (2002) V: Gutman (2020), Arora et al. (2015), Sugland et al. (1993), Smith and Carlson (1997)
	Good	Quality of couple relationship of parents/caregivers	Bad/no relationship	R: Cutuli et al. (2020), Franke (2014), Zolkoski and Bullock (2012), Waller (2001) V: Smith and Carlson (1997)
Familial				
… material resources	Sufficient material resources	Financial and material resources	Poverty, material deprivation	RV: Hall et al. (2022), Gutman (2020), Zolkoski and Bullock (2012), Terrisse (2000) R: Masten et al. (2023), Cutuli et al. (2020), Waller (2001), Daniel and Wassell (2002) V: Vision (2019), Ferenczi et al. (2015), Kumpfer (1999), Arora et al. (2015), Arafat et al. (2019), Hornor (2017), Sugland et al. (1993), Smith and Carlson (1997), OECD (2019)
… quality of relationships	High	Family cohesion and interaction	Low	RV: Gutman (2020), Terrisse (2000) R: Hall et al. (2022), Howard et al. (1999), Masten et al. (2023), Luthar (2015), Zolkoski and Bullock (2012), Waller (2001), Noltemeyer and Bush (2013), Masten (2018) V: Smith and Carlson (1997)

(continued)

Table 2.2 (continued)

	Resilient	Factors	Vulnerable	Source
… safety/violence	Low (family harmony)	Family violence and conflicts (including interparental)	High	RV: Hall et al. (2022) R: Newman and Blackburn (2002), Howard et al. (1999), Cutuli et al. (2020), Daniel and Wassell (2002), Ungar and Liebenberg (2005) V: Kumpfer (1999), Gutman (2020), Zolkoski and Bullock (2012), Hornor (2017), Sugland et al. (1993), Arora et al. (2015), OECD (2019), Arafat et al. (2019)
… support	High	Perceived social/psychosocial and emotional support (also from extended family, e.g., grandparents)	Low (e.g., lack of person to share ones emotions)	R: Hall et al. (2022), Newman and Blackburn (2002), Masten et al. (2023), Luthar (2015), Gutman (2020), Zolkoski and Bullock (2012), Ungar and Liebenberg (2005), Howard et al. (1999) V: Ferenczi et al. (2015), Arora et al. (2015)
… engagement	Yes	Opportunities for meaningful family involvement	No	V: Hall et al. (2022) R: Newman and Blackburn (2002), Kumpfer (1999), Waller (2001), Howard et al.(1999)
… influence	Positive	Having a mentor/role model to follow	Lack/Negative	RV: Sugland et al. (1993) R: Kumpfer (1999), Howard et al. (1999), Waller (2001), Ungar and Liebenberg (2005) V: Arora et al. (2015)
… identity	Yes	Existence of family routines and traditions		R: Howard et al. (1999), Gutman (2020), Masten et al. (2023), Masten (2018), Cutuli et al. (2020)
Friends and schoolmates				
… quality of relationships	Good, stable	Quality of peer relationships/friendships		R: Hall et al. (2022), Ferenczi et al. (2015), Gutman (2020), Arafat et al. (2019), Hornor (2017), Smith and Carlson (1997)

… safety/violence	Low	Bullying	High	R: Ungar and Liebenberg (2005) V: Hall et al. (2022), Gutman (2020), Arora et al. (2015)
… support	High	Peers support: perceived social/ psychosocial and emotional support from peers	Low	V: Hall et al. (2022), Ferenczi et al. (2015), Arora et al. (2015), Arafat et al. (2019) R: Newman and Blackburn 2002, Masten et al. (2023), Waller (2001), Noltemeyer and Bush (2013), Smith and Carlson (1997), Daniel and Wassell (2002)
… engagement	No	Social isolation, peer rejection	Yes	R: Ungar and Liebenberg (2005) V: Hall et al. (2022), Arora et al. (2015), Gutman (2020), Smith and Carlson (1997)
… influence	No	Delinquent peers	Yes	V: Hall et al. (2022), Arora et al. (2015), Gutman (2020) R: Cutuli et al. (2020)
Teachers				
… relationship quality with child	Good	Quality of child-teacher relationship		R: Hall et al. (2022), Franke (2014), Noltemeyer and Bush (2013), Arafat et al. (2019), Howard et al. (1999)
… care	High/encouragement from teachers	Care/encouragement	Low/little encouragement from teachers	RV: Sugland et al. (1993) R: Howard et al. (1999) V: Arora et al. (2015)
… support	High	Perceived social support	Low	R: Masten et al. (2023), Gutman (2020), Smith and Carlson (1997), Daniel and Wassell (2002), Ungar and Liebenberg (2005) V: Ferenczi et al. (2015), Arora et al. (2015)
School				
… safety/violence	Safe	Safety of school environment/ exposure to violence	Unsafe	R: Ungar and Liebenberg (2005) V: Luthar (2015), Arora et al. (2015)

(continued)

Table 2.2 (continued)

	Resilient	Factors	Vulnerable	Source
… support	Supportive	School climate	Unsupportive	R: Masten et al. (2023), Howard et al. (1999) V: Hall et al. (2022)
… engagement	Yes	To be listened and express views freely/ Engagement in a well-functioning school/having responsibilities and tasks	No/low	RV: Hall et al. (2022) R: Masten (2018), Noltemeyer and Bush (2013), Smith and Carlson (1997), Howard et al. (1999)
… influence	Positive	Having a mentor/role model to follow	Lack/Negative	RV: Sugland et al. (1993) R: Newman (2002), Zolkoski and Bullock (2012), Waller (2001), Ungar and Liebenberg (2005) V: Arora et al. (2015)
… professional quality	High/practical and relevant	Quality of curriculum		R: Howard et al. (1999), Noltemeyer and Bush (2013), Waller (2001)

Table 2.3 Most common indirect environmental level factors contributing to child resilience (R), vulnerability (V) or both (RV)

	Resilient	Factors	Vulnerable	Source
Indirect environmental				
Local area				
… material resources	No	Community poverty	Yes/high	R: Noltemeyer and Bush (2013) V: Hall et al. (2022), Gutman (2020), Smith and Carlson (1997)
… sustainability/access to opportunities	Yes	Economic, employment opportunities for families	No	R: Hall et al. (2022), Masten et al. (2023), Zolkoski and Bullock (2012), Waller (2001) V: Smith and Carlson (1997)
	Yes	Access to good-quality child institutions like school and education, information, learning resources	No access, crowded	R: Hall et al. (2022), Masten et al. (2023), Waller (2001), Noltemeyer and Bush (2013), Smith and Carlson (1997), Ungar and Liebenberg (2005) V: Ferenczi et al. (2015)
	Good	Access to trustworthy/affordable/effective emergency and healthcare services (medical, police, fire)	Poor	RV: Terrisse (2000) V: Vision (2019) R: Zolkoski and Bullock (2012), Waller (2001), Masten et al. (2023), Cutuli et al. (2020)
	Good	Access to recreational facilities and programs	Poor	RV: Terrisse (2000) R: Hall et al. (2022), Zolkoski and Bullock (2012), Masten et al. (2023)
… quality of relationships	Good/strong	Community cohesiveness: social relationships among neighbourhood/community members and organisations	Weak/non-existent (social isolation)	R: Hall et al. (2022), Waller (2001), Gutman (2020), Noltemeyer and Bush (2013) V: Ferenczi et al. (2015), Arafat et al. (2019), Smith and Carlson (1997)

(continued)

Table 2.3 (continued)

	Resilient	Factors	Vulnerable	Source
… safety	High	Safety of the surrounding environment	Low	RV: Sugland et al. (1993) R: Masten et al. (2023), Cutuli et al. (2020), Zolkoski and Bullock (2012), Noltemeyer and Bush (2013), Ungar and Liebenberg (2005) V: Vision (2019), Arora et al. (2015), Smith and Carlson (1997)
	Low	Crime and violence level in neighbourhood	High	V: Arora et al. (2015), Arafat et al. (2019), Gutman (2020) R: Masten et al. (2023), Ungar and Liebenberg (2005)
… care	Yes	Caring relationships with mentors, helping professionals and other adults		R: Howard et al. (1999), Hall et al. (2022), Luthar (2015)
… support	High	Supportive community environment/relevant support services/perceived social, psychosocial and emotional support	Low	RV: Sugland et al. (1993) R: Hall et al. (2022), Masten et al. (2023), Cutuli et al. (2020), Newman (2002), Gutman (2020), Zolkoski and Bullock (2012), Waller (2001), Noltemeyer and Bush (2013), Daniel and Wassell (2002), Ungar and Liebenberg (2005), Howard et al. (1999) V: Ferenczi et al. (2015), Arora et al. (2015)
… engagement	Yes (job, volunteering, helping neighbours)	Valued social role, meaningful involvement		R: Newman and Blackburn 2002, Newman (2002), Waller (2001), Ungar and Liebenberg (2005), Howard et al. (1999)
… influence	Positive	(Adult) role models/mentors	Lack/Negative	RV: Sugland et al. (1993) R: Masten et al. (2023), Newman (2002), Zolkoski and Bullock (2012), Daniel and Wassell (2002), Waller (2001), Ungar and Liebenberg (2005) V: Arora et al. (2015)

… identity	Yes	Feelings of belonging, identity in community, sense of community		R: Waller (2001), Noltemeyer and Bush (2013), Luthar (2015)
Country/Society				
… safety		Likelihood of disaster, including catastrophic natural and health emergency events	High	V: Hall et al. (2022), Vision (2019), Gutman (2020)
	High/peaceful political environment	National security/War/armed conflict	Low/Yes	R: Masten et al. (2023) V: Arora et al. (2015), Gutman (2020)
… care	High/protective child policies	Care	Low	RV: Terrisse (2000) R: Masten et al. 2023 V: Arora et al. (2015)
… support	Good	Availability and access to governmental structures and support services	Poor	RV: Terrisse (2000) R: Ungar and Liebenberg (2005) V: Arora et al. (2015)
… tolerance	Low	Discrimination	High	RV: Terrisse (2000) R: Masten et al. (2023) V: Hall et al. (2022), Gutman (2020)

2.3.2 Direct Environmental Vulnerability/Resilience Factors

There are many direct environmental risks and resources which make a child more vulnerable or resilient (see Table 2.2, also for references). Direct environmental vulnerability/resilience is related to the quality of a child's relationship with his/her parent(s)/caregiver(s), friends and schoolmates, teachers, and the quality of the relationship(s) between parents/caregivers and in the wider family. Poor relationships between parent and child and between parents or caregivers as a couple, and also low family cohesion can increase a child's vulnerability. However, high family cohesion, including good relationships between parent and child and between parents or caregivers as a couple, and also good relationships with friends, schoolmates and teachers may boost a child's resilience. In the context of family, it is important to have a close bond with at least one person in the family (Daniel & Wassell, 2002); for example, with one parent (Newman & Blackburn, 2002) or grandparent (Daniel & Wassell, 2002).

Safety with parent(s)/caregiver(s), friends, and schoolmates, but also more widely in the family and school is important. Living in a family environment with high levels of violence and conflict, including experiencing maltreatment by a parent/caregiver, but also an unsafe school environment and experiencing bullying from peers may increase a child's vulnerability. Safe home and school environment, including not experiencing violence may enhance a child's resilience. According to Masten (2018), emotional safety in the family especially enhances a child's resilience.

Care provided by parent(s)/caregiver(s) and teachers is important. Harsh parenting, characterised by inappropriate and inconsistent discipline and parental monitoring, but also a lack of care, including no or little encouragement from teachers can increase a child's vulnerability. Authoritative parenting—characterised by a balance of parental warmth and appropriate and consistent discipline—and experiencing care, including attentive and encouraging teachers can enhance a child's resilience. It is important that parent(s)/caregiver(s) establish consistent expectations, rules, and consequences for behaviour (Smith & Carlson, 1997; Masten et al., 2023).

Support from parent(s)/caregiver(s), friends and schoolmates, teachers, but also a supportive family and school environment more widely is important for a child. A lack of social and emotional support from parent(s)/caregiver(s), the wider family, but also from friends, schoolmates and teachers, and an unsupportive school climate may increase a child's vulnerability. Not having any person to share emotions, especially inside the family, can be an important vulnerability enhancer. However, having social and emotional support from family members, friends, schoolmates, teachers, and being in a supportive school climate may boost a child's resilience.

A child's engagement in family and school, and with friends and schoolmates is important. If a child is not engaged in family and school settings, and they experience peer rejection and social isolation, it may increase the child's vulnerability. On the other hand, feeling engaged may increase a child's resilience.

In addition, poor mental and/or physical health, alcohol/drug abuse, and a low level of education in the parent(s)/caregiver(s), material deprivation/poverty of the family, having no or a negative mentor/role model to follow in the family or school, and being influenced by delinquent peers can increase a child's vulnerability. However, good mental and/or physical health, no alcohol/drug abuse, and a high level of education in the parent(s)/caregiver(s), sufficient family material resources, having a positive mentor/role model to follow in the family or school, the existence of family routines and traditions, not being influenced by delinquent peers, and having a high-quality curriculum in school can increase a child's resilience.

2.3.3 Indirect Environmental Vulnerability/Resilience Factors

Indirect environmental vulnerability/resilience is related to the material resources in a child's local area, sustainability of and access to opportunities, quality of relationships, safety, care, support, engagement, influence and identity, while also safety, care, support, and tolerance at the country/societal level (see Table 2.3, also for references). High levels of poverty in the community, lack of economic or employment opportunities for families, poor access to good-quality child institutions, trustworthy, affordable and effective emergency and healthcare services, and recreational facilities and programmes, weak community cohesiveness, low safety in the surrounding environment, including high levels of crime and violence in the neighbourhood, low social support in the community, lack of adult role models or existence of negative adult role models in the local area, high likelihood of disaster, including catastrophic natural and health emergency events in the country, low national security, including being in war or armed conflict, low care, poor availability and access to government structures and support services, and high levels of discrimination in the country can increase a child's vulnerability. However, living in a non-poor community where there is economic and employment opportunities for families, good access to good-quality child institutions, trustworthy, affordable and effective emergency and healthcare services, and recreational facilities and programmes, strong community cohesiveness, high safety in the surrounding environment, including low levels of crime and violence in the neighbourhood, having caring relationships with mentors, helpful professionals and other adults, high social support in the community, having a valued social role, meaningful involvement in the local area, positive adult role models in the local area, feelings of belonging to the local community, living in a country with high national security, high levels of care for children in the country, including protective child policies, good availability and access to government structures and support services, and low discrimination in the country may increase a child's resilience.

2.4 Conceptual Framework of Child Vulnerability

Based on the ecological model of child development by Bronfenbrenner (1979), the social-ecological model of resilience by Ungar et al. (2013), and the mapping exercise (see Tables 2.1, 2.2 and 2.3), the following conceptual framework of child vulnerability (Fig. 2.1) is proposed. Child vulnerability and resilience are linked. In Fig. 2.1, the conceptual framework for understanding child vulnerability on a more abstract level is presented. In this framework, child vulnerability, as a high level of the risk of harm, and resilience, as a low level of the risk of harm to child well-being, form a continuum suggested as such also by Arora et al. (2015) and Daniel and Wassell (2002). In accordance with Masten et al. (2023) and Gutman (2020), the *vulnerability and resilience factor mapping exercise* showed that most factors were bipolar in nature, representing two extremes on a single continuum. For example, low teacher encouragement (Sugland et al., 1993) can be considered a (direct environmental) vulnerability factor, while high teacher encouragement (Sugland et al., 1993) is a (direct environmental) resilience factor. However, according to some scholars (Luthar, 2015; Luthar & Zelazo 2003; Rutter, 2003), there are also a few *pure* vulnerability or resilience factors, and some factors are most beneficial at medium levels rather than at either low or high extremes. The present mapping exercise uncovered some *pure* resilience factors; for example, having hobbies, extracurricular activities or the existence of family routines and traditions.

The risk of harm may vary at different points in a child's life depending on the interaction and accumulation of individual, direct and indirect environmental vulnerability and resilience factors (see Tables 2.1, 2.2 and 2.3). The risk of harm to a child's well-being is high when risks accumulate, and child vulnerability outweighs resilience. According to the World Bank's downward spiral of childhood vulnerability (Arora et al., 2015), each shock leads to a new level of vulnerability, and each new level opens up a host of new risks. For example, children experiencing parental neglect (direct environmental vulnerability) will be more likely to develop a communication problem (individual vulnerability), and then both the communication problem and the neglect increase the risk of developing a mental health problem

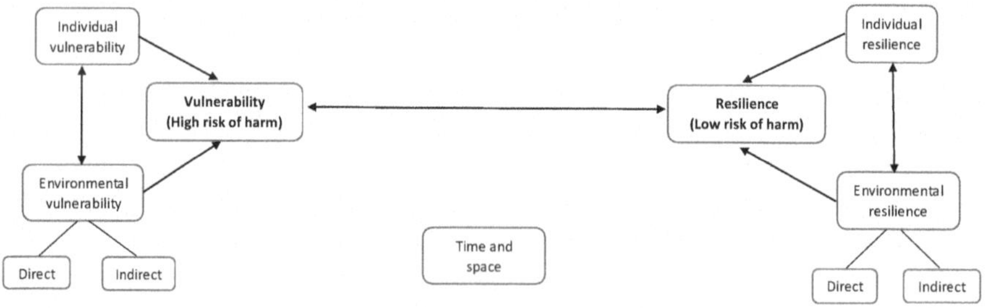

Fig. 2.1 Conceptual framework for understanding child vulnerability as a risk of harm to a child's well-being in relation to their resilience

(individual vulnerability; Andresen, 2014). However, the risk of harm to a child's well-being is low when resources accumulate, and resilience outweighs child vulnerability.

In addition to being dynamic, it is also a context-specific process. For example, in some contexts adopted or fostered children may be at risk of exploitation or abuse while in others they are considered to have an advantage because they have multiple adults in parental roles who care for and invest in them (Leinaweaver, 2014).

2.5 Conclusion

The present conceptual framework for understanding child vulnerability as the risk of harm to a child's well-being in relation to their resilience—stemming from the ecological model of child development by Bronfenbrenner (1979), the social-ecological model of resilience by Ungar et al. (2013) and previous multidisciplinary knowledge on the most common vulnerability and resilience factors—can be considered a step forward from existing risk-centric conceptualisations, where the primary critique centred around the "danger of using it in a stigmatising, labelling, marginalising and objectifying way, denying the agency and voice of those seen as vulnerable" (Virokannas et al., 2020, p. 336). Although there are some conceptualisations linking child vulnerability and resilience, this framework goes further, considering them as a continuum. This conceptual framework has been empirically tested in the process of the development of a new child vulnerability measure, presented in Chap. 4.

Competing Interests The author has no conflicts of interest to declare that are relevant to the content of this chapter.

Acknowledgement Work on this chapter was supported by a grant from the Estonian Research Council (PRG700).

References[1]

Andresen, S. (2014). Childhood vulnerability: Systematic, structural, and individual dimensions. *Child Indicators Research, 7*(4), 699–713.

*Arafat, S. Y., Papadopoulos, K., Mullick, M. S., & Uddin, M. S. (2019). The vulnerability and resiliency of childhood. *Global Psychiatry, 2*(2), 113–120.

[1] Papers from the literature search for the most common vulnerability and/or resilience factors (see Tables 2.1, 2.2 and 2.3) are marked with an asterisk.

*Arora, S. K., Shah, D., Chaturvedi, S., & Gupta, P. (2015). Defining and measuring vulnerability in young people. *Indian Journal of Community Medicine, 40*(3), 193–197.

Ben-Arieh, A., Casas, F., Frønes, I., & Korbin, J. E. (2014). Multifaceted concept of child well-being. In A. Ben-Arieh, F. Casas, I. Frønes, & J. Korbin (Eds.), *Handbook of child well-being*. Springer. https://doi.org/10.1007/978-90-481-9063-8_134

Brandon, M. (2009). Child fatality or serious injury through maltreatment: Making sense of outcomes. *Children and Youth Services Review, 31*(10), 1107–1112.

Bronfenbrenner, U. (1979). *The ecology of human development*. Harvard University Press.

Brown, K. (2011). 'Vulnerability': Handle with care. *Ethics and Social Welfare, 5*(3), 313–321.

Brown, K., Ecclestone, K., & Emmel, N. (2017). The many faces of vulnerability. *Social Policy and Society, 16*(3), 497–510.

Chambers, R. (1989). Vulnerability, coping and policy-introduction. *Ids Bulletin-Institute of Development Studies, 20*(2), 1–7.

*Cutuli, J. J., Herbers, J. E., Masten, A. S., & Reed, M. G. J. (2020). Resilience in development. In C. R. Snyder, S. J. Lopez, L. M. Edwards & S. C. Marques (Eds.), *The Oxford handbook of positive psychology* (3rd ed., pp. 171–188). Oxford University Press.

Daniel, B. (2010). Concepts of adversity, risk, vulnerability and resilience: A discussion in the context of the 'Child Protection System'. *Social Policy and Society, 9*(2), 231–241.

*Daniel, B., & Wassell, S. (2002). *Assessing and promoting resilience in vulnerable children*. Jessica Kingsley Publishers.

*Ferenczi, S. C., Csákvári, J., & Tánczos, É. (2015). *Vulnerability and resilience in early childhood interventions*. Paper presented at the annual meeting for the INTCESS15–2nd international conference on education and social sciences, Istanbul, February.

Fineman, M. A. (2010). The vulnerable subject and the responsive state. *Emory Law Journal, 60*(2), 251–275.

*Franke, H. A. (2014). Toxic stress: Effects, prevention and treatment. *Children, 1*(3), 390–402. https://doi.org/10.3390/children1030390

Giesinger, J. (2019). Vulnerability and autonomy–children and adults. *Ethics and Social Welfare, 13*(3), 216–229.

*Gutman, L. M. (2020). Risk and resilience. In J. B. Benson (Ed.), *Encyclopedia of infant and early childhood development* (2nd ed, pp. 14–24). Elsevier. https://doi.org/10.1016/B978-0-12-809324-5.21835-X

*Hall, W. J., Lanier, P., Jenson, J. M., & Fraser, M. W. (2022). *Social policy for children and families: A risk and resilience perspective*. Sage Publications.

Herring, J. (2016). *Vulnerable adults and the law*. Oxford University Press.

*Hornor, G. (2017). Resilience. *Journal of Pediatric Health Care, 31*(3), 384–390. https://doi.org/10.1016/j.pedhc.2016.09.005

*Howard, S., Dryden, J., & Johnson, B. (1999). Childhood resilience: Review and critique of literature. Oxford Review of Education, 25(3), 307–323. doi:https://doi.org/10.1080/030549899104008.

Jopling, M., & Vincent, S. (2016). Vulnerable children: Needs and provision in the primary phase. *Cambridge Primary Review Trust.*

*Kumpfer, K. L. (1999). Factors and processes contributing to resilience: The resilience framework. In M. D. Glantz & J. L Johnson (Eds.) *Resilience and development: Positive life adaptations* (pp. 179–224). Kluwer Academic/Pienum Publishers.

Leinaweaver, J. (2014). Informal kinship-based fostering around the world: Anthropological findings. *Child Development Perspectives, 8*(3), 131–136.

*Luthar, S. S. (2015). Resilience in development: A synthesis of research across five decades. In D. Cicchetti & D. J. Cohen (Eds.), *Developmental psychopathology: Volume 3; Risk, disorder, and adaptation* (2nd ed., pp. 739–795). Wiley. https://doi.org/10.1002/9780470939406.ch20

Luthar, S. S., & Zelazo, L. B. (2003). Research on resilience: An integrative review. In S. S. Luthar (Ed.), *Resilience and vulnerability: Adaptation in the context of childhood adversities* (pp. 510–550). Cambridge University Press.

*Masten, A. S. (2018). Resilience theory and research on children and families: Past, present, and promise. *Journal of Family Theory & Review, 10*(1), 12–31. https://doi.org/10.1111/jftr.12255

Masten, A. S. (2021). Resilience in developmental systems: Principles, pathways, and protective processes in research and practice. In M. Ungar (Ed.), *Multisystemic resilience: Adaptation and transformation in contexts of change* (pp. 113–134). Oxford University Press.

Masten, A. S., & Garmezy, N. (1985). Risk, vulnerability, and protective factors in developmental psychopathology. In B. B. Lahey & A. E. Kazdin (Eds.), *Advances in clinical child psychology* (pp. 1–52). Springer.

*Masten, A. S., Narayan, A. J., & O'Dougherty-Wright, M. (2023). Resilience processes in development: Multisystem integration emerging from four waves of research. In S. Goldstein & R. B. Brooks (Eds.), *Handbook of resilience in children*. Springer.

*Newman, T. (2002). *Promoting resilience*. Centre for Evidence Based Social Services.

*Newman, T., & Blackburn, S. (2002). *Transitions in the lives of children and young people: Resilience factors*. Scottish Executive Education Department.

*Noltemeyer, A. L., & Bush, K. R. (2013). Adversity and resilience: A synthesis of international research. *School Psychology International, 34*(5), 474–487.

*OECD. (2019). *Changing the odds for vulnerable children: Building opportunities and resilience*. OECD Publishing.. https://doi.org/10.1787/a2e8796c-en

Rogers, W., Mackenzie, C., & Dodds, S. (2012). Why bioethics needs a concept of vulnerability. *IJFAB: International Journal of Feminist Approaches to Bioethics, 5*(2), 11–38.

Rutter, M. (1987). Psychosocial resilience and protective mechanisms. *American Journal of Orthopsychiatry, 57*(3), 316–331.

Rutter, M. (2003). Genetic influences on risk and protection: Implications for understanding resilience. In S. S. Luthar (Ed.), *Resilience and vulnerability: Adaptation in the context of childhood adversities* (pp. 489–509). Cambridge University Press.

Schweiger, G. (2019). Ethics, poverty and children's vulnerability. *Ethics and Social Welfare, 13*(3), 288–301.

*Smith, C., & Carlson, B. E. (1997). Stress, coping, and resilience in children and youth. *Social Service Review, 71*(2), 231–256.

Soffia, M., & Turner, A. (2021). *Measuring children and young people's subjective well-being*. What works Centre for Wellbeing. https://whatworkswellbeing.org/negatiive/measuring-children-and-young-peoples-subjective-wellbeing/

*Sugland, B. W., Zaslow, M., & Nord, C. W. (1993). *Risk, vulnerability, and resilience among youth: In search of a conceptual framework*. Child Trends.

*Terrisse, B. (2000). *The resilient child: Theoretical perspectives and review of the literature*. The Council of Ministers of Education. http://www.cmec.ca/stats/pcera/symposium2000

*Ungar, M., & Liebenberg, L. (2005). The international resilience project. In M. Ungar (Ed.), *Handbook for working with children and youth: Pathways to resilience across cultures and contexts* (pp. 211–229). Sage Publications.

Ungar, M., Ghazinour, M., & Richter, J. (2013). Annual research review: What is resilience within the social ecology of human development? *Journal of Child Psychology and Psychiatry, 54*(4), 348–366. https://doi.org/10.1111/jcpp.12025

Virokannas, E., Liuski, S., & Kuronen, M. (2020). The contested concept of vulnerability – A literature review. *European Journal of Social Work, 23*(2), 327–339.

*Vision, W. (2019). Mapping child vulnerability dimensions in the Lao PDR. *World Vision*.

*Waller, M. A. (2001). Resilience in ecosystemic context: Evolution of the concept. *American Journal of Orthopsychiatry, 71*(3), 290–297.

*Zolkoski, S. M., & Bullock, L. M. (2012). Resilience in children and youth: A review. *Children and Youth Services Review, 34*(12), 2295–2303. https://doi.org/10.1016/j.childyouth.2012.08.009.

Oliver Nahkur is a research fellow of Research of Social Wellbeing at the University of Tartu, Institute of Social Studies, Estonia. He is a member of the International Society for Child Indicators (ISCI) and the Estonian team of the International Survey of Children's Well-Being (ISCWeB); secretary-treasurer of the International Sociological Association, Research Committee No 55—Social Indicators. He actively contributes to the development of child well-being data in Estonia. His research interests include child well-being and vulnerability research and social indicators research, including from a cross-national comparative studies perspective. In one of his latest research publications, he studied the change in children's subjective relational social cohesion with family and friends during the Covid-19 pandemic in 18 countries across the globe.

Chapter 3
Child Participation in Social Research: Ethical and Methodological Considerations

Mai Beilmann and Judit Strömpl

3.1 Introduction

Along with the development of the sociology of childhood and the improvement of children's rights, the question of child participation in social scientific research has also arisen. There is an unavoidable need to ask the children themselves what they think about this or that issue that concerns their lives. Without opening the child's perspective, it is no longer possible to carry out in-depth and broad research on children's lived experiences and opinions (Alves et al., 2022; Dubois et al., 2021; Lundy, 2007, 2018; Hammersley & Traianou, 2012). At the same time, involving children in research requires the adoption of new data collection methods and presents a series of ethical dilemmas for researchers. These dilemmas have primarily been the following. First, children do not form a homogeneous group. Children belong to different age groups, and age in childhood implies differences as it is linked to the rapid development of the child. Children's language skills, their experiences, and their ability to express their experiences and views are different. At the same time, children are social beings and members of social networks from the first moments of their lives, meaning that they interact with the people around them and can express their needs (Alderson et al., 2005; Perry, 2009; Perry & Szalavitz, 2017; Siegel, 2001, 2012). Therefore, children have opinions from a very early age, and it is essential to listen to and study their views and experiences regardless of their age, and this requires an appropriate methodological approach.

Second, children are status-dependent on adults, which means that their direct involvement in the study is made more difficult by the adult-parent or guardian filter. Of course, it is true that the adults responsible for the child's well-being should

M. Beilmann (✉) · J. Strömpl
Institute of Social Studies, University of Tartu, Tartu, Estonia
e-mail: mai.beilmann@ut.ee; judit.strompl@ut.ee

D. Kutsar et al. (eds.), *Child Vulnerability and Vulnerable Subjectivity*, Children's Well-Being: Indicators and Research 27,
https://doi.org/10.1007/978-3-031-61333-3_3

be aware of what the child is doing, who the investigators are, and the purpose and subject of the study, to prevent harm to the child (Neufeld & Maté, 2007). However, there are research topics that may not be to the liking of the adults in charge, especially when these topics relate to the subjective well-being of the child at home, in a substitute home, or in an educational setting. Namely, adults can refuse to allow children to participate in research that may reveal violations in their area of responsibility, such as child abuse at home, in foster care, or at school.

Third, children are not homogeneous in terms of their development and mental health. There are traumatised and abused children who have lost trust in adults. It is particularly difficult for an unfamiliar researcher to establish meaningful contact with such children and engage them in the research. However, their involvement in research is particularly important because they may be living in a dangerous environment, and learning about their circumstances is particularly important in order to initiate positive change in their lives or policies affecting their lives. These specific children also need special research methodologies that are sensitive to their vulnerabilities.

Ultimately, all these factors contribute to a child's vulnerability in social research. Although the personal characteristics of the child (e.g., prone to mental health problems, academic ability) may make some children more vulnerable than others (see Chap. 2), we are of the opinion that the conditions in which children live play a key role in making them vulnerable (or protecting them from becoming vulnerable). It is the obligation of every researcher working with child participants to make sure that their research does not increase the vulnerability of participating children, but rather that their participation would improve their well-being and resilience.

3.2 Agency, Well-being, Vulnerability and Ethics

Agency has become a core concept of the new sociology of childhood. Such a perspective requires that we consider children as *actors*, as *beings*, and not only as *becomings* (Qvortrup et al., 2009). Agency is an important ingredient of the well-being of children. Indeed, when asked about their thoughts about what constitutes well-being, children attribute high importance to the feeling of agency (Fattore et al., 2009). Participation in a well-planned and child-friendly study can provide children with a platform to express their agency (and therefore, increase their well-being).

Participation is not just data collection, but an important situation where researchers communicate with the child/children in a specific situation and discuss topics that are important to the children and show deep interest in the child's life and thoughts. That is why we need to discuss ethical considerations connected to the process of finding and inviting children, and enabling opportunities for children living in vulnerable situations (e.g., out-of-home care, see also Chap. 13; adoption, in exile, see also Chap. 12) to participate.

Unfortunately, children who are considered more vulnerable may also be more often denied the opportunity to participate in research, express their agency, and share their thoughts. For example, the number of children with disabilities would suggest that they are much more prevalent in the research literature than they actually are (Stalker, 2012). Stalker (2012) suggests that the lack of representation of children with disabilities in the mainstream literature may result from the difficulties in conducting research with this group of children as their caretakers and gatekeepers tend to be particularly concerned about their vulnerability.

In the case of disabled children, the reluctance of gatekeepers to allow the children to participate in research may be motivated both by their genuine fear that participation may not be a pleasant experience for a child (e.g., because their previous experience suggests that a child does not like talking to strangers) or by the belief that child is not capable of participating in research because of his/her disability. Davis et al. (2017) report that in the ethnographic study of disabled children in special schools, "the staff appeared to reject the premise that the children would know what was going on. /…/ The staff appeared to challenge the research team's idea that John [one of the researchers] should explain the research to the children and were attempting to influence John's view to have him believe that these children were incapable of thinking for themselves" (p. 123). Therefore, the views of some of the staff conflicted with the researchers' understanding that regardless of age or disability, children are perfectly capable of making up their own minds about participation in research if what is expected from them is explained in a manner that is appropriate to their age and development level.

One of the authors of this chapter (Judit), had a similar experience during an ethnographic study in a special reformatory school for girls (Strömpl, 2002). The school management hired her as an educator and allowed her to conduct the study with only one condition—that she not tell the girls that she was conducting a study. This was a serious breach of research ethics, which presented many ugly moments during and after the research. For example, Judit had to somehow explain to the girls why she came to work in their school when she was a university lecturer. So as not to lie too much, she explained that young people's problems were her topic of study and she had worked with it in the theoretical sense and now she wanted to see how things worked in practice. In tackling the ethical problem, she turned the focus of her study on the functioning of the institution and, above all, on the activities of the staff. However, it was impossible to do this without shedding light on interactions between the staff and the children. To overcome this ethical problem, Judit promised that in the future she would use every opportunity to warn other novice researchers not to accept such a condition from the gatekeepers because every research subject needs to know that they are being studied.

The ban by the gatekeepers shows how the staff doubted that the children in their institution could be trusted to knowingly take part in a study without breaking the school's rules. Therefore, it was impossible for the children to participate in the survey knowingly, and, at the same time, the children's informed choice not to participate was also made impossible. Of course, the possibility of the informed choice not to participate is always doubtful in an ethnographic study if the gatekeepers allow the study to be conducted (Traianou & Hammersley, 2023). However, in this case, one of the gatekeepers' arguments for not letting the girls know that Judit was a researcher was that "the girls would exploit her for their own ends". There was a kind of a demonisation of girls with multiple troubles—as they have broken various norms of behaviour, they cannot be trusted, and they must always be insincere and selfish. However, the children's manipulative behaviour is a clear sign of the trauma they all experienced in their earlier childhood (Maté & Maté, 2022). At this point, the management was most probably simply afraid of having someone in the institution who was outside the routine. In the literature, we can also encounter situations where child participation and child protection are contrasted, which is particularly characteristic of research on children and young people removed from their birth family and growing up in out-of-home care (Garcia-Quiroga & Agoglia, 2020; Hammersley & Traianou, 2012; Strömpl & Luhamaa, 2020; van Bijleveld et al., 2013).

Our standpoint is that children are entitled to make up their own minds about their participation in research regardless of their development level or age. There is every reason to doubt that some children are too young or otherwise incapable of understanding what researchers expect of them and deciding whether they want to be part of the research or not. Mayne et al. (2017) report that with an approach called *interactive nonfiction narrative*, children as young as 3 years old are capable of providing meaningful informed consent. They report that children even understood that they could cease their participation, and one boy in their pilot study actually exercised his right to opt out towards the end of the study.

Therefore, labelling some children as particularly vulnerable (or troublesome) and preventing them from making their own decisions about participation in research may prove counterproductive and deprive groups of children of their agency. Andresen and Ben-Arieh (2016) stress that the concept of vulnerability confronts childhood studies with several challenges. First, a vulnerable child can simultaneously be a strong child because vulnerability does not annul agency. Second, there is a question of whether children and adolescents differ from adults in their vulnerability. Third, it is paramount to avoid stigmatising vulnerable children and adolescents by presenting them as vulnerable. "Protecting" children from participating, however, denies their agency, differentiates them not only from adults but also from other children and adolescents, and therefore, stigmatises some children as particularly vulnerable (or troublesome). Therefore, leaving certain groups of children unstudied can be considered unethical, whereas an ethical solution would be to develop approaches that make it possible to ask for children's informed consent in ways that are understandable and meaningful for them and respectful towards them.

We are convinced that informing children about the research and asking for their consent in a way that is child-friendly and respectful towards them and their situation is important not only in the case of studying particularly vulnerable groups of children but every time when conducting research with children. Children's lives are intersected by different factors such as age, gender, ethnicity, experience, and livelihood circumstances, which means that informing them about the research as well as the research methods has to accommodate these differences. In addition to these factors, it is important to consider the interdependent social relationships in which children find themselves (Abebe, 2019). It is important not to forget that agency is expressed in very different ways by different children in different settings (Greene & Nixon, 2020) and following research protocol in an overly strict manner, for example, may prevent some children from expressing their agency.

Furthermore, even when following a rather strict research protocol, it is important to consider the heterogeneity of children. For example, designing a questionnaire appropriate for children of different ages, from diverse cultural backgrounds and language groups can prove extremely complex (cf. Lobe et al., 2008). The questions in such international questionnaires should comply with ethical guidelines and also be age-appropriate (Görzig, 2012). However, besides age, it would be advisable to also consider differences in livelihood circumstances, level of development, etc. Therefore, sometimes it may prove almost impossible to design a questionnaire appropriate for a very heterogeneous group of children. In being aware of the limits of survey-based research, Andresen and Ben-Arieh (2016) suggest that ethnographic methodology may hold particularly strong potential for studying differences among children shaped by class, gender, and ethnicity. However, they also underline that this potential has not been fully utilised in research on children's worlds.

3.3 Gatekeepers

As noted above, the sociology of childhood views children as competent participants in their social worlds rather than individuals who are merely developing toward adulthood (James & Prout, 1997). However, children are always in an unequal hierarchical subordination compared to adults, and researcher willingness to grant children as much agency as possible (regarding the consent procedures, question design, etc.) is often restrained by the layers of gatekeepers who have the power to decide whether children can participate in the study (Tinson, 2009; Traianou & Hammersley, 2023). Therefore, the researcher is not only balancing their relationships with the children involved in the study but also with the gatekeepers (Tinson, 2009).

There are few exceptions, but in general, children cannot freely agree to participate in research without parental consent (Davies, 2017). Therefore, research with children inevitably involves their parents or guardians in the research in order to get their consent for the children to participate. As the examples above demonstrate, securing guardian consent can prove problematic in cases where children will be asked about their life in school, but it can be even more problematic when family life is the focus of the research. Davies (2017), who does family research with children, claims that the consenting procedure may become complicated when children participating in the research are likely to be discussing and even evaluating some of the very people who have to consent to their participation in the research. In other words, their guardians are basically asked to agree to be the objects of research and may feel uncomfortable with that prospect. A similar situation can appear in school—when children are supposed to evaluate their educational progress, their teacher may feel under examination (Davies, 2017). However, the school is a public institution and teachers are used to being examined and evaluated by the school administration, whereas family is considered a much more private institution, and therefore, parents may feel particularly anxious about having their privacy compromised by letting their children participate in research (Davies, 2017).

Davies (2017) draws attention to a significant consequence of asking parents for consent for their children to participate in research. By asking for parental or carer consent, children are stripped of some of their privacy as research participants because it means that relative to the adults, the children are known participants in the research. While some children want to talk to their parents about what they did or said throughout the research process, other children prefer to use the research situation as a space where they may discuss and reflect upon the complexities of their family relationships (Christensen, 2002; Davies, 2012). Therefore, not all children may be overly happy that their parents or guardians know about their participation in the research and that they may ask them what they confided to the researchers.

We became agonisingly aware of the contradictions related to parental consent for children's participation in research when conducting a survey on the abuse of children and young people in Estonia (Soo et al., 2016). On the one hand, the survey was on a very sensitive topic, which definitely requires parental consent for a child's participation, but on the other hand, the topic of the survey made us question the ethics of asking the parents for consent knowing that there may well be cases where a parent is also a person abusing a child. Therefore, asking the parents' permission in these cases would be asking the perpetrator whether their victim can participate in the survey and provide information about their misconduct. In every likelihood, asking for parental consent in this case may lead to a situation where some of the most vulnerable children and adolescents are stripped of the opportunity to provide information about their traumatic experiences. This, in turn, can lead to a biased sample, underestimation of the problem by the authorities, and as a result, less support services available for children who have experienced abuse at home.

Fortunately, asking for parental consent does not raise such fundamental and severe ethical dilemmas every time as the ones we faced when studying child abuse. However, it is important to contemplate the gatekeepers' role and their impact on the research regardless of the research topic, because doing research with children usually means having to find a way to remain simultaneously responsive to the needs and concerns of the children and their guardians. For example, Davies (2012) draws attention to an interesting paradox concerning those parents who are concerned about the family's privacy. There are parents who want to be in the room while their child is interviewed or to read what their child has written in the questionnaire. For those parents, family privacy overrides the child's right to privacy in the research context (Davies, 2012). It is also a methodological concern because children being aware of the gatekeeper may also influence the data collected. The extent to which the children believe the gatekeeper is watching and listening to them can influence how they react and respond to questions and behave throughout the study (see, for example, Irwin & Johnson, 2005). Therefore, the gatekeepers (who usually only want to protect the child and have the child's best interests at heart) always have an impact on the research process and it can be challenging to find out how a child participant feels about the active protection they are provided (e.g., when a parent attends their interview or reads their written answers).

3.4 The Fine Line Between Child Protection and Restricting the Child's Agency

With the child's best interests at heart, many regulations have been created to protect children participating in social research. The regulations protecting the (child) participants in research are important, as social research that involves human participants can potentially bring both beneficial and harmful consequences to participating individuals (see e.g., Blaikie & Priest, 2019). However, just as social research can be both beneficial and harmful for participants, so can the regulations that have been developed to protect the research participants. Regulations around child participation in social research both protect the well-being of children and, at the same time, limit their right to participate. Researchers of sensitive topics with a wish to involve vulnerable children must continuously balance between the child's well-being (i.e., protection from difficult topics) and rights (to express their own opinion); between vulnerable children and their parents and caregivers; between the general regulations and concrete living situations of a specific child.

To protect the research participants, researchers must follow codes of research ethics and obtain approval from research ethics committees that provide ethical clearance for the research. Blaikie and Priest (2019) note that such requirements are a relatively recent development. They consider the predominant role of ethics committees problematic and express concern that satisfying ethical requirements may start to hinder the advancement of knowledge. Hammersley (2009, p. 217–218) questions the need for evermore draconian ethical regulations considering that there is no evidence of substantial or systematic unethical behaviour in the social sciences. Hammersley (2009) goes even further noting that ethics committees have immense power and the right to decide about things that are yet to come. According to Hammersley (2009, p. 217), "they [ethics committees] require researchers to spell out what they are going to do, and the committee then decides whether or not this is legitimate… There are few other areas of life in which adult citizens are subjected to such a severe form of ethical regulation".

The problem is that this regulatory logic is in stark contrast to the logic of interpretative research, which covers a diverse array of approaches and research methods, and therefore, there exists a particularly great risk that general human research ethics committees lack the necessary knowledge that "is essential in order to make sound ethical judgments about what is proposed" (Hammersley, 2009, p. 216). All ethical issues cannot be foreseen in the application to the ethics committee because social researchers can never fully predict the situations they and their research participants will find themselves in during the research project. This is particularly true in the case of qualitative researchers, where regardless of the research methodology, "ethical judgments are essentially situational" (Hammersley, 2015, p. 445).

The strong regulation of ethical requirements imposed by the committees sometimes calls into question, and even prevents, active participation and co-investigation by participants. In the case of children, the role of co-researcher may be even more difficult for the ethics committee to allow. For this reason, there is a significant risk that target population-driven social science research will not be approved by the ethics committee, even though their right to participate is guaranteed by law (e.g., Garcia-Quiroga & Agoglia, 2020). Innovative participatory research methods are being developed to understand the problems of particularly vulnerable groups from the inside (Hammersley & Traianou, 2012), but the aim of these studies is not just to understand what is happening in the lives of vulnerable participants, but to dignify it. Dignity, however, always involves empowering the participants. Horgan (2017, p. 245) is concerned that "an overly paternalistic framework adopted by ethical review bodies can hamper participatory research with children". If ethics committees, in their bureaucratic approach, only adhere to the precepts of non-harming, confidentiality, and anonymity, a number of marginalised and vulnerable groups will remain excluded (Horgan, 2017; see also Hugman et al., 2011).

It has been claimed that "processes adopted by research ethics committees have been excessively bureaucratic and arbitrary" (Israel & Hay, 2006, p. 137). This is somehow inevitable in the case of general ethics committees evaluating research proposals from clinical psychiatry to pharmaceutics. However, social scientists are faced with a situation where, in order to receive an assessment of a standard social science study, the application must go through a meeting of the ethics committee, where the representatives of different (often not social science) disciplines must reach a consensus among themselves regarding the ethical aspects of the study (Masso & Beilmann, 2022). However, it is very difficult for representatives of different disciplines to reach a consensus due to their different theoretical, methodological, and practical experiences and understandings. Therefore, it often leads to a situation where only the data protection aspects of the study are evaluated (Masso & Beilmann, 2022). This does not do any justice to the children in vulnerable life situations whose right to be heard may be sacrificed due to the lack of the committee's knowledge of innovative participatory research methods.

Without a doubt, ethical committees play an important role in protecting children's rights and well-being in the research process. However, if the ethical committees apply very rigid rules and protocols borrowed from bio-medical research, children's opportunities to participate and make their voices heard may be hampered. To avoid the rigid following of bureaucratic rules, the individuals assessing the ethics of research projects need to be highly knowledgeable of the principles of conducting research in the field according to different paradigms. The lack of knowledge and appreciation of different social research paradigms can prove particularly problematic if the ethics committees go beyond ethical issues in their instructions to researchers and "make suggestions and even demands regarding how research should be restricted and redesigned, regardless of researcher's intent or the nature of fit between the research problem and methodology" (Lincoln, 2009, p. 158).

Obtaining informed consent and ensuring the anonymity and confidentiality of research participants cannot surely be the single most important issues in social research ethics, even though these topics are at the centre of the attention of ethics committees. Of course, obtaining informed consent and ensuring participant anonymity and confidentiality is of utmost importance and cannot be dismissed by researchers, but we agree with different authors (e.g., Blaikie & Priest, 2019; Bourke, 2017; Hammersley, 2009) who have suggested before us that research ethics and ethical considerations of researchers should go way beyond just satisfying strict predefined requirements of ethics committees.

In fact, Bourke (2017) warns that a complacent view of *being ethical* (which includes working through ethics committees and having comprehensive consent forms) might be a form of self-delusion, which prevents researchers from seeing what restrictions are placed on them by *outsiders* of groups and communities within which and with whom these researchers work. Bourke (2017) goes even further by suggesting that being compliant with the rules set by the ethics committees may give researchers general confidence that they are acting ethically and the belief that their research agenda benefits the child. The problem is that such general confidence can be a false confidence that may prevent researchers from asking important questions, like whether the chosen research agenda really benefits the child and gives them a voice.

Bourke (2017) stresses the reflexive nature of ethics, which implies that researchers must be ready to make sophisticated ethical decisions themselves and should not rely solely on the standard ethics committee process. Ethical procedures guided by codified regulations are a good starting point, but different issues that arise during the research necessitate a reflexive revisiting of ethics-related decisions in order to act ethically in a given situation (Bourke & Loveridge, 2014). Therefore, research ethics is always a living, changing, and dynamic process, especially in the case of qualitative research (Bourke et al., 2017). Effective research processes do not follow a template, are often unpredictable, and cannot be planned in advance (Davis et al., 2017; Gallacher & Gallagher, 2008). Therefore, the researchers must be flexible in their reactions to certain situations that arise in the research process. Jadue Roa (2017) lists respecting children's timing and children's choice of information as the fundamental ethical prerequisites in the research process involving young children. It is not possible to give young children a voice in a very strict research process. Furthermore, negotiated ethical practices with children, young people, and their families must be responsive, reflexive, and culturally astute (Bourke et al., 2017).

3.5 New Methodologies and Age-Old Ethical Dilemmas

The range of new digital research methods as well as the use of digital devices for storing research data have created and exaggerated several issues that researchers face when working with children and young people (Cowie & Khoo, 2017). These issues concern the privacy of young research participants, for example, and the worry that access to data on vulnerable children may fall into the wrong hands. However, as emphasised throughout this chapter, while it is important to protect young research participants from potential harm, harm can also be done by avoiding working with a particular child or group of children thereby silencing their voices and experiences (Cowie & Khoo, 2017). Even though digital media has expanded the methodological toolbox for researchers by "adding a new means of communicating with children and a new source of data about their lives" (Livingstone & Blum-Ross, 2017, p. 54), it is not conceivable to rely only on big data to obtain information about children's lives. Much of what is happening in children's lives may be visible on social networking sites, but it is only half of the story if we do not ask children how they feel about their online and offline lives.

The spread of open science requirements and the expectation of making the data publicly available may further damage the possibility of giving a voice to children in vulnerable life situations in research. As the research of the most vulnerable groups is often qualitative and exhibits the very personal stories of participants, it means that the requirement to make data publicly available severely contradicts not only data protection rules but also the very basis of research ethics. Open data requirements pose several ethical issues in qualitative research, including a contradiction with the researcher's responsibility to protect participant confidentiality and give participants a voice without putting them at unnecessary risk (Beilmann & Roots, 2020). Furthermore, Beilmann and Roots (2020) stress that qualitative data is contextual and making, for example, the transcripts of qualitative interviews publicly available would require extremely lengthy descriptions of the contextual and methodological considerations, and even then, the transcripts may be misleading because they do not feature the participant's mimics and body language. These problems may be amplified when studying children in vulnerable life situations as, on the one hand, they may not be very vocal about their experiences and feelings in the first place and if they know that everything they say will be written down and made public, it definitely does not help generate trust in researchers, and on the other hand, ethical researchers would probably back off from doing research in such terms as they would not consider it ethical to make full transcripts public as it may allow the participants to be identified and put some of them in risk now or in the future.

That would be a loss for both research and children as today's research on and with children has the potential of not only exploring children's agency and participation but also *developing* their agency and participation. Increasingly, participatory research design is being used. In these research designs, children themselves are involved in the development of the planning of the research methodology (Clark,

2011; Horgan, 2017; Meininger, 2006; Simmons & Watson, 2015; Watson et al., 2021; Watts, 2021). Clark, for example, used a multi-sensory communication method—the Mosaic approach—while studying young children. The Mosaic approach makes use of "visual and kinaesthetic modes of communication alongside speech in order to broaden the range of modes of expression which are given status within the research—playing to the strengths of the young children involved" (Clark, 2011: 313). The term *mosaic* indicates the use of the assembly of research elements (=tiles), which together form more of a whole (Clark, 2011). The participatory nature of this method leaves a lot of room for children's agency (Clark, 2011). Through the use of a variety of activities and tools—elements of multimodal communication—children can not only express their views on and attitudes towards the important things in their lives but also interact with adults and practice storytelling and meaning-making.

In order to truly benefit children participating in research, participatory research must be combined with high ethical standards. Therefore, we close up this chapter with a recipe or a checklist for ethical considerations when conducting participatory research with children. Swartz (2011) outlined six ethical strategies in qualitative research that may contribute to exceeding the ethical expectations of consent, confidentiality and child protection. All these are dimensions of emancipatory ethics, and these recommendations can be seen as guidelines, especially for young researchers working with vulnerable populations, in particular vulnerable children and young people, or when research participants come from different ethnocultural backgrounds. The strategies promoting an emancipatory approach to researching sensitive issues are (Swartz, 2011):

1. choosing the right methods. Research methods must be child-friendly and consider the specific characteristics of the children and young people participating in the research. Fortunately, qualitative methods include a variety of creative methods that are worth adopting (and adapting according to the particular needs of research participants);
2. building up a relationship between the researcher and the research participants. Before starting data collection, the researcher needs to establish a relationship of trust with the research participants. This may take time, but it is essential that children and young people come into the research process with a clear understanding of what they can expect and that they are adequately prepared to take part;
3. the researcher must be sufficiently open with the participants. The researcher must first acknowledge that they are in a stronger and higher position compared to the research participants and it is their task to present themselves more as an equal to the children participating in the research. This can be achieved by making oneself more vulnerable as well. For example, face-to-face meetings in qualitative research make the researcher more vulnerable and therefore more equal with the research participants as the participant(s) can also ask questions that force the researcher to open up just as the researcher expects the participant(s) to open up and share their experiences;

4. the levelling playing field, which is essential for emancipatory research, can be best achieved by using different games throughout the research process. Play is the domain of children, and when they can play with an adult researcher, it allows them to feel more confident and competent;
5. considering language and representation. The researcher has to regulate their own use of language as well as examine whether as a researcher they have adequately understood what the participants are saying and how adequate is this representation of the participants' perspectives;
6. planning the research as an intervention. The research must bring about positive change in the lives of those being researched.

3.6 Conclusion

Children's vulnerability is not only an academic but most of all a social and political issue (Andresen & Ben-Arieh, 2016), which requires complex ethical decisions to be made by the researchers conducting research on and with children in general and on and with groups of the most vulnerable children in particular. However, the ethical issues around the research of vulnerable children can prove tricky as the researchers have to carefully balance the fine line between child protection and child agency as well as the needs and concerns of gatekeepers and children participating in the research.

It is impossible to stress enough that research with vulnerable children must be reflexive in nature and the researchers must be ready and willing to alter their research according to the needs of the children involved. This makes a qualitative approach particularly suitable for studying children in vulnerable life situations. The relational nature of qualitative research practices in turn necessitates that research ethics is a living, changing, and dynamic process (Bourke et al., 2017). Ethical research practice is negotiated with children, young people, and their families (Bourke et al., 2017). Only by negotiating the terms of participation with children and giving room for their agency, can the researcher fulfil the obligation to make sure that their research would not increase the vulnerability of participating children but rather that children's participation would boost their resilience.

Acknowledgement Work on this chapter was supported by a grant from the Estonian Research Council (PRG700).

Competing Interests The authors have no conflicts of interest to declare that are relevant to the content of this chapter.

References

Abebe, T. (2019). Reconceptualising children's agency as continuum and interdependence. *Social Sciences, 8*(81). https://doi.org/10.3390/socsci8030081

Alderson, P., Hawthorne, J., & Killen, M. (2005). The participation rights of premature babies. *International Journal of Children's Rights, 1*, 31–35. https://doi.org/10.1163/1571818054545231

Alves, H., Gibbs, L., Marinkovic, K., Brito, I., & Sheikhattari, P. (2022). Children and adolescents' voices and the implications for ethical research. *Childhood, 29*(1), 126–143. https://doi.org/10.1177/09075682211061230

Andresen, S., & Ben-Arieh, A. (2016). Can we compare children's well-being across countries? Lessons from the Children's worlds study. In C. Hunner-Kreisel & S. Bohne (Eds.), *Childhood, youth and migration: Connecting global and local perspectives* (pp. 15–29). Springer. https://doi.org/10.1007/978-3-319-31111-1_2

Beilmann, M., & Roots, A. (2020). Avaandmete kasutusvõimalused ja piirangud [Uses and limitations of open data]. In A. Masso, K. Tiidenberg, & A. Siibak (Eds.), *Kuidas mõista andmestunud maailma? Metodoloogiline teejuht [Making sense of the datafied world—a methodological guide]* (pp. 97–118). TLÜ Kirjastus.

Blaikie, N., & Priest, J. (2019). *Designing social research: The logic of anticipation* (3rd ed.). Polity Press.

Bourke, R. (2017). The ethics of including and 'standing up' for children and young people in educational research. *International Journal of Inclusive Education, 21*(3), 231–233. https://doi.org/10.1080/13603116.2016.1260823

Bourke, R., & Loveridge, J. (2014). Exploring informed consent and dissent through children's participation in educational research. *International Journal of Research and Method in Education, 37*(2), 151–165. https://doi.org/10.1080/1743727X.2013.817551

Bourke, R., Loveridge, J., O'Neill, J., Erueti, B., & Jamieson, A. (2017). A sociocultural analysis of the ethics of involving children in educational research. *International Journal of Inclusive Education, 21*(3), 259–271. https://doi.org/10.1080/13603116.2016.1260819

Christensen, P. H. (2002). Why more 'quality time' is not on the top of children's lists: The 'qualities of time' for children. *Children and Society, 2*, 77–88. https://doi.org/10.1002/chi.709

Clark, A. (2011). Multimodal map making with young children: Exploring ethnographic and participatory methods. *Qualitative Research, 11*(3), 311–330. https://doi.org/10.1177/1468794111400532

Cowie, B., & Khoo, E. (2017). Accountability through access, authenticity and advocacy when researching with young children. *International Journal of Inclusive Education, 21*(3), 234–247. https://doi.org/10.1080/13603116.2016.1260821

Davies, H. (2012). Affinities, seeing and feeling like-family: Exploring why children value face-to-face contact. *Childhood, 19*(1), 8–23. https://doi.org/10.1177/0907568211400453

Davies, H. (2017). Researching children's complex family lives and respecting inter-generational relationships. In P. Christensen & A. James (Eds.), *Research with children: Perspectives and practices* (3rd ed., pp. 87–103). Routledge.

Davis, J., Watson, N., & Cunningham-Burley, S. (2017). Disabled children, ethnography and unspoken understandings. In P. Christensen & A. James (Eds.), *Research with children: Perspectives and practices* (3rd ed., pp. 121–141). Routledge.

Dubois, A.-C., Lahaye, M., & Aujoulat, I. (2021). From research 'on' to research 'with' children about their family lives: A scoping review of ethical and methodological challenges. *Child: Care, Health and Development, 48*(2), 203–216. https://doi.org/10.1111/cch.12937

Fattore, T., Mason, J., & Watson, E. (2009). When children are asked about their well-being: Towards a framework for guiding policy. *Child Indicators Research, 2*(1), 57–77. https://doi.org/10.1007/s12187-008-9025-3

Gallacher, L.-A., & Gallagher, M. (2008). Methodological immaturity in childhood research? Thinking through 'participatory methods'. *Childhood, 15*(4), 499–516. https://doi.org/10.1177/0907568208091672
Garcia-Quiroga, M., & Agoglia, I. (2020). Too vulnerable to participate? challenges for meaningful participation in research with children in alternative care and adoption. *International Journal of Qualitative Methods, 19*. https://doi.org/10.1177/1609406920958965
Görzig, A. (2012). Methodological framework: The EU kids online project. In S. Livingstone, L. Haddon, & A. Görzig (Eds.), *Children, risk and safety on the internet. Research and policy challenges in comparative perspective* (pp. 15–32). Policy Press. https://doi.org/10.1332/policypress/9781847428837.003.0002
Greene, S., & Nixon, E. (2020). *Children as agents in their worlds: A psychological-relational perspective*. Routledge.
Hammersley, M. (2009). Against the ethics: On the evils of ethical regulation. *International Journal of Social Research Methodology, 12*, 211–225. https://doi.org/10.1080/13645570802170288
Hammersley, M. (2015). On ethical principles for social research. *International Journal of Social Research Methodology, 18*, 433–449. https://doi.org/10.1080/13645579.2014.924169
Hammersley, M., & Traianou, A. (2012). *Ethics in qualitative research*. Sage. https://doi.org/10.4135/9781473957619
Horgan, D. (2017). Child participatory research methods: Attempts to go 'deeper'. *Chidlhood, 24*(2), 245–259. https://doi.org/10.1177/0907568216647787
Hugman, R., Pittaway, E., & Bartolomei, L. (2011). When 'do no harm' is not enough: The ethics of research with refugees and other vulnerable groups. *British Journal of Social Work, 41*, 1271–1287. https://doi.org/10.1093/bjsw/bcr013
Irwin, L. G., & Johnson, J. (2005). Interviewing young children: Explicating our practices and dilemmas. *Qualitative Health Research, 15*(6), 821–831. https://doi.org/10.1177/1049732304273862
Israel, M., & Hay, I. (2006). *Research ethics for social scientists: Between ethical conduct and regulatory compliance*. Sage. https://doi.org/10.4135/9781849209779
Jadue Roa, D. S. (2017). Ethical issues in listening to young children in visual participatory research. *International Journal of Inclusive Education, 21*(3), 332–345. https://doi.org/10.1080/13603116.2016.1260829
James, A., & Prout, A. (1997). Introduction. In A. James & A. Prout (Eds.), *Constructing and reconstructing childhood: Contemporary issues in the sociological study of childhood* (pp. 1–5). Falmer Press.
Lincoln, Y. S. (2009). Ethical practices in qualitative research. In D. M. Mertens & P. E. Ginsberg (Eds.), *The handbook of social research ethics* (pp. 150–169). Sage. https://doi.org/10.4135/9781483348971
Livingstone, S., & Blum-Ross, A. (2017). Researching children and childhood in the digital age. In P. Christensen & A. James (Eds.), *Research with children: Perspectives and practices* (3rd ed., pp. 54–70). Routledge.
Lobe, B., Livingstone, S., Ólafsson, K., & Simões, J. A. (Eds.) (2008). *Best practice research guide: How to research children and online technologies in comparative perspective*. EU Kids Online, London School of Economics and Political Science. http://eprints.lse.ac.uk/21658/
Lundy, L. (2007). 'Voice' is not enough: Conceptualizing Article 12 of the United Nations Convention on the Rights of the Child. *British Educational Research Journal, 33*(6), 927–942. https://doi.org/10.2307/30032800
Lundy, L. (2018). In defence of tokenism? Implementing children's right to participation in collective decision-making. *Childhood, 25*(3), 340–354. https://doi.org/10.1177/0907568218777292
Masso, A., & Beilmann, M. (2022). Eetiline vaakum Eesti sotsiaalteadustes [Ethical vacuum in Estonian social sciences]. *Sirp, 40*(3912), 18–19, 07.10.2022. https://www.sirp.ee/s1-artiklid/c21-teadus/eetiline-vaakum-eesti-sotsiaalteadustes/
Maté, G., & Maté, D. (2022). *The myth of normal – Trauma, illness and healing in a toxic culture*. New York.

Mayne, F., Howitt, C., & Rennie, L. J. (2017). Using interactive nonfiction narrative to enhance competence in the informed consent process with 3-year-old children. *International Journal of Inclusive Education, 21*(3), 299–315. https://doi.org/10.1080/13603116.2016.1260833

Meininger, H. P. (2006). Narrating, writing, reading: Life story work as an aid to (self) advocacy. *British Journal of Learning Disabilities, 34*(3), 181–188. https://doi.org/10.1111/j.1468-3156.2006.00416.x

Neufeld, G., & Maté, G. (2007). *Hold on to your kids*. Ballantine Books.

Perry, B. (2009). Examining child maltreatment through a neurodevelopmental lens: Clinical applications of the neurosequential model of therapeutics. *Journal of Loss and Trauma, 14*, 240–255. https://doi.org/10.1080/15325020903004350

Perry, B., & Szalavitz, M. (2017). *The boy who was raised as a dog and other stories from a child psychiatrics notebook. What traumatized children can teach us about loss, love, and healing*. Basic Books.

Qvortrup, J., Corsaro, B., & Honig, M.-S. (Eds.). (2009). *The Palgrave handbook of childhood studies*. Palgrave Macmillan.

Siegel, D. (2001). Toward an interpersonal neurobiology of the developing mind: Attachment relationships, "mindsight," and neural integration. *Infant Mental Health Journal, 22*(1), 67–94. https://doi.org/10.1002/1097-0355(200101/04)22:1<67::AID-IMHJ3>3.0.CO;2-G

Siegel, D. (2012). *Pocket guide to interpersonal neurobiology. An integrative handbook of the mind*. W.W. Norton & Company.

Simmons, B. R., & Watson, D. L. (2015). From individualism to co-construction and back again: Rethinking research methodology for children with profound and multiple learning disabilities. *Child Care in Practice, 21*(1), 50–66. https://doi.org/10.1080/13575279.2014.976179

Soo, K., Lukk, M., Ainsaar, M., Beilmann, M., Sammul, M., Tamm, G., Espenberg, K., Murakas, R., Arak, T., Aksen, M., Vahaste-Pruul, S., & Kutsar, D. (2016). *Laste ja noorte seksuaalse väärkohtlemise leviku uuring* [Study of prevalence of sexual abuse of children and young people]. Justiitsministeerium.

Stalker, K. (2012). Researching the lives of disabled children and young people. *Children and Society, 26*, 173–180. https://doi.org/10.1111/j.1099-0860.2012.00430.x

Strömpl, J. (2002). The K-school. *Residential Management of Troublesome Girls in Transition-time Estonia*. Academic dissertation. University of Tampere.

Strömpl, J., & Luhamaa, K. (2020). Child participation in child welfare removals through the looking glass: Estonian children's and professionals' perspectives compared. *Children and Youth Services Review, 118*, 105421. https://doi.org/10.1016/j.childyouth.2020.105421

Swartz, S. (2011). 'Going deep' and 'giving back': Strategies for exceeding ethical expectations when researching amongst vulnerable youth. *Qualitative Research, 11*(1), 47–68. https://doi.org/10.1177/1468794110385885

Tinson, J. (2009). *Conducting research with children and adolescents: Design, methods and empirical cases*. Goodfellow.

Traianou, A., & Hammersley, M. (2023). InterrogatIng the concept of vulnerability in social research ethics. *Diametros.*. 10.33392/diam.1891.

van Bijleveld, G. G., Dedding, C. W., & Bunders-Aelen, J. F. (2013). Children's and young people's participation within child welfare and child protection services. A state-of-the art review. *Child & Family Social Work, 20*(2), 129–138. https://doi.org/10.1111/cfs.12082

Watson, D. L., Staples, E., & Riches, K. (2021). 'We need to understand what's going on because it's our life': Using sandboxing to understand children and young people's everyday conversations about care. *Children & Society, 35*, 663–679. https://doi.org/10.1111/chso.12432

Watts, R. (2021). Relationships, reviews and recording: Developing practice for children in care. *Practice, 33*(3), 207–222. https://doi.org/10.1080/09503153.2021.1889488

Mai Beilmann is an Associate Professor of Empirical Sociology at the Institute of Social Studies, University of Tartu, Estonia, and a former youth worker. Her research focuses mainly on children and youth studies, particularly child/adolescent vulnerability in the education system, NEET youth and youth work, youth civic and political participation, values, and social capital. After working for seven years for the European Social Survey, she joined the Estonian team of the International Survey of Children's Well-Being (ISCWeB) in 2019. She is a member of the Estonian Young Academy of Sciences and since 2018, she has served as the president of the Estonian Association of Sociologists.

Judit Strömpl is an Associate Professor of Social Work Research at the University of Tartu. Her main areas of research are childhood and youth vulnerability, child protection, especially substitute care, juvenile justice. In her research, she is guided by a child rights and well-being perspective. She has researched sensitive topics such as violence, discrimination and trauma. More recently, she has been focusing on the implementation of support measures for traumatised children in substitute care in Estonia. In her research, she prefers qualitative engaging methods such as ethnography, participatory action research and playful techniques when interacting with children and their caregivers. She also believes in the transformative power of social work research; that is, while studying vulnerability, she seeks not only to understand the situation but to improve it.

Part II
Child Vulnerability from Different Angles

Chapter 4
Child Vulnerability from a Cross-Country Comparative Perspective

Oliver Nahkur

4.1 Introduction: Why Do We Need an International Cross-Country Subjective Child Vulnerability Measure?

Child vulnerability; for example, child poverty and poor health, has long been considered a problem of the Global South. However, the Global North is also increasingly taking this issue onto their agenda. In 2017, England started to conduct annual childhood vulnerability reports, attempting to measure the number of vulnerable children in England. In 2019, the OECD (2019) highlighted the importance of tackling the issue of vulnerable children with their report *Changing the Odds for Vulnerable Children: Building Opportunities and Resilience*. Consequently, child vulnerability has been turning into an issue worthy of global attention. However, there is no precise data about the magnitude of child vulnerability worldwide. According to the estimates of SOS Children's Villages International (2016), at least 1-in-10 children of the 2.2 billion children worldwide can be considered vulnerable. Gaps in data have made it difficult to quantify the magnitude of child vulnerability worldwide, and therefore to undertake global analysis or interventions. Indeed, prevention of and early intervention in child vulnerability entails the need to assess the likelihood of future suffering (Daniel, 2010).

Measuring vulnerability is not an easy task, but it can be mapped, monitored or quantified by means of surveys (Arora et al., 2015). To map and/or monitor child vulnerability internationally, nationally representative international surveys, providing harmonised data are needed. Moreover, to make a starting point for action, Saltelli (2007) suggests forming indices based on such data. According to the former EU Commissioner for Competition, Mario Monti (2005), cross-national

O. Nahkur (✉)
Institute of Social Studies, University of Tartu, Tartu, Estonia
e-mail: oliver.nahkur@ut.ee

D. Kutsar et al. (eds.), *Child Vulnerability and Vulnerable Subjectivity*, Children's Well-Being: Indicators and Research 27,
https://doi.org/10.1007/978-3-031-61333-3_4

scoreboards have played a useful role in bringing peer pressure to bear on national decision-makers.

Recently, composite child indicators based primarily on objective statistical data have been constructed. For example, an international objective[1] indicator—the Child Vulnerability Index (CVI)—has been constructed as a measure of how likely it is for children to be at risk in a particular country (SOS Children's Villages International, 2016). In Lao PDA, using primarily objective indicators, a vulnerability index has been constructed measuring the level of child vulnerability at the village level (Vision, 2019). However, to the author's knowledge, there is no cross-nationally comparable vulnerability measure based on survey data collected from children to facilitate international comparisons.

Indeed, children should not be seen as an *object of concern* (Daniel, 2010). Children's own views and perspectives on their life should be taken seriously when trying to measure their vulnerability. This need is even more explicit because of existing evidence of the disconnect between children's own assessment of their *vulnerable* situation and that of professionals (Coram, 2017). Also, as suggested in Chap. 2, whether risks translate into harm to well-being depends more on the child's perceptions about the risks than the objective circumstances. Moreover, such an approach is aligned with the ideas of the newest wave of the Social Indicators Movement stressing the importance of human agency (Tsai, 2017), the new sociology of childhood and the Child Indicators Movement (Ben-Arieh, 2008) and the UN Convention on the Rights of the Child (www.unicef.org/crc/), Article 12, which states that "children are full-fledged persons who have the right to express their views in all matters affecting them and requires that those views be heard and given due weight in accordance with the child's age and maturity."

Internationally, children's own views about their lives are collected by the Children's Worlds project with the International Survey for Child Well-being (ISCWeB). ISCWeB is not a WEIRD (Western, Educated, Industrialised, Rich, and Democratic societies[2]) survey; for example, in its third wave 35 countries as diverse as Algeria, Nepal, and Wales were included. Other international surveys (e.g., Health Behaviour in School-aged Children (HBSC)) collecting data from children are geographically more limited. The scope of ISCWeB's questionnaire is wide enough to cover factors that increase but also decrease child vulnerability. Therefore, it offers a good basis for developing an international subjective child vulnerability measure that is comparable across nations, and which considers the recent shift from solely being focused on risk and its avoidance to building resilience[3] to overcome child vulnerability (e.g., see OECD, 2019).

---

[1] The CVI reflects data such as Gross National Income (GNI) per capita, the under-5 mortality rate, and other measures of living standards, schooling, and orphanhood.

[2] North America, Europe, Australia, New Zealand and Israel. While children growing up in Western countries comprise only about 10–12% of the world's population of children (Henrich et al., 2010; LeVine and New, 2008), approximately 96% of child development research in the leading peer-reviewed psychology journals in the United States is based on samples from what has come to be called WEIRD societies.

[3] Building resilience requires reducing the number of risks and increasing the number of protective factors in a child's world (OECD, 2019).

The aims of the chapter are as follows: (1) to introduce the first version of the International Child Subjective Vulnerability-Resilience Index (ICSVRI) as a measure that aims to be comparable across nations; (2) to test empirically the conceptual framework for understanding child vulnerability presented in Chap. 2; (3) to provide international comparisons of children's subjective vulnerability; (3) to explore the main contributors to child subjective vulnerability; and (4) to examine inequalities in child subjective vulnerability by age and gender.

4.2 What Is ICSVRI?

ICSVRI is a new subjective vulnerability index measuring a child's perceived risk of harm to his/her well-being, which is constructed in seven steps proposed by Nardo (2008). First, a conceptual framework was developed; second, variables from the dataset of the third wave of ISCWeB were selected; third, the imputation of missing data was conducted; fourth, multivariate analysis was conducted; fifth, data was normalised; sixth, weighting and aggregation was conducted to arrive at the ICSVRI; and finally, the validity of ICSVRI was tested. All these steps are described in the following sub-sections.

4.2.1 Conceptual Framework

This paper follows the OECD's (2019) approach to applying the concept of building resilience to overcome child vulnerability and the conceptual framework for understanding child vulnerability presented in Chap. 2. In this framework, child vulnerability and resilience form a continuum. The focus is solely on child subjective (also 'perceived') vulnerability and resilience. According to the framework, child subjective vulnerability in relation to child subjective resilience forms a child's perceived risk of harm to their well-being. Child subjective vulnerability refers to a high level of perceived risk of harm to a child's well-being, and resilience to a low level of perceived risk of harm to a child's well-being.

Based on its sources, three types of child subjective vulnerability and resilience—individual, direct and indirect environmental vulnerability-resilience are considered, inspired by the ecological model of child development by Bronfenbrenner (1979) and social-ecological model of resilience by Ungar et al. (2013). Direct environments are constituted by important relationships—with parents/caregivers, teachers, schoolmates, peers and friends—in the children's life and family and school as more frequent locations where they live their everyday lives. These are considered the 5 dimensions of direct environmental subjective vulnerability-resilience. Indirect environmental subjective vulnerability-resilience has 2 dimensions—the local area and the country, society or world. The most common factors contributing to child vulnerability and/or resilience were determined in two waves of literature search. The conceptual framework, including the most common individual, direct, and indirect environmental vulnerability-resilience factors, are described in more detail in Chap. 2.

4.2.2 *Operationalisation*

Variable Selection and Adaptation to the Structure of ICSVRI

ISCWeB, as the geographically most widespread international survey of 8, 10 and 12-year-old children, provides every 4–5 years representative cross-nationally harmonised data on the lives of children, their daily activities, time use, and perceptions and evaluations of their well-being. To operationalise the first version of ICSVRI, data was used from the survey's third wave, conducted in 2017/2018, due to the wide range of countries participating. The dataset of the third wave of ISCWeB was screened to find variables measuring the most common individual, direct, and indirect environmental vulnerability-resilience factors. The selection criteria for the variables included face validity and the availability of data on children aged 10 and 12[4] (except England where data was only available for 10-year-olds) from a maximum number of different countries. Overall, 34 different variables were selected measuring 3 types, 7 dimensions and 25 sub-dimensions of subjective vulnerability-resilience[5] (see Table 4.1). Ten variables measure individual dimension, 21 direct environmental dimension (2 parental/caregiver, 5 family, 7 friends/peers/schoolmates, 3 teachers, 4 school sub-dimensions) and 3 indirect environmental dimension

[4] Eight-year-old children were not included due to the tighter scope of the data available, and scale differences compared to older age groups.

[5] No suitable data was found for physical health, temperament, sociability, cognitive ability, sense of competence and self-efficacy, social problem-solving skills, sense of humour, empathy for others, having goals and aspirations, sense of direction and meaning in life, minority status, cultural/spiritual/religious identification, having hobbies, extracurricular activities, recognised talents/accomplishments as *individual vulnerability-resilience* sub-dimensions; mental and physical health of the parent(s), parents' alcohol/drug abuse, attachment with parent/caregiver, child maltreatment by parent/caregiver, parental discipline, perceived social support from parent(s)/caregiver(s), parent(s)/caregiver(s) level of education, quality of couple relationship of parents/caregivers, parental separation/divorce as *parental/caregiver vulnerability-resilience* sub-dimensions; having a mentor/role model in family to follow, existence of family routines and traditions as *family vulnerability-resilience* sub-dimensions; delinquent peers as *friends/peers/schoolmates vulnerability-resilience* sub-dimensions; school climate and having a mentor/role model in school to follow as *school vulnerability-resilience* sub-dimensions; community poverty, economic and employment opportunities for families in local area, access to good-quality child institutions, access to trustworthy/affordable/ effective emergency and healthcare services, quality of social relationships among neighbourhood/community members and organizations, crime and violence level in neighbourhood, caring relationships with mentors, helping professionals and other adults in local area, valued social role and meaningful involvement in local area, having role models/mentors in local area, sense of community as *local area vulnerability-resilience* sub-dimensions; likelihood of disaster in country, including catastrophic natural and health emergency events, national security, care in country, availability and access to governmental structures and support services, discrimination in society as *societal/country/global world vulnerability-resilience* sub-dimensions.

Table 4.1 Individual, direct and indirect environmental subjective vulnerability-resilience and their sub-dimensions' variables, original and ICSVRI scale, and the equations for the ICSVRI dimensional sub-indices (*resilience factor only)

Sub-dimensions	Variable(s)	Original scale	ICSVRI scale	ICSVRI dimensional sub-indices
Individual subjective vulnerability-resilience				
Mental health	I_MH1: Last two weeks: How often feeling happy I_MH2: Last two weeks: How often feeling calm I_MH3: Last two weeks: How often feeling full of energy I_MH4: Last two weeks: How often feeling sad I_MH5: Last two weeks: How often feeling stressed I_MH6: Last two weeks: How often feeling bored	0—not at all … 10—extremely	Happy, calm, full of energy: 0—extremely … 1—not at all Sad, stressed, bored: 0—not at all … 1—extremely Arithmetic mean of these 6 variables	Individual vulnerability-resilience sub-index = (I_MH1 + I_MH2 + I_MH3 + I_MH4 + I_MH5 + I_MH6)/6 + I_SE + I_CON + I_HO + I_SC
Self-esteem	I_SE: Satisfaction with: The way that you look	0—not at all satisfied … 10—totally satisfied	0-totally satisfied … 1—not at all satisfied	
Sense of control over life/ Locus of control	I_CON: Satisfaction with: The freedom you have			
Hope, faith, optimism*	I_HO: Satisfaction with: What may happen to you later in your life		0–5→0.5, 6→0.4, 7→0.3, 8→0.2, 9→0.1, 10→0	
Social competence	I_SC: My friends are usually nice to me	0—I do not agree, 1—agree a little bit, 2—agree somewhat, 3—agree a lot, 4—totally agree	0—totally agree, 0.25—agree a lot, 0.5—agree somewhat, 0.75—agree a little bit, 1—I do not agree	

(continued)

Table 4.1 (continued)

Sub-dimensions	Variable(s)	Original scale	ICSVRI scale	ICSVRI dimensional sub-indices
Direct environmental subjective vulnerability-resilience				
… Parental/caregiver vulnerability-resilience				
Parent-child relationship quality	DE_PRQ: My parents/carers listen to me and take what I say into account	0—I do not agree, 1—agree a little bit, 2—agree somewhat, 3—agree a lot, 4—totally agree	0—totally agree, 0.25—agree a lot, 0.5—agree somewhat, 0.75—agree a little bit, 1—I do not agree	Parental/caregiver vulnerability-resilience sub-index = DE_PRQ + DE_PC
Parental care	DE_PC: There are people in my family who care about me			
Developmental support*	Is there a place in your home where you can study?	1—Yes, 2—no, 3—not sure	*Excluded*	
… Family vulnerability-resilience				
Financial and material resources of the family	DE_FRES: How often do you worry about how much money your family has	0—Never, 1—sometimes, 2—often, 3—always	0—never, 0.33—sometimes, 0.67—often, 1—always	Family vulnerability-resilience sub-index = DE_FRES + DE_FCOH + DE_FCON + DE_FaSUP + DE_FINV
Family cohesion and interaction	DE_FCOH: We have a good time together in my family	0—I do not agree, 1—agree a little bit, 2—agree somewhat, 3—agree a lot, 4—totally agree	0—totally agree, 0.25—agree a lot, 0.5—agree somewhat, 0.75—agree a little bit, 1—I do not agree	
Family violence and conflicts	DE_FCON: I feel safe at home			
Perceived social/psychosocial/emotional support from family	DE_FaSUP: If I have a problem, people in my family will help me			
Opportunities for meaningful family involvement	DE_FINV: My parents and I make decisions about my life together			

… Friends/peers/schoolmates vulnerability-resilience				
Quality of peer relationships/friendships*	DE_FrRQ: Me and my friends get along well together	0—I do not agree, 1—agree a little bit, 2—agree somewhat, 3—agree a lot, 4—totally agree	0—totally agree, 0.25—agree a lot, 0.5—agree somewhat + agree a little bit + I do not agree	Friends/peers/schoolmates vulnerability-resilience sub-index = DE_FRQ + (DE_ScMBUL*0.5 + DE_ScMVBUL*0.5) + (DE_ScMREJ*0.5 + DE_FrSI*0.5) + (DE_FrSUP*0.5 + DE_ScMSUP*0.5)
Bullying by peers	DE_ScMBUL: How often: Hit by other children in your school	0—Never, 1—once, 2—two or 3 times, 3—more than 3 times	0—never, 0.33—once, 0.67—two or 3 times, 1—more than 3 times	
	DE_ScMVBUL: How often: Called unkind names by other children in your school			
Social isolation, peer rejection	DE_ScMREJ: How often: Left out by other children in your class			
	DE_FrSI: I have enough friends	0—I do not agree, 1—agree a little bit, 2—agree somewhat, 3—agree a lot, 4—totally agree	0—totally agree, 0.25—agree a lot, 0.5—agree somewhat, 0.75—agree a little bit, 1—I do not agree	
Perceived social/psychosocial/emotional support from peers	DE_FrSUP: If I have a problem, I have a friend who will support me			
	DE_ScMSUP: If I have a problem at school other children will help me			
… Teachers' vulnerability-resilience				
Quality of child-teacher relationship*	DE_TRQ: My teachers listen to me and take what I say into account	0—I do not agree, 1—agree a little bit, 2—agree somewhat, 3—agree a lot, 4—totally agree	0—totally agree, 0.25—agree a lot, 0.5—agree somewhat + agree a little bit + I do not agree	Teachers vulnerability-resilience sub-index = DE_TRQ + DE_TC + DE_TSUP
Care and encouragement from teachers	DE_TC: My teachers care about me		0—totally agree, 0.25—agree a lot, 0.5—agree somewhat, 0.75—agree a little bit, 1—I do not agree	
Perceived social support from teachers	DE_TSUP: If I have a problem at school my teachers will help me			

(continued)

Table 4.1 (continued)

Sub-dimensions	Variable(s)	Original scale	ICSVRI scale	ICSVRI dimensional sub-indices
… School vulnerability-resilience				
Safety of school environment	DE_SSAF: I feel safe at school	0—I do not agree, 1—agree a little bit, 2—agree somewhat, 3—agree a lot, 4—totally agree	0—totally agree, 0.25—agree a lot, 0.5—agree somewhat, 0.75—agree a little bit, 1—I do not agree	School vulnerability-resilience sub-index = DE_SSAF + DE_SENG + (DE_SQC1*0.5 + DE_SQC2*0.5)
Engagement in school	DE_SENG: At school I have opportunities to make decisions about things that are important			
Quality of curriculum*	DE_SQC1: Satisfaction with: Things you have learned	0—not at all satisfied … 10—totally satisfied	0–5→0.5, 6→0.4, 7→0.3, 8→0.2, 9→0.1, 10→0	
	DE_SQC2: Satisfaction with: Your life as a student			
Indirect environmental subjective vulnerability-resilience				
… Local area vulnerability-resilience				
Access to recreational facilities and programmes in local area	IE_LAC: In my area there are enough places to play or to have a good time	0—I do not agree, 1—agree a little bit, 2—agree somewhat, 3—agree a lot, 4—totally agree	0—totally agree, 0.25—agree a lot, 0.5—agree somewhat, 0.75—agree a little bit, 1—I do not agree	Local area vulnerability-resilience sub-index = IE_LAC + IE_LSAF + IE_LSUP
Safety of the surrounding environment in local area	IE_LSAF: I feel safe when I walk in the area I live in			
Supportive community environment	IE_LSUP: If I have a problem there are people in my local area who will help me			

(the local area) of subjective vulnerability-resilience. No suitable variables were found for the society/country/global world dimension. However, according to Lee and Yoo (2015), Klocke et al. (2014), and Nahkur and Kutsar (2019), societal/country factors are not so important for children's perceptions about their life.

Out of 35 countries,[6] 20 countries remained in the dataset. On the basis of the United Nations world regions, the Eastern Asian region is represented by Hong Kong, Taiwan, and South Korea, the Southeast Asian region by Indonesia and Vietnam, Southern Asia by Nepal and Sri Lanka, Northern Africa by Algeria, Southern Europe by Malta, Italy, Spain, Albania, and Croatia, Eastern Europe by Hungary, Northern Europe by Estonia, England, and Wales, Western Europe by Belgium, and Southern America by Brazil and Chile. In most cases, representative samples for a whole country exist. However, in some countries only some region(s) are covered—in Algeria (western), Belgium (Flanders), Brazil (cities: Porto Alegre, Florianópolis, Curitiba, São Paulo, Rio de Janeiro), Chile (Metropolitan and Bío-Bío Region), Indonesia (West Java), Italy (Liguria), Nepal (Dolakha, Dhading, Chitwan districts), Spain (Catalonia), and Sri Lanka (central).

Imputation of Missing Data

Data imputation was needed to get a complete dataset for index construction. First, case deletion was used—children having missing data in more than five variables out of 34 were deleted from the dataset. Out of 61,337, the data of 58,853 children remained. Then, by country, imputation of missing data for each variable was conducted using the Expectation Maximation method, which is a slightly more complex solution than using sample mean, median or mode.

Multivariate Analysis

Next, after assuring that the scales of the selected variables had the same direction, the relationships between the selected variables were explored using Spearman correlation analysis and Cronbach's coefficient alpha. These analyses showed that all the variables were positively and not too strongly (maximum Spearman $r = 0.628$) related, and supported the grouping of variables into (1) individual, (2) parental/caregiver, (3) family, (4) friends, peers and schoolmates, (5) teachers, (6) school, and (7) local area dimensions. The variables were most strongly associated with other variables belonging to the same dimension.[7] Two variables, *Is there a place in your home where you can study* (max $r = 0.180$) and *How often do you worry about*

[6]Bangladesh, Finland, France, Germany, Greece, India, Israel, Malaysia, Namibia, Norway, Poland, Romania, Russia, South Africa, and Switzerland were not included due to not meeting variable selection criteria, e.g., missing data on some relevant variable.

[7]Except *My friends are usually nice to me* being more strongly related to the 'friends, peers and schoolmates' dimension instead of the 'individual' dimension variables. As the Cronbach's alpha for the 'individual' dimension was 0.743, and it did not increase when excluding this variable, it was decided to retain it in the index as a measure of social competence.

how much money your family has (max r = 0.164) were very weakly related to all other selected variables, including those in the same dimensions. In 17 out of 20 countries, the Cronbach's alpha for the parental/caregiver dimension was lower than 0.6, but when the variable *Is there a place in your home where you can study* was excluded, it reduced to 10 countries. Therefore, it was decided to exclude this variable from the index. The decision was made to retain the variable *How often do you worry about how much money your family has*, because Cronbach's alpha was lower than 0.6 with this variable in only five countries.[8]

Overall, no major cross-national differences were noticed. For all the selected variables, Cronbach's alpha ranged from 0.814 in Indonesia to 0.915 in Wales. The values for Cronbach's alpha for different dimensions of subjective vulnerability-resilience did not differ much by country and between children of 10 and 12 years.[9]

Normalisation

As the original scales of different variables were not comparable, all their values were transformed between 0 and 1 (see the 'ICSVRI scale' in Table 4.1). Values below 0.5 indicate subjective resilience, and above 0.5 subjective vulnerability. There are four variables measuring a factor reported as a common resilience (but not vulnerability) factor. In these cases, values indicating vulnerability equalled 0.5—midpoint of the 0 to 1 scale.[10]

Weighting and Aggregating

Before computing the values of ICSVRI and its sub-indices, it was necessary to decide if some variables and dimensions were more important than others. Most composite indicators rely on equal weighting; that is, all variables are given the same weight (Nardo et al., 2008). At the variable level, equal weighting (1.0) was used as we do not have enough robust evidence showing which factors are more important than others and to what extent. If a vulnerability-resilience sub-dimension was measured using two variables, both were weighted 0.5. At the dimensional level, equal weights (1.0) were also used. However, this means that direct environmental dimensions of subjective vulnerability-resilience contribute more to the overall index than individual and indirect environmental dimensions. This is in accordance with Lee and Yoo (2015), Klocke et al. (2014), and Nahkur and Kutsar (2019), who emphasise the importance of family, school and community in children's lives across countries.

---

[8] It would have been so in two countries when excluding it.

[9] In all subjective vulnerability-resilience dimensions, Cronbach's alpha tended to be a little higher for 12-year-olds.

[10] Also the index version, where these four variables were considered resilience and vulnerability factors, was computed, and an extremely strong correlation (Spearman r = 0.999) was found between the two index versions.

To compute the values of ICSVRI and its sub-indices, the linear additive aggregation method was used, which involves the summation of normalised and weighted variables (Nardo et al., 2008, p. 103). This method is compensatory for each dimension/sub-dimension—a deficit in one dimension/sub-dimension can be compensated for by a surplus in another, which is not considered problematic in ICSVRI. For example, a lack of parental/caregiver care can be compensated for by care from a teacher or adult in the local area. In Table 4.1, the equations for ICSVRI dimensional sub-indices are shown. ICSVRI is computed with the following equation:

$$\begin{aligned}\text{ICSVRI} = {} & \text{Individual vulnerability} - \text{resilience sub} - \text{index} \\ & + \text{Parental / caregiver vulnerability} - \text{resilience sub} \\ & - \text{index} + \text{Family vulnerability} - \text{resilience sub} - \text{index} \\ & + \text{Friends / peers / schoolmates vulnerability} \\ & - \text{resilience sub} - \text{index} + \text{Teachers' vulnerability} \\ & - \text{resilience sub} - \text{index} + \text{School vulnerability} \\ & - \text{resilience sub} - \text{index} + \text{Local area vulnerability} \\ & - \text{resilience sub} - \text{index}\end{aligned}$$

ICSVRI values range from 0 to 23, where a higher value indicates a higher level of subjective vulnerability, meaning a higher level of the child's perceived risk of harm to their well-being. More precisely, values 0–5.75 indicate the child is subjectively 'very resilient', 5.75–11.5 'somewhat resilient', 11.5–17.25 'somewhat vulnerable', and 17.25–23.0 'very vulnerable'.[11]

Validity

The internal consistency of ICSVRI is very good, as Cronbach's alpha was 0.890 based on country-pooled data. It varied a bit by age group—being 0.882 for 10-year-olds and 0.896 for 12-year-olds. By country, it ranged from 0.813 in Albania to 0.915 in Wales.

In general, the vulnerability-resilience dimensions have good internal consistency—Cronbach's alpha was 0.718 for individual, 0.582 for parental/caregiver, 0.631 for family, 0.697 for friends/peers/schoolmates, 0.811 for teachers, 0.684 for school, and 0.668 for local area dimensions based on country-pooled data. The internal consistency was a bit better among 12-year-olds compared to 10-year-olds—Cronbach's alpha for the parental vulnerability-resilience dimension was 0.619 and 0.540, respectively.

As expected, ICSVRI is strongly and negatively (Pearson $r = -0.668$) associated with the 5-item version of the Children's Worlds Subjective Well-Being Scale (CW-SWBS5), which has shown good cross-cultural comparability (Casas & González-Carrasco, 2021). Therefore, children with a higher level of subjective vulnerability, meaning higher perceived risk of harm to their well-being, report lower

[11] These technical cut-off points were chosen to ensure ICSVRI comparability across time.

overall subjective well-being. The *individual* vulnerability-resilience sub-index had the strongest (r = 0.706) and the *friends/peers/schoolmates* vulnerability-resilience sub-index the weakest (r = −0.392) association with CW-SWBS5.

4.3 International Comparisons

In this section, I will provide international comparisons of mean overall subjective vulnerability-resilience, but also proportions of subjectively very or somewhat resilient and somewhat and very vulnerable children. Following this, I will explore the main contributors to child subjective vulnerability, followed by a comparison of mean individual, direct and indirect environmental subjective vulnerability-resilience, and then determine the main vulnerability contributors. Finally, inequalities in child subjective vulnerability-resilience by age group and gender are examined by country.

4.3.1 *Overall Subjective Vulnerability-Resilience*

In all the selected countries, most children can be described as subjectively very or somewhat resilient (Fig. 4.1), thus having low overall perceived risk of harm to their well-being. Based on the ICSVRI country average, every 20th child can be considered subjectively somewhat or very vulnerable. However, in some countries the proportion of subjectively vulnerable children is notably higher. Children's overall

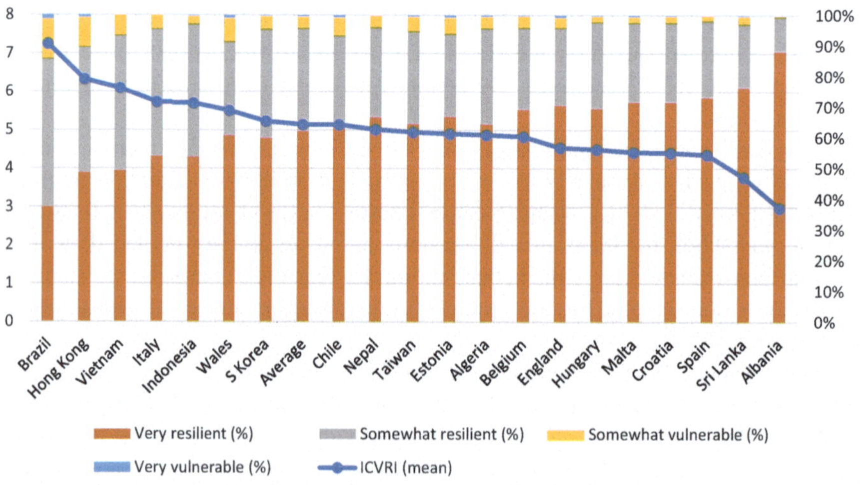

Fig. 4.1 Overall subjective vulnerability-resilience (ICSVRI) mean value (marked with blue line; scale on the left side) by country and proportion (% scale on the right side) of very resilient (ICVRI values 0–5.75), somewhat resilient (5.75–11.5), somewhat vulnerable (11.5–17.25), very vulnerable (17.25–23.0)

perceived risk of harm to their well-being is highest in Brazil and Hong Kong, where 13.0 and 9.6% of children, respectively, are subjectively somewhat vulnerable, and 1.2% and 0.7% very vulnerable. The figures are also above average, based on country means, in Vietnam, Italy, Indonesia, Wales and South Korea, and based on proportion of somewhat and very vulnerable children, in Chile, Estonia and Taiwan. Children's overall perceived risk of harm to their well-being is lowest in Albania, where only 0.4% of children can be considered subjectively somewhat vulnerable, but it is relatively lower also in Sri Lanka, Spain, Croatia, Malta and Hungary. Therefore, children from countries in Southern American, Eastern Asian, Southeastern Asian, but also Northern European (except England) regions seem to have higher perceived risk of harm to their well-being than children from Southern Asian and Southern European (except Italy) countries.[12]

What global and national interventions are needed to tackle child vulnerability? In Table 4.2, the contribution of each ICSVRI component (also 'sub-dimension') to a child's overall subjective vulnerability is presented by country. Regarding global interventions, based on country averages, ICSVRI suggests addressing the financial and material resources of children's family, mental health, bullying by peers, engagement in school, access to recreational facilities and programmes in the local area, community environment supportiveness, and safety of the surrounding environment in the local area. As expected, countries vary in terms of which component contributes more to children's overall subjective vulnerability. In Brazil, a country with the highest overall child subjective vulnerability, there are many sources of vulnerability worthy of the attention of researchers, practitioners, and policymakers (16 out of 25 components having values above the selected countries' average). The financial and material resources of the family, parent-child relationship quality, and opportunities for meaningful family involvement emerge as important contributors. Specific to Brazilian children, local area related components—access to recreational facilities and programmes in the local area, safety of the surrounding environment, supportive community environment in the local area—are important contributors to their high perceived risk of harm. This may possibly be explained by the fact that Brazil had a representative sample of city children. In Eastern Asian countries, the most notable contributor to relatively high overall child subjective vulnerability is mental health.

A more detailed focus on child individual, direct and indirect subjective vulnerability-resilience and its sources are provided next.

4.3.2 Individual Subjective Vulnerability-Resilience

Based on country means of individual ICSVRI sub-indices, children's individual perceived risk of harm to their well-being is highest in Vietnam and Hong Kong, but is above average also in Brazil, South Korea, Taiwan, Nepal, Wales, and Italy

[12] Possibly also Northern Africa, Western Europe, Eastern Europe, but these are represented only by 1 country.

Table 4.2 Overall mean of subjective vulnerability-resilience (ICSVRI; scale 0–23) and the values of the sub-dimensions (scale 0–1, those marked with an asterisk 0–0.5) by country (higher than all countries' average marked in **bold**)

	AL	DZ	BE	BR	CL	HR	EN	EE	HK	HU	ID	IT	MT	NP	KR	ES	LK	TW	WA	VN	All
Mental health	0.1	0.2	0.3	0.3	0.3	0.2	0.3	0.3	**0.4**	0.3	0.3	0.3	0.3	0.3	**0.4**	0.3	0.3	**0.4**	0.3	0.3	0.3
Self-esteem	0.0	0.1	0.2	0.2	0.1	0.1	0.2	0.2	**0.3**	0.2	0.2	0.2	0.1	0.2	**0.3**	0.1	0.2	0.2	**0.3**	0.2	0.2
Sense of control	0.0	0.2	0.1	0.2	0.1	0.1	0.1	0.1	0.2	0.1	0.2	0.1	0.1	0.2	0.2	0.1	0.2	0.2	0.1	0.2	0.2
Hope*	0.1	0.1	0.1	**0.2**	0.1	0.1	0.1	0.1	**0.2**	0.1	0.1	**0.2**	0.1	**0.2**	**0.2**	0.1	0.1	**0.2**	**0.2**	**0.2**	0.1
Social competence	0.1	0.2	0.2	**0.3**	0.2	0.2	0.2	0.2	0.2	0.2	0.2	**0.3**	0.2	0.2	0.2	0.1	0.2	0.2	0.2	**0.3**	0.2
Parent-child relationship quality	0.2	0.2	0.2	**0.4**	0.2	0.2	0.2	0.2	**0.3**	0.1	0.2	0.2	0.2	0.1	0.2	0.2	0.1	**0.3**	0.2	**0.3**	0.2
Parental care	0.1	0.1	0.1	**0.2**	0.1	0.1	0.1	0.1	**0.2**	0.1	**0.2**	0.1	0.1	0.1	0.1	0.1	0.1	0.1	0.1	0.1	0.1
Financial and material resources of the family	0.3	0.3	0.2	**0.6**	0.4	0.3	0.3	0.4	0.3	0.2	0.4	0.4	0.3	**0.5**	0.3	0.4	0.3	0.3	0.3	0.4	0.4
Family cohesion and interaction	0.1	0.1	0.1	0.2	0.1	0.1	0.1	0.1	**0.3**	0.1	0.2	0.2	0.1	0.2	0.1	0.1	0.1	0.2	0.2	0.2	0.2
Family violence and conflicts	0.0	0.1	0.1	0.1	0.1	0.1	0.1	0.1	**0.2**	0.0	**0.2**	0.1	0.1	0.1	0.1	0.1	0.1	0.1	0.1	**0.2**	0.1
Perceived support from family	0.1	0.1	0.1	**0.2**	0.1	0.1	0.1	0.1	**0.2**	0.1	**0.2**	0.1	0.1	0.1	0.1	0.1	0.1	0.1	0.1	**0.2**	0.1
Opportunities for meaningful family involvement	0.1	0.2	0.2	**0.4**	**0.3**	0.2	0.2	0.2	**0.3**	0.2	**0.3**	**0.3**	0.2	0.1	0.2	0.2	0.1	0.2	0.2	**0.3**	0.2
Quality of peer relationships/ friendships*	0.1	0.2	0.2	0.2	0.1	0.1	0.2	0.1	0.2	0.1	0.2	0.1	0.1	0.1	0.1	0.1	0.1	0.1	0.2	0.2	0.2
Bullying by peers	0.1	0.2	0.3	0.3	0.2	0.3	0.3	0.3	0.2	0.3	**0.4**	0.2	0.2	**0.4**	0.1	0.3	0.3	0.2	0.3	0.3	0.3
Social isolation. Peer rejection	0.1	0.2	0.2	**0.3**	0.2	0.2	**0.3**	0.2	0.2	0.2	**0.3**	0.2	0.2	0.2	0.1	0.2	0.2	0.1	**0.3**	0.2	0.2
Perceived support from peers	0.1	**0.3**	0.2	**0.3**	0.2	0.2	0.2	**0.3**	0.2	0.2	**0.3**	0.2	0.2	0.2	0.2	0.1	0.1	0.2	0.2	**0.3**	0.2
Quality of child-teacher relationship*	0.1	0.2	0.2	**0.3**	0.2	0.2	0.2	0.2	**0.3**	0.2	0.2	**0.3**	0.2	0.2	0.2	0.2	0.1	0.2	0.2	0.2	0.2

Care and encouragement from teachers	0.1	0.2	0.2	**0.3**	**0.3**	**0.3**	0.1	**0.3**	0.2	**0.3**	0.2	**0.3**	0.1	0.2	0.2	0.2	0.1	0.2	**0.3**	0.2	0.2
Perceived support from teachers	0.1	0.2	0.2	**0.3**	**0.3**	0.2	0.2	0.2	0.2	0.2	0.2	0.2	0.1	0.1	0.2	0.2	0.1	0.1	**0.3**	0.2	0.2
Safety of school environment	0.1	0.2	0.2	**0.3**	0.2	0.2	0.1	0.2	**0.3**	0.2	0.2	0.2	0.2	0.1	**0.3**	0.1	0.1	0.2	0.2	0.2	0.2
Engagement in school	0.2	0.3	0.3	0.3	0.2	0.2	0.2	0.3	0.3	0.3	0.3	0.3	0.2	0.3	0.3	0.2	0.2	0.2	0.3	0.3	0.3
Quality of curriculum*	0.0	0.1	**0.2**	0.1	0.1	0.1	0.1	**0.2**	**0.2**	**0.2**	0.1	0.1	0.1	0.1	**0.2**	0.1	0.1	**0.2**	**0.2**	**0.2**	0.1
Access to recreational facilities and programmes in local area	0.3	0.3	0.3	**0.4**	0.2	0.2	0.2	0.2	0.3	0.2	0.2	**0.4**	0.3	0.3	0.3	0.2	0.2	0.3	0.3	0.3	0.3
Safety of the surrounding environment in local area	0.2	0.2	0.2	**0.4**	0.2	0.2	0.2	0.1	0.2	0.2	0.3	0.3	0.2	0.2	0.3	0.2	0.3	0.2	0.2	0.3	0.3
Supportive community environment	0.2	0.3	0.3	**0.5**	0.3	0.3	0.3	0.3	**0.4**	0.3	0.3	0.3	0.3	0.2	0.3	0.3	0.2	0.3	**0.4**	0.3	0.3
ICSVRI country mean value	3.0	4.9	4.8	**7.3**	5.1	4.4	4.6	4.9	**6.3**	4.5	**5.7**	**5.7**	4.4	5.0	**5.2**	4.4	3.8	5.0	**5.5**	**6.1**	5.1

AL-Albania, DZ-Algeria, BE-Belgium, BR-Brazil, CL-Chile, HR-Croatia, EN-England, EE-Estonia, HK-Hong Kong, HU-Hungary, ID-Indonesia, IT-Italy, MT-Malta, NP-Nepal, KR-S Korea, ES-Spain, LK-Sri Lanka, TW-Taiwan, WA-Wales, VN-Vietnam, All-average for all countries

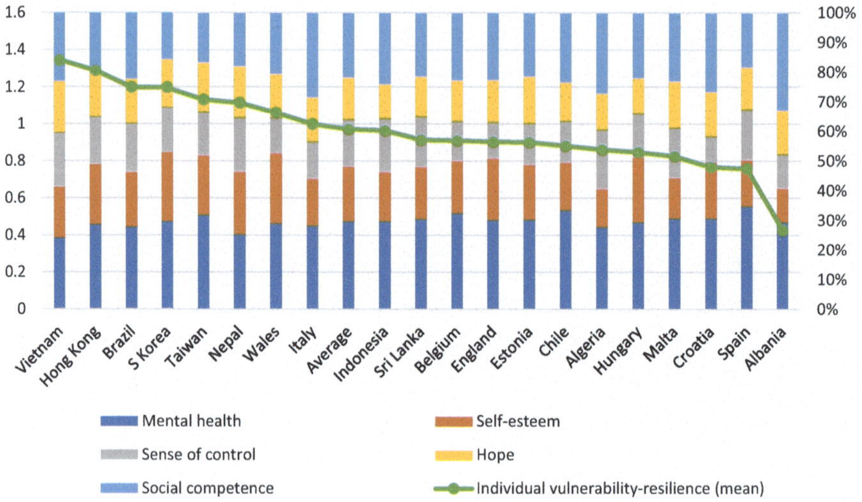

Fig. 4.2 The mean value of children's individual subjective vulnerability-resilience (marked with green line; scale ranging from 0 to 4.5 on the left side) by country and proportion (% scale on the right side) of the contribution of each sub-dimension

(Fig. 4.2). Children's individual perceived risk of harm to their well-being is clearly lowest in Albania. In all countries, mental health was the main contributor to children's individual perceived risk of harm. Only in Albania was the main contributor social competence, while being the second most important contributor in almost all other countries, except in Eastern Asian countries, Nepal, Wales, and Hungary. In these countries, self-esteem was the second most important contributor. Sense of control and hope contributed less to children's individual risk of harm in all countries.

4.3.3 *Direct Environmental Subjective Vulnerability-Resilience*

Based on the means of the direct environmental sub-index of ICSVRI by country, children's direct environmental perceived risk of harm to their well-being is highest in Brazil, but it is above average also in Hong Kong, Vietnam, Indonesia, Italy, Wales, and Chile (Fig. 4.3). The direct environmental perceived risk of harm to children's well-being is clearly lowest in Albania and Sri Lanka. In most countries, the parental dimension combined with the family dimension was the main contributor to direct environmental subjective vulnerability, being especially the case in Taiwan, Hong Kong, and Albania. However, in South Korea and Hungary, but also in Estonia, Wales, Croatia, Algeria, and Belgium, the main contributor was the teacher dimension combined with the school dimension. The friends, peers and school mates dimension was not the main contributor in any of the countries.

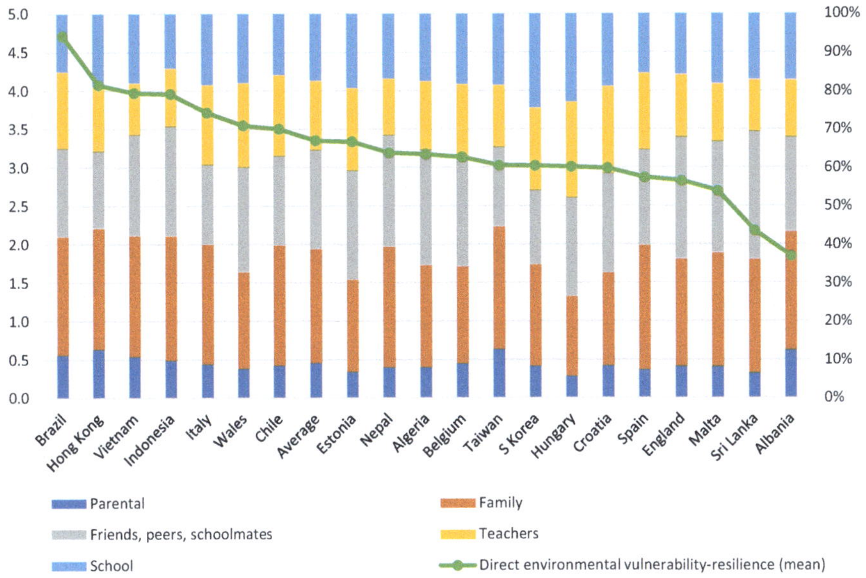

Fig. 4.3 The mean value of children's direct subjective environmental vulnerability-resilience (marked with green line; scale ranging from 0 to 15.5 on the left side) by country and the proportion (% scale on the right side) of the contribution of each dimension

4.3.4 Indirect Environmental Subjective Vulnerability-Resilience

Based on the means of the local area sub-index of ICSVRI by country, children's perceived risk of harm to their well-being from the local area is clearly highest in Brazil, but above average also in South Korea, Italy, Hong Kong, Wales, Malta, and Algeria (Fig. 4.4). Children's perceived risk of harm to their well-being from the local area is lowest in Hungary, Croatia, Estonia and Sri Lanka. In most countries, community environment supportiveness was the main contributor to children's perceived risk of harm from the local area. This was especially the case in Estonia, Hungary, Croatia, and Hong Kong. However, in Nepal, but also in South Korea, Italy, Malta, Vietnam, and Albania, the main contributor to children's perceived risk of harm from the local area was access to recreational facilities and programmes in the local area. Only in Indonesia and Sri Lanka, was the main contributor to children's perceived risk of harm from local area the safety of their surrounding environment.

4.3.5 Inequalities in Child Subjective Vulnerability-Resilience

In each country, it is important to detect the groups of children with relatively higher subjective vulnerability. Next, as an example, inequalities in overall, individual, direct and indirect environmental subjective vulnerability-resilience by age group and gender are examined.

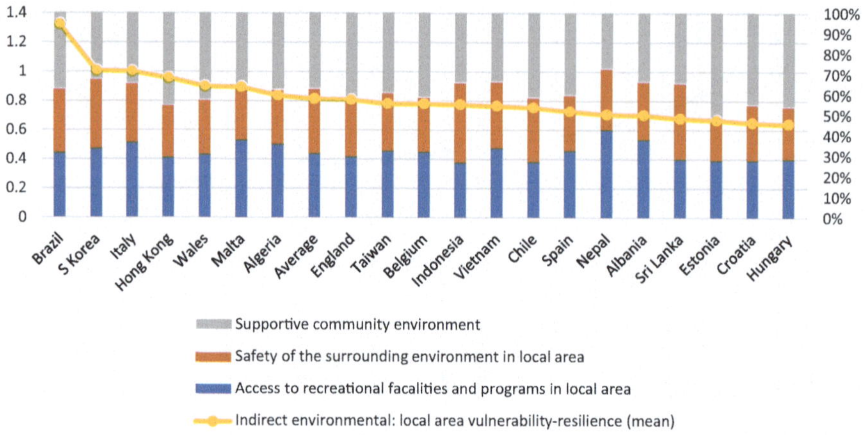

Fig. 4.4 The mean value of the children's indirect subjective environmental-local area vulnerability-resilience (marked with yellow line; scale ranging from 0 to 3 on the left side) by country and the proportion (% scale on the right side) of the contribution of each sub-dimension

In almost every country, based on country means, 12-year-old children had higher overall, including individual, direct and indirect (local area) environmental perceived risk of harm to their well-being than 10-year-old children. Mostly, this difference is present for both boys and girls. However, there are some exceptions; for example, this was true in South Korea but only among girls. Also, the difference between age groups overall, including individual, direct and indirect (local area) environmental perceived risk of harm, was more notable among girls in Brazil, Chile, Estonia, Wales, Hong Kong (except in the local area) and Croatia (except overall and the local area). The gender difference is particularly notable among 12-year-old South Korean and Brazilian children—girls had higher overall, individual, direct and indirect (local area) environmental perceived risk of harm to their well-being compared to boys of the same age. Moreover, among all genders and age groups, based on country means, Brazilian 12-year-old girls have the highest overall (8.6), individual[13] (1.5), direct environmental (5.5) and indirect environmental-local area (1.6) perceived risk of harm to their well-being. There are some countries where boys had a higher perceived risk of harm than girls; for example, in Nepal, mostly among 12-year-olds, boys had higher overall, including individual, direct and indirect (local area) environmental perceived risk of harm to their well-being compared to girls.

Interestingly, in a few countries, 10-year-olds had higher perceived risk of harm compared to 12-year-old children. For example, in Belgium and Nepal, 10-year-olds had higher overall and direct environmental perceived risk of harm to their well-being than 12-year-old children; in Nepal, also a higher individual perceived risk of harm; in Sri Lanka, 10-year-old girls had a higher perceived risk of harm from the local area than 12-year-old girls. In a few countries, statistically significant

[13] Together with 12-year-old Hong Kong girls.

(95%) age group and gender differences did not exist. For example, in Albania, there were no age-group differences, and in Hong Kong and England, no gender differences in the overall, individual, direct and indirect (except Albania) environmental perceived risk of harm.

4.4 Discussion and Conclusions

Measuring child vulnerability, especially internationally in a cross-country comparative manner, is not an easy task. In previous efforts, mostly statistical data was used (e.g., CVI by SOS Children's Villages International, 2016). The first version of the ICSVRI aims to be a new international child subjective vulnerability indicator for comparing countries constructed as an impetus for action. It offers children's own perspective on their vulnerability, boding well with the newest wave of the Social Indicators Movement stressing the importance of bringing human agency to the foreground (Tsai, 2017). Child vulnerability is considered together with resilience, which is also in accordance with the latest developments in the field (e.g., OECD's report *Changing the Odds for Vulnerable Children: Building Opportunities and Resilience* in 2019). Moreover, research, practice and policy need to reach beyond WEIRD societies to understand vulnerability from a wider perspective on children's experiences around the world (Nadan & Korbin, 2018), and the International Survey of Children's Well-being provides data for both the Global North and South.

ICSVRI's potential as a relevant child vulnerability indicator, including its conceptual framework presented in Chap. 2, is supported by strong negative correlation with a child's overall subjective well-being, and the internal consistency analysis, which indicated that ICSVRI is an internally consistent index. Moreover, although there were small differences, ICSVRI seems to function well enough in every selected country. Different vulnerability and resilience factors may be more important at different times during the development of children (e.g., Masten et al., 2023), but ICSVRI seems to work similarly well among 10 and 12-year-old children. One of the strengths of ICSVRI is that each individual child is given their own subjective vulnerability score, and this offers an opportunity to do highly disaggregated analyses.

The first version of ICSVRI provides a snapshot of the subjective vulnerability-resilience of 10 and 12-year-old children as a level of the perceived risk of harm to their well-being and its sources from their own perspective in WEIRD and non-WEIRD countries from East Asia, Southeast Asia, Southern Asia, North Africa, Southern Europe, Eastern Europe, Northern Europe, Western Europe, and South America. ICSVRI provides a rather optimistic picture of child vulnerability, as every 20th child, as opposed to the estimate of every 10th by SOS Children's Villages International (2016), can be considered vulnerable[14] worldwide. This can at least partly be explained by the fact that ICSVRI is a child subjective

[14] However, caution is needed in labelling children as resilient or vulnerable.

vulnerability measure based on their own perceptions. Child subjective well-being studies have shown that children assess their lives quite optimistically; for example, at the national level, the average well-being ratings on a ten-point scale are not five, but rather between seven and eight (Casas, 2019). These optimistic assessments by children seem to also show the high proportion of subjectively resilient children based on ICSVRI. Children from Southern Europe—Malta, Spain, Albania, and Croatia—had the lowest perceived risk of harm to their well-being (except for Italy). This is in accordance with Rees et al. (2020), who show that children‘s overall subjective well-being (measured by CW-SWBS5) is highest in Southern Europe.

However, in some countries the proportion of subjectively vulnerable children is notably higher. For example, in Brazil and Hong Kong at least every 10th child is subjectively vulnerable. An important strength of ICSVRI is that it provides important information for policymakers and practitioners on the main contributors to child vulnerability, which can be used for planning global and national interventions. For example, in Brazil more notable contributors to higher child subjective vulnerability compared to other countries are related to the financial and material resources of the family, the quality of the parent-child relationship, opportunities for meaningful family involvement, (un)supportive community environment, access to recreational facilities and programmes in the local area, and the safety of the surrounding environment in the local area.

As another major strength, ICSVRI allows us to detect the groups of children whose subjective vulnerability level is relatively high, thus, needing the attention of policymakers. For example, ICSVRI and its sub-indices indicated in many countries, most notably in Brazil, Chile, Estonia, Hong Kong, and Wales, that a child's perceived risk of harm to their well-being increases with age, especially among girls. This is in accordance with recent findings from the Health Behaviour in School-aged Children 2021/2022 survey (Cosma et al., 2023), showing that in Europe, Central Asia and Canada, the gender difference in mental health and well-being increases with age—among 11–15-year-old children, 15-year-old girls report the lowest mental health and well-being scores. Therefore, it is important for national policymakers and practitioners to design new or adjust existing services specifically for teenage girls to build their resilience to overcome vulnerability. Moreover, ICSVRI allows us to detect specific sources of vulnerability, including for 10 and 12-year-old girls, providing information about what types of services are needed. On the national level, addressing the group of teenage girls is important to reduce the rise of inequality among children, which is an important challenge also for international organisations (Casas, 2019). However, this requires a shift in the understanding of policymakers—money invested in children is usually planned to achieve well-being in the future rather than to ensure their current well-being (Casas, 2019).

ICSVRI has its limitations. A major one is that ICSVRI does not cover several groups of relatively vulnerable children. Most international harmonised surveys, including ISCWeB, are school-based surveys that do not cover specific groups of children; for example, children living in institutions or not attending school. Unfortunately, this is an even deeper problem, as according to Casas (2019), research has neglected whole groups of children and even forgotten about them when researching children's well-being. Therefore, in the near future it would be difficult to make international child vulnerability measurement more inclusive regarding these neglected groups. Other limitations are that ICSVRI includes only 10 and 12-year-old children, not all world regions are covered and not all countries have a sample representative of the whole country. For example, in Spain a representative sample only exists for Catalonia, but children's subjective vulnerability may vary between different parts of the country.

In this chapter, the first version of ICSVRI is presented. This measure needs further development. In the next steps the number of countries and geographical coverage should be increased, and the regularity aspect of the index developed. It needs additional robustness checks, including further investigation on how ICSVRI is related to other child vulnerability measures. There is also a need for a child vulnerability measure that is not purely subjective (e.g., ICSVRI) or objective (e.g., CVI), but combines children's subjective assessments with objective indicators. Developing such a hybrid measure can also be one of the further steps in developing ICSVRI. For example, globally available child statistics and also other nationally representative international survey data in addition to ISCWeB could be used. However, such a measure would be more limited in terms of disaggregation possibilities.

Competing Interests The author has no conflicts of interest to declare that are relevant to the content of this chapter.

Ethics Approval This study was performed in line with the principles of the Declaration of Helsinki. Approval was granted by the Ethics Committee of the University of Tartu (21.08.2017/No. 272/T-4).

Acknowledgement Work on this chapter was supported by a grant from the Estonian Research Council (PRG700).

References

Arora, S. K., Shah, D., Chaturvedi, S., & Gupta, P. (2015). Defining and measuring vulnerability in young people. *Indian Journal of Community Medicine, 40*(3), 193–197.

Ben-Arieh, A. (2008). The child indicators movement: Past, present, and future. *Child Indicators Research, 1*(1), 3–16.

Bronfenbrenner, U. (1979). *The ecology of human development*. Harvard University Press.

Casas, F. (2019). Kas kõik lapsed on väga õnnelikud? Sissejuhatus laste subjektiivse heaolu teemasse rahvusvahelises vaates. In D. Kutsar & K. Raid (Eds.), *Laste subjektiivne heaolu kohalikus ja rahvusvahelises vaates* (pp. 6–17). Statistikaamet.

Casas, F., & González-Carrasco, M. (2021). Analysing comparability of four multi-item well-being psychometric scales among 35 countries using Children's Worlds 3rd wave 10 and 12-year-olds samples. *Child Indicators Research, 14*(5), 1829–1861.

Coram. (2017). *Constructing a definition of vulnerability—Attempts to define and measure*. Children's Commissioner for England. https://www.childrenscommissioner.gov.uk/wp-content/uploads/2018/07/Vulnerability-Technical-Paper-1-2017-Constructing-a-Definition-of-Vulnerability.pdf

Cosma, A., Abdrakhmanova, S., Taut, D., Schrijvers, K., Catunda, C., & Schnohr, C. (2023). *A focus on adolescent mental health and wellbeing in Europe, Central Asia and Canada.* Health Behaviour in School-aged Children international report from the 2021/2022 survey (Volume 1). WHO Regional Office for Europe.

Daniel, B. (2010). Concepts of adversity, risk, vulnerability and resilience: A discussion in the context of the 'Child Protection System'. *Social Policy and Society, 9*(2), 231–241.

Henrich, J., Heine, S. J., & Norenzayan, A. (2010). The weirdest people in the world? *Behavioral and Brain Sciences, 33*(2–3), 61–83.

Klocke, A., Clair, A., & Bradshaw, J. (2014). International variation in child subjective well-being. *Child Indicators Research, 7*(1), 1–20.

Lee, B. J., & Yoo, M. S. (2015). Family, school, and community correlates of children's subjective well-being: An international comparative study. *Child Indicators Research, 8*(1), 151–175.

LeVine, R. A., & New, R. (2008). *Anthropology and child development: A cross-cultural reader.* Wiley-Blackwell.

Masten, A. S., Narayan, A. J., & O'Dougherty-Wright, M. (2023). Resilience processes in development: Multisystem integration emerging from four waves of research. In S. Goldstein & R. B. Brooks (Eds.), *Handbook of resilience in children.* Springer.

Monti, M. (2005, March 21). Toughen up EU reform agenda and make it count. *Financial Times.*

Nadan, Y., & Korbin, J. (2018). Cultural context, intersectionality, and child vulnerability. *Childhood Vulnerability Journal, 1*(1–3), 5–14.

Nahkur, O., & Kutsar, D. (2019). Social ecological measures of interpersonal destructiveness impacting child subjective mental well-being: Perceptions of 12-year-old children in 14 countries. *Child Indicators Research, 12*(1), 353–378. https://doi.org/10.1007/s12187-018-9542-7

Nardo, M., Saisana, M., Saltelli, A., Tarantola, S., Hoffmann, A., & Giovannini, E. (2008). *Handbook on constructing composite indicators: Methodology and user guide.* OECD.

OECD. (2019). *Changing the odds for vulnerable children: Building opportunities and resilience.* OECD Publishing. https://doi.org/10.1787/a2e8796c-en

Rees, G., Savahl, S., Lee, B. J., & Casas, F. (2020). Children's views on their lives and well-being in 35 countries: A report on the Children's Worlds project, 2016–19. Children's Worlds Project (ISCWeB). https://isciweb.org/wp-content/uploads/2020/07/Childrens-Worlds-Comparative-Report2020.pdf

Saltelli, A. (2007). Composite indicators between analysis and advocacy. *Social Indicators Research, 81*(1), 65–77.

SOS Children's Villages International. (2016). *Child at risk: The most vulnerable children, who they are and why they are at risk.* SOS Children's Villages International.

Tsai, M.-C. (2017). Social indicators movement and human agency: Comment on Land and Michalos. *Social Indicators Research, 135*(3), 991–999.

Ungar, M., Ghazinour, M., & Richter, J. (2013). Annual research review: What is resilience within the social ecology of human development? *Journal of Child Psychology and Psychiatry, 54*(4), 348–366. https://doi.org/10.1111/jcpp.12025

Vision, W. (2019). *Mapping child vulnerability dimensions in the Lao PDR.* World Vision.

Oliver Nahkur is a research fellow of Research of Social Wellbeing at the University of Tartu, Institute of Social Studies, Estonia. He is a member of the International Society for Child Indicators (ISCI) and the Estonian team of the International Survey of Children's Well-Being (ISCWeB); secretary-treasurer of the International Sociological Association, Research Committee No 55—Social Indicators. He actively contributes to the development of child well-being data in Estonia. His research interests include child well-being and vulnerability research and social indicators research, including from a cross-national comparative studies perspective. In one of his latest research publications, he studied the change in children's subjective relational social cohesion with family and friends during the Covid-19 pandemic in 18 countries across the globe.

Chapter 5
Child Vulnerability Within the Complexity of the Family

Dagmar Kutsar

5.1 Introduction

> There are some things that I as a kid certainly did not want to experience, and do not want my children to go through, and there are some patterns of behaviour that are so ingrained in me that it has been difficult to break and change them. (Reflection of a young adult from 2023)

Mental health concerns and declining subjective well-being among populations have become widespread particularly in the western world. The World Health Organization (2022) asserts that individuals bear accumulated vulnerabilities and trauma from their childhood, which can influence their well-being as they mature. Over time, the family as a social institution has undergone numerous changes in Europe, leading to increased complexity in its structures and especially in terms of relationships. This includes various types of blended families living together or forming multiple households to create a family network consisting of biological, half-biological, and non-biological members. Considering the decreasing number of families based on marriage, growing evidence of cohabitation and the instability of family relationships expressed in the frequency of separations and divorces, the new forms of living together challenge mutual relationships. Thomson (2014, p. 245) concludes that the "transitions that occur in the lives of adults and their children produce families and households that are complex". The complexity of relationships is the pivotal factor that affects the subjective well-being of those involved (Thomson, 2014). It unveils existing and emerging vulnerabilities and requires the development of life skills as a source of resilience when tackling troublesome situations and relieving negative future outcomes.

D. Kutsar (✉)
Institute of Social Studies, University of Tartu, Tartu, Estonia
e-mail: dagmar.kutsar@ut.ee

D. Kutsar et al. (eds.), *Child Vulnerability and Vulnerable Subjectivity*, Children's Well-Being: Indicators and Research 27,
https://doi.org/10.1007/978-3-031-61333-3_5

The expectations towards the family remain high despite changing and diversifying family structures and challenging mutual relationships, even as the personal meaning of family becomes less clear. This is particularly significant for children who depend on and follow the decisions of adults: there are children who live with parents with inadequate social skills and limited parenting abilities, which is further exposed in periods of family transition; many children have to endure the separation or divorce of their parents and relocate between different household arrangements. However, children hold immense social value, especially in contemporary ageing societies where parenting standards are particularly elevated. It challenges adults to be good parents even if they do not live with their children. Children have the right to communicate with both their resident and non-resident parents, while the parents acknowledge their right to equal parenthood, even if a new parental figure enters the child's life. Despite the character and speed of family transitions, with reference to Newland (2015), the family remains the primary life environment for children and the basic source of their subjective well-being.

This chapter provides a brief overview of family change in Estonia and examines children's perspectives on various family arrangements and relationships as potential sources of vulnerability. The conclusions are drawn from an assortment of small-scale quantitative and qualitative studies executed with children—being socially competent actors based on their age and dependable sources of information (Mason & Danby, 2011).

5.2 Families and Children in Estonia: A Short Insight into the Background

5.2.1 The Traditional Family Setting

Before World War II, Estonia enjoyed independent statehood, and like other European countries, marriage-based families constituted the conventional social setting. Compared to now, family relations were relatively stable: up to 10% of all marriages ended in divorce (Eesti arvudes…, 1937). The formal stability of marriages relied on external factors such as different standards applied to men and women and close kinship networks. Community interests were prioritised over personal preferences, in line with social norms and control through social imperatives and strengthened by close ties to family units within the community. In family relationships, fathers played a dominant role and the economic and social reliance of women on men limited women's ability to initiate family transitions. Finally, children did not have a say in family decision-making.

5.2.2 *De-traditionalisation of Families*

The Soviet occupation in 1940–1991 brought about an ideological shift in Estonian society, with the formal equalisation of the genders and the demand for full employment. Women's participation in the labour force increased rapidly and exceeded the share of men. For example, in 1985, the proportion of women in the labour force had reached to 55% with the majority of them engaged in full-time work (Kutsar, 1991). Soviet family policy supported employed mothers in balancing domestic and professional responsibilities by providing short childcare leave exclusively to women, without offering them any choice on the matter. In addition to bearing the double burden of both work and care, women retained a dominant role in the upbringing of children as well as performing other daily household chores, including cooking and cleaning.

In the family portrait (an example of a research method commonly employed in studies involving children; see Fig. 5.1), a sketch by an anonymous teenager in the 1980s (unknown student paper, author's collection), she illustrates the visible mothers and invisible fathers of that time (see Fig. 5.1). The child portrays the father as lacking power and visibility at home: his facial features are hidden, he lies on a sofa and watches TV, disconnecting himself from the rest of the family. However, the father is situated in the middle of the image, suggesting that he is a significant character to the artist. The mother still fulfils the traditional role of preparing food for the family. She has detailed features that resemble the artist herself and her brother.

Women becoming more self-aware due to their dominant role in the family and increased extra-familial activities (education and employment) signalled the de-traditionalisation of family life. The external forces that kept families tight were

Fig. 5.1 A family portrait drawn by an Estonian teenage girl in the 1980s

losing their power and in the case of bad marital relationships, women became increasingly encouraged to initiate divorce. Notably, in 1988, women made over 75% of the applications for divorce, while mutual agreement accounted for only 18% of proceedings (Kutsar, 1991). The fathers also remained unseen after the divorce or separation; in most cases, the children stayed in the care of their mothers who acted as primary caregivers and rigorous gatekeepers, overseeing and underestimating the value of father-child interactions. However, the role of a father figure remained crucial for children. According to research evidence from a 1972 study of couples intending to marry, relationships with fathers, retrospectively rated as good or very good during childhood, significantly impacted following the parental home as a model for their own family life, particularly in the case of daughters (Tavit & Tiit, 1978). The common sense that children are *not yet adults*, that they are *human becomings* (Qvortrup, 1991) was characteristic of family life at that time.

5.2.3 Entering the Twenty-First-Century Risk Society

The restoration of independent statehood from the collapsing Soviet Union in 1991 brought about enormous social and political changes. By the mid-1990s, a new democratic state was established, and Estonia had entered a modern risk society (a term introduced by Beck, 1986) with a precarious labour market, diffusion of norms and values, and insecurity concerning the future. The complexity of the major societal transitions was reflected in statistics. There was a dramatic drop of the number of births—bottoming out in 1998. Informal networks declined and external forces continued losing power over family stability. However, the family kept a prominent position in the hierarchy of personal values, alongside good health, and active participation in the labour force (Heidmets, 2007), despite the increased social complexities. By 2000, the marriage rate had dropped to its lowest rate ever recorded and unmarried cohabitation was partly and increasingly replacing marriage (Hansson, 2000).

The ratification of the UN Convention on the Rights of the Child in 1991 significantly impacted Estonian society. The Child Protection Act issued in 1992 (RT 1992, 28, 370) followed the main principles of the UN CRC. Both texts advocate for children to be active social actors and encourage parents to develop their parenting skills. Indeed, compared to 1972, the 2007 study identified a significant shift in parenting practices towards democratic negotiation with the child, replacing the previously dominant parental influence (Kutsar et al., 2012). Moreover, Estonia's family policy has implemented effective practices for involving fathers in child rearing. Today, parents are invited to agree on who will stay at home with small children and for how long, while also combining this with part-time work. Fathers have returned from *invisibility*—the prevalent image during the Soviet past.

The existence of *active fathers* is currently widespread, particularly among young parents. In the new social and political context that values egalitarian parenting, mothers, who have traditionally been seen as the primary caregivers and *gatekeepers*, are experiencing a loss of power as shared parenting becomes more prevalent and socially valued not only while married but also after a separation or divorce. The study by Kallaste et al. (2023) showed that three-quarters of separated or divorced parents have agreed on joint custody, and more than half of the parents discuss their children's living arrangements and parenting issues among themselves. Roughly one-third of the separated parents have a fixed visitation order for their children, and approximately half of the children have input on when and for how long they stay with the other parent. Unfortunately, the study also revealed that roughly one-third of the children of separated parents had not met their other parent in the last 12 months. In addition, approximately 14% had no contact whatsoever, even by telephone or Skype, for example (Kallaste et al., 2023). However, in addition to the idea of the *active father* who engages in their children's lives, there also exists the notion of a *harmful father* who is violent and abusive. In the latter case, the separation or divorce of parents may increase the child's well-being if this has ended the maltreatment in the child's life.

The evolving landscape of society, including shifting gender norms, the status of children in the family and society, and broader social conventions, has contributed to the diversification of family structures and an increase in familial vulnerabilities. Today, children have the potential to actively participate in conversations with their parents about their needs and desires, while parents can assist in organising children's activities outside of the home. Dedication to the family is based on ethical standards of justice and closeness rather than uncritically adhering to external moral codes. Although it is vital to foster togetherness and spend time together as a family, it can be demanding to maintain these aspects due to each member pursuing their individual careers and objectives.

In brief, circumstances predisposing children to vulnerabilities begin with routine interactions within the family unit. However, the risk of harm spikes during family transitions that muddy subjective family membership and relationships, commencing with the question of who now constitutes their family.

5.3 Who Is Part of the Family from the Perspective of Children?

5.3.1 Studies of Children's Views of Diverse Family Arrangements

Irene Levin and Jan Trost (1992a, 1992b) and Jan Trost (1990) acknowledge issues in grasping the multifaceted implications of the term *family* during the early 1990s. In particular, they raise questions regarding what individuals mean when they discuss or envisage their own family and when they refer to families in a broader sense without specifying their own. In addition, they questioned whether departing from the household would lead to the end of one's family (Levin & Trost, 1992a). The concept of family is not fixed or standardised, and therefore being part of a family is a dynamic process. Trost (1990) argued that family membership could change at different points in time, as household members create defined borders for their families. The study by Castrén and Widmer (2015) demonstrated that a separated individual could stay as part of the subjective family group, and not all members of one's household may qualify as family members. Their investigation of diverse family arrangements offers valuable insights into the characteristics of family units and the importance of subjective perception in defining familial relationships. These matters are becoming increasingly significant as family structures become more varied and living arrangements more intricate, resulting in potential harm and vulnerabilities for both adults and children. For instance, by the age of 12, children may have experienced various changes in their domestic arrangements, such as the addition of new family members or the departure of customary ones. A biological parent may have departed, and a non-biological parent may have arrived. Children may live with one parent and move between the dwellings of their separated biological parents, among other adjustments. A child has the potential to acquire a comprehensive family network comprising both biological and non-biological parents, full or half-biological siblings and non-biological siblings. Moreover, they may benefit from the increasing complexities within their large family group. However, this is not always the case, and the child may instead acquire vulnerabilities, particularly because their subjective family spans multiple households and has multiple nuclei.

The issue of *who my family consists of* falls within the domain of individual psychology that deals with subjective notions of family and familial boundaries and has, besides academic interest, also clear practical implications. Here, however, we are interested in the factors that influence children's identification of family members in the case of sample structures. Trost and Levin originally created a collection of family sample structures (Trost, 1990; Levin & Trost, 1992b). The participants indicated *yes* to denote that the provided structure is a family and *no* to signify disagreement. Roots (2010) updated this compilation and conducted a survey among 104 schoolchildren in Estonia aged between 12 and 13 years in 2009. In 2023, Nurmik conducted a follow-up study to monitor changes in the conceptualisations of families among children in Estonia. Her sample comprised 225 students aged 12–13 years (Nurmik, 2023). In both studies, children appended their reasoning to their responses of *yes* or *no*. Can cohabiting parents form a family? Is a departed parent still a family member? Is a parent's partner a family member? Can a family consist of both biological and non-biological parents at the same time? What are the notable transformations in children's understandings over 14 years, and do they align with the escalating variations of family arrangements? The investigations carried out by Roots (2010) and Nurmik (2023) offer insights into these enquiries and are outlined below.

5.3.2 Household Vs. Family

State statisticians in Estonia have debated the definition of the family, encountering difficulties in the process. They arrived at the term *household* defined as a group of individuals who reside together, share resources, and self-identify as a household (Tiit, 2011). The term *family* is not covered by this definition. Roots (2010) and Nurmik (2023) asked their child respondents the following: "Helle and Rasmus are married, and they have a daughter living with them and an adult son who lives in another town. Are these four a family?" Nearly all children in both surveys said they were a family due to them sharing common genes and blood. However, some children no longer perceived an adult brother in this case, who lives independently, as a member of the family. The authors then gave the following example: "Maarja is a divorced lone mother and lives with her son Tiit. Tiit's father lives separately but in the same town. Are these three a family?" In 2010, 18% and in 2023, 29% of the children stated that the separated father remains a family member. Children brought moral and emotional reasons, "...no, they are divorced and do not love each other, and they do not wish to be a family" /GIRL/; "...not a family because he left them... the boy can have two families instead." /BOY/ However, some children offered a conflicting explanation, "... the father may have left even to China, but they are still the same family." /BOY/

As previously stated, genetic heritage and shared ancestry are important in identifying family groups from the perspective of children. The research conducted by Plakso (2023) reinforces prior findings. Plakso interviewed 11–13-year-old children living with a single parent in Estonia. Children who had a positive relationship with their other parent identified themselves as belonging to a birth family with two parents even when the parents had formed separate households. The results suggest that a child views family members and significant others as their own personal family, regardless of whether they live together or separately. However, moral and emotional considerations may also play a decisive role in distinguishing between present and departed family members: in the case of divorce or separation and a single parent relocating, the family may potentially become disconnected. In sum, families may reside both within and expand outside the household in the perceptions of the children.

5.3.3 Marriage Vs. Cohabitation

There is a growing trend of individuals cohabiting in Estonia, and consensual unions increasingly resemble traditional married families as an alternative form of family arrangement. At the beginning of the twentieth century, 70% of young people started their unions with a marriage, but among the birth cohorts of the 1960s and 1970s, more than 90% of couples started their unions as a cohabitation (Puur & Rahnu, 2011), and more than half of all children are born to cohabiting parents. When children are asked about cohabitation as a foundation for a family, they are given the following sample structure: "Katariina and Tarmo have cohabited for a decade but have refrained from marrying each other. They have a son Jürgen and a daughter Juta. Are they a family of four?" With no change over the time of observation (2010 vs. 2023), 93% of children agreed that these individuals constitute a family. They explained, "…yes, love and togetherness are the most important things, and not just what is written on a paper, that you are a family" /GIRL/; "…nowadays marriages have become less popular, my parents are not married either"/BOY/. Moreover, 7% of children upheld conventional views about families and favoured married couples as the optimal family arrangement. They gave moral and personal safety reasons why people should get married. For example, "…yes, for instance mother or father may find someone else but when married and you have given a promise that there will not be any other person in your life, it feels more safe" /BOY/ or they expressed direct traditional attitudes, saying "…otherwise the child cannot be happy" /BOY/; "marriage binds parents together." /GIRL/

Children from both waves of the study (Roots, 2010; Nurmik, 2023) agreed that a married couple with children constitutes a family. They offered comparable justifications to the instance of an unmarried couple who have offspring. Some arguments were as follows, "…yes, they are emotionally related and share a living space; and they have a daughter" /GIRL/; "…yes, because they are married, they have a daughter and share a common family name, both have the daughter, marriage made them a family." /BOY/ The researchers next asked, "How important is it for you personally that your parents are married?" In 2010, 30% of the children rated this as very important compared to 25% in 2023, while 17% in 2010 and 28% in 2023 assessed this as not important at all. This evidence cannot be statistically verified due to small, non-representative samples. Nevertheless, these figures indicate a tendency for children to follow the increasing trend of adult cohabitation, particularly if the couple has children in common or if the respondent child lives with cohabiting parents.

In the 2023 study (Nurmik, 2023), the interviewer asked the opinions of the children on same-sex couples: "Mati and Taavi [two men] live together. Are these two a family?" This sample structure resulted in confusion for the children, who required additional information on the daily arrangement of these two individuals. Only 20% of the respondents agreed, but with the condition that a family necessarily should involve raising a child. In the following sample: "Jüri and Margus [two men] cohabit and raise a child. Are they considered a family?"—82% of the girls and 50% of the boys responded affirmatively. They explained, "… yes, because they are the child's parents, they constitute the child's family. Therefore, they are a family" /BOY/; "…there is no reason why not because the child connects all three of them" /GIRL/.

In summary, children are conforming to the growing trend of cohabitation, which is becoming increasingly widespread. In addition, as they more frequently live with unmarried parents, this trend continues to gain traction. Children prioritise closeness and affection over a formal agreement. Still, boys highlight that the institution of marriage establishes clearer moral standards, imposes greater obstacles to ending the relationship, and offers enhanced legal protection compared to cohabitation.

5.3.4 A New Parent Figure in the Household

Statistics indicate a slight decrease in the number of single-mother households and an increase in both single-father households and households with a stepfather in Estonia. In 2021, 77% of families in Estonia with children consisted of two birth parents, approximately 10% of families were single-parent households, and the remaining 13% of families were stepfamily households (Märtsin et al., 2023). The addition of a parent's partner to the household can have a significant impact on a child's life. Can the new parent figure be a family member for the child? In 2023, 82% (75% in 2010) answered "yes" to the following example: "Merike and Merje [two sisters] live with their mother and her partner. Are these four a family?" However, the children provided various arguments, "... yes, because he is in the father's place" /GIRL/; "...depends, what relations they have" /GIRL/; "...somehow yes and somehow not...he is still a stepfather, not your own father." /GIRL/ Boys were more reluctant; for example, "...no, because this new man is not the father of these children. This is just a mother with two children and a stranger." / BOY/ If the mother marries the newcomer and they have a child, then over three-quarters of the children consider this group to be a family. Some explained, "... yes, because they live together, and they have children... I have a stepfather and he IS a family member" /GIRL/; "...if the mother loves this man and they live together and they have a daughter then this all makes the family" /GIRL/. Still one-fifth were not happy, arguing, "...surely not, this is all confusing... because there is a new father..." /GIRL/; "...I do not know, actually this is not a family because mother and father have separated and you are like in a stranger's family, not all people around are your relatives anymore, they are almost strangers" /BOY/. Boys place greater emphasis on blood and genes, whereas girls prioritise love and closeness. Both studies (from 2010 and 2023) suggest that children living with step-parents have a greater likelihood of accepting a new parental figure as a member of their family. In conclusion, children possess potential adaptability when it comes to embracing new parental figures and handling the possible vulnerability in family transitions, particularly when they cultivate positive mutual relationships.

Mägi (2016) conducted interviews with children in blended families in Estonia. Several of them expressed vulnerability by omitting the new parental figure from their family mapping exercise due to insufficient familiarity with them. It is the responsibility of the newcomer to be empathetic to the child's vulnerability and make an effort to establish positive relationships with the child and become a member of the child's subjective family. The structure of a family may become more complex and mixed if there are biological children accompanying the new parent from a previous relationship, or if there are biological children living apart (and commuting between two homes). However, the aforementioned studies did not investigate such potential family setups.

5.3.5 Expansion of the Birth Family Nucleus Beyond the Household

Plakso's (2023) study showed that broadening a child's family beyond the household is less difficult and precarious when the separated parent fulfils the role of a single parent in an alternative living situation and when both parents maintain friendly relations. However, living in separate homes and the emotional connections can become unclear or disrupted, particularly if the separated parent starts a new family. This can be a complex issue for a child to grasp. Roots (2010) and Nurmik (2023) revised the previous sample structure in their respective studies as follows. "Merike and Merje reside with their mother and visit their father, who lives in a separate town and has a new spouse and child, every other week. Are Merike, Merje, their mother and father a family?" Only 31% of the children in 2023 (20% in 2010) responded affirmatively, suggesting their capacity to maintain the father's position in their perception of a family. They explained, "…yes because the father meets his daughters, he cares about the girls, a child keeps the family together." /GIRL/ Maintaining a strong bond and regular communication with the father can benefit the child's family and mitigate the potential harm, demonstrating the importance of shared parenting for separated parents. However, it is noteworthy that the child did not mention a mother in this statement, indicating the concealed predicament of having two mothers—one natural and the other handpicked by the father—which could potentially complicate the child's situation. Still, most of the children responded "no" to this example of a family structure. Some explanations, "…no, the father is a betrayer" /GIRL/; "…no, because the father has a new family with a new wife" /BOY/; "… a child may say that yes, they are my family but difficult to say that THE SAME family" /GIRL/. Children may experience moral and emotional obstacles when accepting their separated parent as a familial member, particularly if they perceive that the parent replaced their former family with a new one. However, regular communication with the father could reduce the child's vulnerability to the effects of the family transition.

5.3.6 Children's Attitudes Concerning Their Own Family

In traditional Estonian family customs, women adopt the surnames of their future spouses. Over time, and particularly in cases of consensual unions, fewer families share the same surname, and a considerable number of children take on the surname of only one parent. Is the common surname important for children? Of all respondents in 2023 (Nurmik, 2023), 26% felt that the surname shared by the child and parents was very important, while 18% felt that it was not important at all (33% and 19% respectively in 2010; Roots, 2010). Children who deemed the shared surname with their parents to be of great significance frequently cited the common name as a unifying factor for the family. In several cases, they stressed that without a common name, children and parents would not seem to be connected, "...where else do you get your surname from, and if you have a family, it could be the same surname" /GIRL/. Over time, however, the importance of having a common surname tends to diminish. Children argue, "...the child may not always be the offspring of the same parents, in which case the surname may not be the same" /GIRL/; "...name doesn't change anything, they are still your parents" /BOY/ (Roots, 2010; Nurmik, 2023).

The final question posed to children in the Roots (2010) and Nurmik (2023) studies was whether they envisage themselves marrying, cohabiting, or remaining single in the future. In 2010, 70% of children expressed an inclination towards getting married in the future, while only one voiced a preference for remaining single and pursuing their own career. By 2023, the proportion of children who favoured marriage had dropped to 55%, and a slight increase was observed in the group that preferred singlehood and not the other two options. Returning to the previously discussed question in this chapter, children are adjusting to a range of family structures. However, there are challenges associated with dealing with vulnerability. The most notable changes in children's understanding over the 14 years between the studies are the acceptance of cohabitation as an alternative to marriage, of a new parent figure in a reconstituted family, and of a family that expands beyond the birth parents' household after a divorce or separation. However, children bring moral considerations to family structural change and may condemn the departing parent as a betrayer. Nevertheless, good and loving relationships and maintaining close contacts are a powerful key to children's flexibility and acceptance of family diversity.

5.4 Families and Child Vulnerability

5.4.1 Multifaceted Images of a Child

Families have always been complex in some ways, providing a vital survival network and being a main source of joys and worries for members. Over time, the view of children has become more diverse, resulting in greater vulnerabilities in their lives and increased challenges for parents in meeting higher parenting standards. Anniste et al. (2018) investigated how historical and contemporary views have shaped the perception of children from the perspective of children and adults. The authors based their work on the depictions of children presented by Ariès (1979). Ariès' seminal work recognised children as vulnerable and in need of protection during sixteenth century Europe, but also noted their potential to be *dangerous*, their inability to be responsible, and their need for control and discipline during seventeenth and eighteenth century Europe. Contrary to this, Bühler-Niederberger (2010) presented a current social depiction of children as active, having distinctive experiences, perceptions, attitudes, and interests, and possessing age-appropriate social competence. Anniste et al. (2018) conducted a study with children aged 10 and 17 which discovered that 66% of the child respondents perceived themselves as fragile and vulnerable, with 93% believing that they require protection. It is noteworthy that the sense of safety and security is a fundamental emotional requirement for children, and the absence of this feeling can be directly attributed to inadequate parenting that neglects the child's basic emotional needs and makes the child vulnerable.

Contrary to the widely accepted belief that children are vulnerable and need protection, 35% of child respondents hold the view that they cannot take responsibility for their actions, which perpetuates the idea of a potentially *dangerous* child, as noted by Ariès (1979). It is worth noting that 71% of children attribute their misbehaviour to their immaturity, lack of competence and deficient understanding, regarding it as unintentional. Furthermore, 57% of children agree that adult supervision plays an essential role in children's lives. However, children do not consider themselves deliberately misbehaving. Jürgenson (2017) conducted interviews with 16 kindergarten children aged five to seven regarding rules and punishment. Her research findings demonstrate that children possess a clear understanding of the meaning and significance of rules, "…if there are no rules, you can do what you want and accidents can happen" /GIRL, 6 years old/. Children agreed to corporal punishment only in extreme circumstances: when the child had deliberately done something unbelievably bad; for example, broken something (a new doll, a parent's car, set fire to something with matches). However, children offer the advice that before punishing, parents should try to find out why their child had broken the rules—talk to the child and try to understand the child's point of view. Jürgenson (2017) argues that effective parenting is integral to disciplining a child, and a failure to do so results in punishment that not only reflects a parent's incompetence but also places the child in a vulnerable position susceptible to harm.

Being a protective parent is easier than dealing with the child's misbehaviour without verbal or physical violence. The latter is a challenge, especially if the parent has an image of the child as *dangerous* and in need of discipline (i.e., punishment). In Estonia, corporal punishment of children has been banned since 2016. Nonetheless, according to Anniste et al. (2018), 42% of adult respondents perceive it as an indispensable and justifiable method of managing children in specific circumstances (in comparison, only 19% condone physical violence between adults).

A significant majority (96%) of both child and adult respondents (in an alternative study by Anniste et al., 2018) agreed with the image of a child as a competent subject: they agreed that children have their individual preferences and opinions, which are noteworthy and need to be considered. Moreover, 85% of the child respondents considered themselves intelligent and bright, while 74% of them thought that they can make autonomous decisions (Anniste et al., 2018). An affirmation of children's competence is, for example, the ability of children to a certain extent to be resilient in complicated situations that reveal the risk of harm (Boyden & Mann, 2005). Still, children can challenge parents to accept them as competent. This means moving away from traditional hierarchical power and developing negotiation skills with the child. This is particularly important today where family life is increasingly full of choices and is complex.

5.4.2 Fathers Are Back

Fathers are influential figures in children's lives as indicated above by child respondents from different studies. According to the main principle of the Convention on the Rights of the Child, prioritising children's best interests and involving both parents in their upbringing is crucial, both at home and beyond. In contemporary Estonia, there has been a normative shift where fathers have become more visible. First, there has been a rise in the number of fathers taking paternity leave to look after their young children. Second, fathers are advocating for equal parental rights following separation or divorce. Although modern family life in Estonia has many positive aspects, not all parents are capable of implementing democratic values in their relationships and approach to parenting. Nearly 300 children per year are removed from their homes due to the parents' inability to meet their basic needs (Kutsar et al., 2022).

It is challenging to maintain the stability of familial bonds in modern times. Nevertheless, the rate of marital splits has ceased to escalate; although, the frequency of non-spousal separations remains unquantified. There is a substantial body of research into the impact on children of parental separation (see, e.g., meta-analysis by Auersperg et al. 2019) and remarriage (e.g., Jeynes, 2006). The research has confirmed that co-parenting is important for the psychological adjustment of children to new life arrangements (e.g., meta-analysis by Teubert & Pinquart, 2010). The separation of parents can lead to distress and anxiety in children, increasing their vulnerability. This is especially true when parents are unable to split amicably and maintain a cohesive structure that extends beyond the child's home. In Estonia, court statistics from 2017 to 2021 indicate a decrease in litigations related to child sustenance and litigations related to custody (Chancellor of Justice, 2023). This signifies a movement toward shared parental responsibility following separations and relates to the ability to negotiate. As a result, the quantity of children travelling between separated or divorced parents may be on the rise. However, a child may have many questions and few answers. Did my father and mother tell me about their decision to separate? Where is my home today? What about MY needs and interests? Not all parents are able to come to an agreement regarding shared custody, resulting in a court process to establish the visiting order of their child. Is this arrangement in the child's best interests? It is important to seek the views of children who have experienced parental separation and are now moving between their mother's and father's homes.

Ilves (2021) conducted semi-structured interviews with eight children aged 9–13 who travel between their parents' separate homes. The children additionally created a drawing of their family to represent their family unit after the separation and evaluated their subjective well-being. Before the study, Ilves sought active and informed consent from both parents and children. However, some parents refused to give consent because they did not believe in the child's competence, arguing: "...you don't get enough information from the child anyway, the child doesn't agree to go to the father just because he wants to be with his friends, even though he says he wants us to be together again, ah, that's just his story". The children who were able to take part in the research expressed their joy at feeling valued and recognised as competent experts in their own lives.

Ilves' analysis revealed that children feel confused by their parents' separation. They remembered parents having arguments and their own regular crying. When asked to retrospectively rate their well-being using a scale from zero to ten, they indicated a low score of around four to six. The children explained that the family transition was unexpected and insufficiently communicated to them, "…I was confused as to why he was leaving /…/ they didn't tell me what was going on." /BOY, 13 years old/ Parents of some children have not resolved their mutual problems, "…I can talk to both of them any time I want, but it's just that they don't want to get along with each other." /BOY, 11 years old/ Moreover, the study's results suggest that the parents did not fully consider their children's opinions or input when making decisions about access rights. A wall of silence appeared to be forming, with parents failing to provide explanations and the children concealing their feelings to prevent additional conflict between the parents and a return to court to modify visiting arrangements.

Ilves' study demonstrated that children want their birth parents to be reunited in order to restore a sense of the completeness of the family. For example, Liisa/GIRL, 11 years old/kept her birth family together on her drawing of the family (see Fig. 5.2). She explained, "…I would definitely want my parents to live together and have a really good marriage, to treat each other well". A boy (11 years old) argued,

Fig. 5.2 A family portrait of Liisa (from left): mother, father, sister, brother and Liisa (source: Ilves 2021)

"...the family still stays together, as I understand they are separated and so, but it is still a family". Two equally shared parenting arrangements increasingly embody separating adults' understanding of co-parenting, whereby neither parent is deemed the major or minor parent. The child experiences this situation as a constant need to travel between two homes. The children discuss the problems that arise in their everyday logistics, such as finding their school bag or leaving their sports clothes at the *wrong* house. In addition, they may experience confusion about their true home, emotional distress from missing a parent, and ethical dilemmas about causing confusion for another parent due to their affection towards a new parental figure. For example, one boy (11 years old) says, "...and if I'm with one; for example, I'm with my dad, my mum is offended, and if I'm with my mum, my dad is offended, and so on". They prefer to have primary residence at either the mother's or the father's home, as opposed to dividing their living arrangements equally between the two homes. As socially active actors, children require adaptable access rights regulations to accommodate their changing plans and preferences. However, to maintain control over the lives of both the child and the former partner, the study suggests that a set routine is beneficial for the parents.

Children can be flexible and adapt to the transitions in the family and to the new arrangements in their lives (e.g., Castrén & Widmer, 2015). Children's appraisals of parenting practices revealed that living with step-parents provide less stable lives; however, not all children living with step-parents are unhappy (Nahkur & Kutsar, 2022). Going back to the early 1990s and Levin's study (Levin, 1994), children then kept mother's and father's homes separate in their family portraits. In accordance with the growing prevalence of equal parenting, children in the 2020s may view their updated family arrangements as a network of multiple households, consisting of both biological and non-biological members, as depicted in their drawings. In Ilves' study (2021), one girl (9 years old) drew her mother, her sister, father and stepfather on her family portrait. She explained, "...In the beginning I didn't want my parents to split up and when I saw my stepfather, I didn't get on with him very well at first but now I do /.../ Sometimes I even get on better with him. He shares time with me more than my father". However, a boy (12 years old), argues, "...those bad things [in my life], for example... this stepfather, a complete idiot /.../ if he left us ... it would improve my life". The best illustration of the children's adaptability to a new life arrangement is in Karl's (10 years old) family portrait (see Fig. 5.3). Karl is content that his parents are divorced because they had conflicts with each other. He explains, "... they made the right choice. If they were together right now, they'd be fighting and then I don't think I'd feel very good. Today everything is fine". Karl has an extensive family that encompasses individuals with diverse biological connections and spanning multiple generations. He rates his life as 9 out of 10 on a scale ranging from 0 to 10.

Ilves' study (2021) confirmed that the children's subjective well-being is weakened by a generally poor relationship background, whether with their peers and friends or with their parents, foster parents and the over-regulation of social interactions. In contrast, the child's ability to manage his or her own life; that is, to make decisions about interactions with parents, increased the satisfaction rating. The

Fig. 5.3 Karl's family portrait (from left): Karl, mother, small brother, the smallest brother, stepfather, father, grandfather, stepmother, and two grandmothers (source: Ilves, 2021)

study also showed that parenthood shared equally between parents may not be in the best interests of the child; for example, in a situation where a child does not want to be with one parent because, for whatever reason, the child has not developed or maintained a close relationship with that parent. However, it is in the best interests of the child that the parents get on well together. The children's narratives showed that children's familial vulnerability can decrease, and well-being is enhanced by reconciliation and friendly interaction between their parents.

5.5 Conclusion: What Did We Learn from the Children?

According to Donati (2011), society is made up by individuals but is not made of individuals. The same applies to families, that people, whether adults or children, become social actors through mutual relations, and are interconnected in various relational environments and related structures, with repeated interactions. Effective communication can be challenging for a child without a stable and secure upbringing, such as the presence of caring parents or trusted individuals. Research highlighted in this chapter has indicated that children place significant value on biological connections within their family. Furthermore, they can identify several reasons why they perceive marriage between parents to be safer than cohabitation. However, children appear to be adept at adapting to changes in the family structure due to their prevalence as subjects of such changes; for example, living with parents who are in a cohabiting relationship or in a blended family that extends beyond the confines of one home.

The studies with children showed that vulnerability is a relational aspect of family complexity. It arises from everyday interactions and requires attention, just like relational well-being (see e.g., White, 2015). It is worth mentioning that not only children but also adults carry their own vulnerabilities as inputs in relationships (Giesinger, 2019).

In the context of ageing societies that assert a high societal value on children, being a proficient parent is a challenge. Accepting a democratic way of family life, acknowledging children's rights, and developing effective conflict resolution and parenting skills are the first steps towards achieving this goal. Second, it involves possessing effective coping strategies to manage family adjustments initiated by the adults themselves, such as separation, divorce, or the arrival of a new parental figure within the family arrangement. Children expect and hope that their parents will successfully resolve their conflicts (i.e., overcome their personal and relational vulnerabilities) and be capable of amicably co-parenting, regardless of whether they live in the same or separate residences and irrespective of the nature of their biological relationship with the child. It is essential for adults to take responsibility for effectively managing the challenges of family transitions in the best interests of their offspring. Child protection professionals and judges should value children's input in family concerns: their perspectives should be considered as part of the decision-making process. Whatever family changes occur, Madge and Willmott (2007) assert that children can overcome stressful circumstances when they feel loved and cared for. In sum, parents bear primary responsibility for handling complex and vulnerable situations and preserving familial closeness for the child.

Acknowledgements The author is grateful to all the children who participated in the different social studies referred to in this chapter. Special thanks go to my students with whom we conducted this research as part of their Bachelor or Master's studies: Eva Jürgenson, Eva Mägi, Kelly Nurmik, Marika Roots and Helen Plakso.

Work on this chapter was supported by a grant from the Estonian Research Council (PRG700).

Competing Interests The author has no conflicts of interest to declare that are relevant to the content of this chapter.

Ethics Approval This study was performed in line with the principles of the Declaration of Helsinki. Approval was granted by the Ethics Committee of the University of Tartu (18.05.2020/ No. 315/T-10).

References

Anniste, K., Biin, H., Osila, L., Koppel, K., & Aaben, L. (2018). *Lapse õiguste ja vanemluse uuring 2018. Uuringu aruanne*. Poliitikauuringute Keskus Praxis. https://www.praxis.ee/wp-content/uploads/2017/11/Lapsed-vanemad-aruanne.pdf

Ariès, P. (1979). *Centuries of childhood*. Penguin.

Auersperg, F., Vlasak, T., Ponocny, I., & Barth, A. (2019). Long-term effects of parental divorce on mental health—A meta-analysis. *Journal of Psychiatric Research, 119*, 107–115.

Beck, U. (1986). *Risk society. Towards a new modernity*. Sage.

Boyden, J., & Mann, G. (2005). Children's risk, resilience, and coping in extreme situations. In M. Ungar (Ed.), *Handbook for working with children and youth: Pathways to resilience across cultures and contexts* (pp. 3–25). Sage.

Bühler-Niederberger, D. (2010). Childhood sociology – Defining the state of the art and ensuring reflection. *Current Sociology, 58*(2), 155–164.

Castrén, A.-M., & Widmer, E. D. (2015). Insiders and outsiders in stepfamilies: Adults' and children's views on family boundaries, *63*(1), 35–56. https://doi.org/10.1177/0011392114551650
Chancellor of Justice of Estonia homepage. https://www.oiguskantsler.ee/et/statistika-ja-uuringud [visited on 15 September 2023].
Child Protection Act issued in 1992 (RT 1992, 28, 370).
Donati, P. (2011). *Relational sociology. A new paradigm for the social sciences*. Routledge.
Eesti arvudes 1920–1935. (1937). Riigi Statistika Keskbüroo.
Giesinger, J. (2019). Vulnerability and autonomy–children and adults. *Ethics and Social Welfare, 13*(3), 216–229. https://doi.org/10.1080/17496535.2019.1647262
Hansson, L. (2000). The changing family in Estonia and Europe. In *Estonian human development report 2000* (pp. 42–48). UNDP.
Heidmets, M. (2007). *Where is Estonia? In Estonian human development report 2006* (pp. 108–118). Eesti Koostöö Kogu.
Ilves, E. (2021). *Mitme koduga lapsed: kes, kus, mis on minu kodu? Suhtluskorra retoorika ja praktika.* Magistritöö TÜ. https://dspace.ut.ee/server/api/core/bitstreams/da005bd4-1ab4-40e7-b13f-7c4717090fbc/content
Jeynes, W. H. (2006). The impact of parental remarriage on children. *Marriage & Family Review, 40*(4), 75–102. https://doi.org/10.1300/J002v40n04_05
Jürgenson, E. (2017*). Reeglid ja karistused kodus 5-7-aastaste laste arusaamad reeglitest ja karistustest.* Magistritöö TÜ. https://dspace.ut.ee/bitstream/handle/10062/57561/jyrgenson_eve_ma.pdf?sequence=1&isAllowed=y
Kallaste, E., Lang, A., Rentel, A., Kadarik, K., & Sõmer, M. (2023). Lastega perede leibkonnapilt (centar.ee) CentAR, 2023-06-02.
Kutsar, D. (1991). Marriage breakdown in Estonia. *Finnish Yearbook of Population Research, 29*, 73–82. https://doi.org/10.23979/fypr.44850
Kutsar, D., Kasearu, K., & Kurrikoff, T. (2012). Family trends and changing parenting practices in Estonia. *Cognition Brain Behavior. An Interdisciplinary Journal, 16*(2), 171–190.
Kutsar, D., Beilmann, M., Luhamaa, K., Nahkur, O., Soo, K., Strömpl, J., & Rebane, M. (2022). https://arenguseire.ee/pikksilm/laste-heaolu-tulevik/. Arenguseirekeskus, 2022-31-01.
Levin, I. (1994). *Stefamilien—variasjon og mangfold.* Aventura.
Levin, I., & Trost, J. (1992a). Understanding the concept of family. *Family Relations, 41*(3), 348–351. https://www.jstor.org/stable/585202
Levin, I., & Trost, J. (1992b). Women and the concept of family. *Familjerapporter/Family Reports 21.* Uppsala University.
Madge, N., & Willmott, N. (2007). *Children's views and experiences of parenting*. Joseph Rowntree Foundation.
Mägi, E. (2016). *Kärgperes elavad lapsed: lapse perspektiiv*. Bakalaureusetöö. TÜ. https://dspace.ut.ee/server/api/core/bitstreams/0915059a-96e2-4dd1-9f42-e4fcba42c789/content
Märtsin, M., Nahkur, O., & Abuladze, L. (2023). Family relationships and family members' self-reported mental health and wellbeing. In M. Sisask, K. Konstabel, D. Kutsar, H. Sooväli-Sepping, K. Tiidenberg, & K. Pärna (Eds.), *Estonian human development report 2023* (pp. 173–185). SA Eesti Koostöö Kogu.
Mason, J., & Danby, S. (2011). Children as experts in their lives: Child inclusive research. *Child Indicators Research, 4*(2), 185–189.
Nahkur, O., & Kutsar, D. (2022). Family type differences in children's satisfaction with people they live with and perceptions about their (step)parents' parenting practices. *Social Sciences, 11*(5), 223. https://doi.org/10.3390/socsci11050223
Newland, L. A. (2015). Family well-being, parenting, and child well-being: Pathways to healthy adjustment. *Clinical Psychologist, 19*, 3–14. https://doi.org/10.1111/cp.12059
Nurmik, K. (2023). *Mis on perekond? 6. klasside õpilaste hoiakud perestruktuuride suhtes TÜ.* Käsikiri.

Plakso, H. (2023). Kes on üksikvanemaga elava lapse perekond? *Lapse perspektiiv*. Magistritöö. TÜ. https://dspace.ut.ee/bitstream/handle/10062/91014/plakso_hele_ma_2023.pdf?sequence=1&isAllowed=y

Puur, A., & Rahnu, L. (2011). Teine demograafiline üleminek ja Eesti rahvastiku nüüdisareng. *Akadeemia, 23*(12), 2225–2272.

Qvortrup, J. (1991). *Childhood as a social phenomenon. An introduction to a series of national reports*. EUROSOCIAL reports, 36. European Centre for Social Welfare Policy and Research.

Roots, M. (2010). *Perepiirid laste käsitluses*. Bakalaureusetöö TÜ.

Tavit, A., & Tiit, E.-M. (1978). Vanemate perekonnaelu laste abielu- ja perekonnaideaali kujundajana. In *Perekonnaprobleemid 3* (pp. 92–104). Tartu Riiklik Ülikool.

Teubert, D., & Pinquart, M. (2010). The association between coparenting and child adjustment: A meta-analysis. *Parenting: Science and Practice, 10*(4), 286–307. https://doi.org/10.1080/15295192.2010.492040

Thomson, E. (2014). Family complexity in Europe. *The Annals of the American Academy of Political and Social Science, 654*, 245–258.

Tiit, E.-M. (2011). *Eesti rahvastik. Viis põlvkonda ja kümme loendust*. Statistikaamet.

Trost, J. (1990). Do we mean the same by the concept of family? *Communication Research, 17*(4), 431–443.

White, S. C. (2015). *Relational wellbeing: A theoretical and operational approach, Bath Papers in International Development and Wellbeing*, 43, University of Bath, Centre for Development Studies (CDS), Bath.

World Health Organisation. (2022). *World mental health report: Transforming mental health for all*. World Health Organization. https://www.who.int/publications/i/item/9789240049338

Dagmar Kutsar is an Associate Professor of Social Policy at the University of Tartu, Estonia. Her research interests are family, childhood, and welfare research and policies. She was a board member of the International Society for Child Indicators (ISCI) and is a principal researcher for the International Survey of Children's Worlds. She is also a board member of the Children's Rights Academic Network (CREAN) and the International Commission on Couple and Family Relations (ICCFR). She has partnered in several international research projects (e.g., EU 6FP PROFIT, IPROSEC, NoE EQUALSOC and EU FP7 FLOWS). She has been a member of the Standing Committee of Social Sciences of the European Science Foundation, the Executive Committee and Chair of the National Associations Council of the European Sociological Association, and an expert for the EU FP7 Youth Social Inclusion Cluster at the European Commission. She was a member of the Advisory Group for the Widening Programme at the EU Horizon 2020 and an Advisory Group member for the UNICEF Report Card Nr 16.

Chapter 6
Child Vulnerability in the School Environment

Kadri Soo

6.1 Introduction

Nowadays, childhood is more and more institutionalised (Qvortrup, 2011); children spend a significant part of their time in school developing their knowledge, skills and values to become autonomous, self-respecting, creative and responsible citizens, future workers and promoters of social life. The goals of education are rather forward-looking. Education is a cornerstone of economic prosperity in society and an indicator for comparing social development and the academic achievements of countries. Kutsar and Kasearu (2017) critically state that education systems have occupied children as agents of knowledge production, making them responsible for the *goodness* of the future society (p. 141). For children, school is both a work environment, often leading to stress and poor health due to academic demands and the assessment of performance, and a social arena where the formation of friendships and status hierarchies, as well as exclusion and bullying takes place (Östberg et al., 2015). Layard and Hagell (2015) criticise over-emphasising academic success and paying less attention to children's well-being while attending school. For example, Estonia, where students are academically successful in ranking at the top in PISA tests (Program for International Student Assessment; OECD, 2023), aims to attain both high levels of achievement and well-being of children. The Education Strategy of Estonia for 2021–2035 has set an ambitious objective to increase the share of top performers in the PISA test by about eight percentage points and the share of students satisfied with school (the outcome not specified) in 15 years (Ministry of Education and Research, 2021). Vision documents, such as OECD Education 2030 project (OECD, 2018) and the policy glossary *Learning for Well-being* (Kickbusch,

K. Soo (✉)
Institute of Social Studies, University of Tartu, Tartu, Estonia
e-mail: kadri.soo@ut.ee

D. Kutsar et al. (eds.), *Child Vulnerability and Vulnerable Subjectivity*, Children's Well-Being: Indicators and Research 27,
https://doi.org/10.1007/978-3-031-61333-3_6

2012), have addressed the issue of prioritising children's well-being and sense of agency in education as key components of having a secure and flourishing childhood.

However, in practice, the school experiences of children may not be in line with the ambitious goals in policy and vision documents formulated by adults. Children's academic success does not always equate to high subjective well-being. The WHO collaborative cross-national study of adolescent health and well-being *Health Behaviour of School-Aged Children* (HBSC) displays a problematic decline in children's assessments of the liking of going to school and an upturn in the proportion of students feeling pressured by schoolwork over time (Inchley et al., 2020). During the last decade, the biggest drop in happiness with schoolwork was observed among adolescents (The Children's Society, 2022)—an age group which grapples most with mental health problems. Education is a right of the child designed to improve the child's life and development in the present and in the future, but in realising this right, the child seems to face situations that, instead of enhancing or maintaining well-being, can make them vulnerable.

Using children's views of their school experiences, this chapter explores the sources of vulnerability in the school environment that create or undermine children's subjective well-being. I understand vulnerability of children as a relational phenomenon that can harm their subjective well-being at school, and stems from children's developmental needs, including the need to have positive relationships with others (parents, teachers and peers), and to participate and be respected in order to be (and become) a self-efficient and self-valuing social agent (Giesinger, 2019). I examine vulnerability by presenting examples mainly from Estonia as an outstanding case characterised by high-quality education, minimal impact of family affluence on children's educational achievements and school-related well-being, but very low ratings of school liking in international comparisons (see: Inchley et al., 2020).

The analysis is based on the National Satisfaction and School Environment Survey (referred to below as the School Satisfaction Survey) that was carried out among children from more than 350 regular schools all over Estonia (about 85% of all schools with a basic school level), and their teachers and parents in 2021 (Lutsoja et al., 2022). Here, I use the responses of 11,365 fourth-grade students (mostly aged 10) and 9460 eighth grade students (mostly aged 14), that constitute 74% and 64% of their corresponding age cohorts. Using self-administered electronic questionnaires, children evaluated their academic, social and physical learning environments, self-efficacy and self-image, as well as relationships with parents and engagement with hobbies. I supplement the results of the School Satisfaction Survey with findings from eight semi-structured focus group interviews, conducted among 12-year-old children studying in urban and rural schools in Estonia in 2016 (Mandel, 2016). Altogether 55 children (29 girls and 26 boys) from grade 6 participated in the study.

6.2 Education in Estonia

Basic education (grades 1–9) is the minimum compulsory general education in Estonia. Children generally start attending school at age 7 and usually transition from primary to lower secondary school in grade 5, depending on the arrangements of the particular school. During this transition, children must cope with many changes, including a higher homework load, receiving marks instead of former customary qualitative assessments, and having several subject teachers instead of predominantly one class teacher. National proficiency tests in fourth and seventh grades are held to map students' knowledge, plan learning and develop the curriculum. At the end of lower secondary school, students have to pass exams in three subjects.

Estonian education policy aims to provide high-quality and inclusive education, ensuring primary education (grades 1–6) are as close to home as possible (Ministry of Education and Research, 2021). In the last 20 years, the number of school-age children has remarkably decreased, particularly in remote counties of Estonia (even up to 50%; Statistics Estonia, 2023). The national education policy has therefore undertaken a plan to optimise the school network and adapt it to demographic changes (Haridus- ja teadusministeerium, 2023). Many rural schools with a small number of students have been closed or the number of grades has been reduced (e.g., 6 or 4 grades instead of 9 grades). This trend has been accelerated by the centrally distributed subsidies to local governments—the owners of municipal schools—on the condition that they contract the school network. The school reform has caused anxiety and resentment among rural communities and particularly among school principals, teachers and parents. For children, this can mean longer distances to school or a change of school with the need to adapt to a new learning environment and new relationships.

Estonian education suffers from personnel problems: the Estonian teaching staff is ageing, shrinking and overworked, and the recruitment of qualified teachers and support specialists is not sufficient (Leijen et al., 2021; Taimalu et al., 2020). The shortage of teachers is particularly acute in some subjects (e.g., mathematics, physics) and in rural areas. According to the OECD Teaching and Learning International Survey (TALIS), nearly a fifth of teachers complain about a high level of stress in their work (Taimalu et al., 2020). Burnout and turnover rates are high among beginning teachers (Taimalu et al., 2020).

6.3 General Sources of Vulnerability at School

6.3.1 Relationships at School

The process of teaching and learning is primarily relational (Thapa et al., 2013). In the learning context, relationships imply much more than interpersonal communication between students, teachers and other school staff. Relationships constitute an essential frame for instructional interactions, including motivating engagement in learning, reducing task-related anxiety, fair treatment, recognising students' participation and efforts, providing feedback, and listening to and considering their views (Kutsyuruba et al., 2015; Murray-Harvey, 2010). Social support is a central characteristic of positive interpersonal relationships, functioning as a social resource in the child's network that provides emotional understanding, advice, information, and monitoring of well-being in order to enhance their ability to cope with adversity (Thompson, 2014) and prevent vulnerability. Mutual feelings of support, trust, respect, and caring are pivotal in shaping a positive school climate (Wang & Degol, 2016) and sense of agency. Agency is a dynamic and relational feature denoting a child's capability to responsibly participate in the world, set goals and find means to achieve them and influence people and events for the better (OECD, 2018). Enabling a child's agency in school relies on relationships with teachers, schoolmates and parents, in so-called co-agency that refers to the "interactive, mutually supportive relationships that help learners to progress towards their valued goals" (OECD, 2018, p. 4).

Twelve-year-old Estonian children authentically depicted in the interviews (Mandel, 2016) how students and teachers act as co-agents in the formation of school experiences that can be perceived more positively or negatively, and that promote or inhibit their agency. For instance, friendly classmates and caring and flexible teachers who tried to understand the children's views and the reasons for their behaviour were the sources of good feelings and a sense of agency at school. Students disturbing lessons lead to angry reactions from teachers; furthermore, cruel, moody and often (unreasonably) reprimanding teachers caused fear and anxiety and the children attempt to avoid these teachers during recess: "Every time you go to this teacher's class, you basically bite your nails, because you worry about what's next, what you're guilty of now" (a girl; Mandel, 2016).

The findings from the School Satisfaction Survey in Estonia indicate that relationships at school are positive for most students (Fig. 6.1). On average, children agreed most strongly that they get along well with teachers and that they get along well with classmates. Equal recognition of all students regardless of their achievements and encouragement of children to express their opinions are less common practices among teachers. Children are also less likely to have experienced caring by fellow students. The age differences in the evaluations of relationships with peers are small, but the ratings about teachers drop substantially with age. Compared to younger children, eighth graders consider teachers significantly less caring and interested in how they are doing. Based on the Self-Determination Theory (Ryan & Deci, 2000), the indicators of the quality of the relationships with teachers and peers reflect the satisfaction of students' basic psychological needs—sense of autonomy (in this analysis understood as expressing one's opinion), competence (i.e., being recognised) and connectedness (i.e., experiencing care, support and good communication). According to the children's responses, the satisfaction of these needs, especially connectedness with teachers, seems to be better promoted in the school life of the majority of younger children. The experiences of older children on the other hand demonstrate a moderate level of connectedness with teachers, and

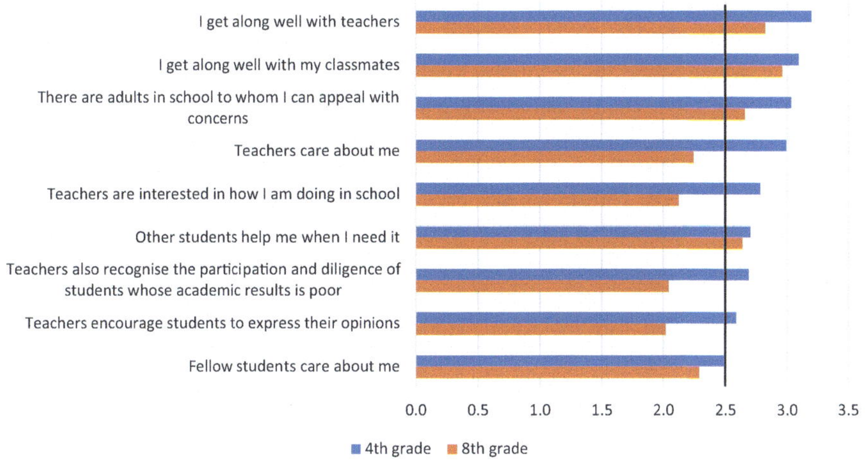

Fig. 6.1 Average ratings of relationships with teachers and fellow students among fourth and eighth grade students. Note. Scale of items: 0—"I do not agree at all", 1—"I rather disagree", 2—"A little agree and a little disagree", 3—"I rather agree", 4—"I totally agree". The values above the solid line indicate a good level in the components of the relationships (more than half of children agreed)

slightly lower levels of participation and recognition. As these different components of children's needs are interlinked (the Spearman's correlation analysis between the statements in Fig. 6.1 reveals a significant positive correlation), I will henceforth refer to them together using the generic term of quality of relationships.

The decline in ratings of the quality of relationships with age can be viewed within the frame of two intertwined changes in the lives of children: educational and developmental transitions. Research on educational transition (Spernes, 2022; Trotman et al., 2015) has revealed that attached relationships are more likely to occur in younger grades where teacher-student contact is more frequent throughout the school year, enabling the teacher to get to know students better and communicate on personal topics as well. At the primary school level, the teacher embodies a stable non-parental attachment subject and role model for children (Wentzel, 2016). Having such a model and the provision of support concerning emotional, social and academic problems are important in ensuring developmental competence and can facilitate coping and adjustment in later years of schooling.

Moving from primary into lower secondary school, requires children to adapt to larger class sizes, new teachers and higher educational demands, and sometimes even to a new school environment. Although most children experience these transitions easily or the transition may involve positive changes, a substantial number of children struggle with anxiety, stress and a decrease in learning motivation (Eccles & Roeser, 2011). Educational transition in parallel with pubertal development may pose a serious challenge especially for children with little social support from home and school (Duchesne et al., 2009; Waters et al., 2014) and a poor socio-economic family background (Moore et al., 2021), leading even to school failure and dropping out (Neild et al., 2008).

During adolescence, in becoming socially and cognitively mature, there is a growth in children's sense of autonomy, and effort to be an independent and competent person whose decision-making would be respected by parents and other adults (Inguglia et al., 2015). Having a say in decisions at school boosts children's happiness with school (The Children's Society, 2022). The interviews with 12-year-olds (Mandel, 2016) showed that asking children's opinions on matters concerning them (e.g., school meals) and taking their opinions into account is rare at school. Only one positive initiative appeared in the study conducted by Mandel (2016)—the organisation of open forums, where students can make suggestions to improve school life: "For example, they [the management] have changed some classrooms and hired more teachers". Bjerke (2011) found in his research that compared to eight-to-nine-year-olds, teenagers perceive a low level of participation at school as a problem causing them frustration and anger, especially towards teachers, leading even to conflicts. Thus, developmentally important respect and participation, especially for students in older grades, can be detrimental to a child's dignity and sense of well-being at school if they remain unsatisfied.

Good relationships with teachers can compensate for deficiencies in relationships with fellow students and vice versa. Based on the responses of Estonian children in the School Satisfaction Survey, I looked at what patterns of the quality of relationships appear in children's school experiences. By summarising children's answers to the statements about the quality of relationships with teachers and fellow students (see Fig. 6.1) into an aggregate variable,[1] it turns out that 43% of fourth grade children and 23% of eighth graders consider their relationships both with teachers and fellow students very good. Less than half of the participants In both grades reported moderately or fairly good relationships with both teachers and students. Among younger children, there are more of those (9%) whose relationships are poor only with students than those who identified that their relationships with teachers were bad but good with peers (3%). In the older age group, the opposite trend is evident—14% of children judged their relationships with peers as pleasant but not with teachers, however, 8% regarded their relationships good only with teachers. Particularly vulnerable are children—4% of the younger age group and twice as high in grade 8—who reported a low level of caring, support, inclusion and

[1]The aggregate variable of the quality of relationships with teachers and schoolmates consists of the following groups. The group 'poor relationship with both' includes children who disagreed with almost all items in Fig. 6.1 (answered with the scale points 0 or 1). Children with poor relationships only with teachers mostly disagreed with the statements related to teachers or adults at school but chose scale points 2–4 ("a little agree and a little disagree", "rather agree", "totally agree") concerning peer-related items. Children with poor relationships only with fellow students mostly disagreed with the statements related to students but chose scale points 2–4 concerning teacher-related items. Moderate or fairly good relationships refer to children who responded "a little agree and a little disagree" to most of the statements or agreed with the statements about either the relationships with teachers or students. Children with very good relationships with both are those who agreed to all the statements (the scale points 3 and 4).

recognition by teachers and peers, being at risk of unfulfillment of their basic psychological needs by important others at school.

Gender differences between these groups in the quality of relationships are small. An exception are girls in fourth grade, who, compared to boys, are more likely to consider their relationships with teachers and students very good (47% and 39%, respectively). The absence of such a difference in grade 8 reflects a greater decline in school-related well-being for girls than for boys (see Kutsar & Kasearu, 2017). Children attending small schools (less than 300 students; mostly located in a rural area) tend to evaluate relationships more positively, especially with teachers, than those who study in a school with 600 students or more. In smaller schools, it is easier to create a school climate that provides a sense of safety, inclusion and belongingness (Thapa et al., 2013). Having fewer children in the classroom, teachers have more opportunities to pay attention to each child, notice their problems, recognise their achievements, and maintain personal contact, thereby enhancing students' engagement and happiness with school experiences.

The quality of relationships is a key factor shaping a child's attitude towards school. Figure 6.2 illustrates the large variability in school liking between children with very high and very low ratings of the quality of relationships at school. Children in both grades having good relationships with teachers and classmates enjoy school attendance. The greater sensitivity of fourth grade children concerning the lack of supportive, caring, and involving relationships is evident. Specifically, 60% of children in grade 4 with poor relationships with both teachers and fellow students disagree that they like going to school, compared to 4% of children with very good relationships. Of the latter, four fifths (81%) report liking school. The findings in the figure also highlight how the role of teachers is more crucial than of fellow students in making school attendance enjoyable.

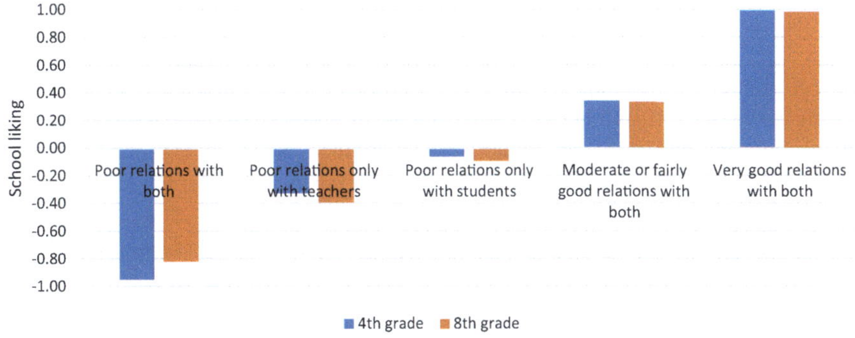

Fig. 6.2 Children's estimations of school liking by the quality of relationships with teachers and fellow students (group average ratings compared to the average value of all groups). Note. A value greater than 0 indicates experiencing a higher level of school liking than the average of all groups, a value less than 0 indicates a lower level of school liking

6.3.2 School Bullying

A sense of unsafety and being bullied at school is a clear manifestation of vulnerability. Although the findings of international studies have shown a decline in school bullying over time, it is still widespread, particularly in Estonia (Inchley et al., 2020). Bullying is more present in schools where relationships between peers, and particularly between children and teachers, are distant and conflictual (Bouchard & Smith, 2017; Harel-Fisch et al., 2011). For instance, the findings of the School Satisfaction Survey show that the majority (81%) of fourth grade children having poor relationships with both teachers and students informed of bullying experiences at school, two thirds of them having been victimised repeatedly. Among children with very good relationships, only a third have experienced bullying.

Bullying is a traumatic experience that affects the well-being of many children, undermining their sense of self-worth (Sarkova et al., 2014), academic motivation and success in school performance (Erath et al., 2008). Students being exposed to bullying tend to dislike going to school, as revealed in the focus groups carried out by Mandel (2016). Interviewed children described bullying as humiliating and frightening experiences that harmed their autonomy and exercise of agency through (self) isolation and school avoidance or absenteeism. For example, a girl who was teased about her appearance daily started lying about having a headache to avoid attending school and being revictimised. A dislike for school can be a short-term attitude, lasting until the end of the unpleasant situation; however, it can also become pervasive if induced by a self-perception of academic failure (Graham et al., 2022) or recurrent school bullying, and can result in early school leaving (Cornell et al., 2013). The extent to which bullying experiences may harm children's sense of well-being at school depends on the availability of assistance and the resilience of children.

Teachers play a central role in creating a safe and non-aggressive classroom atmosphere and mitigating the negative effects when bullying does occur (Veenstra et al., 2014). The results of the interviews with 12-year-olds (Mandel, 2016) demonstrated few positive situations where teachers' activities had prevented and/or stopped bullying. In a story with a positive ending, the teacher paid attention to the student in concern, listening to him/her empathically, and solved the situation by talking to the bully. In another positive example, children studying at a school where an anti-bullying program was implemented described how teachers' constant visibility in the corridors signalled that bullying was taken seriously. Research on the effectiveness of such programmes (Gaffney et al., 2021; Kärnä et al., 2013) indicates that the joint and consistent contribution of students and school staff to raising awareness, prevention, detection, and intervention creates a social norm that condemns bullying and reduces the number of incidents. In Mandel's study (2016) interviewed children also discussed similar effects, as in the following quote from children from a large school.

> Boy 1: Teachers have KiVa[2] vests on and then they go back and forth here [in the corridor].
> Boy 2: Teachers make sure no one is bullied.
> Researcher: Do you think it works?
> Children together: Yes!
> Boy 3: I think there was more bullying last year or the year before this.

In most cases, interviewed children described bullying experiences where the victims receive no help, or they do not believe in the possibility of it. Children felt abandoned when they needed assistance. Teachers, in their narrations, rarely noticed a child with a bullying problem, did not find time nor take measures to resolve the situation, as happened with a bullied child who avoided contacts with classmates:

> I often spent my breaks there under the table /…/ just sitting. Then the teacher noticed it and asked if there was something wrong with me that I was sitting there all the time. But she only asked. I told her [about bullying] and she did nothing (Mandel, 2016).

Some interviews also revealed a lack of support staff in the school or students' unawareness of their existence.

Although the evidence on whether bullying is more common in large or small schools is conflicting (Azeredo et al., 2015), the results from the interviews with 12-year-olds in Estonia (Mandel, 2016) indicate a tendency that in larger schools, due to greater anonymity and places hidden from teachers, bullying tends to remain unnoticed. In contrast, in smaller schools, teachers can more easily monitor the students' activities during breaks, and in addition, the greater closeness between teachers and students facilitates the flow of information about cases of bullying and the provision and asking for help.

Children narrated in the interviews (Mandel, 2016) that some teachers were unable to deal with bullying effectively or disbelieved the victim. In addition, children's fear of the teacher, particularly in the case of moody, strict and authoritarian teachers, prevented children from disclosing the bullying incident or addressing them with another concern.

> Boy 1: They [teachers] say it's your business. And then they say like this: stop it [bullying], it's your business, solve it yourself how you want.
> Boy 2: Yeah, and then they go away.
> Girl: Because the teachers don't care about the children. (Mandel, 2016)

The problematic functioning of co-agency in the child-teacher relationships and not listening to the child's voice (their concerns) makes children feel like a secondary person in the school system, whose rights are not important. Failure to meet the rights and psychological needs of children can increase their vulnerability and supresses a sense of agency. However, complicated and harmful situations can make a child strong and resilient and look for solutions independently. The understanding that children have to deal with their own problems emerged from the interviews (Mandel, 2016), mainly due to children's disappointment in and distrust of adults.

---

[2] KiVa is an acronym of the Finnish expression "Kiusaamista Vastaan" that means "against bullying". The acronym signifies the theory-based anti-bullying intervention program developed in Finland (Kärnä et al., 2013).

There were also opinions reflecting children's desire and effort to be an autonomous person who manages their lives even in difficult situations. Girl: "I try to be like that, I try to solve my problems myself, not to be like so that others should solve my problems."

The teacher-student relationship shapes children's mental representations of themselves and others, which in turn are the basis for interpretations and assessments of others' behaviour, intentions, and trustworthiness (Wentzel, 2016). In the school setting, teachers are the most important primary adults who are able to provide multiple forms of social support to bullied children to keep them engaged in school and buffer a decline in school liking (Troop-Gordon & Kuntz, 2013). Experiencing support from parents and teachers, children develop skills and courage to ask for assistance (from another person) at some point in time (Thompson, 2014). Failing to receive help from a teacher concerning bullying diminishes faith in pedagogues as trustworthy and caring adults. Children narrated in the interviews (Mandel, 2016) how distrust of one teacher can spread to others and make children avoid asking for assistance from those with whom they have had no unpleasant incidents, even when help was needed.

> Girl 1: I've thought about going to a school psychologist or a real psychologist, but I don't know, I don't really trust anyone recently.
> Girl 2: Yeah, me neither.
> Researcher: But for what?
> Girl 2: Everyone we've trusted has betrayed us. (Mandel, 2016).

Therefore, children instead rely on peers who may compensate for a lack of teachers' assistance by providing protection, support or comfort in case of bullying. The findings of a Swedish study (Thornberg et al., 2017) showed that fellow students are more likely to defend victimised classmates when the student-student relationships are perceived as warm, caring, and friendly. However, victims often do not have friends at school because "nobody wants to become someone who would be bullied next", leading thus to the accumulation of trauma experiences, where aggression is accompanied by social exclusion from significant others without social support.

Children's descriptions of bullying and its intervention in Mandel's (2016) study reflected the degree of the expression of their agency and the quality of co-agency. In a school collective with well-functioning relationships, agency manifests in the prevention of bullying, disclosure of incidents, as well as in protection and support from fellow students. But the more there are power asymmetries in the relationships between students or between students and teachers, the worse co-agency works and children's courage to stand up for their well-being decreases. To conclude, children are especially vulnerable when they experience bullying and poor-quality relationships with teachers and peers with little prospect of receiving support.

6.3.3 School Stress and Motivation to Learn

At school, students are faced with relational and normative stressors that influence their physiological and psychological stability. School stress is generally understood as the imbalance between experienced academic demands or challenges and a student's capacity to deal with them (Östberg et al., 2015). School-related stress can threaten children's well-being, causing tension, restlessness, exhaustion, sleeping difficulties, and negative feelings (Östberg et al., 2015; Scrimin et al., 2014).

Compared to younger children, older ones are more likely to experience school stress. For instance, the findings of the School Satisfaction Survey show that by grade 8, the share of children reporting high levels of feeling overburdened due to schoolwork has doubled (up to 44%).[3] The children in the interviews (Mandel, 2016) also complained about high schoolwork loads as one of the aspects causing bad feelings, strain and reducing their liking of school. According to them, doing homework, including at weekends, took a lot of time, limited their free time to spend with friends or relax, and led them to give up their hobbies. Non-working co-agency is especially expressed in children's assessments of teachers' lack of interest in asking children's opinions about the amount of homework or consulting them (or other teachers) to avoid taking multiple tests on the same day. The children were especially disturbed by social pressure to get good marks and concerns about failure, while insufficient attention was paid to their actual knowledge and effort (Mandel, 2016). Fattore et al. (2022) state that the part of the harm children experience from stress and anxiety refers to the way school systems put increasing pressure on children to perform at a high level, by monitoring their achievements with different standards of normal development and ranking the results.

A noticeable gender difference can be observed in the perception of school-related stress (Inchley et al., 2020). In the School Satisfaction Survey, 21% of boys and 36% of girls in the eighth grade reported feeling stress to a great degree. Girls in the interviews conducted by Mandel (2016) described how, due to the perceived excessive amount of homework and preparing for tests, they had to study at nights or wake up earlier in the morning, being therefore exhausted. In contrast to boys' more relaxed attitude towards schoolwork and social comparison, girls tend to internalise a higher standard concerning educational achievements, set by themselves and/or others, and try to perform well. Östberg et al. (2015) conclude that dealing with the developmental challenges of puberty (e.g., how a girl should look like) in parallel with different academic expectations for boys and girls may enlarge the gender variation in the perception of stress and makes girls more vulnerable to accumulated stress.

[3] Perception of school stress was measured by two items ("I often sleep badly due to school problems" and "I feel overburdened with schoolwork") and decline in learning motivation was measured by three items ("I don't want to study at school anymore", "I feel I have lost interest in studying", "I constantly doubt whether my studies make sense"), using the scale 0—"I do not agree at all", 1—"I rather disagree", 2—"A little agree and a little disagree", 3—"I rather agree", 4—"I totally agree". I calculated two indices by averaging the corresponding items.

Poor relationships with teachers and students seem to be a serious source of school stress at any age. In the School Satisfaction Survey, if the quality of relationships with one or all parties at school is good, the level of perceived stress decreases (Fig. 6.3). A feeling of being supported and respected functions as a useful resource for children, promoting their motivation and resilience, and thereby increasing their ability to cope with stressors in the school environment and promoting personal growth (Tong et al., 2019; Wentzel, 2016). However, if the stress response is prolonged with inadequate support from caregivers or teachers, stress may become toxic, increasing vulnerability to adverse health and educational outcomes (Franke, 2014).

In the judgements of younger and older children in Fig. 6.3, different patterns of association between the quality of relationships and perceived stress emerge. Eighth grade children reported slightly more school stress when their relationships with peers were good but poor with teachers. Children's negative assessments about teachers can be linked to their expectation of greater support from adults at school in coping with increasing study loads and their resentment towards the insufficient involvement, recognition and enabling of their agency. Adolescents' pursuit of autonomy can clash with some teachers' authoritarian, directive and obedience-oriented teaching style, resulting in either student passivity or more frequent conflicts (Soo, 2023). Thus, emotionally cold, unsupportive and unrespectful connections with teachers are stressful and worsen school satisfaction.

In the case of the children in fourth grade, school stress is more related to poor relationships with peers, referring to their greater exposure of bullying as a severe school-stressor. At this age, a child's friendships are often school-centred. Without friends and supportive peers, a child lacks an important stress reliever and is more vulnerable to adversities in the school environment (Arafat et al., 2019). If children's concerns (e.g., bullying) and school stress in younger grades are not responded to rapidly and adequately, then worries about the educational transition may increase

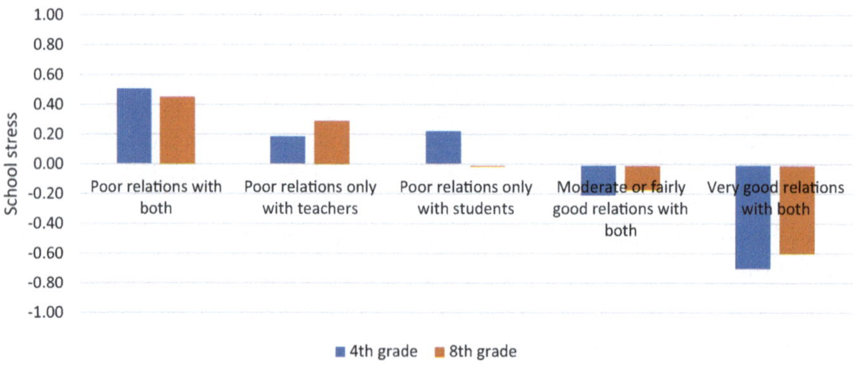

Fig. 6.3 Children's perception of school stress by the quality of relationships with teachers and fellow students (group average ratings compared to the average value of all groups). Note. A value greater than 0 indicates experiencing a higher level of school stress than the average of all groups, a value less than 0 indicates a lower level of stress

(Evans et al., 2018), and stress and anxiety can accumulate and manifest in school burnout or mental health problems in older grades (Lester et al., 2013; Salmela-Aro & Upadyaya, 2014). However, high-quality relationships that underlie a sense of belonging at school can provide children with a foundation for healthy functioning at school.

School-related stress tends to jeopardise students' motivation for learning (af Ursin et al., 2020). During the transition to lower secondary school, a decline in children's motivation to learn can be observed. According to the School Satisfaction Survey, 6% of children had a low interest in learning in grade 4, however, by grade 8, this share has more than tripled. Less motivated students are at risk of harm. They are likely to be disengaged in learning activities, have lower academic achievements and feel negative affect (Hornstra et al., 2018). The interviews with students (Mandel, 2016) revealed that their learning motivation was reduced by unattractive and non-inclusive teaching methods and too fast learning tempo that left children few opportunities to ask questions and supressed their creativity, curiosity and sense of agency. However, individual contact with teachers and attention to the student's progress, as well as learning in small groups, were more likely to arouse interest in schooling. Children also narrated that lessons full of self-directed activities or those where they can talk about real life issues, such as communication skills, inspired them to learn.

Differential treatment and expectation from a teacher (e.g., favouring some students over others) can have essential cumulative positive or negative effects on interest in learning, achievements (see Hornstra et al., 2018) and expression of agency. Eccles and Roeser (2011) conclude that when students move to secondary school, teachers tend to use more differential recognition and performance-oriented instructional practice, which can stimulate the learning motivation and school engagement of high-achieving students but has an opposite effect on low achievers. Lower levels of a sense of competence, particularly among high school students, can increase children's vulnerability to negative affect and a decline in school satisfaction (Tian et al., 2014).

The effect of the quality of relationships on learning motivation is even greater than on the perception of school stress (see Fig. 6.4). If quality of relationships at school is inadequate, the child's interest in studies declines. Children in lower grades are particularly vulnerable to the impact of negative relationships. Relationships with teachers play a more important role in maintaining learning motivation than relationships with fellow students. In their study with a longitudinal research design, Jang et al. (2012) found that children who experience an autonomy-supportive instructional style by teachers; that is, providing freedom of choice, encouraging children to express opinions, and adopting students' perspectives, are more committed in learning later in the semester. Students' motivation to be agentic and actively engaged in classroom activities and achieve academic goals is a product of social reciprocity between members of the learning process. Teachers' supportiveness and inclusive and motivating style improve the children's agency and motivation in class, which, in turn, can lead to an increase in teachers' support for autonomy (Reeve & Tseng, 2011). Specifically, teachers, fulfilling student's needs

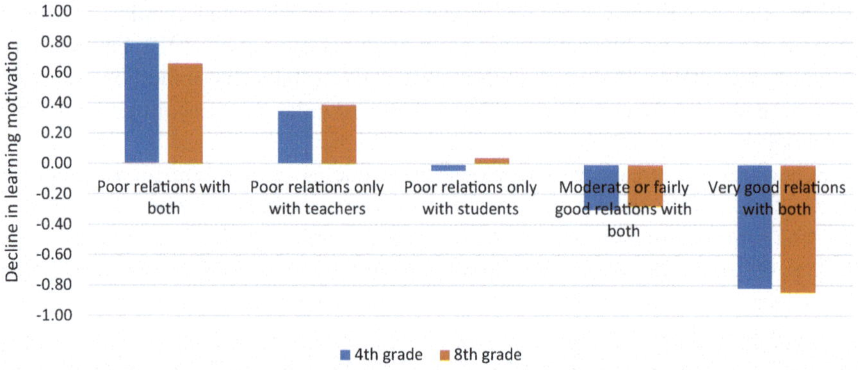

Fig. 6.4 Decline in learning motivation by the quality of relationships with teachers and fellow students (group average ratings compared to the average value all groups). Note: A value greater than 0 indicates experiencing a higher level of decline in learning motivation than the average of all groups, a value less than 0 indicates a lower level of decline

for autonomy, competence, and connectedness, support their motivation to learn as well as contribute to their psychological and academic growth and enjoyment of going to school. Thus, the instructional interaction that encourages children to learn is relational and requires effectively functioning co-agency.

6.4 Conclusion

This chapter demonstrated how the creation of both well-being and vulnerability are relational. The qualities of relationships, such as support, care, respect and trust, in student-student and particularly in student-teacher relationships reduce or prevent children's vulnerability and contribute to the enjoyment of the learning environment.

Social relations (re)producing vulnerability occur and are influenced by three dynamic interconnected dimensions. The first dimension is societal, which provides a wider political, cultural and social framework to understand children as human beings and define their needs, rights and position in the social order, including the school system. Compared to adults, children's vulnerability is revealed in their more limited freedom to choose their own supportive social networks and avoid those not perceived as such (Thompson, 2014). Parents, school authorities and teachers can act as gatekeepers, deciding on the school, class and sometimes even deskmates for children, or using assessment tools to place them into study groups with different levels. Policymakers and teachers assign tests to evaluate children's knowledge and progress, impose learning tempo and give assignments according to the content of the curriculum. The children's opportunity to influence the circumstances in the learning environment is limited depending on the extent to which children are included in decision-making processes and their opinions are taken into account; that is, children are enabled to be autonomous and express their agency. But children's agency is related to culturally constructed ideas about the extent of agency performance that is appropriate for them (Bordonaro, 2012), and is restricted by the educational institution and the exercise of the power of their parents and teachers (Sirkko et al., 2019).

Although the child's right to participate is explicitly formulated in the adult-led documents (e.g., the UN Convention on the Rights of the Child, laws and development plans of education), based on children's assessments, the realisation of this right is not common at school, depending on the initiative of a particular school or a teacher and the desire to listen to children. The ability to have a say and express one's agency does not arise by itself, it is learned and practised primarily in supportive and respectful relationships. However, when there is an emotional distance in children-teacher relationships, due to the teacher's unprofessionalism or authoritarianism, then children's interest in voicing their thoughts and wishes and actively engage in the classroom, and even more, their courage to ask for help at moments directly endangering their well-being, diminishes. Thus, socially structured patterns of relationships that inhibit children's autonomy and agency embrace a vulnerability-enhancing effect. However, agency and vulnerability are not mutually exclusive. This chapter provided evidence that challenging and damaging situations children face can make them stronger, develop their capacities and coping skills, and, in turn, reduce their vulnerability.

The second—the dimension of transitions—contains coinciding developmental and institutional changes in the child's (school) life. Andresen (2014) claims that socially determined transition alongside the transition from childhood to adolescence have an essential impact on producing or avoiding vulnerability in childhood. Being supported, involved, and esteemed in trusted and stable relationships at school (and at home) is important both from the perspective of socially and emotionally healthy development and in adapting to increasing demands concerning moving to secondary school. But, low fulfilment of fundamental needs disrupts the child's adjustment to the educational changes, causes distress and challenges the maintenance of learning motivation. A poor start to schooling; for example, struggling with stressful and traumatic situations without social support, can lead to a cumulation of vulnerability. Low-quality relationships among students and between students and teachers in primary school can increase children's anxiety and dissatisfaction with school, which, in turn, worsen their mental well-being, academic performance and aversion to going to school at the subsequent school levels (Kiuru et al., 2020; Lester et al., 2013).

The third dimension refers to school as an environment, with its material, physical and human resources, in which social relationships and school culture are created and maintained. The organisational aspects of the school (e.g., school or class size), enough professional teachers and availability of support staff provide the favourable conditions to create a supportive school climate that values learning. Shared positive values and a well-functioning co-agency, regardless of the number of children at the school, ensure a safe and cohesive environment, preventing harmful school experiences for children or intervening quickly and effectively to reduce vulnerability. However, if vulnerability manifests at the level of school or teachers;

for example, a school is at a risk of closure or reorganisation, teachers are overburdened, fatigued, under-supported and with low agency, then it can impact on relationships between all parties and be transferred to students. In a situation where vulnerability is pervasive in the school environment, it can be particularly difficult for a student to realise their rights and satisfy needs.

The chapter suggests that children's sense of well-being is not keeping pace with the adult-directed educational requirements about the amount of knowledge children should acquire and the expectations of children's success, raising the question of whether all the requirements in the curricula are necessary and realistic. Secondly, the quality of relationships creates inequalities in attainment of education. In realising their right to education, many children experience unhealthy relationships that jeopardise their learning motivation and well-being at school and make them vulnerable. Children feel good and do good (the terms used by Norrish et al., 2013) at school if their other rights are realised as well, including the right to be cared for, treated fairly, protected from violence, receive assistance, and the right to express their views and be heard (see Convention on the Rights of the Child, United Nations, 1989). The state, schools and teachers, being guided by the rights of the child and avoiding aspects producing vulnerability, will contribute to children's secure and flourishing school life, that is in line with the priorities set out in vision documents of education. School as a child's work environment, is then less stressful and unpleasant, and as a social arena, less frightening.

Acknowledgement Work on this chapter was supported by a grant from the Estonian Research Council (PRG700).

Competing Interests The author has no conflicts of interest to declare that are relevant to the content of this chapter.

References

af Ursin, P., Järvinen, T., & Pihlaja, P. (2020). The role of academic buoyancy and social support in mediating associations between academic stress and school engagement in Finnish primary school children. *Scandinavian Journal of Educational Research, 65*(4), 661–675. https://doi.org/10.1080/00313831.2020.1739135

Andresen, S. (2014). Childhood vulnerability: Systematic, structural, and individual dimensions. *Child Indicators Research, 7*(4), 699–713. https://doi.org/10.1007/s12187-014-9248-4

Arafat, S. Y., Papadopoulos, K., Mullick, M. S., & Uddin, M. S. (2019). The vulnerability and resiliency of childhood. *Global Psychiatry, 2*(2), 113–120. https://doi.org/10.2478/gp-2019-0010

Azeredo, C. M., Rinaldi, A. E. M., de Moraes, C. L., Levy, R. B., & Menezes, P. R. (2015). School bullying: A systematic review of contextual-level risk factors in observational studies. *Aggression and Violent Behavior, 22*, 65–76. https://doi.org/10.1016/j.avb.2015.04.006

Bjerke, H. (2011). 'It's the way they do it': Expressions of agency in child–adult relations at home and school. *Children & Society, 25*, 93–103. https://doi.org/10.1111/j.1099-0860.2009.00266.x

Bordonaro, L. I. (2012). Agency does not mean freedom. Cape Verdean street children and the politics of children's agency. *Children's Geographies, 10*(4), 413–426. https://doi.org/10.1080/14733285.2012.726068

Bouchard, K. L., & Smith, J. D. (2017). Teacher–student relationship quality and children's bullying experiences with peers: Reflecting on the mesosystem. *The Educational Forum, 81*(1), 108–125. https://doi.org/10.1080/00131725.2016.1243182

Cornell, D., Gregory, A., Huang, F., & Fan, X. (2013). Perceived prevalence of teasing and bullying predicts high school dropout rates. *Journal of Educational Psychology, 105*(1), 138–149. https://doi.org/10.1037/a0030416

Duchesne, S., Ratelle, C. F., Poitras, S.-C., & Drouin, E. (2009). Early adolescent attachment to parents, emotional problems, and teacher-academic worries about the middle school transition. *The Journal of Early Adolescence, 29*(5), 743–766. https://doi.org/10.1177/0272431608325502

Eccles, J. S., & Roeser, R. W. (2011). Schools as developmental contexts during adolescence. *Journal of Research on Adolescence, 21*(1), 225–241. https://doi.org/10.1111/j.1532-7795.2010.00725.x

Erath, S. A., Flanagan, K. S., & Bierman, K. L. (2008). Early adolescents school adjustment: Associations with friendship and peer victimization. *Social Development, 17*, 853–870. https://doi.org/10.1111/j.1467-9507.2008.00458.x

Evans, D., Borriello, G. A., & Field, A. P. (2018). A review of the academic and psychological impact of the transition to secondary education. *Frontiers in Psychology, 29*(9), 1482. https://doi.org/10.3389/fpsyg.2018.01482

Fattore, T., Fegter, S., & Hunner-Kreisel, C. (2022). The value of transnational, qualitative comparative research on children's vulnerability: Methodological and epistemological reflections. In H. Tiliouine, D. Benatuil, & M. K. W. Lau (Eds.), *Handbook of children's risk, vulnerability and quality of life: Global perspectives* (pp. 33–51). Springer International Publishing.

Franke, H. A. (2014). Toxic stress: Effects, prevention and treatment. *Children, 1*, 390–402. https://doi.org/10.3390/children1030390

Gaffney, H., Ttofi, M. M., & Farrington, D. P. (2021). Effectiveness of school-based programs to reduce bullying perpetration and victimization: An updated systematic review and meta-analysis. *Campbell Systematic Reviews, 17*(2), 1–102. https://doi.org/10.1002/cl2.1143

Giesinger, J. (2019). Vulnerability and autonomy—Children and adults. *Ethics and Social Welfare, 13*(3), 216–229. https://doi.org/10.1080/17496535.2019.1647262

Graham, L. J., Gillett-Swan, J., Killingly, C., & Van Bergen, P. (2022). Does it matter if students (dis)like school? Associations between school liking, teacher and school connectedness, and exclusionary discipline. *Frontiers in Psychology, 13*, 825036. https://doi.org/10.3389/fpsyg.2022.825036

Harel-Fisch, Y., Walsh, S. D., Fogel-Grinvald, H., Amitai, G., Pickett, W., Molcho, M., Due, P., Gaspar de Matos, M., & Craig, W. (2011). Negative school perceptions and involvement in school bullying: A universal relationship across 40 countries. *Journal of Adolescence, 34*(4), 639–652. https://doi.org/10.1016/j.adolescence.2010.09.008

Haridus- ja teadusministeerium. (2023). *Haridus- ja noorteprogramm 2023–2026*. Accessed October 20, 2023, from https://www.hm.ee/ministeerium-uudised-ja-kontakt/ministeerium/strateegilised-alusdokumendid-ja-programmid#haridus-ja-noortepr

Hornstra, L., Stroet, K., van Eijden, E., Goudsblom, J., & Roskamp, C. (2018). Teacher expectation effects on need-supportive teaching, student motivation, and engagement: A self-determination perspective. *Educational Research and Evaluation, 24*(3–5), 324–345. https://doi.org/10.1080/13803611.2018.1550841

Inchley, J., Currie, D., Budisavljevic, S., Torsheim, T., Jåstad, A., Cosma, A., et al. (Eds.). (2020). *Spotlight on adolescent health and well-being. Findings from the 2017/2018 Health Behaviour in School-aged Children (HBSC) survey in Europe and Canada. International report. Volume 2. Key data*. WHO Regional Office for Europe. License: CC BY-NC-SA 3.0 IGO.

Inguglia, C., Ingoglia, S., Liga, F., Lo Coco, A., & Lo Cricchio, M. C. (2015). Autonomy and relatedness in adolescence and emerging adulthood: Relationships with parental support and psychological distress. *Journal of Adult Development, 22*, 1–13. https://doi.org/10.1007/s10804-014-9196-8

Jang, H., Kim, E. J., & Reeve, J. (2012). Longitudinal test of self-determination theory's motivation mediation model in a naturally occurring classroom context. *Journal of Educational Psychology, 104*(4), 1175–1188.

Kärnä, A., Voeten, M., Little, T. D., Alanen, E., Poskiparta, E., & Salmivalli, C. (2013). Effectiveness of the KiVa Antibullying program: Grades 1–3 and 7–9. *Journal of Educational Psychology, 105*(2), 535–551. https://doi.org/10.1037/a0030417

Kickbusch, I. (2012). *Learning for well-being: A policy priority for children and youth in Europe. A process for change with the collaboration of Jean Gordon & Linda O'Toole, drafted on behalf of the learning for well-being consortium of foundations in Europe*. Universal Education Foundation.

Kiuru, N., Wang, M. T., Salmela-Aro, K., Kannas, L., Ahonen, T., & Hirvonen, R. (2020). Associations between adolescents' interpersonal relationships, school well-being, and academic achievement during educational transitions. *Journal of Youth and Adolescence, 49*, 1057–1072. https://doi.org/10.1007/s10964-019-01184-y

Kutsar, D., & Kasearu, K. (2017). Do children like school—Crowding in or out? An international comparison of children's perspectives. *Children and Youth Services Review, 80*, 140–148. https://doi.org/10.1016/j.childyouth.2017.06.052

Kutsyuruba, B., Klinger, D. A., & Hussain, A. (2015). Relationships among school climate, school safety, and student achievement and well-being: A review of the literature. *Review of Education, 3*(2), 103–135. https://doi.org/10.1002/rev3.3043

Layard, R., & Hagell, A. (2015). Healthy young minds: Transforming the mental health of children. In J. F. Helliwell, R. Layard, & J. Sachs (Eds.), *World happiness report 2015*. Sustainable Development Solutions Network.

Leijen, Ä., Pedaste, M., & Baucal, A. (2021). Assessing student teachers' agency and using it for predicting commitment to teaching. *European Journal of Teacher Education, 45*(5), 600–616. https://doi.org/10.1080/02619768.2021.1889507

Lester, L., Waters, S., & Cross, D. (2013). The relationship between school connectedness and mental health during the transition to secondary school: A path analysis. *Australian Journal of Guidance and Counselling, 23*(2), 1–15. https://doi.org/10.1017/jgc.2013.20

Lutsoja, K., Matina, J., & Rebane, M. (2022). Üldhariduskoolide 2021. aasta rahuloluküsitluse tulemused. Aruanne. Accessed May 20, 2023, from https://harno.ee/sites/default/files/documents/2022-01/%C3%9Cldhariduskoolide%20rahulolu-%20ja%20koolikeskkonna%20k%C3%BCsitluste%20riiklik%20aruanne%202021.pdf

Mandel, L.-M. (2016). *Laste heaolu koolis ja heaolu loov kool: laste perspektiiv*. Tartu Ülikool, ühiskonnateaduste instituut.

Ministry of Education and Research. (2021). *Education strategy 2021–2035*. Republic of Estonia, Ministry of Education and Research. Accessed May 12, 2023, from https://www.hm.ee/ministeerium-uudised-ja-kontakt/ministeerium/strateegilised-alusdokumendid-ja-programmid

Moore, G., Angel, L., Brown, R., van Godwin, J., Hallingberg, B., & Rice, F. (2021). Socioeconomic status, mental health difficulties and feelings about transition to secondary school among 10–11-year-olds in Wales: Multi-level analysis of a cross-sectional survey. *Child Indicators Research, 14*, 1597–1615. https://doi.org/10.1007/s12187-021-09815-2

Murray-Harvey, R. (2010). Relationship influences on students' academic achievement, psychological health and well-being at school. *Educational & Child Psychology, 27*(1), 104–115.

Neild, R. C., Stoner-Eby, S., & Furstenberg, F. (2008). Connecting entrance and departure: The transition to ninth grade and high school dropout. *Education and Urban Society, 40*(5), 543–569. https://doi.org/10.1177/0013124508316438

Norrish, J. M., Williams, P., O'Connor, M., & Robinson, J. (2013). An applied framework for positive education. *International Journal of Wellbeing, 3*(2), 147–161. https://doi.org/10.5502/ijw.v3i2.2

OECD. (2018). *The future of education and skills 2030*. Education 2030. The future we want. Accessed April 20, 2022, from http://www.oecd.org/education/2030/E2030%20Position%20Paper%20(05.04.2018).pdf

OECD. (2023). *PISA 2022 results (volume I): The state of learning and equity in education*. PISA. OECD Publishing, Paris. Accessed January 10, 2024, from https://doi.org/10.1787/53f23881-en

Östberg, V., Almquist, Y. B., Folkesson, L., Låftman, S. B., Modin, B., & Lindfors, P. (2015). The complexity of stress in mid-adolescent girls and boys. *Child Indicators Research, 8*, 403–423. https://doi.org/10.1007/s12187-014-9245-7

Qvortrup, J. (2011). Childhood as a structural form. In J. Qvortrup, W. Corsaro, & M. Honig (Eds.), *The Palgrave handbook of childhood studies* (pp. 21–33). Palgrave Macmillan.

Reeve, J., & Tseng, C.-M. (2011). Agency as a fourth aspect of students' engagement during learning activities. *Contemporary Educational Psychology, 36*, 257–267. https://doi.org/10.1016/j.cedpsych.2011.05.002

Ryan, R. M., & Deci, E. L. (2000). Self-determination theory and the facilitation of intrinsic motivation, social development, and well-being. *American Psychologist, 55*(1), 68–78.

Salmela-Aro, K., & Upadyaya, K. (2014). School burnout and engagement in the context of demands-resources model. *British Journal of Educational Psychology, 84*, 137–151. https://doi.org/10.1111/bjep12018

Sarkova, M., Bacikova-Sleskova, M., Madarasova Geckova, A., Katreniakova, Z., van den Heuvel, W., & van Dijk, J. P. (2014). Adolescents' psychological well-being and self-esteem in the context of relationships at school. *Educational Research, 56*(4), 367–378. https://doi.org/10.1080/00131881.2014.965556

Scrimin, S., Mason, L., & Moscardino, U. (2014). School-related stress and cognitive performance: A mood-induction study. *Contemporary Educational Psychology, 39*, 359–368. https://doi.org/10.1016/j.cedpsych.2014.09.002

Sirkko, R., Kyrönlampi, T., & Puroila, A.-M. (2019). Children's agency: Opportunities and constraints. *International Journal of Early Childhood, 51*, 283–300. https://doi.org/10.1007/s13158-019-00252-5

Soo, K. (2023). *School as a source of child subjective well-being in the framework of children's rights: Perspectives of children and young adults*. (Doctoral thesis, University of Tartu). University of Tartu Press.

Spernes, K. (2022). The transition between primary and secondary school: A thematic review emphasising social and emotional issues. *Research Papers in Education, 37*(3), 303–320. https://doi.org/10.1080/02671522.2020.1849366

Statistics Estonia. (2023). *HT18: Students in stationary general education by grade, language of instruction and county*. Accessed August 2, 2023, from https://andmed.stat.ee/et/stat/sotsiaalelu__haridus__uldharidus/HT18

Taimalu, M., Uibu, K., Luik, P., Leijen, Ä., & Pedaste, M. (2020). *Õpetajad ja koolijuhid väärtustatud professionaalidena. OECD rahvusvahelise õpetamise ja õppimise uuringu TALIS 2018 tulemused. 2. osa*. Tartu Ülikool, SA Innove. Accessed November 25, 2022, from https://dspace.ut.ee/bitstream/handle/10062/70216/TALIS_raporti_II_osa.pdf?sequence=1&isAllowed=y

Thapa, A., Cohen, J., Guffey, S., & Higgins-D'Alessandro, A. (2013). A review of school climate research. *Review of Educational Research, 83*, 357–385. https://doi.org/10.3102/0034654313483907

The Children's Society. (2022). *The good childhood report 2022*. Accessed August 23, 2023, from https://www.childrenssociety.org.uk/sites/default/files/2022-09/GCR-2022-Full-Report.pdf

Thompson, R. A. (2014). Why are relationships important to children's well-being? In A. Ben-Arieh, F. Casas, I. Frønes, & J. Korbin (Eds.), *Handbook of child well-being* (pp. 1917–1954). Springer.

Thornberg, R., Wänström, L., Hong, J. S., & Espelage, D. L. (2017). Classroom relationship qualities and social-cognitive correlates of defending and passive bystanding in school bullying in Sweden: A multilevel analysis. *Journal of School Psychology, 63*, 49–62. https://doi.org/10.1016/j.jsp.2017.03.002

Tian, L., Chen, H., & Huebner, E. S. (2014). The longitudinal relationships between basic psychological needs satisfaction at school and school-related subjective well-being in adolescents. *Social Indicators Research, 119*(1), 353–372. https://doi.org/10.1007/s11205-013-0495-4
Tong, L., Reynolds, K., Lee, E., & Liu, Y. (2019). School relational climate, social identity, and student well-being: New evidence from China on student depression and stress levels. *School Mental Health, 11*, 509–521. https://doi.org/10.1007/s12310-018-9293-0
Troop-Gordon, W., & Kuntz, K. J. (2013). The unique and interactive contributions of peer victimization and teacher-child relationships to Children's School Adjustment. *Journal of Abnormal Child Psychology, 41*, 1191–1202. https://doi.org/10.1007/s10802-013-9776-2
Trotman, D., Tucker, S., & Martyn, M. (2015). Understanding problematic pupil behaviour: Perceptions of pupils and behaviour coordinators on secondary school exclusion in an English city. *Educational Research, 57*(3), 237–253. https://doi.org/10.1080/00131881.2015.1056643
United Nations. (1989). *United Nations Convention on the Rights of the Child*. United Nations.
Veenstra, R., Lindenberg, S., Huitsing, G., Sainio, M., & Salmivalli, C. (2014). The role of teachers in bullying: The relation between antibullying attitudes, efficacy, and efforts to reduce bullying. *Journal of Educational Psychology, 106*(4), 1135–1143. https://doi.org/10.1037/a0036110
Wang, M.-T., & Degol, J. L. (2016). School climate: A review of the construct, measurement, and impact on student outcomes. *Educational Psychology Review, 28*, 315–352. https://doi.org/10.1007/s10648-015-9319-1
Waters, S., Lester, L., & Cross, D. (2014). How does support from peers compared with support from adults as students transition to secondary school? *Journal of Adolescent Health, 54*(5), 543–549. https://doi.org/10.1016/j.jadohealth.2013.10.012
Wentzel, K. R. (2016). Teacher-student relationships. In K. R. Wentzel & D. B. Miele (Eds.), *Handbook of motivation at school* (2nd ed., pp. 211–230). Routledge.

Kadri Soo is a lecturer of social welfare at the Institute of Social Studies, University of Tartu, Estonia. Her research interests include child well-being, children's rights, child abuse and domestic violence. She has also studied reconciliation of work and family life and family policies in local governments. Kadri has long-term experience in researching children using both quantitative and qualitative survey methods. She is a member of the International Society for Child Indicators and has conducted Children's Worlds surveys (ISCWeB, International Survey on Children's Well-Being) in Estonia.

Chapter 7
Child Autonomy and Vulnerability in Healthcare

Kristi Paron

7.1 Introduction

In healthcare, the child's general right to autonomy deriving from Article 12 of the UN Convention on the Rights of the Child (CRC) is interlinked with a fundamental principle of medical ethics—patient autonomy—which requires any medical intervention to be based on the patient's free and informed choice. Child patients usually exercise their patient autonomy together with their parent(s), or other guardian(s). In other words, the patient is *represented* by two individuals (a dual patient), and autonomy is shared between the child and the parent, as I argue in this chapter. Physicians and other health professionals therefore face a challenging exercise of respecting the autonomy of children and honouring parental rights at the same time. In this process the child must be attributed adequate autonomy—giving the child too much autonomy that is not in accordance with their maturity and competence may render the child vulnerable; the same may happen when the child's autonomy is excessively limited.

Even though the principles of international law and Estonian regulations both require that children should be heard in any matter concerning them, the social reality of the participation of child patients in decision-making may diverge from these requirements. Child patients in Estonia and elsewhere often report that they have not been involved in decision-making or they have felt that their opinion did not matter enough (Coyne & Gallagher, 2011; Kilkelly & Donnelly, 2006; Paron, 2018). According to a survey completed in the Council of Europe member states, 60% of children reported that health professionals should talk to children more and 68% of

K. Paron (✉)
Children's Rights Department, Office of the Chancellor of Justice/Ombudsperson for Children, Tallinn, Estonia
e-mail: kristi.paron@oiguskantsler.ee

D. Kutsar et al. (eds.), *Child Vulnerability and Vulnerable Subjectivity*, Children's Well-Being: Indicators and Research 27,
https://doi.org/10.1007/978-3-031-61333-3_7

children found that health professionals should listen to children more (Kilkelly, 2011). The above views of children mirror the deficiencies in the knowledge, attitudes and behaviours of adults, both health professionals and parents. Several studies demonstrate that health professionals are not trained to involve children in decision-making, and they lack the tools to support them in that process (Boland et al., 2016; Coyne & Gallagher, 2011; Paron, 2018). Studies also demonstrate that parents' attitudes and behaviour may be an essential barrier to child participation in decision-making. Research in Estonia shows that 40% of adults are either not sure whether a child has the right to be informed about decisions regarding their health or the right to participate in making such decisions, or they even believe that a child does not have such rights (Praxis, 2018).

Against this background, a monumental educational task must be accomplished in order to improve children's lives and promote every child's right to have a say in matters concerning their life. Adults understanding what it means to be heard under Article 12 of the CRC is a prerequisite of a child's right to health (Article 24 of the CRC). Being aware of one's rights as a patient is a key component in accessing appropriate healthcare (Council of Europe, 2023).

Children exercising their patient's rights depends significantly on their level of competence. Under the legal framework of the CRC, the child's competence is understood as a complex set of knowledge, experience and understanding. Gathering knowledge, experience and understanding is conceptualised as the maturation process, which enables gradually increasing levels of child autonomy. How to assess a child's maturity and competence and adjust the amount of autonomy afforded to the child is still an extremely complex exercise for practitioners making decisions that affect children's lives. Such an exercise is even more delicate in healthcare since children visit physicians, as a general rule, with their parents, and the autonomy is shared between the child and the parent. The discussion in this chapter draws on data collected within a 2021 qualitative study in Estonia that explored how health professionals understand child-patient autonomy and the involvement of children in decision-making (Paron & Kutsar, 2023; hereinafter: Autonomy Study).

The chapter starts by briefly introducing the concept of autonomy from the perspective of legal theory, medical ethics and psychology (self-determination theory). In the second part, the CRC principles describing the child's right to be heard in healthcare are discussed, followed by a discussion of the theoretical criteria of assessing patient competence and decision-making capacity, reflecting on how Estonian physicians understand what is important in assessing a child's maturity. The third part demonstrates how a certain age is often automatically a mark of maturity (age-maturity paradox). Finally, the last part of the chapter offers an approach to child-patient autonomy that considers both normativity and relationality.

7.2 What Is Human Autonomy?

The idea of human autonomy is a core concept of many research fields. The discussion in this chapter about child autonomy in healthcare touches upon three of them—legal scholarship, medical ethics and psychology.

The legal concept of human autonomy—the right to self-determination or the right to determine one's own destiny and to decide how to live one's life—has its roots in moral philosophy. In the history of moral philosophy, Immanuel Kant is given the honour of the *invention* of (private) autonomy (Schneewind, 1998). According to Kant, human beings are self-governing because they are autonomous—we ourselves legislate the moral law which guides our actions; it is the power of choice that enables us to decide between the call of desire and that of morality (Schneewind, 1998). The other prominent foundation of human autonomy is John Stuart Mill's utilitarian liberalism, the central idea of which is liberty of will and the wrongfulness of interfering in that, except to prevent harm to others (Donnelly, 2010; Christman, 2003). It is outside the scope of this chapter to give a proper account of the historic evolution of the concept of autonomy. There have been many other philosophers who have elaborated the idea and developed it to where it stands today. Christman (2003) summarises in the Stanford Encyclopedia of Philosophy that the concept of autonomy is the product of Enlightenment humanism and contemporary liberal political philosophy, in short: "to be autonomous is to be one's own person, to be directed by considerations, desires, conditions, and characteristics that are not simply imposed externally upon one, but are part of what can somehow be considered one's authentic self." The manifestation of the free will that is guided by reason and conscience lies within Article 1 of the Universal Declaration of Human Rights (1948) that stipulates: "All human beings are born free and equal in dignity and rights. They are endowed with reason and conscience and should act towards one another in a spirit of brotherhood." This, evidently, is an ideal; contemporary scholarship on autonomy acknowledges the fact that autonomy depends on context, social norms, interpersonal relations and nobody is ever fully autonomous (Daly et al., 2019; Donnelly, 2010; Donnelly et al., 2022; Christman, 2003; Baylis et al., 2008).

Autonomy is also a core principle of medical ethics. Beauchamp and Childress (2001), who are regarded as the creators of principlism, one of the most influential approaches to bioethics (Herring, 2018, p. 24), determine respect for autonomy as one of four principles of biomedical ethics (the other three being non-maleficence, beneficence and justice). Beauchamp and Childress (2001, p. 58) argue that:

> Personal autonomy is, at minimum, self-rule that is free from both controlling interference by others and from limitations, such as inadequate understanding, that prevent meaningful choice. The autonomous individual acts freely in accordance with a self-chosen plan, analogous to the way an independent government manages its territories and sets its politics.

Hence, in other words, being autonomous means not being under any external control, manipulation or coercion, and not lacking understanding or authenticity (Beauchamp & Childress, 2001; Varelius, 2006; Walker, 2008). In addition to free will and self-rule, the component of responsibility is an important but often neglected aspect of human autonomy. I agree with Morreim's (1993) view that the central moral value of autonomy lies in its connection with responsibility. It is hard to regard someone as autonomous in decision-making if they held others accountable for the consequences of their decisions (be they good or bad) and blame others for not avoiding their bad decisions. Consequently, being autonomous means taking responsibility for one's decisions and actions. It is also important that even though the principle of autonomy in medical ethics requires that the person's choice be honoured whatever the choice is, there is an important qualification—only choices made by competent patients have to be respected (Goold & Herring, 2018). The assessment of competence and capacity is therefore a fundamental issue in healthcare that is relevant both for adult[1] and child patients (see also Sect. 7.4).

Why is human autonomy important? Is there any direct psychological benefit that people gain from being autonomous and having their autonomy respected? Self-determination theory (SDT) in studying human motivation (Deci & Ryan, 1985; Ryan & Deci, 2000, 2006) asserts that autonomy is an innate psychological need of a human being (along with the need for competence and relatedness). According to Ryan et al. (1997, p. 702) "in human personality, the construct of autonomy concerns the processes through which action and experience are initiated and governed by 'the self'". Fulfilment of that innate psychological need for autonomy directly impacts the health and well-being of human beings (Ryan et al., 1997; Ryan & Deci, 2000). According to Ryan and Deci (2000), even highly efficacious people may experience less than optimal well-being if they follow goals that do not fulfil basic psychological needs, like autonomy, competence and relatedness. As the feeling of relatedness is directly linked to well-being, it is important to emphasise in the context of children's autonomy that SDT-research has continually found that people feel most related to those who support their autonomy (Ryan & Deci, 2006). Being autonomous also affects the quality of action the person undertakes. As Ryan et al. (1997) demonstrate, when a certain behaviour or action is not self-initiated but stems from external control then there is a diminished likelihood that a person will use all their internal resources to complete such an action. This is a relevant aspect also in the context of patient behaviour as, for example, in order to adhere to a treatment plan, a patient should be internally motivated to follow the plan.

To summarise, respect and support for the autonomy of a person, be they an adult or child, enhances that person's motivation, sense of relatedness and general well-being. In the context of child healthcare, supporting children's autonomy, by involving them in decision-making about their health, increases their self-esteem, reduces their fear and makes them more satisfied with the treatment (Adewumi et al., 2001; Kelly et al., 2017).

[1]A thorough account on adult patient autonomy in healthcare, that is relevant in many ways with regard to children, is given by Donnelly (2010) in "Healthcare Decision-Making and the Law. Autonomy, Capacity and the Limits of Liberalism", and Donnelly, Harding and Tascioglu (Eds) (2022) in "Supporting Legal Capacity in the Socio-Legal Context."

7.3 Child Autonomy Under the CRC

The CRC does not address children's autonomy explicitly. Nevertheless, the principle of human autonomy is tacitly included in the preamble to the CRC which manifests that everyone, without distinction of any kind, is entitled to all the rights as agreed in the Universal Declaration of Human Rights and in the International Covenants on Human Rights. Therefore, children are regarded under the framework of the CRC as equal subjects of human rights who, however, are in need of "special care and assistance" (wording of the preamble) for which purpose the CRC provides specific provisions creating "special human rights" for children.[2]

Within the CRC framework, children exercise their autonomy by participating in the process of decision-making (CRC Committee, General Comment No 12, para 3). According to Article 12 of the CRC, "States parties shall assure to the child who is capable of forming his or her own views the right to express those views freely in all matters affecting the child, the views of the child being given due weight in accordance with the age and maturity of the child." For this purpose, the CRC requires that the child must be heard in any proceedings affecting the child. The above means that it is always an adult who decides how much weight is given to the child's opinion or in other words how autonomous the child is allowed to be in decisions about their life. It is therefore disputable whether the CRC considers children as full subjects of their rights. This is why Daly (2018) asks rhetorically whether the CRC really stipulates children's autonomy and concludes that it is an "obscured autonomy idea" that the CRC encompasses.

In healthcare, the child's autonomy is closely related to the principle of informed consent (patient autonomy). A child's right to health, that is stipulated in Article 24 of the CRC, does not, however, encompass the right to give free and informed consent to their medical treatment. Even though some authors have argued that informed consent is a derivative of the principle of bodily integrity, which is included in the right to health (Tobin, 2019), it is up to the domestic laws of countries to regulate the exact conditions of the informed consent of the child. In addition, the Oviedo Convention[3] leaves it open to the signatory states to determine the relevant threshold of the capacity of minors for informed consent. According to Article 6 of the Oviedo Convention:

> Where, according to law, a minor does not have the capacity to consent to an intervention, the intervention may only be carried out with the authorisation of his or her representative or an authority or a person or body provided by law. The opinion of the minor shall be taken

[2] In children's rights' scholarship it is discussed whether creating children's special rights could actually lead to discrimination of children in comparison to adults and their human rights (e.g., Hanson, K. (2012). Schools of Thought in Children's Rights. M. Liebel, K. Hanson, I. Saadi & W. Vandenhole (Eds.), *Children's rights from below: Cross-cultural perspectives*, pp. 63–79.

[3] Council of Europe's 1997 Convention for the Protection of Human Rights and Dignity of the Human Being with Regard to the Application of Biology and Medicine: Convention on Human Rights and Biomedicine.

into consideration as an increasingly determining factor in proportion to his or her age and degree of maturity.

The CRC Committee has given its recommendation to Member States with regard to children's autonomy in healthcare in its General Comment No. 20 (2016) about adolescents' rights, where the committee for the first time explicitly touches upon the topic of adolescent's informed consent. In this general comment the committee states that the informed consent of the adolescent should be obtained whether or not the consent of a parent or guardian is required (by domestic law) for any medical treatment. The committee (2016) calls on states to "review or introduce legislation recognising the right of adolescents to take increasing responsibility for decisions affecting their lives" and recommends that states introduce minimum legal age limits that "recognise the right to make decisions in respect of health services or treatment".

To conclude, Articles 12 and 24 of the CRC do provide children a certain degree of autonomy, requesting that children's views must be taken into account in their health matters. However, it depends on the internal laws of Member States how autonomous children really are in their decision-making. In countries where the regulation does not stipulate an age limit (e.g., in Estonia) but leaves it to be decided on a case-by-case basis whether the child is mature enough to decide by themselves about health issues, it is the responsibility of specialists, like health professionals to evaluate the child's maturity. In reality, the same challenge may arise in any situation where decisions are taken about the child's health, as in accordance with Article 12 of the CRC, due weight must be given to the child's own view. This means that the assessment or evaluation of children's maturity (CRC framework) and capacity (medical ethics framework) is of vital importance in guaranteeing children their autonomy rights. This has been acknowledged by the CRC Committee, who has expressed the need to develop good practice for assessing the capacity of the child (CRC Committee, General Comment No 12, 2009).

7.4 Giving Due Weight to the Child's Opinion and Assessing the Child's Decision-Making Capacity in Healthcare: Examples from the Autonomy Study in Estonia

The only key that Article 12 of the CRC offers to understand how due weight should be given to the child's view, is that the weight should be in accordance with the child's age and maturity. Whereas age is a matter of fact, maturity, a personal characteristic that often has legal significance, has no exact legal content and is therefore open to interpretation. The CRC Committee has given an interpretation in its General Comment No 12 (2009) stating that "maturity refers to the ability to understand and assess the implications of a particular matter" and that "it is the capacity of the child to express her or his views on issues in a reasonable and independent manner." Therefore, according to the CRC Committee, maturity includes three components: (1) ability to understand implications; (2) ability to assess those implications, and (3) ability to express one's position in a reasonable and independent manner.

The above conceptualisation is largely in accordance with the common framework for the assessment of a patient's decision-making capacity (the term competence is also used) in medical ethics. The model by Grisso and Appelbaum (1998) that has become one of the most influential frameworks for patient capacity assessment (Hass, 2022) envisages that in order to be competent to give a consent, the patient should be able to (1) communicate a choice, (2) understand relevant information, (3) appreciate the medical consequences of the situation, and (4) reason about treatment choices. The same concept for the assessment of patient competence is used by researchers in child healthcare (Ruhe et al., 2015; Grootens-Wiegers et al., 2017). However, it has also been demonstrated by research that in addition to the above criteria, interpersonal relations between children, parents and health professionals play a crucial role in the involvement of children in decision-making and that those relations affect children's competence (Darabos et al., 2021; Mårtenson & Fägerskiöld, 2008; Pyke-Grimm et al., 2019). The findings of the Autonomy Study (Paron & Kutsar, 2023) confirm that health professionals themselves understand that their manner of communication with child patients is one of the most influential factors with regard to the child's involvement; 39 physicians out of 52 fully agreed with the statement that a child's involvement in decision-making depends on the way the physician communicates with the child.

The Autonomy Study (Paron & Kutsar, 2023) aimed to explore, among other things, how clinicians make judgements about children's maturity and decision-making capacity, as there are no guidelines for such assessments. For physicians, criteria connected with the child's abilities and age are the most important when judging their maturity. With one to two exceptions, all of the physicians participating in the study fully agreed or rather agreed that they judge the child's maturity by:

1. the child's ability to understand information they are given (38 physicians out of 52 fully agreed and 12 rather agreed);
2. the child's ability to form a view based on that information (32 physicians out of 52 fully agreed and 17 rather agreed);
3. the child's age (30 physicians out of 52 fully agreed and 21 rather agreed), and
4. the child's intellectual abilities (29 physicians out of 52 fully agreed and 19 rather agreed).

It is worth noting that only 8 out of 52 physicians fully agreed (22 rather agreed) with the statement that they would consider the parents' judgement on their child's maturity when making an assessment. Such a modest readiness to trust the parent's judgement is surprising since, generally, parents know their child the best and the parents' knowledge of their child would be a valuable source of information for physicians. This may reflect physicians' understanding that parents would not be able to make an impartial judgement on their child's maturity or would not have enough expertise for a relevant evaluation. Such a suggestion may be supported by the finding of the Autonomy Study that a child's own opinion about their maturity is more relevant to physicians than the parent's evaluation.

A certain level of mistrust towards parents by the physicians is also suggested by other findings of the Autonomy Study. The majority of the physicians that participated in the study found, when asked about obstacles to assessing the child's maturity, that such assessment is hindered by the parent's excessive intervention in the decision-making process (43 physicians out of 52 agreed or rather agreed with this statement). The physicians also agreed that the assessment of the child's maturity is hindered by a lack of time (34 physicians agreed or rather agreed), a lack of relevant knowledge and training (31 physicians agreed or rather agreed) and the routines and documents of the health institution (23 physicians agreed or rather agreed). The physicians also felt that assessing maturity is affected by the degree of risk involved, they are reluctant to make a clinical decision on a complicated health issue based only on the child's explanations. The physicians participating in the Autonomy Study emphasised the role and example of parents in developing the child's ability to take responsibility for their own health and well-being. This conforms with recommendations from other studies; for example, Ruhe et al. (2016) concluded in their study on child-patient participation in paediatric oncology, that paediatricians have a central role in guiding parents as to how their child could be involved in decision-making. With regard to possible conflicts of child-parent autonomy, in the case of their dissenting opinions, it is remarkable that according to the Autonomy Study, the physicians are rarely ready to intervene in parental authority. This is problematic, both morally and legally, as the child and the parent are not equal in their power (Kuczynski, 2003). In the healthcare context, a physician has to respect the child's autonomy (Article 12, CRC) and may be the only person able to influence the parents and encourage them to consider the child's position. By distancing themselves from the child-parent autonomy conflict, physicians may increase the child's vulnerability. This may also mean that the child will not receive adequate treatment.

Another important finding revealed by the Autonomy Study is that there is a need for additional training and awareness raising among physicians about the framework of child-patient consent and child maturity assessment. The majority of physicians participating in the study said that they know about the regulations of the CRC and domestic law regarding the child's right to participate in decision-making but not enough, whereas some physicians said that they are not aware of such regulations.

To summarise, whether a child is assessed to be mature enough to decide on health issues depends on several factors, such as age and the cognitive capacities of the child, and child-parent relationship. Moreover, the evaluation of a child's maturity is essentially dependent on the training, values and attitudes of the adults, such as physicians, whose professional duties may encompass giving such an assessment. Therefore, awareness raising among professionals working with children about child development and child maturity assessment should be a key issue in guaranteeing respect to children's right to autonomy (see also Committee on the Rights of the Child, 2009). I agree with Daly (2020) that, in any event, the goal in the process realising the autonomy of the child (Article 12 of the CRC) should be to maximise the child's capacity, not the reverse.

7.5 Age-Maturity Paradox

Under Article 12 of the CRC, the child's age is one criterion among others according to which due weight must be given to the child's view. Nevertheless, it is important to emphasise that age alone cannot determine the significance of the child's view, as children's maturation process is not uniformly linked to their biological age (CRC Committee, General Comment No 12, para. 29).

There is an understandable ambition in the field of medicine to find clear evidence about the age from which children could be regarded competent to make independent decisions about their health (see Hein et al., 2015; Grootens-Wiegers et al., 2017). Such age limits would relieve physicians from the burdensome assessment of children's competence. However, regardless of scientific evidence about children's capacities at a certain age, or the development of standardised tools for assessing competence, it remains the responsibility of the physician to make a judgement on a particular child's decision-making capacity in a particular situation (Ruhe et al., 2015).

The results of the Autonomy Study revealed the tendency among physicians to relate competence to a certain age. In the questionnaire, the physicians were given two hypothetical scenarios where a child comes alone to the appointment and asks the physician not to involve their parents. The first scenario was about a child who needs a low-risk medical intervention (surgery) and the second scenario was about a child who needs a prescription for pills. The physicians had to choose how they would act from four possible alternatives, where three of those alternatives were about accepting the child's autonomous consent and the last alternative involved asking the child to come back with the parent, and so not acting upon the child-patient's consent. In the question following the hypothetical case, physicians were asked whether they had a certain age limit in mind when selecting alternatives based on the child's autonomy. In a low-risk medical intervention scenario, the majority of the physicians said that there is no specific age limit for them to accept the child-patient's autonomous consent. Fourteen physicians gave a specific age limit for accepting the child-patient's autonomous consent in this hypothetical scenario of a low-risk medical intervention—18 years (2 physicians), 16 years (7 physicians), 15 years (1 physician) and 14 years (4 physicians). In the prescription pills scenario, the majority of the physicians said that there is no specific age limit for them to accept the child-patient's autonomous consent. Eleven physicians gave a specific age limit for accepting the child-patient's autonomous consent in this hypothetical scenario—16 years (5 physicians), 15 years (2 physicians), 14 years (3 physicians) and 12 years (1 physician). These findings allow us to suggest that the age limit of 16-years is most often regarded as the threshold of full capacity for those specialists who link children's competence more strongly to a child's age.

The Autonomy Study also aimed to explore whether physicians associate a certain age with a particular competence in children. In the questionnaire, the physicians were asked from which age (on average) children are competent to decide independently on (1) vaccination, (2) low-risk medical intervention, and (3) high-risk medical intervention. The physicians' responses differed considerably but two age limits stood out most prominently—16 and 18. Twenty physicians out of 46 found that 16-years-olds are able to decide on vaccinations; 22 physicians out of 46 found that 16-years-olds are able to decide on low-risk medical interventions. Remarkably, the majority of the physicians (30 out of 46) found that children are not able to decide independently on high-risk medical interventions, as they associated such a competence with 18-years-olds. It would be of interest in further sociological studies to identify the attitudes and understandings behind these associations between competence and age limits in children.

To summarise, the findings of the Autonomy Study demonstrate that physicians may assess children's competence primarily based on age. This is in accordance with the research findings of Kilkelly and Donnelly (2006). If physicians' perceptions about the relation between age and competence are too rigid, it may leave children under certain ages without the opportunity to indicate their maturity. This resonates with Archard's position that when "presumed unable to do something, children may simply not be allowed to show that they can" (Archard, 2015, p. 91). As Archard plausibly argues, it may be that competence in something can only be acquired by doing that something. Making decisions in important matters in their lives, weighing all the pros and cons, is something that children should be allowed to practice. Therefore, it is important to give a child ample opportunity to participate in decision-making, regardless of their age.

7.6 A New Way of Conceptualising Child-Patient Autonomy Through Relationality and Child-Centredness

The uniqueness of patient autonomy in child healthcare is that it operates, as a general rule, in a triadic relationship which involves a dual patient, as the patient is represented in most cases by two (or three) individuals—the child and the parent(s). This makes patient autonomy a complex relational process (Paron & Kutsar, 2023). Focusing on the relational nature of rights and autonomy is a relatively recent development in children's rights' scholarship (Daly, 2020; Reynaert & Roose, 2017; Tobin, 2017; Varadan, 2020). Nevertheless, this is in line with the understandings of longstanding research conducted within the framework of self-determination theory, which emphasises the behavioural and experiential nature of human autonomy (Ryan et al., 1997). The relational approach to autonomy acknowledges that autonomy is produced in relationships and that the child and adult parties to a relationship are *coproducers* of child autonomy (Paron & Kutsar, 2023). Healthcare is a vivid example of such coproduction; in healthcare three parties—the child, his/her parent and the physician meet to solve a child's health issue. As the Autonomy Study demonstrated, they communicate, express views, and make decisions, where in this process they have effect on each other's behaviour. In this process the child's autonomy is tacitly negotiated. What is important here, however, is that the child and adult parties are unequal in terms of their resources of power in the process of negotiating their autonomy (Kuczynski et al., 2014). Adults, the parent(s) and the physician, should be aware and cautious about this power imbalance; they must support and guide the child through the decision-making process, holding the power to co-create the child's autonomy. Conversely, unresolved or unbalanced power relations between the physician and the parent(s) may deepen the child's dependent status and vulnerability.

In supporting children's autonomy, adults must consider the child's evolving capacities as envisaged in Article 5 of the CRC. Article 5 stipulates the right and the duty of a parent to provide appropriate direction and guidance to the child, in a manner consistent with the evolving capacities of the child. The CRC Committee has explained the concept of evolving capacities as "an enabling principle that addresses the process of maturation and learning through which children progressively acquire competencies, understanding and increasing levels of agency to take responsibility and exercise their rights" (CRC Committee, General Comment No 20, para. 18). The more the child "knows, has experienced and understands", the more the parents have to withdraw their parental authority and guidance (CRC Committee, General Comment No 12, para. 84). Therefore, within the CRC framework, the child's maturation process is understood as the gathering of knowledge, experience and understanding. In this maturation process the child moves towards full autonomy—in legal terms Articles 5 and 12 of the CRC operate in symbiosis. The more mature the child, the more weight must be given to the child's opinion. This means that at some point in their development, children acquire maturity equal to that of adults and then the child's view must be determinative when making a decision about their life (Tobin, 2019).

In real life situations, however, such as, for example, in the child healthcare context, the process of the realisation of autonomy may not function like a smooth gradual shift as in the interpretation above. When a child-patient visits a physician with their parent to solve the child's health issue, decisions must often be made about what has to be done. In this decision-making process the patient is represented by two individuals—the child and the parent—they both have the right to participate in the decision-making—the child as the subject of health rights within the framework of the child's autonomy and the parent within his/her parental authority. This leads us to the acknowledgement of their shared autonomy in the exercise of patient rights—the idea of the CRC is neither to repel parents from children's lives, nor to deny children the right to decide according to their age and maturity. However, it is mostly out of the control of the specialists working with the families how the child and the parent resolve the inner autonomy balancing exercise (Article 5 of the CRC) within their relationship. The basis for intervening in parental authority is normally only when the parent clearly undermines the child's best interests

(Article 3 of the CRC).[4] Nevertheless, in everyday healthcare, the threshold for medical intervention is usually not that clear that it would justify the physician reporting the parent to child protection services if they suspect the overuse of parental power either in refusing their child's treatment or pushing for it. This means that physicians and other health professionals can only capitalise their professional authority and communication skills to guide and encourage parents to support the health autonomy of their children. Research evidence demonstrates that the way physicians talk with their patients can influence treatment resistance and promote patient acceptance (Bergen & McCabe, 2021; McCabe, 2021; Stivers & Timmermans, 2020). This would allow us to suggest that physicians may also influence the parental resistance to involving their child in decision-making. This, in turn, means that health professionals must be educated about children's autonomy rights and about the importance of involving children in decision-making. Similarly, parents and children should be educated about children's autonomy rights in order to be able to enforce those rights. At the same time, some research demonstrates that gaps in the knowledge of health professionals and parents is the main barrier to shared decision-making in paediatric hospitals (Boland et al., 2016). What is also important in framing child-patient autonomy as a shared process is that the children themselves see their autonomy as relational (Abebe, 2019; Mayall, 2000) and they often prefer shared decision-making with their family instead of deciding independently (Darabos et al., 2021; Paron, 2018; Pyke-Grimm et al., 2019).

To summarise, child-patient autonomy usually evolves in a triadic relationship involving the child, the parent(s) and the physician. All three parties "are involved in communication and negotiations, and their interaction produces the child's autonomy in constant circulation" (Paron & Kutsar, 2023, p. 12). The dual patient renders the patient autonomy a shared phenomenon which accords with the child autonomy framework under the CRC, whereby the degree of involvement in decision-making is constantly changing between the child and the parent. Against this background, patient autonomy is not clearly attributed to either the child or the parent (Paron, 2023).

7.7 Conclusion

Child-patient autonomy is not just a child's right to participate in decision-making about their health and the right to have their opinion considered according to their age and maturity. It is rather a relational process of reciprocal interaction and communication between the child, the parent(s) and the health professional(s). Within this process patient autonomy is not clearly attributed either to the child or to the parent but is shared between them. This means that child-patient autonomy is

[4] The analysis of the interlinkage between Article 3 and Article 12 together with Article 5 would fall outside the scope of this chapter.

constantly changing within the larger maturation process of the child, where the child moves from dependence towards independence until they acquire full autonomy.[5]

Even though the CRC (Article 12) is considered to guarantee children respect for their autonomy by giving them the right to be heard in any matter concerning them, it is a right with a qualification—it is always an adult who decides how much weight is given to the child's opinion or in other words how autonomous the child is allowed to be in decisions about their life. This means that the assessment of children's maturity (CRC framework) and capacity (medical ethics framework) is of vital importance in guaranteeing children their autonomy rights. Furthermore, awareness raising about the assessment of child development and child maturity among professionals working with children should be a future key-agenda in promoting respect for children's right to autonomy. It is not, however, only a matter for specialists. Parents are and should be the primary guarantors of their children's autonomy. Close and supportive relationships with their family and friends is a primary source of child well-being. Therefore, parents must also be included in educational agendas and CRC Member States must continuously raise awareness among parents with regard to child development and sensitise parents to children's need for autonomy. Specialists working with children have, in turn, a challenging exercise in promoting children's autonomy, and intervening in parental power if necessary; and at the same time not harming the child-parent relationship. This balancing exercise is not simple—giving the child too much autonomy that is not in step with their maturity and competence may render the child helpless and vulnerable, the same may occur when limiting the child's autonomy excessively. What is important, is the goal in the process of realising child autonomy (Article 12 of the CRC), that should be to maximise the child's capacity, not the reverse. Within the educational agenda of promoting children's autonomy rights, children's own role should not be underestimated. There is enough evidence that children themselves may be human rights activists, initiate necessary societal changes and educate adults (e.g., Greta Thunberg or Malala Yousufzai). However, to be a human rights activist, one must know that such rights exist. Therefore, educating children about their rights is of fundamental importance.

The relationality of child-patient autonomy, as conceptualised in this chapter, does not contradict its normativity. On the contrary, relationality is theorised in this chapter as an enabling and empowering concept, which emphasises the importance of autonomy support and the responsibility of adults to allow and guide children's autonomous decision-making within reciprocal interactions. To become a competent decision-maker, the child must be given ample opportunity to practice decision-making in a secure and supportive environment.

[5]The age from which the child becomes fully autonomous in healthcare decision-making depends on domestic laws of CRC member states. In some countries, this age limit is set below 18 years, in some countries, a patient is given the right to decide independently only after becoming an adult (see for more in European Union Agency for Fundamental Rights, 2018).

Acknowledgement Work on this chapter was supported by a grant from the Estonian Research Council (PRG700).

Competing Interests The author has no conflicts of interest to declare that are relevant to the content of this chapter.

References

Abebe, T. (2019). Reconceptualising children's agency as continuum and interdependence. *Social Sciences, 8*(3), 81.

Adewumi, A., Hector, M. P., & King, J. M. (2001). Children and informed consent: A study of children's perceptions and involvement in consent to dental treatment. *British Dental Journal, 191*(5), 256–259. https://doi.org/10.1038/sj.bdj.4801157

Archard, D. (2015). *Children: Rights and childhood* (3rd ed.). Routledge.

Baylis, F., Kenny, N.P. & Sherwin, S. (2008). A Relational Account of Public Health Ethics. Public Health Ethics, 1(3), 196–209.

Beauchamp, T., & Childress, J. F. (2001). *Principles of biomedical ethics* (5th ed.). Oxford University Press.

Bergen, C., & McCabe, R. (2021). Negative stance towards treatment in psychosocial assessments: The role of personalised recommendations in promoting acceptance. *Social Science & Medicine, 290*, 114082.

Boland, L., McIsaac, D. I., & Lawson, M. L. (2016). Barriers to and facilitators of implementing shared decision making and decision support in a paediatric hospital: A descriptive study. *Paediatrics & Child Health, 21*(3), e17–e21.

Christman, J. (2003). *Autonomy in moral and political philosophy*. Retrieved from https://plato.stanford.edu/ENTRIES/autonomy-moral/

Committee on the Rights of the Child. (2009). General Comment No 12. 2009: The right of the child to be heard. UN Doc. CRC/C/GC/12.

Committee on the Rights of the Child. (2016). General Comment No 20: on the implementation of the rights of the child during adolescence. UN Doc. CRC/C/GC/20.

Council of Europe. (2023). Guide to health literacy - contributing to trust building and equitable access to healthcare. Retrieved from https://www.coe.int/en/web/bioethics/health-literacy

Coyne, I., & Gallagher, P. (2011). Participation in communication and decision-making: Children and young people's experiences in a hospital setting. *Journal of Clinical Nursing, 20*(15–16), 2334–2343.

Daly, A. (2018). *Children, autonomy and the courts: Beyond the Right to be Heard*. Brill.

Daly, A. (2020). Assessing children's capacity: Reconceptualising our understanding through the UN convention on the rights of the child. *The International Journal of Children's Rights, 28*(3), 471–499. https://doi.org/10.1163/15718182-02803011

Daly, A., Heah, R., & Liddiard, K. (2019). Vulnerable subjects and autonomous actors: The right to sexuality education for disabled under-18s. *Global Studies of Childhood, 9*(3), 235–248.

Darabos, K., Berger, A. J., Barakat, L. P., & Schwartz, L. A. (2021). Cancer-related decision-making among adolescents, young adults, caregivers, and oncology Poviders. *Qualitative Health Research, 31*(13), 2355–2363.

Deci, E. L., & Ryan, R. M. (1985). *Intrinsic motivation and self-determination in human behavior*. Plenum Press.

Donnelly, M. (2010). *Healthcare decision-making and the law: Autonomy, capacity and the limits of liberalism* (Vol. 12). Cambridge University Press.

Donnelly, M., Harding, R., & Tascioglu, E. (Eds.). (2022). *Supporting legal capacity in socio-legal context*. Bloomsbury Publishing.

European Union Agency for Fundamental Rights. (2018). Mapping minimum age requirements concerning the rights of the child in the EU. Retrieved from https://fra.europa.eu/en/publication/2017/mapping-minimum-age-requirements-concerning-rights-child-eu

Goold, I., & Herring, J. (2018). *Great debates in medical law and ethics*. Palgrave Macmillan.
Grisso, T., & Appelbaum, P. S. (1998). *Assessing competence to consent to treatment: A guide for physicians and other health professionals*. Oxford University Press.
Grootens-Wiegers, P., Hein, I. M., van den Broek, J. M., et al. (2017). Medical decision-making in children and adolescents: Developmental and neuroscientific aspects. *BMC Pediatrics, 17*(1), 1–10. https://doi.org/10.1186/s12887-017-0869-x
Haavi Morreim, E. (1993). Impairments and impediments in patients' decision making: Reframing the competence question. *The Journal of Clinical Ethics, 4*(4), 294–307.
Hass, B. (2022). The values and rules of capacity assessments. *Journal of Medical Ethics, 48*(11), 816–820.
Hein, I. M., De Vries, M. C., Troost, P. W., Meynen, G., Van Goudoever, J. B., & Lindauer, R. J. (2015). Informed consent instead of assent is appropriate in children from the age of twelve: Policy implications of new findings on children's competence to consent to clinical research. *BMC Medical Ethics, 16*(1), 1–7. https://doi.org/10.1186/s12910-015-0067-z
Herring, J. (2018). *Medical law and ethics* (7th ed.). Oxford University Press.
Kelly, K. P., Mowbray, C., Pyke-Grimm, K., & Hinds, P. S. (2017). Identifying a conceptual shift in child and adolescent-reported treatment decision making: "Having a say, as I need at this time". *Pediatric Blood & Cancer, 64*(4), e26262. https://doi.org/10.1002/pbc.26262
Kilkelly, U. (2011). *Child-friendly health care: The views and experiences of children and young people in Council of Europe member States*. Retrieved from https://www.researchgate.net/publication/363579331_Child-friendly_health_care_the_views_and_experiences_of_children_and_young_people_in_Council_of_Europe_member_States
Kilkelly, U., & Donnelly, M. (2006). *The Child's right to be heard in the healthcare setting: Perspectives of children, parents and health professionals*. Retrieved from https://www.researchgate.net/publication/279638240_The_child's_right_to_be_heard_in_the_healthcare_setting_perspectives_of_children_parents_and_health_professionals_Ursula_Kilkelly_Mary_Donnelly
Kuczynski, L. (2003). Beyond Bidirectionality: Bilateral conceptual frameworks for understanding dynamics in parent-child relations. In L. Kuczynski (Ed.), *Handbook of dynamics in parent-child relations* (pp. 1–24). Sage.
Kuczynski, L., Parkin, M., & Pitman, R. (2014). Socialization as dynamic process: A dialectical, transactional perspective. In J. E. Grusec & P. Hastings (Eds.), *Handbook of socialization* (2nd ed., pp. 135–157). Guilford Press.
Mårtenson, E. K., & Fägerskiöld, A. (2008). A review of children's decision-making competence in health care. *Journal of Clinical Nursing, 17*(23), 3131–3141.
Mayall, B. (2000). The sociology of childhood in relation to children's rights. *The International Journal of Children's Rights, 8*(2000), 243–259.
McCabe, R. (2021). When patients and clinician (dis)agree about the nature of the problem: The role of displays of shared understanding in acceptance of treatment. *Social Science & Medicine, 290*, 114208.
Praxis (2018). Lapse Õiguste ja Vanemluse Uuring. Study on Children's Rights and Parenting. Retrieved from: https://www.praxis.ee/wp-content/uploads/2017/11/Lapsed-vanemad-aruanne.pdf
Paron, K. (2018). *Child's informed consent to medical intervention—Illusion or reality? The Estonian experience.* Master Thesis. University of Geneva.
Paron, K. (2023). Exploring child-patient autonomy: Findings from and ethnographic study of clinic visits by children. *Child Indicators Research*, 1–23.
Paron, K., & Kutsar, D. (2023). Creation of child-patient's autonomy in a child-parent-doctor relationship: Medical doctors' perspectives. *Childhood, 30*(2), 145–160.
Pyke-Grimm, K. A., Franck, L. S., Kelly, K. P., Halpern-Felsher, B., Goldsby, R. E., Kleiman, A., & Rehm, R. S. (2019). Treatment decision-making involvement in adolescents and young adults with cancer. In *Oncology nursing forum* (Vol. 46, No. 1, p. E22). NIH Public Access. https://doi.org/10.1188/19.ONF.E22-E37

Reynaert, D., & Roose, R. (2017). Children's rights: A framework to eliminate social exclusion? Critical discussions and tensions. In *Handbook of children's rights* (pp. 36–52). Routledge.

Ruhe, K. M., Wangmo, T., Badarau, D. O., Elger, B. S., & Niggli, F. (2015). Decision-making capacity of children and adolescents—Suggestions for advancing the concept's implementation in pediatric healthcare. *European Journal of Pediatrics, 174*, 775–782. https://doi.org/10.1007/s00431-014-2462-8

Ruhe, K. M., Wangmo, T., De Clercq, E., Badarau, D. O., Ansari, M., Kühne, T., Niggli, F., Elger, B. S., & on behalf of the Swiss Pediatric Oncology Group (SPOG). (2016). Putting patient participation into practice in pediatrics—Results from a qualitative study in pediatric oncology. *European Journal of Pediatrics, 175*, 1147–1155.

Ryan, R. M., & Deci, E. L. (2000). Self-determination theory and the facilitation of intrinsic motivation, social development, and well-being. *American Psychologist, 55*(1), 68–78.

Ryan, R. M., & Deci, E. L. (2006). Self-regulation and the problem of human autonomy: Does psychology need choice, self-determination, and will? *Journal of Personality, 74*(6), 1557–1586.

Ryan, R. M., Kuhl, J., & Deci, E. L. (1997). Nature and autonomy: An organizational view of social and neurobiological aspects of self-regulation in behavior and development. *Development and Psychopathology, 9*(4), 701–728.

Schneewind, J. B. (1998). *The invention of autonomy. A history of modern philosophy*. Cambridge University Press.

Stivers, T., & Timmermans, S. (2020). Medical authority under siege: How clinicians transform patient resistance into acceptance. *Journal of Health and Social Behavior, 61*(1), 60–78.

Tobin, J. (2017). Fixed concepts but changing conceptions: Understanding the relationship between children and parents under the CRC. In *Handbook of children's rights* (pp. 53–67). Routledge.

Tobin, J. (2019). The right to health. In J. Tobin (Ed.), *The UN convention on the rights of the child: A commentary*. Oxford University Press.

Varadan, S. (2020). Article 5: The role of parents in the proxy informed consent process in medical research involving children. *The International Journal of Children's Rights, 28*(3), 521–546.

Varelius, J. (2006). The value of autonomy in medical ethics. *Medicine, Health Care and Philosophy, 9*, 377–388.

Walker, R. L. (2008). Medical ethics needs a new view of autonomy. *Journal of Medicine and Philosophy, 33*(6), 594–608.

Kristi Paron is a children's rights lawyer. For the last ten years, she has worked as an adviser to the Children's Ombudsperson in Estonia. She holds a PhD in sociology and master's degree in law from the University of Tartu, and MCR (Master of Advanced Studies) in children's rights from the University of Geneva, the Centre for Children's Rights Studies. Her dissertation explored child-patient autonomy, focusing on the interplay between its normativity and relationality. In her research, she bridges children's rights and childhood sociology, focusing on the relationality of rights. In her daily practice, she is devoted to raising awareness on children's rights and sensitising society to children's views and needs.

Chapter 8
Child Vulnerability in the Digital World

Veronika Kalmus, Susana Batista, Signe Opermann, Natalie Tercova, and Marie Jaron Bedrosova

8.1 Introduction

Today's social world is characterised by "far reaching entanglement of media technologies with the everyday practices" (Hepp, 2016, p. 918). In this ongoing process, called *mediatisation*, using various digital technologies, and engaging in online activities have become thoroughly embedded into children's daily lives (e.g., Livingstone, 2013). In line with these socio-technical changes, there is a growing need for research on the interconnections between children's offline and online vulnerabilities, and protective factors.

This chapter focuses on vulnerability during *adolescence*—in the socially shaped and immature phase of life (Andresen, 2014)—in relation to teenagers' digital environment, and activities and experiences therein. *Vulnerability*, in general, means that a person is at risk of harm to their well-being and is unable to sufficiently protect themself or to be sufficiently protected by others (Mackenzie et al., 2014). Vulnerability is not necessarily harmful—it is a likelihood of experiencing one or more types of harm (Schweiger, 2019) that varies between individuals. Being more vulnerable than others can mean different things: besides a greater likeliness of

V. Kalmus (✉) · S. Opermann
Institute of Social Studies, University of Tartu, Tartu, Estonia
e-mail: veronika.kalmus@ut.ee; signe.opermann@ut.ee

S. Batista
Interdisciplinary Centre of Social Sciences (CICS.NOVA), NOVA FCSH, Lisbon, Portugal
e-mail: susanabatista@fcsh.unl.pt

N. Tercova · M. Jaron Bedrosova
Interdisciplinary Research Team on Internet and Society, Masaryk University, Brno, Czech Republic
e-mail: natalieterc@mail.muni.cz; marie.bedrosova@mail.muni.cz

D. Kutsar et al. (eds.), *Child Vulnerability and Vulnerable Subjectivity*, Children's Well-Being: Indicators and Research 27,
https://doi.org/10.1007/978-3-031-61333-3_8

vulnerability toward a particular harm, it can mean being vulnerable to being harmed more severely (describing the depth of vulnerability) or being vulnerable towards more different types of harm (describing the width of vulnerability; Schweiger, 2019). In this chapter we focus mainly on the likelihood and depth of vulnerability to differentiate between more and less vulnerable adolescents offline and online.

Regarding child vulnerability in the offline and online worlds, another distinction is relevant—between inherent and situational vulnerability. The first refers to natural or ontological features of children such as particular age-related developmental needs and the lack of certain cognitive, emotional, or physical strengths and abilities. Situational vulnerabilities are based on social practices and norms, for instance, the vulnerability children face from road traffic (Schweiger, 2019). As children's negative and potentially harmful online experiences are related to the scope and nature of their digital practices as well as social norms (Livingstone, 2013; Livingstone et al., 2022), online vulnerability can be conceptualised as situational. Inherent and situational vulnerabilities, however, are often intertwined (Schweiger, 2019), also in online environments.

Child vulnerability as a concept has several dimensions and many sub-dimensions on the individual and environmental levels. On the environmental level, previous literature on child vulnerability and resilience in medicine, psychology, childhood studies and the sociology of childhood has mostly focused on family, school, peers, local area, and country/society (see Chaps. 2 and 4 in this volume for an overview) while largely neglecting the dimension of the online world. The latter has been a relevant research area in media studies, with a prominent focus on children's online risks, harm, coping and resilience (e.g., Livingstone, 2013). Online vulnerability as a concept, however, tends to be used in a rather loose and common-sense meaning in media studies, and would benefit from a clearer definition and empirical operationalisation.

This chapter proposes an operational definition of online vulnerability and explores its relationships with subjective vulnerability. We proceed from the theoretical models of the EU Kids Online network (Livingstone et al., 2011; Smahel et al., 2020) and the EU Horizon 2020 project ySKILLS (Haddon et al., 2020) and make use of the models' central concepts that characterise child personality and resources (including individual strengths and vulnerabilities, and socio-demographic variables such as age, gender and socio-economic status), children's online lives (including digital practices and skills, and positive and negative online experiences, that is, opportunities and risks, and coping and harm), and child well-being. We suggest complementing these models with the concepts of online vulnerability and online resilience. Based on Livingstone (2013, p. 22), we understand *online vulnerability* as the conceptual opposite of *online resilience*, defined as positive patterns of adaptation and coping in the context of online risks (cf. Vandoninck et al., 2012). Online vulnerability, thus, is a probability of poor adaptation to online risks and the experiencing of harm (as a consequence of deficient coping). As vulnerability, by definition, refers to a likelihood of harm, not to harm itself, it is difficult to measure the concept empirically. We suggest using deficient coping with online risks, and experiences of harm as actual *manifestations of online vulnerability* in empirical operationalisations. *Harm* may be experienced as a feeling of being upset, threatened, or distressed to a different degree or severity, which may have short-, medium- or long-term consequences for the individual's *well-being* in its psychological, cognitive, social, and physical dimensions, as envisioned in the ySKILLS model (Haddon et al., 2020). Our conceptualisation of online vulnerability is also in accordance with the framework of child vulnerability as a risk of harm to a child's well-being in relation to his/her resilience (as defined in Chap. 2), thus building a bridge between media studies, child indicators research and childhood studies.

We assume that harm experienced in the digital world most likely influences children's *subjective well-being*, which covers affective, cognitive and eudaimonic aspects of well-being (Soffia & Turner, 2021). Previous research (e.g., Laurinavičius et al., 2012; Vandoninck et al., 2012), furthermore, has shown that children with more emotional, psychological, social, and behavioural problems are more likely to encounter online risks and to report being harmed by them. Most probably there are bidirectional relationships between harmful risky experiences online (that we conceptualise as manifestations of online vulnerability) and subjective well-being (or *subjective vulnerability* as its reconstructed opposite; cf. Andresen, 2014, p. 707). Based on this presumption, the chapter aims to explore the relationships between adolescents' subjective vulnerability and manifestations of online vulnerability.

Previous theoretical models on children's online lives and well-being involve two further components relevant for our conceptualisation and study—the intensity of *internet use* and *digital skills*. The latter are defined in the ySKILLS project as the set of competencies that allow individuals to use information and communication technologies in ways that help them "to achieve beneficial, high-quality outcomes in everyday life for themselves and for others, and to reduce potential harm associated with more negative aspects of digital engagement" (Helsper et al., 2021, p. 9). Digital skills, furthermore, are seen as a presumably crucial mediator between internet use on the one hand, and the online risks and opportunities that influence well-being outcomes on the other (Livingstone et al., 2022).

Previous literature (e.g., Livingstone, 2013) has often called for longitudinal research designs that would permit the assessment of online risks, harm, and vulnerability over time, and capture accumulation and repeated manifestations of these phenomena as stronger and more reliable indicators. This chapter makes use of the data from the first two waves of the longitudinally designed survey conducted in 2021 and 2022 within the ySKILLS project focusing on young people's well-being and digital skills in six European countries (Estonia, Finland, Germany, Italy, Poland, and Portugal). The repeated measurements enable us to observe children's subjective vulnerability at two different times and to explore recurrent experiences of online risks and harms. We assume that the children who reported high levels of subjective vulnerability (measured with a scale of negative thoughts and emotional experiences) in both waves are subjectively more vulnerable compared to their peers, and that recurrent unintentional experiences of online risks and harms refer to higher online vulnerability, related to deficient coping strategies and low resilience. The longitudinal design enables us to estimate the likelihood of children's subjective and online vulnerability (by means of recurrency and frequency) while the measurement scales (of subjective vulnerability and online harms) indicate the depth of vulnerabilities.

In aiming to explore the relationships between children's subjective and online vulnerability and the role of digital skills in reducing unintentional experiences of online risks and harms, we pose the following research questions:

1. What characterises more subjectively vulnerable children? How do they differ from less vulnerable peers in terms of internet use and digital skills?
2. Which online risks are more frequent and more likely to recur, and which are more likely to lead to harm? How is children's subjective vulnerability related to their experiences of online risks and harms?
3. Do digital skills help subjectively vulnerable children in preventing unintentional experiences of online risks and harms?

8.2 Online Risks, Harms, and Vulnerabilities

According to the conceptual models of EU Kids Online and ySKILLS, adapted for this chapter, online opportunities and risks tend to be interconnected; thus, both positive and negative experiences are common among children. Moreover, as Livingstone et al. (2011, p. 3) clearly distinguish, depending on one's age, psychological resources, and digital skills, different strengths and vulnerabilities play a role in an individual's inner coping mechanisms with (a) various online risks that often accompany increased digital media use, and (b) harm these risky experiences may cause.

In this section, we define the main online risks and harms that previous literature has shown to be related to an individual's strengths and vulnerabilities, and subjective well-being. Children can purposefully search for risky online content; however, they can also encounter it unintentionally and experience unwanted interactions with others during their routine online activities. We focus on *unintended experiences* with online risks as these might be especially harmful for subjectively vulnerable children with coping problems. In particular, previous research (Livingstone et al., 2015) shows linkages between vulnerabilities and risky online experiences such as different forms of *cybervictimisation* (e.g., Livingstone & Smith, 2014), *cyberhate* (e.g., online hate speech and hateful expressions), exposure to potentially *harmful online content* (e.g., promotion of unhealthy lifestyles and behaviour; Smahel et al., 2020), being targeted with inappropriate content (e.g., *sexually explicit material* or SEM), or facing potentially harmful conduct (e.g., *sexting*). To date, however, longitudinal research exploring the links between these online risks and vulnerability is scarce.

8.2.1 Cybervictimisation

One of the most serious risks in the digital world is cybervictimisation, which can include behaviours like online harassment, peer victimisation or cyberbullying (Wright & Wachs, 2020). Research has shown that cybervictimisation can cause severe psychological and emotional harm, such as depression, anxiety, and low self-esteem (Fischer et al., 2016). Further, some researchers argue that the relationship between cybervictimisation and negative emotional outcomes is bidirectional (Görzig et al., 2023; Wang & Wang, 2023). Youth with emotional problems or lower life-satisfaction may be more vulnerable to cybervictimisation due to cognitive vulnerabilities and lack of interpersonal communication and problem-solving skills (Görzig et al., 2023). Moreover, cybervictimisation can also be linked to other types of risky online behaviour (Ponte et al., 2021).

8.2.2 Cyberhate

Cyberhate, or online hate speech, is a form of cyberaggression that involves attacks against individuals and groups due to their group characteristics and identities (Kansok-Dusche et al., 2023). Cyberhate is motivated by negative intergroup stereotypes and prejudice (Mondal et al., 2017) and it justifies or incites intolerance and discrimination toward minorities and vulnerable groups (Council of Europe, 2022). Children may encounter it via social media, online discussions, direct messages, or in online games. Exposure to cyberhate is associated with lower psychological well-being (Keipi et al., 2018) and can lead to psychological adjustment problems such as depression and anxiety (Tynes et al., 2008). Low life-satisfaction is also connected to cyberhate victimisation (Görzig et al., 2023) and youth with low life-satisfaction are more likely to be exposed to extremist and hateful online content (Stoilova et al., 2021).

8.2.3 Harmful Online Content

Children may also be exposed to harmful online content that depicts or promotes psychologically and physically harmful attitudes, behaviours, and experiences (Keipi et al., 2017), such as alcohol or drug consumption, risky sexual behaviours, or unhealthy dieting. Findings from studies show that exposure to harmful content is associated with lower subjective well-being (Keipi et al., 2017) and emotional problems (Kvardova et al., 2021). Exposure to harmful content may result in engaging in risky offline behaviour (Branley & Covey, 2017), as well as evoking symptoms of post-traumatic stress disorder in youths (McHugh et al., 2018).

8.2.4 Sexually Explicit Material and Sexting

Exploring sexuality and romantic relationships is a normal aspect of adolescent development (Steinberg et al., 2019). However, this exploration may also increase the likelihood of exposure to sexually explicit material, commonly referred to as pornography, which is readily available offline and online for both adults and children (Alexandraki et al., 2018). Adolescents are the biggest consumers of online pornography (Peter & Valkenburg, 2006), and although viewing such content may lead to positive effects (Litsou et al., 2021), it may also be associated with mental health issues (Mattebo et al., 2018) and threaten aspects of adolescent development and well-being (Owens et al., 2012).

Sending sexually explicit texts and/or photographs (completely or semi-nude images) via the internet or digital devices is known as *sexting* (Klettke et al., 2014), commonly desired and practised during the adolescent developmental period (Kosenko et al., 2017). Although some adolescents engage in sexting to receive desired romantic attention, others may receive sexual content unintentionally. The receipt of unwanted sexting messages has been linked to adverse outcomes, such as depression (Dake et al., 2012), low self-esteem (Sorbring et al., 2014), and sexting-triggered online harassment (Festl et al., 2019).

8.3 Data and Methods

This chapter explores data collected through a longitudinally designed school-based survey administered to adolescents in six European countries within the scope of the ySKILLS project. The first wave was carried out between April and November 2021 (T1, $N = 6221$, age range 12–17) and the second wave between February and July 2022 (T2, $N = 5890$), with the same (and new) participants 1 year older. Although schools were selected by a purposive, non-probability sampling method in each country, diversity of participants was ensured considering the schools' and/or regions' socio-economic background. The same online questionnaire, translated into the languages of the participating countries, was self-completed during school classes on standard computers with the presence of researchers (in person, or digitally during the COVID-19 pandemic) or with the presence of teachers, following thorough guidelines set by the research teams (in two countries—Estonia and Finland).

We focus our analysis on a total of 3899 adolescents who participated in both waves of the survey, including participants from Estonia ($n = 807$), Finland ($n = 618$), Germany ($n = 465$), Italy ($n = 671$), Poland ($n = 584$) and Portugal ($n = 754$). In this sub-sample, participants in T1 were 49% female, with an average age of 14.34 years ($SD = 1.19$).

8.3.1 Measures

Subjective vulnerability was assessed with three statements on negative thoughts and emotional experiences: "I felt dissatisfied with my life", "I felt cheerless", "I felt that life was meaningless". These statements were derived from the negative dimension of the short psychological scale by Joseph et al. (2010), originally developed to measure the continuum of depression-happiness. The response scale ranged from 1—Not true to 4—Very true. The scale scores were computed as mean values of the three statements, where higher values represent higher levels of subjective vulnerability (T1: $M = 2.38$, $SD = 0.87$, $\alpha = .82$; T2: $M = 2.46$, $SD = 0.87$, $\alpha = .83$). The two measurements (at T1 and T2) were used as classifiers in a cluster analysis with K-means procedure to identify three groups of adolescents, which significantly differ from each other on the two measurements scales ($p < .001$; see Table 8.1). The Least vulnerable group ($n = 1013$, 34%) persistently reports lower values (below 2.00) at T1 and T2, in contrast to the Most vulnerable ($n = 843$, 28%), with a mean score above 3.00 in both waves. The Average group ($n = 1163$, 39%) represents intermediate values at both T1 and T2.

To measure *manifestations of online vulnerability*, we used the indicators of *repeated unintentional exposure* to five types of *online risks*, and the related experiences of *harm*, applied in the ySKILLS survey as shown below. Not all questions were asked from all participants: in Germany and Portugal, the risk section of the survey was used only with older children (aged 14–15 at T1, and 15–16 at T2); two countries did not ask all of the questions in both waves (Finland did not ask about cybervictimisation in 2021; Poland asked about sexual content and sexting from a part of the sample only in 2021).

Four types of content-related risks and harm (*cyberhate, harmful content, sexual content,* and *sexting*) were measured similarly. After a brief introductory note exemplifying the respective risk, participants were asked whether they had seen or received that type of content online or on a phone. Those who answered *yes* were asked about unintentional exposure on a 6-point frequency scale: "How often have you seen something like this when you did not intend/expect to see it?" For analytical purposes, the answers were recoded into dichotomous variables ("never/once" and "at least a few times"). Further questions in the case of each of these four risks assessed whether and how often the experience was perceived as upsetting, thus resulting in *harm*.

The fifth risk—*cybervictimisation*—is conceptualised as always unintentional and upsetting. Thus, it was measured with only one item—the frequency of "being treated in a hurtful or nasty way on the internet". The original scale was transformed into a dichotomous variable ("never/once" and "at least a few times").

To measure *repeated exposure* to five online risks, we used the data from T1 and T2 and distinguished three categories: those who had never or only once experienced the risk; those who had experienced it at least a few times in one wave; and those who had experienced it at least a few times in the two consecutive waves. A similar logic was applied in categorising *repeated experiences of online harm*:

Table 8.1 Characterisation of the clusters of subjective vulnerability

		Clusters[a]		
	Total[b]	Most vulnerable	Average	Least vulnerable
N	3019	843	1163	1013
%	100.0	27.9	38.5	33.6
Mean score of the 3 items of subjective vulnerability (scale 1–4)				
Year 2021	2.38	3.42	2.33	1.55
Year 2022	2.46	3.35	2.57	1.56
Gender[a,c]*				
Boys (%)	49.0	16.6	37.8	45.6
Girls (%)	49.7	38.1	39.6	22.3
Other (%)	1.3	64.1	25.6	10.3
Age[a,c]*				
12–13 (%)	26.7	25.3	37.3	37.3
14–15 (%)	50.1	27.0	38.1	34.8
16–17 (%)	23.2	32.9	40.7	26.4
M	14.37	14.50	14.41	14.22
SD	1.21	1.22	1.20	1.21
Country*				
Estonia	19.3	26.0	40.4	33.6
Finland	11.4	17.4	31.6	51.0
Germany	12.7	13.1	28.3	58.6
Italy	20.0	32.3	46.1	21.6
Poland	14.3	43.9	33.6	22.5
Portugal	22.3	29.2	42.6	28.2
Family living standard[c,d]*				
Higher (%)	72.2	26.0	38.0	36.0
Average (%)	26.1	32.6	39.8	27.6
Lower (%)	1.7	56.3	35.4	8.3
Mean time spent online (hours per day)				
Year 2021*	3.89	4.39	3.89	3.49
Year 2022*	3.97	4.39	3.92	3.67
Overall mean level of digital skills (5-point scale)				
Year 2021	4.04	4.05	4.03	4.06
Year 2022	4.17	4.16	4.19	4.16

Note: The differences between the clusters were tested by using chi-square (for categorical variables) and ANOVA (for scales); $*p < .001$

[a]In the total column, we report column percentages for variables gender, age, country, and family living standard. The base was children with linked data from both waves of the ySKILLS survey ($N = 3899$); due to missing data on the classifier variables we performed the cluster analysis with a sample of 3019 children

[b]In the clusters' columns, we report row percentages for variables gender, age, country, and family living standard

[c]Wave 1 of the survey (2021)

[d]Family living standard was measured by self-assessed consumption resources on a scale from 1—We struggle to get by: We sometimes do not have enough money to afford basic needs, such as

(continued)

Table 8.1 (continued)

food and clothes to 5—We live very well: We can purchase luxury items, like [local examples], and still have money left over. For analytical purposes, the scale was recorded into three categories by merging the two highest and two lowest categories

Table 8.2 Unintentional exposure to online risks reported in both survey waves (Based on the derived variables)

		Never/once		At least a few times in one wave		At least a few times in two waves	
	N	*n*	%	*n*	%	*n*	%
Cyberhate	1617	429	26.5	471	29.1	717	44.3
Harmful content	1747	633	36.2	548	31.4	566	32.4
Sexual content	1681	830	49.4	471	28.0	380	22.6
Sexting	1946	1135	58.3	476	24.5	335	17.2
Cybervictimisation	1869	1202	63.4	425	22.4	269	14.2

Note: The base was children with linked data from both waves of the ySKILLS survey ($N = 3899$). Valid % are reported

never; sometimes (in one or two waves); and at least half of the times in both waves. Descriptive variables are presented in Tables 8.2 and 8.3.

Time spent online was measured with one item asking respondents to estimate the time spent on the Internet during a regular weekday, from which we computed average hours spent online (T1: $M = 3.92$, $SD = 1.90$; T2: $M = 4.00$, $SD = 1.77$).

Digital skills were measured by the average of the scores on the five items in each of the four dimensions as proposed by Helsper et al. (2021), namely *technical and operational*, *information navigation and processing*, *communication and interaction*, and *content creation and production*, resulting in an overall digital skills level. Items included statements like "I know how to choose the best keywords for online searches", and the options ranged from 1—Not true of me to 5—Very true of me.

8.4 Results

8.4.1 Clusters of Subjective Vulnerability

Using cluster analysis based on the 2-year consecutive data (from the respondents who participated in both waves of the survey) we distinguished three groups of children: (1) *most vulnerable*, (2) *average*, and (3) *least vulnerable*. Table 8.1 displays the clusters, the children's socio-demographic characteristics, average time spent online, and overall digital skills.

The group of most vulnerable children, though being the smallest, forms more than a quarter of adolescents in our sub-sample. Subjective vulnerability is significantly related to gender: while adolescents with non-binary gender identity form a

Table 8.3 Harm from content-related online risks reported in both survey waves (based on the derived variables)

		Never	Sometimes	At least half of the times (in both waves)
	N	%	%	%
Cyberhate	727	5.2	23.7	71.1
Harmful content	583	11.0	39.6	49.4
Sexual content	416	10.1	35.3	54.6
Sexting	357	12.9	25.5	61.6

Note: The base was children with linked data from both waves of the ySKILLS survey and who reported the experience of the respective risk (cyberhate: $n = 1617$; harmful content: $n = 1747$; sexual content: $n = 1681$; sexting: $n = 1946$; cybervictimisation: $n = 1869$). Valid % are reported

tiny proportion of the sample (1.3%), they are strongly over-represented in the most vulnerable group (64%), and boys are over-represented in the least vulnerable cluster (46%). Although the biggest proportion of girls belongs to the average cluster (40%), they, too, are over-represented among the most vulnerable group (38%).

Subjective vulnerability increases with children's growing age: one-third of the 16–17 years old respondents are in the most vulnerable group, while the share of the 12–13-year-olds and the 14–15-year-olds among the most vulnerable is around one-quarter. As previous research (e.g., OECD, 2019) has revealed, the level of life-satisfaction and sense of meaning in life tends to decrease in the middle of adolescence; that is, during the period of life when rapid changes occur in the body but also in emotional and social life. Our findings are in line with this developmental phenomenon.

We also found a statistically significant relationship between subjective vulnerability and children's self-evaluated living standard of their families. While participants with poorer material conditions represent a small minority (below 2%) in the total sample, more than half of them belong to the most vulnerable cluster. At the same time, the share of those with the best material conditions is the highest in the least vulnerable group.

When comparing the clusters by country, we see Polish, Italian and Portuguese children being over-represented in the most vulnerable group, while German and Finnish children have the smallest proportions in that cluster (13% and 17%, respectively). Due to the non-probability sampling of schools and slightly varying approaches to sampling by countries, it is difficult and problematic to interpret the cross-cultural differences.

Our analysis demonstrates a significant relationship between subjective vulnerability and the intensity of internet use: the most vulnerable children spend approximately one more hour on a regular weekday on the internet than the least vulnerable group does (4.4 vs. 3.5 h in 2021, and 4.4 vs. 3.7 in 2022). The data show a slight increase in overall digital skills between the two measurements in all three clusters; there are, however, no significant differences in skills between the vulnerability clusters.

8.4.2 Manifestations of Online Vulnerability: Experiences of Risks and Harm

Among the five online risks we analysed, *cyberhate* was the most frequent and most repeatedly experienced. Table 8.2 shows that 44% of children reported in both waves that they had encountered content that attacks groups of people or individuals because of their race, nationality, gender, sexuality, or religion. Moreover, cyberhate exposure harms adolescents the most compared to other content-related risks. About two-thirds reported in both waves that they had felt upset about cyberhate at least half of the times they saw such content or situations online (Table 8.3). Very few (5%) responded that they had never felt upset about cyberhate.

Sexting (i.e., receiving sexual messages online or on a phone) was the second most upsetting risk after cyberhate. About 62% of those participants who had unintentionally experienced sexting felt upset in at least half of the cases in both waves, and a quarter felt that way sometimes after encountering sexting incidents. However, more than half of the participants (58%) never experienced this risk; 17% reported repeated exposure, and a quarter had experienced sexting at least a few times in one of the waves.

Almost one-third of the respondents had encountered *harmful content* (texts, images or videos that include information about taking drugs, alcohol, unhealthy dieting or eating and other potentially harmful behaviour) in both survey waves. Nearly half of them (49%) repeatedly perceived such content as upsetting.

Nearly a quarter of the sample (23%) reported in both waves that they had seen *sexual content* (pictures, photos or videos of naked people or of people having sex) online or on their phones which made half of them (55%) feel bad.

Cybervictimisation, the most severe risk, was least frequent among the children: 14% of the respondents reported in both waves the experience of being treated in a hurtful or nasty way on the internet. Almost a quarter (22%) had encountered this risk at least a few times in one survey wave.

Our analysis shows that large proportions of children in our sample had repeatedly faced unintentional exposure to online risks, and the experience was generally felt as harmful for those who had undergone it. Overall, adolescents' online vulnerability is rather high.

8.4.3 Relationships Between Subjective Vulnerability, and Online Risks and Harm

The most vulnerable group of children in our survey experienced all five risks in both waves more often than their peers belonging to the average or the least vulnerable cluster (Fig. 8.1).

The most frequently encountered risk—cyberhate—had repeatedly hit slightly less than two-thirds of the vulnerable youth (62%), compared to 42% of the average

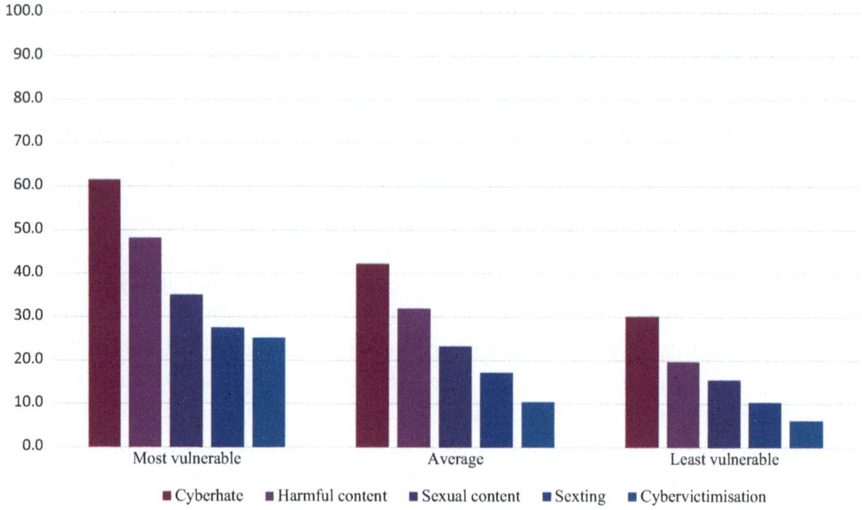

Fig. 8.1 Unintentional exposure to online risks reported in both survey waves across the three clusters of subjective vulnerability (%). Note. Differences between the clusters are statistically significant (all at $p < .001$)

group and 30% of the least vulnerable one. The most vulnerable children, furthermore, had experienced repeated harm from cyberhate significantly more often (78% at least half of the times on both waves) compared to the least vulnerable (64%) and the average group (69%; $p < .05$).

Experiencing repeated exposure to harmful content was reported by 48% of the most vulnerable children, which is a more than twice higher frequency compared to the least vulnerable adolescents (20% had experienced this risk in both waves).

The other three risks are less reported, but nevertheless affect the most vulnerable children to a greater extent than the average and least vulnerable group. Around one-third of the most vulnerable adolescents reported repeated exposure to sexual content or sexting, while these proportions remain below one-fifth in the case of the average and least vulnerable groups. The most vulnerable children also reported significantly more experiences of harm from sexting: 73% of them had been upset at least half of the times on both waves, while only 48% of the least vulnerable and 58% of the average group reported repeated harmful experiences from this risk ($p < .05$).

A quarter of the most vulnerable children also reported repeated cybervictimisation, while only 6% of the least vulnerable youth and 11% of the average cluster had had similar experiences.

8.4.4 The Role of Digital Skills in Preventing Online Risks and Harm

As seen in previous studies (e.g., Smahel et al., 2020), the more time children spend online, the more likely they are to experience any kind of risk. In our sample, the largest difference in time spent online is found between those who had never (or once) experienced cybervictimisation and those who had suffered from this at least a few times in both waves (3.6 vs. 4.9 h in T1).

To see whether digital skills matter in preventing online risks, we also analysed the distribution of the overall skills score across the frequency categories of reported online risks. Interestingly, in all risks, the overall digital skills score (in T1 or T2), is slightly but significantly higher among those who reported repeated exposure to the risk. For example, the average skills score for those who have never, or once, experienced unintended sexting is 4.02, compared to 4.22 among those who have experienced it at least a few times in both waves.

Taking a closer look at the most vulnerable group ($n = 843$), we created two subgroups based on the whole sample median of the overall digital skills scale (4.17): those with a higher skills level (equal to or above the median; $n = 450$, 53%), and those with below the median skills level ($n = 392$, 47%). Then we compared the exposure to risks and perceived harm in both groups.

Higher skills did not help the most vulnerable children to avoid risks, rather on the contrary. The differences between the two groups were small, and those with higher skills had more often experienced risks repeatedly (in two waves): in the case of sexting (31% vs. 24%), sexual content (39% vs. 30%) and cybervictimisation (29% vs. 20%, the only statistically significant difference at $p < .05$). Similar conclusions can be drawn regarding harm. Despite the small number of cases, there is no evidence which supports the idea that higher skills would help the most vulnerable children to prevent harm. The only exception is exposure to obviously sexual content: 14% of the most vulnerable youth with higher skills had never suffered harm from sexual content, compared to 2% of the most vulnerable youth with lower skills. Inversely, the share of the most vulnerable children with lower skills who had sometimes experienced this type of harm was 10% larger than the proportion of those with higher skills (35% vs. 25%). However, the difference between the most vulnerable children with lower and higher digital skills was not remarkable regarding the repeated harm from this risk (62% and 61%, respectively).

8.5 Concluding Discussion

By analysing data collected through a longitudinally designed survey in six European countries, this chapter focused on vulnerability during adolescence in relation to the digital environment. Our analysis contributes to understanding the interconnections between subjective and online vulnerabilities, by conceptualising online vulnerability as a probability of poor adaptation to online risks and experiencing harm (as a consequence of deficient coping) and operationalising the concept in the form of its manifestations—as unintentional encounters with online risks and experiences of harm.

Findings indicate that different levels of subjective vulnerability are related to individual demographic characteristics. Not surprisingly, non-binary youth, girls, and older adolescents are more susceptible than their peers to having negative thoughts and emotional experiences, confirming the results of earlier research on gender and age as inherent characteristics influencing children's subjective vulnerability (or well-being; e.g., OECD, 2019). The perceived condition of facing financial difficulties also increases the likelihood of being subjectively vulnerable, as it impacts "the spaces and times of vulnerability where and within children grow up" (Schweiger, 2019, p. 292) and increases the exposure to situational vulnerabilities and threats.

Subjective vulnerabilities are also related to the intensity of online activities. The most vulnerable children spend more time online than their peers, which is in line with various studies linking the intensity of internet use to negative mental and emotional consequences for young people (Vissenberg et al., 2022). It is, however, crucial to understand the bidirectionality of this relationship. According to our data, more and less subjectively vulnerable children do not differ in terms of their overall digital skills. Challenging the common assumption that digital skills would facilitate well-being, this finding reflects the ambiguous role of digital skills in the subjective outcomes for children and young people (Livingstone et al., 2023).

Cyberhate was the risk most frequently experienced by children in our sample, especially in the most vulnerable group, and it was also the risk most likely to be faced repeatedly. Almost half of the participants reported they were unintentionally exposed to cyberhate at least a few times during the two waves. This is in line with research showing that cyberhate is becoming prevalent on mainstream online platforms and social media (e.g., Reichelmann et al., 2021). Hateful content is reaching wider audiences, including children and young people, who most often encounter it unintentionally as bystanders or audiences during their everyday online interactions. Indeed, young people report the normalisation of hate online and worry about desensitisation towards it (Cohen et al., 2020). However, our findings suggest that adolescents do not easily build resilience toward cyberhate and that it has adverse effects on their well-being, as it was the risk that upset children in our sample the most. Furthermore, due to its prevalence on mainstream platforms and discussions, avoidance might not be possible. There is an emerging line of research investigating coping strategies focusing on cyberhate victims (e.g., Gámez-Guadix et al., 2020; Schultze-Krumbolz et al. 2022). Our findings, however, highlight the need to help to develop appropriate coping strategies for bystanders who are also adversely affected.

Unwanted *sexting and exposure to sexual content* were the next most upsetting experiences after cyberhate. Even though exploring one's sexuality online can have positive effects (e.g., Litsou et al., 2021), our focus was on unsolicited experiences, and according to our expectations and previous research, these have negative effects on adolescents' well-being, including self-harm and depression (e.g., Festl et al., 2019; Mattebo et al., 2018; Wachs et al., 2021). Compared to cyberhate, sexting and sexual content exposures were less common, and most children in our sample experienced these risks only once or never. Similar is the case of other types of *harmful online content* that were repeatedly encountered by a third of children, and most of them encountered it only once or a few times. However, their potential detrimental effects should not be underestimated as all three—sexting, sexual content, and harmful content exposure—were most often experienced by the most vulnerable group of children who might lack the emotional or social resources to appropriately cope with them. As shown by recent qualitative research with young people with mental health difficulties, harmful online content may lead to experiences of *triggering* (when particular content proves upsetting because of prior mental health problems) and setbacks in their mental health (Livingstone et al., 2022). Therefore, we recommend future research differentiate more delicately between various types of harmful content, including sexual content, and focus on the potentially more vulnerable groups of children for whom the emotional and developmental consequences might be the most severe.

Cybervictimisation was the least common risk across the two waves of our survey as it was experienced by a minority of children. In our study, experienced harm after cybervictimisation was not assessed, but research suggests that it is one of the most serious online risks in terms of the potential harm and its impact on emotional well-being and mental health (Fischer et al. 2016) and can be further amplified by maladaptive coping strategies (e.g., Schunk et al., 2022). Thus, we suggest future research to investigate the moderating and mediating factors that can further explain the associations between cybervictimisation, other risks, and experienced harm.

Our findings show that *subjective vulnerability* was related to all five types of risks, with the most vulnerable children being significantly more often exposed to repeated experiences of all online risks. The most vulnerable group, furthermore, tended to experience more harm from some risks (cyberhate and sexting). This is in line with previous research, which shows that youth's online risk experiences overlap, and the most vulnerable groups often experience polyvictimisation (El Asam & Katz, 2018). Our findings confirm the assumptions of the bidirectional relationship between subjective vulnerability and risky experiences. The youth experiencing the most online risks also reported the most emotional harm, while being subjectively most vulnerable led to the most experiences of online risks. In previous research, higher life-satisfaction and well-being have been shown to support coping resources, buffer from negative behavioural reactions (Diener et al., 1999) and, thus, serve as a protective mechanism against online risky experiences (e.g., Görzig et al., 2023). In other words, more vulnerable children may lack the necessary resources (cognitive, emotional, or social) to cope with risky experiences, which may lead to further increasing their emotional problems.

In our study, we explored the role of digital skills as a potential protective factor. The data suggest a connection between digital skills and online risk experiences. Children who reported more frequent and repeated exposure to various online risks also self-reported higher digital skills. This observation can be linked to the increased time spent online, potentially leading to both more opportunities to develop digital skills and more chances to encounter risks (Donoso et al., 2020). It is, however, worth further investigation to determine whether different types of digital skills lead to different outcomes in terms of encountering and coping with online risks. According to the recent research with young people with mental health difficulties (Livingstone et al., 2022), some adolescents are developing particular digital skills that interlink technical, informational, communication and content creation skills and even go beyond them: for example, the skill of gaming a callous algorithm to make their feed positive or locate *safe* spaces or trustworthy people. This finding calls for expanding prior definitions of digital competence to enable a more sensitive and up-to-date measurement of digital skills and their relationships with online vulnerability. We, furthermore, suggest conceptualising *online vulnerability* and *online resilience* more firmly and in an explicit and elaborate manner in the theoretical models on children's online lives and digital skills.

In our analysis, we found no significant relationship between digital skills and the subjective vulnerability clusters. This implies that digital skills development and subjective vulnerability may be separate factors that do not necessarily influence each other directly. The findings also reveal that in the most vulnerable group of children, higher digital skills do not prevent repeated experiences of risks and harm. Similarly, the qualitative study with young people with mental health difficulties (Livingstone et al., 2022) revealed that sophisticated digital skills did not necessarily make for better mental health and well-being outcomes. On the one hand, better skills may result in riskier online engagement, at times exceeding the ability of vulnerable youth to cope with harmful consequences. On the other hand, vulnerable young people may not always manage to put their specific skills into practice, especially if a mental health difficulty impacts on their functioning. These findings raise important questions about how to effectively support subjectively vulnerable adolescents in managing online risks. Relying solely on youth digital skills is clearly insufficient. Other factors such as social support and help by mental health professionals, empathetic towards young people's digital lives, probably play a more significant role in enhancing online resilience and preventing harm among this group.

8.5.1 Contextualisation and Limitations

This study has its limitations, some of which may serve as a stimulus for future research and further discussion. Firstly, due to the non-probability sampling strategy, the findings of the ySKILLS survey cannot be generalised to the population of adolescents in six participating countries; for the same reason, we did not aim to draw cross-national comparisons.

Secondly, the survey method provided self-reported data, in which both under-reporting and over-reporting is likely (Livingstone, 2013). Self-reporting, at the same time, has a methodological value in presenting children's own appraisals of their subjective or online vulnerabilities and digital lives.

Thirdly, conducting the survey during the Covid-19 pandemic influenced our fieldwork in schools (see Waechter et al., 2023) and probably also the findings. Although we did not study the direct influence of the pandemic on our participants, it is likely that lockdowns and school closures affected children's subjective vulnerability and increased time spent online, raising, in turn, the probability of exposure to online risks and harms.

Fourthly, the role of gatekeepers (school administrators and parents) in conducting school-based surveys may lead to sample biases. In this study, we had to deal with the difficulties of obtaining active parental consent (see Waechter et al., 2023) and collecting data about more sensitive topics, as in some countries schools restricted asking questions about online risks or sexual content from younger children. Our experience indicates that adult gatekeepers in the research field sometimes predefine children as vulnerable, thus preventing researchers from hearing the voice of young people on their own perceptions of subjective or situational vulnerabilities. We conclude that researching children's subjective and online vulnerabilities is a methodological challenge, yet a much-needed endeavour to provide new cross-disciplinary knowledge to the field.

Acknowledgements Preparation of this publication has received funding from the European Union's Horizon 2020 Research & Innovation programme under Grant Agreement no. 870612. The information in this article reflects only the authors' views and the European Union is not liable for any use that may be made of the information contained therein. Veronika Kalmus' work on this publication was supported by a grant from the Estonian Research Council (PRG1761). Natalie Tercova's and Marie Jaron Bedrosova's work on this publication has received funding from the Czech Science Foundation, project No. 19-27828X.

Competing Interests The authors have no conflicts of interest to declare that are relevant to the content of this chapter.

Ethics Approval This study was performed in line with the principles of the Declaration of Helsinki. Approval was granted by the he Social and Societal Ethics Committee of the project coordinator's university (KU Leuven) (17.03.2021/No. G-2019 11 1813). The project partners responsible for the longitudinal school-based data collection in their countries applied for additional ethical approval according to national regulations. In Germany and Portugal, the survey was approved by the (Federal) Ministry of Education, and in Finland, Italy, and Poland, approval was granted by the ethical commission of the project partners' universities (University of Helsinki; Università Cattolica del Sacro Cuore; Adam Mickiewicz University). The Finnish team obtained another ethical approval by the city of Salo. In Estonia, no further ethical approval was necessary as KU Leuven's procedure was considered adequate and applicable.

References

Alexandraki, K., Stavropoulos, V., Anderson, E., Latifi, M. Q., & Gomez, R. (2018). Adolescent pornography use: A systematic literature review of research trends 2000–2017. *Current Psychiatry Reviews, 14*(1), 47–58. https://doi.org/10.2174/2211556007666180606073617

Andresen, S. (2014). Childhood vulnerability: Systematic, structural, and individual dimensions. *Child Indicator Research, 7*, 699–713. https://doi.org/10.1007/s12187-014-9248-4

Branley, D. B., & Covey, J. (2017). Is exposure to online content depicting risky behavior related to viewers' own risky behavior offline? *Computers in Human Behavior, 75*, 283–287. https://doi.org/10.1016/j.chb.2017.05.023

Cohen, A., Ekwueme, P. O., Sacotte, K. A., Bajwa, L., Gilpin, S., & Heard-Garris, N. (2020). "Melanincholy": A qualitative exploration of youth media use, vicarious racism, and perceptions of health. *Journal of Adolescent Health, 69*, 288–293. https://doi.org/10.1016/j.jadohealth.2020.12.128

Council of Europe. (2022). *Combating hate speech.* https://rm.coe.int/prems-083822-gbr-2018-recommendation-on-combating-hate-speech-memorand/1680a70b37

Dake, J. A., Price, J. H., Maziarz, L., & Ward, B. (2012). Prevalence and correlates of sexting behaviour in adolescents. *American Journal of Sexuality Education, 7*(1), 1–15. https://doi.org/10.1080/15546128.2012.650959

Diener, E., Suh, E. M., Lucas, R. E., & Smith, H. L. (1999). Subjective well-being: Three decades of progress: 1967 to 1997. *Psychological Bulletin, 125*(2), 276–302. https://doi.org/10.1037/0033-2909.125.2.276

Donoso, V., Retzmann, N., Joris, W., & d'Haenens, L. (2020). *Digital skills: An inventory of actors and factors*. ySKILLS, KU Leuven. https://zenodo.org/records/4525639#.YTc37I4zabh

El Asam, A., & Katz, A. (2018). Vulnerable young people and their experience of online risks. *Human–Computer Interaction, 33*(4), 281–304. https://doi.org/10.1080/07370024.2018.1437544

Festl, R., Reer, F., & Quandt, T. (2019). Online sexual engagement and psychosocial well-being: The mediating role of sexual victimization experiences. *Computers in Human Behavior, 98*, 102–110. https://doi.org/10.1016/j.chb.2019.04.010

Fischer, B. W., Gardella, J. H., & Teurbe-Tolon, A. R. (2016). Peer cybervictimization among adolescents and the associated internalizing and externalizing problems: A meta-analysis. *Journal of Youth and Adolescence, 45*, 1727–1743. https://doi.org/10.1007/s10964-016-0541-z

Gámez-Guadix, M., Wachs, S., & Wright, M. (2020). "Haters back off!" Psychometric properties of the coping with cyberhate questionnaire and relationship with well-being in Spanish adolescents. *Psicothema, 32*(4), 567–574. https://doi.org/10.7334/psicothema2020.219

Görzig, A., Blaya, C., Bedrosova, M., Audrin, C., & Machackova, H. (2023). The amplification of cyberhate victimisation by discrimination and low life satisfaction: Can supportive environments mitigate the risks? *The Journal of Early Adolescence, 43*(1), 5–36. https://doi.org/10.1177/02724316221078826

Haddon, L., Cino, D., Doyle, M-A., Livingstone, S., Mascheroni, G., & Stoilova, M. (2020). *Children's and young people's digital skills: A systematic evidence review*. ySKILLS, KU Leuven. doi:https://doi.org/10.5281/zenodo.4274654.

Helsper, E. J., Schneider, L. S., van Deursen, A.J. A. M., & van Laar, E. (2021). *The youth Digital Skills Indicator: Report on the conceptualisation and development of the ySKILLS digital skills measure.* ySKILLS, KU Leuven. doi:https://doi.org/10.5281/zenodo.4608010.

Hepp, A. (2016). Pioneer communities: Collective actors in deep mediatisation. *Media, Culture & Society, 38*(6), 918–933. https://doi.org/10.1177/0163443716664484

Joseph, S., Linley, P. A., Harwood, J., Lewis, C. A., & McCollam, P. (2010). Rapid assessment of well-being: The Short Depression-Happiness Scale (SDHS). *Psychology and Psychotherapy, 77*(4), 463–478. https://doi.org/10.1348/1476083042555406

Kansok-Dusche, J., Ballaschk, C., Krause, N., Zeißig, A., Seemann-Herz, L., Wachs, S., & Bilz, L. (2023). A systematic review on hate speech among children and adolescents: Definitions,

prevalence, and overlap with related phenomena. *Trauma, Violence and Abuse, 24*(4). https://doi.org/10.1177/15248380221108070
Keipi, T., Näsi, M., Oksanen, A., & Räsänen, P. (2017). *Online hate and harmful content: Cross-national perspectives*. Routledge.
Keipi, T., Räsänen, P., Oksanen, A., Hawdon, J., & Näsi, M. (2018). Exposure to online hate material and subjective well-being. *Online Information Review, 42*(1), 2–15. https://doi.org/10.1108/OIR-05-2016-0133
Klettke, B., Hallford, D. J., & Mellor, D. J. (2014). Sexting prevalence and correlates: A systematic literature review. *Clinical Psychology Review, 34*, 44–53. https://doi.org/10.1016/j.cpr.2013.10.007
Kosenko, K., Luurs, G., & Binder, A. R. (2017). Sexting and sexual behavior, 2011–2015: A critical review and meta-analysis of a growing literature. *Journal of Computer-Mediated Communication, 22*(3), 141–160. https://doi.org/10.1111/jcc4.12187
Kvardova, N., Smahel, D., Machackova, H., & Subrahmanyam, K. (2021). Who is exposed to harmful online content? The role of risk and protective factors among Czech, Finnish, and Spanish adolescents. *Journal of Youth and Adolescence, 50*, 2294–2310. https://doi.org/10.1007/s10964-021-01422-2
Laurinavičius, A., Žukauskienė, R., & Ustinavičiūtė, L. (2012). Explaining vulnerability to risk and harm. In S. Livingstone, L. Haddon, & A. Görzig (Eds.), *Children, risk and safety online: Research and policy challenges in comparative perspective* (pp. 297–308). Policy Press.
Litsou, K., Byron, P., McKee, A., & Ingham, R. (2021). Learning from pornography: Results of a mixed methods systematic review. *Sex Education, 21*(2), 1–17. https://doi.org/10.1080/14681811.2020.1786362
Livingstone, S. (2013). Online risk, harm and vulnerability: Reflections on the evidence base for child Internet safety policy. *ZER - Journal of Communication Studies, 18*(35), 13–28. https://eprints.lse.ac.uk/62278/
Livingstone, S., & Smith, P. K. (2014). Annual research review: Harms experienced by child users of online and mobile technologies. *Journal of Child Psychology and Psychiatry, 55*(6), 635–654. https://doi.org/10.1111/jcpp.12197
Livingstone, S., Haddon, L., Görzig, A., & Ólafsson, K. (2011). *EU Kids Online II: Final report 2011*. EU Kids Online, London School of Economics and Political Science. http://eprints.lse.ac.uk/45490/.
Livingstone, S., Mascheroni, G., & Stakstrud, E. (2015). *Developing a framework for researching children's online risks and opportunities in Europe*. EU Kids Online, London School of Economics and Political Science. https://eprints.lse.ac.uk/64470/.
Livingstone, S., Stoilova, M., Stänicke, L. I., Jessen, R. S., Graham, R., Staksrud, E., & Jensen, T. K. (2022). *Young people experiencing internet-related mental health difficulties: The benefits and risks of digital skills. An empirical study*. ySKILLS, KU Leuven. doi:https://doi.org/10.5281/zenodo.6976424.
Livingstone, S., Mascheroni, G., & Stoilova, M. (2023). The outcomes of gaining digital skills for young people's lives and wellbeing: A systematic evidence review. *New Media and Society, 25*(5), 1176–1202. https://doi.org/10.1177/14614448211043189
Mackenzie, C., Rogers, W., & Dodds, S. (2014). Introduction: What is vulnerability, and why does it matter for moral theory? In C. Mackenzie, W. Rogers, & S. Dodds (Eds.), *Vulnerability: New essays in ethics and feminist philosophy* (pp. 1–29). Oxford University Press.
Mattebo, M., Tydén, T., Häggström-Nordin, E., Nilsson, K. W., & Larsson, M. (2018). Pornography consumption and psychosomatic and depressive symptoms among Swedish adolescents: A longitudinal study. *Uppsala Journal of Medical Sciences, 123*(4), 1–10. https://doi.org/10.1080/03009734.2018.1534907
McHugh, B. C., Wisniewski, P., Rosson, M. B., & Carroll, J. M. (2018). When social media traumatizes teens: The roles of online risk exposure, coping, and post-traumatic stress. *Internet Research, 28*(5), 1069–1188. https://doi.org/10.1108/intr-02-2017-0077

Mondal, M., Silva, L. A., & Benevenuto, F. (2017). A measurement study of hate speech in social media. *Proceedings of the 28th ACM Conference on Hypertext and Social Media*, pp 85–94. doi:https://doi.org/10.1145/3078714.3078723.

OECD. (2019). *PISA 2018 results (Vol. III): What school life means for students' lives*. doi:https://doi.org/10.1787/acd78851-en.

Owens, E. W., Behun, R. J., Manning, J. C., & Reid, R. C. (2012). The impact of internet pornography on adolescents: A review of the research. *Sex Addict Compulsivity, 19*, 99–122. https://doi.org/10.1080/10720162.2012.660431

Peter, J., & Valkenburg, P. M. (2006). Adolescents' exposure to sexually explicit material on the internet. *Communication Research, 33*(2), 178–204. https://doi.org/10.1177/0093650205285369

Ponte, C., Carvalho, M. J. L., & Batista, S. (2021). Exploring European children's self-reported data on online aggression. *Communications, 46*(3), 419–445. https://doi.org/10.1515/commun-2021-0050

Reichelmann, A., Hawdon, J., Costello, M., Ryan, J., Blaya, C., Llorent, V., Oksanen, A., Räsänen, P., & Zych, I. (2021). Hate knows no boundaries: Online hate in six nations. *Deviant Behavior, 42*(9), 1100–1111. https://doi.org/10.1080/01639625.2020.1722337

Schultze-Krumbolz, A., Pfetsch, J. S., & Lietz, K. (2022). Cyberbullying in a multicultural context – forms, strain, and coping related to ethnicity-based cybervictimization. *Frontiers in Communication, 7*, 846794. https://doi.org/10.3389/fcomm.2022.846794

Schunk, F., Zeh, F., & Trommsdorff, G. (2022). Cybervictimization and well-being among adolescents during the COVID-19 pandemic: The mediating roles of emotional self-efficacy and emotion regulation. *Computers in Human Behavior, 126*, 107035. https://doi.org/10.1016/j.chb.2021.107035

Schweiger, G. (2019). Ethics, poverty and children's vulnerability. *Ethics and Social Welfare, 13*(3), 288–301. https://doi.org/10.1080/17496535.2019.1593480

Smahel, D., Machackova, H., Mascheroni, G., Dedkova, L., Staksrud, E., Ólafsson, K., Livingstone, S., & Hasebrink, U. (2020). *EU Kids Online 2020: Survey results from 19 countries*. EU Kids Online, London School of Economics and Political Science. doi:https://doi.org/10.21953/lse.47fdeqj01ofo.

Soffia, M., & Turner, A. (2021). *Measuring children and young people's subjective wellbeing: Conceptual framework*. What Works Centre for Wellbeing. https://whatworkswellbeing.org/wp-content/uploads/2021/09/MCYPSW-Conceptual-framework-1.pdf

Sorbring, E., Skoog, T., & Bohlin, M. (2014). Adolescent girls' and boys' well-being in relation to online and offline sexual and romantic activity. *Cyberpsychology: Journal of Psychosocial Research on Cyberspace, 8*(1), 7. https://doi.org/10.5817/CP2014-1-7

Steinberg, D. B., Simon, V. A., Victor, B. G., Kernsmith, P. D., & Smith-Darden, J. P. (2019). Onset trajectories of sexting and other sexual behaviors across high school: A longitudinal growth mixture modeling approach. *Archives of Sexual Behavior, 48*(8), 2321–2331. https://doi.org/10.1007/s10508-019-1414-9

Stoilova, M., Livingstone, S., & Khazbak, R. (2021). *Investigating risks and opportunities for children in a digital world: A rapid review of the evidence on children's internet use and outcomes. Innocenti Discussion Papers, no. 2021-01*. UNICEF Office of Research, Innocenti. https://www.unicef-irc.org/publications/1183-investigating-risks-and-opportunities-for-children-in-a-digital-world.html

Tynes, B. M., Giang, M. T., Williams, D. R., & Thompson, G. N. (2008). Online racial discrimination and psychological adjustment among adolescents. *Journal of Adolescent Health, 43*(6), 565–569. https://doi.org/10.1016/j.jadohealth.2008.08.021

Vandoninck, S., d'Haenens, L., & Segers, K. (2012). Coping and resilience: Children's responses to online risks. In S. Livingstone, L. Haddon, & A. Görzig (Eds.), *Children, risk and safety online: Research and policy challenges in comparative perspective* (pp. 205–218). Policy Press.

Vissenberg, J., d'Haenens, L., & Livingstone, S. (2022). Digital literacy and online resilience as facilitators of young people's wellbeing? A systematic review. *European Psychologist, 27*(2), 76–85. https://doi.org/10.1027/1016-9040/a000478

Wachs, S., Wright, M. F., Gámez-Guadix, M., & Döring, N. (2021). How are consensual, non-consensual, and pressured sexting linked to depression and self-harm? The moderating effects of demographic variables. *International Journal of Environmental Research and Public Health, 18*(5), 2597. https://doi.org/10.3390/ijerph18052597

Waechter, N., Kalmus, V., Mascheroni, G., & Opermann, S. (2023). Large-scale comparative school-based survey research: Challenges and solutions for sampling, fieldwork and informed consent. *Methods, Data, Analyses, 17*(2), 303–324. https://doi.org/10.12758/mda.2023.03

Wang, X., & Wang, S. (2023). The bridge between cybervictimization and suicidal ideation among adolescents: A vicious cycle of hopelessness. *Journal of Youth and Adolescence, 52*, 996–1009. https://doi.org/10.1007/s10964-022-01726-x

Wright, M. F., & Wachs, S. (2020). Adolescents' cyber victimization: The influence of technologies, gender, and gender stereotype traits. *International Journal of Environmental Research and Public Health, 17*(4), 1293. https://doi.org/10.3390/ijerph17041293

Veronika Kalmus is Professor of Sociology at the Institute of Social Studies, University of Tartu, Estonia. Her current research focuses on socialisation, mediatisation, datafication, digital skills, and well-being. She has published the collective monograph *Researching Estonian Transformation: Morphogenetic Reflections* and numerous articles in international journals and collections, including *Childhood, Children & Society*, and *New Media & Society*. She has received several awards, including the National Research Award in Social Sciences (with the research group Me. The World. The Media in 2022), and has been elected a Member of Academia Europaea (MAE), Section of Film, Media and Visual Studies (in 2019). Since 2007, she has been the leader of the Estonian team of the EU Kids Online network.

Susana Batista is Assistant Professor at NOVA FCSH, where she coordinates the MA in Studies in Education, and a researcher at the interdisciplinary Centre of Social Sciences (CICS.NOVA). She also co-coordinates the Sociology of Education section at the Portuguese Sociological Association (APS). Susana has been a member of the Portuguese team of the European network EU Kids Online since 2017 and a researcher at the ySKILLS Project (2020–2023, H2020). She is also a member of CriA.On, a Portuguese digital platform with resources on children's and adolescents' digital contexts, skills, and rights. Mainly focusing on quantitative data analysis, her recent work explores the relationships between children, youth, and media, particularly regarding digital literacy, citizenship, and risks.

Signe Opermann is a research fellow in Media Sociology at the University of Tartu, Estonia. Her research focuses on media use, social and media generations, mediatisation and platformisation, digital skills, and future education. She has participated in international research projects related to the digital literacy of children and young people (e.g. CO:RE, ySKILLS). Her current projects include researching platforming families in a cross-generational and cross-cultural setting (PlatFAMS) and ed-tech imaginaries of learning, communicating, and citizen-making in Estonia and Sweden. Her publications include books such as *Researching Estonian Transformation: Morphogenetic Reflections* (co-edited with Veronika Kalmus, Marju Lauristin, and Triin Vihalemm, 2020) and *The Routledge International Handbook of European Social Transformations* (co-edited with Peeter Vihalemm and Anu Masso, 2018).

Natalie Tercova is a Junior Researcher at the Interdisciplinary Research Team on Internet and Society (IRTIS) and a PhD Candidate in Media Studies at Masaryk University, Czech Republic. Her primary research focus is on the digital skills of children and adolescents. Additionally, she is researching online privacy, sharenting, artificial intelligence, and CSAM. Natalie is also the Founder and Chair of the Internet Governance Forum (IGF) Czechia, and Vice Facilitator within the Internet Society, Youth Standing Group (ISOC YSG).

Marie Jaron Bedrosova is a postdoc researcher at the Interdisciplinary Research Team on Internet and Society (IRTIS) and the Department of Media Studies at the Faculty of Social Studies at Masaryk University in Brno, the Czech Republic. She also works as a Reviews Editor at *Cyberpsychology: Journal of Psychosocial Research on Cyberspace*. Her research interests are cyberaggression, cyberhate, and online discrimination with a focus on children and youth.

Chapter 9
Child Vulnerability Within the Legal System

Katre Luhamaa, Anna Markina, and Kristi Paron

9.1 Introduction

Children navigate their lives within a societal framework where, at times, they may be affected by law and legal proceedings due to unforeseen events through the actions of third parties or through their own actions, often without the child's full understanding or consent. Children act typically within subordinate power structures (families, schools, and other institutions), in which their agency is limited. The law not only contextualises these encounters but also regulates the extent and manner of state intervention in the agency of the child, as well as that of their parents and family. There are instances, where these contacts are direct, as is the case of young offenders and children in conflict with the law, or children whose parents have custody disputes or who are removed from the family because of safety concerns. There are also instances where the regulations or particular decision-making processes influence the position or circumstances of the child but where the child is not a direct participant in the proceedings, such as the child who is exposed to domestic violence.

This chapter discusses the general concepts and norms that define the state's obligation to recognise the child's vulnerabilities and to protect the child and their rights when a child is in contact with the law. In this analysis, the rights protected in the Convention on the Rights of the Child (CRC, 1989), especially the best interests

K. Luhamaa (✉) · A. Markina
School of Law, University of Tartu, Tartu, Estonia
e-mail: katre.luhamaa@ut.ee; anna.markina@ut.ee

K. Paron
Children's Rights Department, Office of the Chancellor of Justice/Ombudsperson for Children, Tallinn, Estonia
e-mail: kristi.paron@oiguskantsler.eeee

D. Kutsar et al. (eds.), *Child Vulnerability and Vulnerable Subjectivity*, Children's Well-Being: Indicators and Research 27,
https://doi.org/10.1007/978-3-031-61333-3_9

of the child (CRC Article 3(2)) together with the child's participation right (CRC Article 12) and evolving capacities of the child (CRC Article 5) are the focal guiding principles and rights that frame the state's actions in most of the world's legal systems (CRC Committee, 2003).

The current chapter brings examples from three legal scenarios that impact the life of the individual child. First, it assesses state-led child welfare proceedings where the child is removed from their biological parents. Second, it analyses the treatment of juvenile offenders and children in conflict with the law, considering whether the system adequately provides for the child's resocialisation, participation and agency, particularly through restorative justice mechanisms that offer a balance of support and accountability. Third, the chapter explores the situation of children witnessing interparental domestic violence, often an overlooked group in legal procedures, and discusses the importance of empowering them with separate legal counsel or advice. Throughout these contexts, the chapter examines the legal system's recognition and support of the individual child's agency, scrutinising the extent to which the child is given a voice, included in decision-making, and provided with both the necessary support services and independent legal advice.

The current chapter builds upon the legal framework of European child rights law, where the requirements of the CRC are paramount (Europarat, 2011). Therefore, the CRC together with the instruments of the Council of Europe form the legal foundation of this chapter, using the Estonian national legal framework only as an example.

9.2 Child Agency Within the Legal System

9.2.1 Interrelation Between Child Agency and Child Rights

Children's agency has been a focal point of childhood studies for decades. Before the 1970s, children were mostly regarded as incompetent and incapable members of society, whereas the new paradigm in childhood sociology saw the rise of the notion of the agentic child (James, 2009). In the field of childhood studies, the conceptualisations of children's agency have developed in tandem with the development of children's rights studies, gaining significant impetus following the adoption and subsequent global ratification of the CRC.

Within the agency framework, children are viewed as active participants in society who have an influence on their lives and on those of others (Corsaro, 2018; James & Prout, 2015; Mayall, 2002, 2015). Children's agency pertains to their capacity to act (James & James, 2004, p. 24). It extends beyond mere decision-making to include active participation in their social environment, expressing views, and negotiating positions even when their decision-making capability might be limited. James (2009) views agency as a concept that extends into societal structures, capturing the child's broader interactions and influence in child-world, child-adult, and child-child relations. This makes agency inherently connected to both shaping their world and meaningful participation in society. Children have such agency both as individuals and as a distinct social group (Peleg, 2019b, p. 167). Greene and Nixon (2020, p. 193) define agency "as a complex, dynamic feature of the engagement of human beings with their internal and external worlds". Therefore, agency is understood as the child's ability to affect changes within the contexts in which they live (Daly, 2018a, p. 76).

The concept of child agency is intrinsically linked to the child's sphere of autonomy and the freedoms within which they can exert influence. Child agency is supported by the full implementation and recognition of children's rights, foremost by the right of the child to participate in decision-making (Art. 12, CRC), whereby children exercise their autonomy (CRC Committee, 2009, para. 3). The law is one of the most significant symbols of legitimacy (Freeman, 2009). Given legal rights, as opposed to moral rights, which children may also have, children are given a recognised status (Archard, 2015) and the state has a duty to guarantee the protection of this status. Michael Freeman (2011, p. 22) has defined the relationship between rights and agency as follows:

> Rights are important because those who have them can exercise agency. Agents are decision-makers. They are persons who can negotiate with others, who can alter relationships and decisions, who can shift social assumptions and constraints. And there is now clear evidence that even the youngest amongst us can do this.

The actualisation of children's agency is reinforced by specific children's rights, which prioritise the child's best interests as the paramount guiding principle and underscore the necessity of the child's participation in any matter concerning them, including legal proceedings (CRC Committee, 2003). These principles not only carve out the child's discretionary space but also impose an obligation on the state to duly consider the child's contribution and perspectives. These principles also require giving due regard to the voice and perspectives of the child. The crux of the implementation of the rights of the child is in balancing the vulnerability of the child with the child's individual agency.

International child rights recognise the child's vulnerable position within society and aim to find an appropriate balance between protection and autonomy. The CRC Committee has noted children's general vulnerability, often linked to the development of the child (e.g., CRC Committee, 2023); there are also groups of children whose life circumstances require special attention; for example, children in migration, living in remote areas, or in poverty (e.g., CRC Committee, 2021). Similarly, the practice of the CRC Committee and the case-law of the European Court of Human Rights (ECtHR) recognise the fundamental principle that the law should protect children's welfare and afford them the protection necessitated by their vulnerability and lack of maturity.[1] The need to protect a child in contact with the law must be balanced against the child's right to participate (Article 12, CRC) and the respect for the child's evolving capacities (Article 5, CRC). As the rights and principles guiding the child's agency and participation within the legal system have

[1] See the summary of the relevant practice in ECtHR, 2022.

received wide substantive academic attention, the current chapter discusses only the essence of these principles in legal proceedings to provide a specific context for the examples used.

9.2.2 Defining the Context of Child Participation Through Age or Capacity?

Article 1 of the CRC defines a child in terms of an upper age limit—everyone under the age of 18 is a child, unless national legislation grants the child earlier maturity. National legislation typically formalises the right and ability to participate in legal proceedings through the concepts of legal capacity. This context is relevant, as the national legal system includes different age limits and connects it with the child's capabilities or responsibilities. The CRC supports this approach in a limited number of cases treating it as presumptive not determinative (Lundy et al., 2019, p. 416; Peleg, 2019a, pp. 138–139). It rather uses the more fluid concepts of maturity and the evolving capacities of the child, as conceptualised in Articles 5, 6 and 12 of the CRC. These provisions attach importance to the evolving capacities of the child. The CRC Committee defines evolving capacities as "an enabling principle that addresses the process of maturation and learning through which children progressively acquire competencies, understanding and increasing levels of agency to take responsibility and exercise their rights" (CESCR Committee, 2009, para. 18). Lansdown (2005) emphasises three dimensions of the concept of evolving capacities: (i) developmental concept, emphasising the child's rights to development; (ii) a participatory or emancipatory concept focusing on the shift of transferring rights from adults to the child; and (iii) a protective concept acknowledging the child's rights to protection while the capacities of the child are still evolving.

National age limits can exclude but also empower children. Therefore, they are appropriate measures only when provided in law, justified and reasonable, also taking into account the appropriateness of individual assessment in the matter and the need to find an appropriate balance between protection and empowerment (Tobin & Varadan, 2019, p. 183). When a state sets age limits in its legislation, the CRC requires that such limitations are justified and based on sufficient and available evidence while protecting the coherence of child rights (Peleg, 2019a, p. 139; Tobin & Varadan, 2019, p. 183). The current chapter discusses such age limits in connection with child protection court procedures and juvenile offenders.

As discussed below, in the context of this chapter, neither Articles 3 nor 12 of the CRC directly connect the implementation of a child's right to their capacities. These provisions require making participation possible for every child "who is capable of forming his or her own views", considering that the direction and guidance given by parents (and other adults) to the child in the process of rights realisation must consider the evolving capacities of the child. Nevertheless, it is typical in national legislations that the child's participation in family law proceedings that concern their welfare include specific age limits from which the state has an obligation to formally hear the child as well as an age limit that grants the child the status of a separate litigant. As an example, the Estonian Code of Civil Procedure (CCP, 2006) included an obligation to hear a child who is at least 10 years of age and left hearing a younger child.

the discretion of the Court. As will be discussed below, this translated into practice so that only a small margin of younger children have been heard by the court. A recent change in the legislation abolished the age limit in family law proceedings and follows more closely the understanding that the court has to take into account the evolving capacities of the child and give the child's views due weight considering their individual level of development and capacity.

In the context of criminal law, national legislation sets the age of criminal responsibility and requires special treatment of juvenile offenders. Therefore, in the Estonian context, offenders younger than 14 are supported through the child welfare system, while children older than 14 can receive special support and treatment typically through the justice system, which implements restorative justice measures, but there is a possibility for stringent criminal law proceedings that include imprisonment as a punishment. While the CRC does not set a minimum age for criminal responsibility (Article 40), the CRC Committee (2019, para. 21) has determined that it should be the age of 14 at the youngest, as children below this age should not be held responsible in penal law proceedings.

When defining the child as well as throughout legal proceedings, parties are under a clear duty not to discriminate against any child within their jurisdiction, irrespective of their or their parents' status. Article 2 of the CRC identifies 11 such statuses, but also forbids discrimination on any other statuses (Kleber & Besson, 2019). Within the context of the legal system and deciding individual cases, this directs the legal system to guarantee access to justice and equality in all legal proceedings, requiring the state to provide legal aid and necessary services to the child irrespective of the economic abilities of the parents.

To summarise, policymakers and specialists working with children must find a delicate balance between a child's age and capacities when making decisions concerning children, as the holistic application of CRC principles assumes.

9.2.3 Child's Best Interests

Article 3(1) of the CRC requires that the child's best interests guide all the decisions relating to the child and obliges the decision-maker to regard it as a "primary consideration" in "all actions concerning children". Article 3 does not differentiate between different types of proceedings but creates a general and overarching obligation to consider the child's best interests in them. The principle of the child's best interests is aimed at ensuring the full and effective enjoyment of all the rights recognised in the Convention. The importance of the best interest's principle is demonstrated by the fact that it is embedded not only in Article 3 of the Convention, but in other Articles as well, notably including those that deal with some types of legal proceedings. These include Article 9 (separation from parents), Article 10 (family reunification), Article 18 (parental responsibilities), Article 20 (deprivation of family environment), Article 21 (adoption), Articles 37 and 40 (juvenile justice).

This is both a substantive as well a procedural right, and countries must include this principle as a substantive right, interpretative principle as well as a procedural requirement in their national legal system (CRC Committee, 2013; Peleg, 2019b, p. 142; Tobin & Eekelaar, 2019). In its core, this principle is a dynamic concept which should be interpreted in context. This interpretation requires that the decision-maker determines the issues at stake, identifies the relevant interests and rights of a specific child, or children, in this situation, obtains the child's views while providing support and information for the child to understand the issue and assessing how the range of decisions that can be made will impact on the child's interests.

There are national variations of the wording as well as differences in the scope of this principle in different countries (Luhamaa et al., 2022; Skivenes & Sørsdal, 2018). As an example, section 5(3) of the Estonian Child Protection Act (CPA, 2016) requires the state to prioritise the child's interests in all actions concerning the child. Therefore, the CPA includes the concept of the *interests of the child* instead of the *best* interests of the child.[2]

The principle of the child's best interests still includes two major problems from the perspective of the concepts of childhood and the child's evolving capacities—subjectivity and adult paternalism. Each child and their circumstances are unique, thus, there is a need to give decision-makers appropriate discretion when deciding on individual cases leaving decisions open to a level of subjectivity and the possibility of paternalism. Both problems can somewhat be remedied through the child's participation and hearing the child.

9.2.4 Supporting Child Agency Through Participation: The Way Forward Towards Child Autonomy

Article 12 of the CRC states that children should be heard in all matters affecting them, and have their views given due weight in accordance with age and maturity. Such an approach has been conceptualised in children's rights studies as participation—the child must be enabled to participate in the decision-making process (CRC Committee, 2009, para. 3). Therefore, Article 12 protects the child's right to be heard as well as requiring the decision-maker to hear the child and give their views due regard. As Peleg (2019b, p. 148) puts it, Article 12 transforms the image of children under the law, conceptualising them as active agents who should have a

[2] The English translation of CPA however, uses the term "best interests" and this is not a correct translation corresponding to the Estonian connotation of the law. See the English translation of the law: https://www.riigiteataja.ee/en/eli/510042023004/consolide

voice in their lives as it is an act of inclusion that recognises children as citizens in their communities. Daly (2018b) proposes that children's actual influence on outcomes should be considered the most important purpose of Article 12, particularly in proceedings where intimate matters about their personal lives are being determined. Nevertheless, a child's right to be heard still requires reconciliation with the fact that it includes a high level of subjectivity and paternalism especially when the child's opinion is given due weight by the adult(s) in the proceedings.

Attributing due weight to children's views in proceedings affecting them is problematic as it includes a high level of discretion by the adult decision-maker, thus, it is claimed that there is no accepted understanding as to how to weight children's views and that the process of giving due weight lacks transparency, consistency and accountability (Daly, 2018a). Nevertheless, the CRC Committee (2013, p. 53) has stressed that "Any decision that does not take into account the child's views or does not give their views due weight according to their age and maturity, does not respect the possibility for the child or children to influence the determination of their best interests." Therefore, there is an inherent connection between the child's participation and the establishment of the best interests of the child. The child's best interests cannot be accurately ascertained if the child has not been heard and their opinion has not been given due weight.

The above explorations reveal that children's agency and autonomy, granted through the participation right under Article 12 of the CRC is limited (Daly, 2018a; Hart, 2008; Reynaert et al., 2009). Legally, there are two qualifications of the child's agency. First, the child must be capable of forming their view; and second, even if the child is capable of forming a view, it is still an adult who gives weight to the child's view in a particular matter. There is abundant scholarship about Article 12 of CRC, and interpretation and shortcomings are possible (see e.g., Doek, 2020; Lundy, 2007; Lundy et al., 2019; Tisdall, 2015). A comprehensive overview of key issues related to child participation is given by McMellon and Tisdall (2020). In light of the above framework, it has been argued that Article 12 of the CRC and child participation as such need novel conceptualisation. Daly (2018a, p. 7) proposes that the principle of the autonomy of the child should be introduced in the best interests assessment proceedings, meaning that: "In legal decisions in which the best interest of the child is the primary consideration, children should get to choose—if they wish—how they are involved (*process autonomy*) and the outcome (*outcome autonomy*) unless it is likely that significant harm will arise from their views". Even though such an approach is likely to face some scepticism (e.g., how would such a principle apply to very young children), it still encompasses essential new thinking for the children's rights field. The rules and procedures of decision-making regarding children should aim at including them as much as possible and at maximising their capacity, not vice versa.

Within the European legal system, the Council of Europe has dedicated special attention to child-friendly justice and has adopted guidelines (2011), which generally focus on all types of judicial proceedings, including civil and criminal law proceedings where a child might be a party. These guidelines operationalise the requirements of Article 12 of the CRC and give practical advice and define best practices that national systems should adhere to.

9.3 Supporting the Child's Agency in Family Law Proceedings

Daly (2018b) calls civil law proceedings relating to the child "child's best interests proceedings" as these proceedings aim to protect the child when parents are not able to agree on the living arrangements or provision of subsistence for the child or when the child has to be protected against harm deriving from the family or its members. These proceedings concern the child often because of life choices or events involving the parents.

9.3.1 Estonian Child Protection System

The current chapter uses the Estonian family law system as an example.[3] As a typical Continental-European legal system, Estonia has three central legal acts regulating family law proceedings and child protection. The Estonian Child Protection Act (CPA, 2016) details general principles of child protection including the child's right to be heard. The CPA section 5(4) acknowledges the child's right to an independent opinion and the right to express their views in all matters affecting the child; this is complemented by section 21(2), which requires the decision-maker to take three main steps to establish the views of the child:

1. ascertain all the relevant circumstances concerning the situation and person of the child and other information which is necessary to evaluate the effect of the decision on the child's rights and well-being;
2. to explain the content and reasons for the planned decision to the child, to hear the child in a manner taking account of their age and development and to account for their opinion based on the child's age and development as one of the circumstances upon ascertaining the best interests of the child;
3. assess all the relevant circumstances in aggregate, to form a reasoned opinion concerning the best interests of the child with regard to the planned decision.

When a decision establishes that the best interests of a child differ from the child's opinion or if a decision does not coincide with the child's opinion, CPA section 21(3) requires that the decision-maker explains the decision to the child.

[3] For comparison with Finnish legal system see Toivonen et al. (2019); for comparison in the context of adoptions from care, see Burns et al. (2019); for global comparative analysis see Berrick et al. (2023a, b).

It is worth mentioning that Estonia is a monist country, thus, the decision-makers can and do rely directly on the CRC as a legal source. This is a more recurring practice at the level of the Supreme Court, whereas reliance on it is less common in the county and circuit courts (Luhamaa, 2020).[4]

Estonian Family Law Act (FLA, 2010) makes matters more complicated and unclear as the FLA section 123 obliges courts in any matter concerning a child to "make a decision primarily in the interests of the child, taking into account all the circumstances and the legitimate interests of the relevant persons." The FLA also recognises at a limited level the need for parents to take into account the evolving capacities of the child as required in section 116(3) that parents take into account that "the ability and need of the child to act independently and responsibly increases". The legal obligation that follows, however, waters down the evolving capacities principle as it requires if "the development level of a child so allows", to "discuss" caring and raising issues with the child. Therefore, the FLA does not separately regulate the child's general right to be heard. It only requires in section 151 that the adoption of the child is allowed only with the consent of the child who is at least 10 (for European comparison see Burns et al., 2019).

Child protection family law proceedings in Estonia combine administrative law and civil law. At the pre-court level, child protection workers follow the Administrative Procedure Act (APA, 2002) when working with child protection cases; the APA does not separately regulate hearing the child, thus, the general regulation of the CPA should apply. Child protection cases are decided following civil procedure on petition, and since 2022, the CCP section 552.1 obliges the court to hear every child, who is capable of holding their own opinions in the cases that concern them. A child who is 14 or older has the capacity to make individual claims or contest the decisions (CCP sec. 553). Otherwise, these rights are vested with the legal guardians of the child.

9.3.2 The Child's Agency in Child Protection Removals

As shown by Berrick et al. (2023a, b), all legal systems include some type of child protection where the state has the right to intervene in the family, when the child is in danger. Berrick et al. (2023a, b) also show how the various child protection systems aim to protect children against different risks on five levels. At the most basic level, all countries attempt to protect children against the risk of child exploitation (e.g., Philippines); going beyond this risk, at the next level some countries also protect against child deprivation (e.g., Mexico); some are further focused on protecting narrowly against child maltreatment (e.g., US, but also Estonia); widening the scope

[4] Estonia has a three-tier court system. County and administrative courts on the first level; circuit courts as appellate courts on the second; and the Supreme court as the court of cassation and constitutional review. Constitution of Estonia (The Constitution of the Republic of Estonia (*Põhiseadus*), 1992) sec. 148. See further Ristikivi et al. (2023, pp. 393–399)

of this coverage, others also seek to protect child well-being (e.g., Belgium); and finally, covering all the levels of risk, a few countries further aspire to protect child rights in a wider sense (e.g., Norway or Finland). They conclude, however, that countries typically have a mix of these discreet systems and combine the protection against maltreatment with the protection of child rights.

Therefore, following Article 19 of the CRC, national child welfare systems have to acknowledge the responsibility of the state to intervene in the child's family life when the child is at risk of maltreatment (Tobin & Cashmore, 2019). In these proceedings, the state should follow the principle of the least intrusive measure and place the child outside the biological family only when other measures are not deemed sufficient. It should also aim to protect the child's rights during such proceedings, and any removal decision should be in the best interests of the child. During the proceedings, the state must balance the child's rights with the parent's rights, setting the child's best interests as the paramount consideration. There is international consensus that any removal decision must be subject to judicial review, which determines that separation is necessary for the child's best interests (*Strand Lobben et al. v. Norway (GC)*, 2019). Previous research has shown that child protection cases do not focus on the individual rights and circumstances of a particular child (Križ et al., 2022) and often lose the voice of the child (e.g., McEwan-Strand & Skivenes, 2020; Pösö & Enroos, 2017; Vis & Fossum, 2013).

According to Statistics Estonia, there were 259,338 children living in Estonia in 2022. In recent years, the state has removed between 255 and 310 children from their biological family every year due to neglect or maltreatment (Statistikaamet, 2023). While some of these children go back to their biological families or to a kinship placement, most remain under state custody. Recent research on the full sample of child protection removal judgements in Estonia in 2018 (n = 154) shows a lack of attention to the individual child, including the agency and vulnerability of the individual child. This sample showed that the focus of the child protection proceedings was primarily on the rights and risks of the parent(s) and whether the parents would be able to deal with their risks and create a safe home for their children. This shift of focus was reinforced by the fact that the state-appointed and financed legal representative for the child typically would represent all the children affected by the decision together (Luhamaa et al., in preparation). Furthermore, the court often discussed the vulnerabilities and interests of the children as a group, mentioning the individual needs of the child only in passing. While this generalisation might be since this research is only able to use formal written judgements as a source, the presumption is nevertheless that the judgements should show the full extent of the court's arguments and considerations in any child protection case.

Only a small proportion of the removal cases is contested in Estonia; nevertheless, in more recent practice, a shift towards focusing on the individual needs and interests of the child can be seen. As an example, the Tallinn County Court resolved an appeal of a 16-year-old child who contested his removal from his biological family (*No. 3-1-2-4-14*, 2023). The court stressed the need to show individual views, interests and the needs of each concerned child separately. While the court did not reverse the removal decision, it used both the court hearing as well as the judgement to establish the views of the child as well as explain to the child the reasons for the decision. In this case, the language and argumentation of the court showed substantive respect toward the child and their agency. Furthermore, the costs set up by the court showed that the child's lawyer discussed the judgement with the child, thus, supplying explanation and information for the child. Further research is needed to show whether there is a shift towards more recognition of the child's agency in removal cases.

9.4 Recognising the Child's Vulnerability in Criminal Law and Criminal Law Proceedings

Children may find themselves engaged with the criminal justice system due to their own actions as offenders, or through the actions of others when they are victims or witnesses. Regardless of how they are involved, the fundamental principles of children's rights discussed above—non-discrimination, the child's best interests, ensuring their right to life and development, and upholding their right to be heard—must be upheld alongside specific procedural protections tailored to their circumstances in the criminal justice system. The importance of a child's agency and empowerment are especially important in criminal law as research shows that the child is much more willing to accept responsibility when the child can freely agree with the special restorative justice measures (FRA, 2017). As will be discussed below, children who are exposed to domestic violence are rarely included in the criminal law measures, as the law is not clear on whether such children should be viewed as victims or witnesses of violence. This often means that the children lack information as well as opportunities to participate in any related proceedings, making secondary victimisation a possibility.

9.4.1 Juvenile Justice System: A Paradigm Shift Towards Restorative Justice

Since Estonia regained independence in 1991, the juvenile justice system has fluctuated between a punitive approach for severe crimes and a more lenient approach coupled with rehabilitation for minor offences. Unlike many other countries (Dünkel, 2017), Estonia does not have specialist juvenile or family courts, leading to these cases being processed within the general court system. The Estonian Penal Code (PC, 2002), the Code of Criminal Procedure (CCrP, 2004), and the Imprisonment Act (IA, 2000) govern the detention of children in Estonia.

From 1998 to 2017, Estonia's juvenile sanctions system empowered juvenile committees—including educational, social welfare, healthcare, police, and probation experts—to offer non-judicial interventions to young offenders aged 7–17, aiming to divert them from formal criminal proceedings. These committees were designed to supply alternative responses to youth offences, allowing the authorities to recommend interventions rather than impose traditional criminal sanctions. However, studies over two decades have shown that these committees had limited success in preventing subsequent criminal activity among the youth (Markina & Märtson, 2008; Rannala, 2014; Rannala et al., 2006).

In 2018, significant reforms were enacted in Estonia's juvenile justice system, leading to the disbandment of the juvenile committees. The reformed system follows the recommendations of the CRC Committee (2014, paras. 48–49) and prioritises delinquency prevention and tailors rehabilitative measures to each child's specific needs, with incarceration being a measure of last resort. The updated legal framework broadens the spectrum of interventions, ranging from warnings to addiction treatment, with many dependent on the minor's consent. This approach is in harmony with the 2016 amendments to the Child Protection Act, which characterise juvenile offenders as children in need of help, and advocates for case management methods. Moreover, closed childcare services have been transformed into welfare services, emphasising child development and applying restrictions on liberty sparingly, reflecting the *ultima ratio* principle from criminal law.

A significant aspect of the reform was the amendment of section 87 of the PC to encompass ten sanctions available to courts or public prosecutors: warnings, referrals to intervention programmes, compensation for offence-related damages, addiction treatment, mediation, conduct supervision, community service, movement restriction via electronic monitoring, placement in a closed childcare facility, or any other voluntarily assumed obligation. Notably, some measures, such as addiction treatment and mediation, require the minor's consent to be implemented.

The 2016 amendments to the CPA supported revisions to Estonia's criminal law and procedure, redefining a child in need of help as one whose behaviour endangers their own well-being or that of others, thus encompassing juvenile offenders. Case management principles guide the assistance of such children, though the Act lacks specific guidelines on operational collaboration details for child protection workers.

The reforms established a closed childcare service through the Social Welfare Act (SWA, 2015) as a welfare-oriented alternative to punitive institutions, with placement reserved for cases where a child's behaviour poses a serious risk. Such decisions can be made by both civil and criminal courts. Here the focus is on developmental support within these services, with restrictions on the child's liberty applied sparingly. The number of children in childcare service institutions has increased (Table 9.1).

An average of 114 applications per year were submitted for placement in a secure children's institution in 2018–2021, the vast majority of which were granted by the court and the child was placed in a closed childcare service. The majority of those who are referred to the service (around 70% in 2022) are referred under the SWA, and the remainder under the PC. More than a third (39%) of children referred to services have a previously diagnosed disability, most often a mental disability (Tarto et al., 2022).

Table 9.1 Number of children in closed childcare institutions in Estonia at year-end, 2018–2022

	2018	2019	2020	2021	2022
Decision by the civil court	28	42	57	46	44
Decision by the Penal Court	18	20	19	14	11
In place of arrest	2	0	4	3	3
Total	48	62	80	63	58

Source: Office of the Chancellor of Justice

As a result of the juvenile justice reform, the prosecutor's office now has greater discretion to terminate proceedings for offenders aged 14–17, favouring interventions over sanctions. Since 2018, there has been a marked increase in the use of proceedings termination by the public prosecutor, with most minors receiving obligatory measures aimed at rehabilitation and the prevention of re-offending.

The reform also allows prosecutors to tailor obligations to the minor's needs and the offence's specifics, extending beyond predefined interventions. Should the public prosecutor determine that an adolescent aged 14 to 17 who has offended might be better influenced outside the sanction system, they have the authority to cease criminal proceedings, deliver a warning, and, with the youth's consent, assign appropriate obligations (CCrP sec. 201). The reform was designed to enhance prosecutorial discretion, enabling prompt intervention to deter re-offending more effectively. Research by Markina et al. (2021) revealed that by 2020, prosecutors' decisions to terminate criminal proceedings for minors increased from 21% to 52% in 2016, with 80% of these cases imposing at least one obligation on the young offenders, including community sanctions, intervention programmes, mediation, or treatment.

Following the reform, prosecutors can personalise the corrective measures to reflect the minor's unique situation and the nature of their offence. For instance, obligations can range from essay writing to animal shelter work, and activities that resonate with the youth. The most common requirement imposed by prosecutors is school attendance and the completion of basic education, often accompanied by reflective writing about the offence (Markina et al., 2021).

By 2020, a mere 20% of juvenile cases proceeded to court, where even there, punitive sentences could be supplanted by measures of influence, with their use increasing from 45% in 2018 to 64% in 2020 (Markina et al., 2021). Concurrently, actual imprisonment has declined, indicating a shift towards more child-centric practices within the justice system even before the official reform. This trend is underscored by a reduction in incarcerated juveniles, a change depicted in Fig. 9.1.

As noted by Zehr (2015), restorative justice aims to remedy the harm caused by criminal acts and address their root causes. The 2018 reforms in Estonia's juvenile justice system resonate with these goals, setting up specialised procedures for minors that prioritise accountability for their actions and respond to their specific risks and needs. The inclusion of mediation in criminal proceedings for juveniles exemplifies this shift, signifying a transition from a penalty-focused system to a more child-friendly, restorative justice-oriented framework. Furthermore, as the

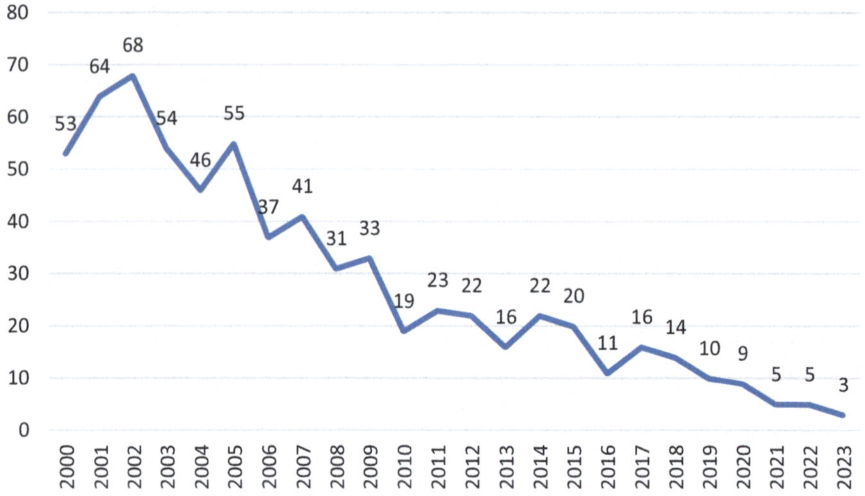

Fig. 9.1 Number of juveniles in prison in Estonia 2000–2023. Source: Estonian Prison Services

measures are developed together with the child, the child consenting to the measures is paramount. Therefore, such an approach empowers the juvenile offender, recognises their agency and allows them to take responsibility for their actions. This is especially so when the measures used include restorative justice measures, such as mediation.

9.4.2 *Children Exposed to Domestic Violence—Unsolved Indirect Victimhood?*

The second criminal law area with new empirical evidence relates to children exposed to domestic violence. In 2021, there were more than 6000 such children in Estonia (Espenberg et al., 2022). In these situations, exposure to violence influences a child directly, even when there are no direct legal remedies available to the child. The Estonian legal system has clear regulations when a child is a direct victim of domestic violence, as it provides the child with necessary protection and support during any such proceedings. Research shows that children exposed to domestic violence are at increased risk of experiencing emotional, physical and sexual abuse, of developing emotional and behavioural problems and of increased exposure to the presence of other adversities in their lives (Holt et al., 2008). Research by Espenberg et al. (2022) analysed how the criminal law and victim protection systems, whose central aim is to deal with violent adults in domestic violence cases, treat and support such children.

Interviews with police officers, prosecutors, lawyers, judges, representatives of NGOs, victim support service workers, and child welfare specialists showed that the systems focus on protecting the child by not involving them. Here, the lack of a holistic approach to child protection was visible as the child welfare and victim support services used different evaluation measures.

The preference of the criminal justice professionals was that such a child was given neither a victim nor a witness status and was excluded from all criminal proceedings when such a procedure was started. The main arguments for such a choice are based on acknowledging the child's vulnerability; however, this vulnerability was unrelated to the need for legal protection and child agency. Instead, the arguments of the professionals posited that participation at any stage of the criminal justice process would re-victimise the child. The criminal justice specialist explained that the child's involvement in the procedure would push them to testify against one of the parents, and therefore, cause a loyalty conflict. The only benefit of participation to consider, according to the professionals, is access to supporting measures related to the victim's status. The support provided to the children by the child welfare system does not require the victim status of the child; hence, they argue that involvement in the criminal procedure is not necessary.

Such an approach is not in conformity with the views of the GREVIO committee (Council of Europe, Group of Experts on Action against Violence against Women and Domestic Violence; GREVIO, 2022), where the committee has stressed the need to view and treat direct and indirect victims of domestic violence holistically, providing them protection and support through legal remedies; for example, the right to receive information and legal representation, as well as through victim and child protection remedies.

The research in Estonia (Espenberg et al., 2022) demonstrated that children with victim status would receive better protection and support because victim support services, compared with general child protection services, are more potent and have more resources to help victims of crime. The quality of assistance provided by child welfare services in local governments is uneven and does not consider the child's specific needs when a child is exposed to violence. The research further established that child protection workers lack special knowledge of the children exposed to domestic violence, and there are cases when the general notification of the child in need of support does not mention the context of domestic violence. As a result, some children may not receive the support they need. When this happens, their sense of agency is also limited, thus making the re-victimisation more likely.

9.5 Conclusion

Empirical examples prove that the Estonian child protection system has taken a substantial step forward and attempts to protect children's agency when the state interferes in the child's life and that of his or her family. The preference towards protection at the expense of agency is still visible in examples discussed in the current chapter. Such a limitation is not surprising, as earlier research also showed that

Estonian child protection workers see child agency and protection as juxtapositions (Strömpl & Luhamaa, 2020; Toivonen et al., 2019).

However, civil law examples showed that the courts slowly recognise the child's individuality, agency and vulnerability as inherent to each child, thus making the child visible in the proceedings.

Similarly, the preliminary view of juvenile justice reforms in criminal law shows that the turn towards alternative and restorative justice measures has already had an effect in decreasing the number of young offenders who are imprisoned. Further research is necessary to analyse the effectiveness of these restorative justice measures both in decreasing repeat offences as well as supporting the agency and rehabilitation of the child.

The example of Estonia still shows that a holistic approach towards child vulnerability, needs and the protection of their rights requires further work—progress has been achieved in the most serious violations of children's rights but is not a common practice in all areas of possible harm and neglect; the justice system needs further development to become more child-friendly and inclusive at all stages of the process. Here, the position of the child welfare workers needs further attention as they have special competence in working with vulnerable children and assisting them, which the court itself lacks. Similarly, further co-operation with victim support services and training in trauma-informed care is needed to support children exposed to domestic violence.

Acknowledgement Work on this chapter was supported by a grant from the Estonian Research Council (PRG700).

Competing Interests The authors have no conflicts of interest to declare that are relevant to the content of this chapter.

References

Administrative Procedure Act (*Haldusmenetluse seadus*), RT I 2001, 58, 354; RT I, 03.02.2023, 14 (2002). https://www.riigiteataja.ee/en/eli/513032023002/consolide

Archard, D. (2015). *Children: Rights and childhood* (3rd ed.). Routledge, Taylor & Francis Group.

Berrick, J. D., Gilbert, N., & Skivenes, M. (2023a). Child protection systems across the world. In J. D. Berrick, N. Gilbert, & M. Skivenes (Eds.), *Oxford handbook of child protection systems*. Oxford University Press.

Berrick, J. D., Gilbert, N., Skivenes, M., Berrick, J. D., Gilbert, N., & Skivenes, M. (Eds.). (2023b). *Oxford handbook of child protection systems*. Oxford University Press.

Burns, K., Križ, K., Krutzinna, J., Luhamaa, K., Meysen, T., Pösö, T., Pösö, T., Segado, S., Skivenes, M., & Thoburn, J. (2019). The hidden proceedings – An analysis of accountability of child protection adoption proceedings in eight European jurisdictions. *European Journal of Comparative Law and Governance, 6*(4), 339–371. https://doi.org/10.1163/22134514-00604002

CESCR Committee. (2009). *General Comment No. 20: Non-discrimination in economic, social and cultural rights (art. 2, para. 2, of the Covenant)*. E/C.12/GC/20.

Child Protection Act (*Lastekaitseseadus*), RT I, 06.12.2014, 1; RT I, 06.01.2023, 1 (2016). https://www.riigiteataja.ee/en/eli/510042023004/consolide

Code of Criminal Procedure (*Kriminaalmenetluse seadustik*), RT I 2003, 27, 166; RT I, 11.03.2023, 3 (2004). https://www.riigiteataja.ee/en/eli/505092023002/consolide

Code of Civil Procedure (2006). (Tsiviilkohtumenetluse seadustik), RT I 2005, 26, 197; RT I, 22.03.2024, 1. https://www.riigiteataja.ee/en/eli/ee/510042024001/consolide/current

Convention on the Rights of the Child. (1989). *United Nations, Treaty Series* (Vol. 1577, p. 3). U.N. General Assembly, UNCRC.

Corsaro, W. A. (2018). *The sociology of childhood* (Fifth edition, international student edition). Sage.

CRC Committee. (2003). *General Comment No. 5. General measures of implementation of the Convention on the Rights of the Child (arts. 4, 42 and 44, para. 6)*. CRC/GC/2003/5.

CRC Committee. (2009). *General Comment No. 12: The right of the child to be heard*. CRC/C/GC/12.

CRC Committee. (2013). *General Comment No. 14 on the right of the child to have his or her best interests taken as a primary consideration (art. 3, para. 1)*. CRC/C/GC/14.

CRC Committee. (2014). *State party report: Second, third and fourth report of Estonia*. CRC/C/EST/2-4. http://vm.ee/sites/default/files/elfinder/article_files/report_of_estonia.pdf

CRC Committee. (2019). *General comment no 24: Children's rights in the child justice system*. CRC/C/GC/24.

CRC Committee. (2021). *General comment no 25: Children's rights in relation to the digital environment*. CRC/C/GC/25.

CRC Committee. (2023). *Draft general comment No. 26: Children's rights and the environment, with a special focus on climate change*. CRC/C/GC/26.

Daly, A. (2018a). *Children, autonomy and the courts: Beyond the right to be heard*. Brill | Nijhoff. doi:https://doi.org/10.1163/9789004355828.

Daly, A. (2018b). No weight for "due weight"? A children's autonomy principle in best interest proceedings. *The International Journal of Children and Rights, 26*(1), 61–92. https://doi.org/10.1163/15718182-02601012

Doek, J. (2020). Child participation. In J. Todres & S. M. King (Eds.), *The Oxford handbook of children's rights law* (p. 0). Oxford University Press. doi:https://doi.org/10.1093/oxfordhb/9780190097608.013.14.

Dünkel, F. (2017). Juvenile justice and crime policy in Europe. In I. Zimring, E. Franklin, M. Langer, & D. S. Tanenhaus (Eds.), *Juvenile Justice in global perspective* (Vol. 1). New York University Press.

ECtHR. (2022). *Guide on Article 8 of the Convention – Right to respect for private and family life*. Council of Europe/European Court of Human Rights. https://www.echr.coe.int/Documents/Guide_Art_8_ENG.pdf

Espenberg, K., Luhamaa, K., Markina, A., & Vain, K. (2022). *Laps perevägivalla pealtnägijana* (Kriminaalpoliitika Uuringute Sari Nr 36). Tartu Ülikool. https://skytte.ut.ee/sites/default/files/2022-04/Laps%20perev%C3%A4givalla%20pealtn%C3%A4gijana_l%C3%B5pparuanne_ISBN.pdf

Europarat (Ed.). (2011). *Guidelines of the Committee of Ministers of the Council of Europe on child-friendly justice*. Council of Europe Publ.

Family Law Act (*Perekonnaseadus*), RT I 2009, 60, 395; RT I, 11.01.2023, 2 (2010). https://www.riigiteataja.ee/en/eli/ee/507022018005/consolide/current

FRA. (2017). *Child-friendly justice: Perspectives and experiences of children involved in judicial proceedings as victims, witnesses or parties in nine EU Member States : Annexes*. Publications Office. https://data.europa.eu/doi/10.2811/516162

Freeman, M. (2009). Children's rights as human rights: Reading the UNCRC. In J. Qvortrup, W. A. Corsaro, & M.-S. Honig (Eds.), *The Palgrave handbook of childhood studies* (pp. 377–393). Palgrave Macmillan Limited. http://ebookcentral.proquest.com/lib/bergen-ebooks/detail.action?docID=485290

Freeman, M. (2011). The value and values of children's rights. In A. Invernizzi & J. Williams (Eds.), *The human rights of children: From visions to implementation*. Ashgate Publishing.

GREVIO. (2022). *3rd General report on GREVIO's activities*. Council of Europe. https://rm.coe.int/prems-055022-gbr-2574-rapportmultiannuelgrevio-texte-web-16x24/1680a6e183
Green, S., & Nixon, E. (2020). Children as agents in their worlds: a psychological-relational perspective. *Routledge.*. https://www.taylorfrancis.com/books/9781315625911
Hart, J. (2008). Children's participation and international development: Attending to the political. *The International Journal of Children's Rights, 16*(3), 407–418. https://doi.org/10.1163/157181808X311231
Holt, S., Buckley, H., & Whelan, S. (2008). The impact of exposure to domestic violence on children and young people: A review of the literature. *Child Abuse and Neglect, 32*(8), 797–810. https://doi.org/10.1016/j.chiabu.2008.02.004
Imprisonment Act (*Vangistusseadus*), RT I 2000, 58, 376; RT I, 18.02.2023, 3 (2000). https://www.riigiteataja.ee/en/eli/531072023005/consolide
James, A. (2009). Agency. In J. Qvortrup, W. A. Corsaro, & M.-S. Honig (Eds.), *The Palgrave handbook of childhood studies* (pp. 34–45). Palgrave Macmillan UK. https://doi.org/10.1007/978-0-230-27468-6_3
James, A., & James, A. L. (2004). Constructing children, childhood and the child. In A. James & A. L. James (Eds.), *Constructing childhood: Theory, policy and social practice* (pp. 10–28). Macmillan Education UK. https://doi.org/10.1007/978-0-230-21427-9_1
James, A., & Prout, A. (Eds.). (2015). *Constructing and reconstructing childhood: Contemporary issues in the sociological study of childhood* (Classic edition). Routledge, Taylor & Francis Group.
Kleber, E., & Besson, S. (2019). Article 2. The RIght to non-discrimination. In *The UN convention on the rights of the child: A commentary* (1st ed., pp. 41–72). Oxford University Press.
Križ, K., Krutzinna, J., Pösö, T., & Skivenes, M. (2022). The invisible child: A comparative study of newborn removal judgments from a child equality perspective (cep). *The International Journal of Children's Rights, 30*(3), 644–674. https://doi.org/10.1163/15718182-30030006
Lansdown, G., UNICEF, & Innocenti Research Centre. (2005). *The evolving capacities of the child. Save the Children*. UNICEF.
Luhamaa, K. (2020). International human-rights supervision triggering change in child-protection systems? The effectiveness of the recommendations of the CRC Committee in Estonia. *Juridica International, 29*, 108–123. https://doi.org/10.12697/ji.2020.29.10
Luhamaa, K., Krutzinna, J., & Skivenes, M. (2022). *Child's best interest in child protection legislation of 44 jurisdictions*. https://doi.org/10.13140/RG.2.2.16641.33129.
Luhamaa, K., Beilmann, M., & Strömpl, J. (in preparation). *Characteristics of vulnerable families in Estonian child protection court proceedings*.
Lundy, L. (2007). 'Voice' is not enough: Conceptualising Article 12 of the United Nations Convention on the Rights of the Child. *British Educational Research Journal, 33*(6), 927–942. https://doi.org/10.1080/01411920701657033
Lundy, L., Tobin, J., & Parkes, A. (2019). Art. 12 The right to respect for the views of the child. In *The UN convention on the rights of the child: A commentary*. Oxford University Press. https://opil.ouplaw.com/display/10.1093/law/9780198262657.001.0001/law-9780198262657
Markina, A., & Märtson, M. (2008). *Alaealiste karistuste tulemuslikkus*. https://www.kriminaalpoliitika.ee/sites/krimipoliitika/files/elfinder/dokumendid/alaealiste_karistuste_tulemuslikkus._tartu_ulikooli_oigusinstituut._2008.pdf
Markina, A., Strömpl, J., Tamm, G., Ilves, K., Luhamaa, K., Ginter, J., Tubelt, E., Puur, S. M., Roos, L., Espenberg, S., TÜ Sotsiaalteaduslike Rakendusuuringute Keskus, & Justiitsministeerium. (2021). *Noorte õigusrikkujate uuring*. https://skytte.ut.ee/sites/default/files/2022-04/noorte_oigusrikkujate_uuring_lopparuanne_22.10.2021.pdf
Mayall, B. (2002). *Towards a sociology for childhood: Thinking from children's lives*. Open University Press.
Mayall, B. (2015). Understanding inter-generational relations: The case of health maintenance by children. *Sociology of Health and Illness, 37*(2), 312–324. https://doi.org/10.1111/1467-9566.12227

McEwan-Strand, A., & Skivenes, M. (2020). Children's capacities and role in matters of great significance for them: An analysis of the Norwegian county boards' decision-making in cases about adoption from care. *The International Journal of Children's Rights, 28*(3), 632–665. https://doi.org/10.1163/15718182-02803006

McMellon, C., & Tisdall, E. K. M. (2020). Children and young people's participation rights: Looking backwards and moving forwards. *The International Journal of Children's Rights, 28*(1), 157–182. https://doi.org/10.1163/15718182-02801002

No. 3-1-2-4-14, 2-21-10886 (Tallinna Ringkonnakohus 9 November 2023).

Peleg, N. (2019a). International children's rights law: General principles. In U. Kilkelly & T. Liefaard (Eds.), *International human rights of children* (pp. 135–157). Springer. https://doi.org/10.1007/978-981-10-4184-6_5

Peleg, N. (2019b). *The child's right to development*. Cambridge University Press.

Penal Code (*Karistusseadustik*), RT I 2001, 61, 364; RT I, 06.01.2023, 1 (2002). https://www.riigiteataja.ee/en/eli/520032023010/consolide

Pösö, T., & Enroos, R. (2017). The representation of children's views in Finnish court decisions regarding care orders. *The International Journal of Children's Rights, 25*(3–4), 736–753. https://doi.org/10.1163/15718182-02503009

Rannala, I.-E. (2014). *Dialoogi olulisus töös riskikäitumisega noortega. Alaealiste komisjonide näitel*. Tallinn University.

Rannala, I.-E., Tiko, A. T., & Rohtla, A. (2006). Käitumisraskustega noored ja neile määratud mõjutusvahendite kohaldamine alaealiste komisjonides. *Justiitsministeerium*. https://www.kriminaalpoliitika.ee/sites/krimipoliitika/files/elfinder/dokumendid/kaitumisraskustega_noored_ja_neile_maaratud_mojutusvahendite_kohandamine_alaealiste_komisjonides._ie._rannala_a.tiko_a._rohtla._2006.pdf

Reynaert, D., Bouverne-de-Bie, M., & Vandevelde, S. (2009). A review of children's rights literature since the adoption of the united nations convention on the rights of the child. *Childhood, 16*(4), 518–534. https://doi.org/10.1177/0907568209344270

Ristikivi, M., Kangur, A., Kull, I., Luhamaa, K., Sedman, M., Siimets-Gross, H., & Värv, A. (2023). An introduction to Estonian legal culture. In S. Koch & M. M. Kjølstad (Eds.), *Handbook on legal cultures* (pp. 389–418). Springer International Publishing. https://doi.org/10.1007/978-3-031-27745-0_11

Skivenes, M., & Sørsdal, L. M. (2018). The child's best interest principle across child protection jurisdictions. In *Human rights in child protection* (pp. 59–88). Palgrave Macmillan. https://doi.org/10.1007/978-3-319-94800-3_4

Social Welfare Act (*Sotsiaalhoolekande seadus*), RT I, 30.12.2015, 5; RT I, 30.06.2023, 73 (2015). https://www.riigiteataja.ee/en/eli/530042020006/consolide

Statistikaamet. (2023). *SK031: Perekonnast eraldatud lapsed*. SK31. https://andmed.stat.ee/et/stat/sotsiaalelu__sotsiaalne-kaitse__sotsiaalabi__vanemliku-hoolitsuseta-lapsed/SK031

Strand Lobben et al v. Norway (GC), 37283/13 (echr 2019). http://hudoc.echr.coe.int/eng?i=001-178877

Strömpl, J., & Luhamaa, K. (2020). Child participation in child welfare removals through the looking glass: Estonian children's and professionals' perspectives compared. *Children and Youth Services Review, 118*, 105421. https://doi.org/10.1016/j.childyouth.2020.105421

Tarto, L., Kalda, L., Haljasmets, K., Kaldmaa, K., Tomla, A., & Pedjasaar, M. (2022). *Kinnise lasteasutuse teenusele suunatud laste riskitegurid*. Haap Consulting.

The Constitution of the Republic of Estonia (*Põhiseadus*), RT 1992, 26, 349 (1992).

Tisdall, E. K. M. (2015). Children and young people's participation: A critical consideration of Article 12. In *Routledge international handbook of children's rights studies*. Routledge.

Tobin, J., & Cashmore, J. (2019). Article 19. The RIght to protection against all forms of violence. In *The UN convention on the rights of the child: a commentary* (1st ed., pp. 687–724). Oxford University Press.

Tobin, J., & Eekelaar, J. (2019). Article 3. The best interests of the child. In *The UN convention on the rights of the child: A commentary* (1st ed., pp. 73–107). Oxford University Press.

Tobin, J., & Varadan, S. (2019). Article 5. The rights to parental direction and guidance consistent with a child's evolving capacities. In *The UN convention on the rights of the child: A commentary* (1st ed., pp. 159–185). Oxford University Press.

Toivonen, V.-M., Toivonen, V., Muhonen, J., Luhamaa, K., Kalliomaa-Puha, L., & Strömpl, J. (2019). Child participation in Estonian and Finnish child welfare removals: Professionals' perceptions and practices. *The International Journal of Children's Rights, 29*(3), 701–730. https://doi.org/10.1163/15718182-29030009

Vis, S. A., & Fossum, S. (2013). Representation of children's views in court hearings about custody and parental visitations—A comparison between what children wanted and what the courts ruled. *Children and Youth Services Review, 35*(12), 2101–2109. https://doi.org/10.1016/j.childyouth.2013.10.015

Zehr, H. (2015). *Little book of restorative justice: Revised and updated* (2nd ed.). Good Books.

Katre Luhamaa is Associate Professor of European and Comparative Law at the University of Tartu. Her main areas of research are international and European protection of child rights and their national implementation. Her second area of research focuses on legal culture and development and the recognition and implementation of values such as human rights and children's rights within the legal system. Her expertise spans law and legal studies, human rights and democracy, EU and European studies, and legal theory. She has made significant contributions to the field of children's rights with her research focusing on international law, EU law, and human rights, particularly children's rights.

Anna Markina is a researcher at the School of Law, University of Tartu. Her research focuses on youth delinquency, juvenile justice system, victims of crime, and trafficking in human beings. She has conducted quantitative and qualitative research with young juvenile offenders on probation and parole, in prisons and reformatories, addressing the rights of the child, the effectiveness of interventions, and young people's response to them. She is a member of a steering committee of the international Self-Report Delinquency Study (ISRD).

Kristi Paron is a children's rights lawyer. For the last 10 years, she has worked as an adviser to the Children's Ombudsperson in Estonia. She holds a PhD in sociology and master's degree in law from the University of Tartu and MCR (Master of Advanced Studies) in children's rights from the University of Geneva, the Centre for Children's Rights Studies. Her PhD at the University of Tartu analyses child-patient autonomy. In her research, she bridges children's rights and childhood sociology, focusing on the relationality of rights. In her daily practice, she is devoted to raising awareness on children's rights and sensitising society to children's views and needs.

Chapter 10
Childhood Vulnerability: Trauma-Aware Approaches for Building Resilience in Traumatised Children

Judit Strömpl and Beata Žarkovski

10.1 Introduction

The beginning of a human life is full of vulnerability linked to the total dependence of infants and young children on their carers. But every human being is born with a capacity to be active—to interact with the people around them. By crying, babies signal that they are present and have needs. It is the first sign of a child's potential agency. The development of a child's agency depends to a large extent on how those around the child—the environment—respond to the child's ability to interact with carers. Relationships imply different qualities of tension. Stress is natural and even necessary to living organisms (Panksepp, 1998). But stress can also be harmful. Resilience to stress is individual to a certain extent—different people react differently to similar stressors. Human childhood can be full of stressful events and relationships. These can be frightening events or unfavourable relationships with immediate caregivers that produce toxic stress in the child (Panksepp & Biven, 2012; Perry, 2008; Siegel, 2012; van der Kolk, 2005, 2015). The experience of toxic stress is referred to as trauma, which can have far-reaching effects on a child's development and the rest of their life (Burke Harris, 2020; Carliner et al., 2016; Choi, 2018; Choi et al., 2017; Danielson et al., 2009; Fang et al., 2022; Fereidooni et al., 2023; Groth et al., 2020; Hoover et al., 2022; Kelleher et al., 2013; Mayer et al., 2021; van der Kolk, 2015; Wang et al., 2022; Yang et al., 2022). Trauma can exacerbate vulnerability and lead to a range of illnesses and behavioural problems.

J. Strömpl (✉)
Institute of Social Studies, University of Tartu, Tartu, Estonia
e-mail: judit.strompl@ut.ee

B. Žarkovski
School of Law, University of Tartu, Tartu, Estonia
e-mail: beata.zarkovski@ut.ee

D. Kutsar et al. (eds.), *Child Vulnerability and Vulnerable Subjectivity*, Children's Well-Being: Indicators and Research 27,
https://doi.org/10.1007/978-3-031-61333-3_10

Untreated childhood trauma is seen as the root of the world's rapidly growing mental health problems (Maté & Maté, 2022; Perry & Winfrey, 2021). However, traumatic events and relationships do not always have a negative impact. Adverse childhood experiences and toxic relationships can be the basis for the development of health problems, on the one hand, but can also support individual strengths and resilience, on the other (Masten, 2015; Masten & Reed, 2002). Humans experience the full range of threats and have access to protective mechanisms, but they do not always know how or are not always able to use them. The key is for adults working with children to be aware of childhood traumas, to eliminate as much as possible toxic stressors when interacting with children, recognise the signs of trauma and know how to respond and cope with them appropriately. Resilience may be the result of an individual's resistance to adverse experiences, but we must not rely on this alone.

Along with an awareness of the impact of childhood trauma, trauma-aware, trauma-informed, trauma-sensitive or trauma responsive approaches[1] have been developed in different areas of children's lives (Blaustein & Kinniburgh, 2019; Burke Harris, 2020; Panlilio, 2019; Strand & Sprang, 2018; Treisman, 2017).

In this chapter, we provide an overview of the concept of childhood trauma, which is the most extreme manifestation of childhood vulnerability; the negative consequences of trauma to child development; the growth of trauma awareness and existing measures to reduce the negative consequences of trauma and support the building of resilience. A trauma-aware approach needs to be mainstreamed in all areas of children's lives, starting with the family, child welfare, education and health policy, children's participation in the justice system and ending with children's involvement in research. We aim to show how skilful trauma-aware approaches can reduce childhood vulnerability and risks of harm and support children's resilience.

10.2 Competing Definitions of Childhood Trauma

Definitions of trauma broadly fall into two categories: an *event-driven* definition, and a *relation-driven* trauma definition. The most used event-driven definition is presented by Substance Abuse and Mental Health Services Administration (SAMHSA). SAMHSA defines trauma as the following:

> Individual trauma results from an event, series of events, or set of circumstances that is experienced by an individual as physically or emotionally harmful or life threatening and that has lasting adverse effects on the individual's functioning and mental, physical, social, emotional, or spiritual well-being. (2014, p. 7)

The event-driven definition is, however, limited and many experts in child psychology and psychiatry apply a more complex definition of childhood trauma

[1] Of the many terms in use, we prefer here to use the term trauma-aware, which we believe, is the broadest, best captures the notion and best fits with the concepts of our book.

introducing the notion of developmental trauma disorder (DTD), which focuses on relationships (D'Andrea et al., 2012; van der Kolk, 2005; van der Kolk & d'Andrea, 2010). These authors provide a relation-driven trauma definition and focus on the impact of interpersonal trauma on child development (Blaustein & Kinniburgh, 2019; D'Andrea et al., 2012; Maté & Maté, 2022; Perry, 2009; Spinazzola et al., 2018; van der Kolk, 2005, 2015). They extend the event-driven definition to include other overwhelming childhood experiences, often occurring within the attachment relationship, such as neglect, psychological maltreatment, attachment separations, and impaired caregiving systems. Authors (Spinazzola et al., 2021; van der Kolk, 2005) speak about traumatic victimisation which is connected not only with one event or a series of events but based on the traumatic relations between children and their direct caregivers. Studies show that exposure to interpersonal trauma in childhood can chronically and pervasively alter the social, psychological, cognitive, and biological development of a child (Blaustein & Kinniburgh, 2019; Cook et al., 2005; D'Andrea et al., 2012; Spinazzola et al., 2018; van der Kolk, 2015). "Developmental trauma disorder (DTD) has been proposed as an integrative framework for assessing and treating children's emotional, biological, cognitive, behavioural, interpersonal, and self/identity dysregulation in the wake of traumatic victimisation and disrupted attachment" (Spinazzola et al., 2018, p. 631). Undoubtedly, all kinds of traumatic events have an impact on a person, whether child or adult. However, DTD emphasises the interpersonal nature of trauma, which has profoundly detrimental effects on a child's development because it destroys the child's trust in other people.

The term post-traumatic stress disorder (PTSD) is used to describe the consequences of both event-driven and relationship-driven trauma (DTD). But DTD specifies PTSD symptoms and adds the very important interpersonal aspect. "Developmental trauma disorder (DTD) is a childhood syndrome that was formulated to complement and extend the post-traumatic stress disorder (PTSD) diagnosis with 15 symptoms of emotional/somatic, cognitive/behavioural, and self/relational dysregulation" (Spinazzola et al., 2021, p. 711). The study presented in the same article (Spinazzola et al., 2021, p. 718) and other sources (Morelli & Villodas, 2022) provide evidence from empirical studies confirming the validity of DTD symptoms.

Along with DTD, the notion of complex childhood trauma was developed. It was first conceptualised by Judith Herman in 1992 and further developed by well-known child development researchers (Briere & Spinnazola, 2005; Courtois, 2004; van der Kolk & Courtois, 2005; van der Kolk, 2015). In short, if long-term child maltreatment—relational stress—is combined with multiple traumatic events, such as violence between parents, bullying at school, loss of a loved one etc. then a complex trauma is indicated (Briere & Spinnazola, 2005; van der Kolk & Courtois, 2005; van der Kolk, 2015; Treisman, 2017). A person who has experienced complex trauma is characterised by several alterations in their sense of self and their understanding of the reality and relationships around them (van der Kolk & Courtois, 2005).

Some authors (Asmussen et al., 2020; Felitti et al., 1998) use another term for expressing childhood trauma—adverse childhood experiences (ACEs). ACEs bring together both event-centred and relationship-centred trauma approaches and focus on the impact of childhood traumatic stress on human development. In 1998 the first publication about a large population study by the Kaiser Permanente's San Diego Health Appraisal Clinic was published where 10 categories of ACEs were indicated, including childhood physical, sexual, and emotional abuse, physical and emotional neglect, witnessing of domestic violence, living with a substance abusing, mentally ill, or incarcerated family member, and parental separation or divorce (Felitti et al., 1998).

Some authors (Burke Harris, 2020; Maté & Maté, 2022), while defining trauma, point to its links with the broader cultural context, which includes the factors that generate toxic stress in human relationships, including relations between family members and specifically parents and children. Toxic stressors in the relationship between a child and their parents or carers are not always conscious and deliberate child abuse. Parents, carers, teachers may think they are acting out of sincere love, scolding, punishing their child or imposing their will (Maté & Maté, 2022).

In any case, the different definitions and the narrower and broader interpretations of childhood trauma show that it is an extremely complex problem that is not easy to prevent (considering the general toxic stress within human culture) and even more difficult to cope with the consequences. Next, we provide a brief overview of how childhood trauma can be harmful to a child's development. We need this to understand more clearly which of the child's needs must be met to support recovery from childhood trauma.

10.3 Childhood Trauma and the Child's Development

Leading child psychologists, brain researchers and psychiatrists have reached a new understanding of the impact of childhood trauma on child development. This knowledge is based on attachment theory (Bowlby, 1953, 1988) and interpersonal victimisation theory (Spinazzola et al., 2021; van der Kolk, 2015).

Spinazzola et al. (2021) distinguish between two types of developmental trauma: one type is associated with interpersonal victimisation, the other with traumatic disruption with an immediate caregiver. The criteria focus on the child's emotional and somatic reactions, behavioural regulation and inability to regulate relationships and the self. The symptoms of DTD are represented in four diagnostic criteria (A, B, C, D) and each of the criteria have 2–6 subcriteria[2] (Spinazzola et al., 2021, p. 712). Research (Carliner et al., 2016; Fereidooni et al., 2023; Lucero et al., 2022; Morelli & Villodas, 2022) confirms the adequacy of these symptoms and shows how untreated childhood DTDs influence the person's whole life. Many publications have been published in recent years exploring the impact of childhood trauma on a range of human physical (Burke Harris, 2020; Felitti et al., 1998; Hughes et al., 2017; Kalmakis & Chandel, 2015; Maté, 2003) and mental health (Choi et al., 2017; de Koning et al., 2022; Fang et al., 2022; Groth et al., 2020; Hong et al., 2023;

[2] Space constraints do not allow us to go into more detail on these criteria.

LeMoult et al., 2020; Mayer et al., 2021; Wiss & Brewerton, 2020), behavioural problems (Danielson et al., 2009; Hoover et al., 2022; Liu et al., 2021), including offending behaviour (Santo et al., 2023; Yang et al., 2022).

As mentioned earlier, traumatic relations are not always conscious acts by a caregiver to harm the child. If the direct caregiver is under too much stress, if they are an addict, depressed, constantly dealing with their own problems, they may not even notice that the child needs their attention and may not respond in time and in the right way to the signals given by the child (van der Kolk & Courtois, 2005). If this happens continuously and over a long period of time, the child learns that their needs are not being met and so they stop signalling their needs and in the long run loses control of the fact that they have any needs (Perry & Szalavitz, 2006/2017; van der Kolk, 2015). If the carer is responsive at times and unresponsive at other times, this also confuses the child. In the long run, the child may lose adequate contact with the outside world, which will be followed by losing contact also with the inside world. This can be an unconscious *unresolved attachment relationship* between parent/carer and child, which also has long-lasting effects on the child's development and is reflected in the child's behaviour; for example, lack of communication skills, mistrust, and tension even in situations that would not cause anxiety in a child who has grown up in a normal attachment relationship (van der Kolk 2015). In any case, when a child experiences physical, sexual, or other forms of abuse, abandonment and neglect, the traumas they have suffered leave deep and long-lasting effects on the child's development and on their life, even if they do not remember them or are not aware of the links between their problems and their past trauma. Why does this happen? Biopsychologists answer this question as follows. In the presence of toxic stress, which is manifested by a strong feeling of fear, cortisol overproduction occurs and can harm a child's brain development. Traumatic events and relationships may be "forgotten" because of cortisol overproduction (Panksepp & Biven, 2012).

Jaak Panksepp (Panksepp & Biven, 2012) studied the effects of stress on brain chemistry in animal experiments and explained the difference between the effects of *normal* and *toxic* stress on the body. During normal stress the body produces cortisol, which helps the body to encode its own strength and react in a threat situation.

> Under optimal conditions when an animal is afraid, the secretion of cortisol mobilizes glucose as an energy supply for the skeletal muscles in case the animal decides to flee. In this way, cortisol secretion is beneficial. However, excessive secretion can begin to damage the body if elevations are sustained for too long. Normally when cortisol has circulated through the blood back up to the brain, the paraventricular nucleus (PVN) of the hypothalamus exerts an inhibitory effect that stops further release of cortisol. If, however, a person or animal is subjected to an excessive amount of stress—when they are chronically frightened or anxious—the PVN may not be able to stop the production of cortisol. (Panksepp & Biven, 2012, p.9)

Cortisol overproduction can severely damage the body and can be the cause of various diseases, including memory deficits.

10.3.1 The Consequences of Childhood Trauma in Adulthood

In the late 90 s, Kaiser Permanente's San Diego Health Appraisal Clinic developed and introduced the adverse childhood experiences (ACEs) survey, which is a self-reported retrospective questionnaire completed by people with health problems (Felitti et al., 1998). All patients who admitted to the hospital with a health problem of any kind were asked to complete the questionnaire with questions about ACEs. It turned out that if a patient experienced four or more childhood adversities, a link between the adversity and the health problem was established (Asmussen et al., 2020). The ACEs questionnaire is now in use around the world and collects evidence on the link between childhood trauma and health problems. However, this method also raises some doubts about whether retrospective information can be taken as ironclad evidence. It is well known that people do not always remember the harsh treatment they experienced in childhood. There are also several ethical challenges regarding ACEs; for example, whether it is appropriate to leave a person alone with such difficult memories when filling in the questionnaire and the fact the anonymity of the respondents is not guaranteed when filling in these questionnaires, to mention just a few (Asmussen et al., 2020). At the same time, since the ACEs screening has been adopted, a very large volume of scientific texts building on the findings of the screening have been published, which are certainly useful in developing trauma-informed prevention and policies for children in various settings.

Childhood trauma is most directly associated with various psychiatric diseases such as depression and anxiety (Lester et al., 2014; Lucero et al., 2022; Mayer et al., 2021; Wang et al., 2022;), panic disorder (Hong et al., 2023), as well as schizophrenia, and rumination (Fang et al., 2022). Associations are found also between childhood trauma and inflammatory, immune and cancer diseases (de Koning et al., 2022; Felitti et al., 1998; Maté, 2003; Maté & Maté, 2022), and eating disorders (Groth et al., 2020). Studies find links between childhood trauma and behavioural problems, particularly offending behaviour (Santo et al., 2023; Yang et al., 2022).

Yang et al. (2022) has investigated associations between childhood trauma and antisocial personality disorder (ASPD) and borderline personality disorder (BPD) among Chinese adult male prisoners. Specifically, the effects of childhood trauma on the development of ASPD and BPD and on the ability of emotional self-regulation (ER) among prisoners were examined (Yang et al., 2022). The study confirms that ASPD and BPD are two common personality disorders among prisoners. Difficulties in ER are key to understanding the links between childhood trauma and personality disorders. Childhood trauma contributes to ASPD, BPD, and suicidal behaviour in adult prisoners. Difficulties in ER play a partial mediating role between childhood trauma, ASPD and BPD, and the mediating effect varies across different dimensions of ER. Researchers suggest that multiple types of ER interventions are needed to reduce mental health problems and increase resilience in vulnerable populations (Yang et al., 2022).

People with a history of childhood trauma are also more likely to become victims of crime, including cyber-victimisation (Fereidooni et al., 2023; Akarsu et al., 2022).

The link between childhood trauma and addictions is increasingly confirmed. Including addictions to various substances and activities (Carliner et al., 2016; Choi et al., 2017; Danielson et al., 2009; Maté & Maté, 2022; Santo et al., 2023) but also food addiction (Groth et al., 2020; Hoover et al., 2022).

To summarise the above brief and limited overview of the impact of childhood trauma, it is important to be aware that childhood trauma, both relational and event-related, creates in children a deep sense of insecurity and distrust of the people around them. This is expressed in inappropriate reactions of children, adolescents, and adults, where there is no real reason to feel threatened. The toxic stress of insecurity turns on the individual, which eventually manifests itself in illness and/or hostility towards those around them. Aggression, manipulation, harming others and oneself, substance abuse and offending behaviour are as a rule the results of untreated childhood trauma (Maté & Maté, 2022).

Fortunately, the risks of childhood trauma are surmountable if there is trauma awareness and potential to deal with childhood vulnerability. In the next subsection, we will explore the signs of trauma and how trauma-aware professionals working with children can help them to heal from trauma and how trauma-informed care can support building resilience in children.

10.4 Trauma Awareness: Noticing the Signs of Trauma, Coping with Childhood Trauma and Building Resilience in Children

Trauma awareness starts with adults knowing the signs of trauma and recognising them in the behaviour of the children they work with. This is not an easy task, as certain peculiarities in children's behaviour may be linked to age-related characteristics and do not always have to be the result of traumatic experiences; for example, non-compliant behaviour, rebellion and testing different norms, including trying prohibited substances. As a rule, these behaviours disappear on their own when the child realises that they are not satisfying and do not lead to the expected goal. But it is worth paying attention to, because if the child has experienced trauma, the response should be quick and appropriate. It is better to err on the side of reacting where there is no risk of harm than to overlook a child in need. The longer children's traumatic experiences and associated symptoms remain neglected, the more likely they are to experience profound psychological problems that will reflect in their behaviours (Cook et al., 2005), including substance use, self-injuries and suicidal behaviour (Scott & Anglin, 2015). In this context, substance use and self-harm are coping mechanisms to mask the pain caused by isolation, anger, loneliness, loss and grief, and emotional pain (Scott & Anglin, 2015). In addition, one must be alert when children's behaviour changes, when they suddenly go from being a good child to a problem child—this change needs to be noticed and responded to. Behavioural problems of all kinds—excessive shyness, self-containment, shutting others out, or, conversely, excessive aggression, clinging to others, imposing one's own will, disobeying adult instructions, arrogant or rude behaviour towards others, squeezing things and money out of others, any kind of delinquent behaviour, manipulative behaviour—all these can indicate that a child is experiencing adversity. There is a widespread belief, especially among teachers, that bad behaviour is a child's way of getting attention. This is a correct statement that needs a trauma-informed response.

There is a rich literature on evidence-based trauma-informed approaches to coping with childhood trauma. They are characterised by a child-centred approach and a deep understanding of what happens to a child when they experience complex relational and developmental trauma.

Blaustein and Kinniburgh (2019) developed their trauma-informed care model on the Attachment, Self-regulation and Competency (ARC) framework. ARC is:

> … a four-level framework, in which overarching goals (i.e., strengthening the caregiving system) are supported by addressing specific treatment targets (i.e., supporting parent-child attunement); which in turn are supported by addressing and building specific skills (i.e., cultivating maternal curiosity about child behaviours) through the use of a range of intervention techniques (i.e., engaging a parent in a structured daily detective activity about his or her child). (Blaustein & Kinniburgh, 2019, p. 40)

According to Blaustein and Kinniburgh (2019), traumatic stress overwhelms developing children's limited emotion management skills and forces them to either disconnect from their emotions and body sensations or use inappropriate or unhealthy coping skills. Children who have experienced inadequate early care and/or inadequate emotional support may never have developed the ability to identify and express emotions. Other children may have developed limited skills that are overloaded and fragmented. Because of these factors, children who have experienced trauma are often disconnected or unaware of their emotional experience. Difficulties in recognising emotions can manifest themselves in several ways. The earliest regulatory problem is mainly physiological (sleeping, attentive communication, eating and toileting). This regulation is largely supported by external or simultaneous caregiver regulation. Over time, the regulation of experience moves from being mainly externally structured to mainly internally directed, although we continue to use significant others as resources for regulation throughout life. All the skills involved in regulation progress from basic to increasingly complex. For example, from a basic internal state of "I feel bad" to a more sophisticated state of "I am frustrated or worried" (Blaustein & Kinniburgh, 2019).

The care system plays an important role in the successful development of the regulatory system. Over time, caregivers contribute to the development of a child's healthy self-regulation. Important behavioural regulation techniques include *reflection, modelling, stimulation and calming*. Reflecting the child's experience (verbally and behaviourally) through the caregiver's facial expressions, words and actions, the child learns to interpret their experience. Competent affect regulation communicates to the child that affect is tolerable and the child is acceptable (Blaustein & Kinniburgh, 2019; see also Siegel & Bryson, 2012; Tomlinson, 2004; Treisman, 2017).

Another important component of trauma-informed care is modelling. Expressing and modelling caregivers' own feelings provides a visual language for understanding as well as coping with the effects. The child learns to *read* verbal expressions, facial expressions as well as other non-verbal signs of emotion with associated experiences. Through modelling, the child learns that intense affect is also normal and that there are strategies that can be used to manage and tolerate it, and that it does not last forever (Blaustein & Kinniburgh, 2019; see also examples of Life Story Work (LSW) in Chap. 13).

Stimulation and calming are the next important elements of trauma-informed care. By providing a harmonised behavioural approach, the carer can support the child to reach an optimal level and provide alternating stimulation and reward. When energy levels become overwhelming, the child will respond appropriately; for example, with high (intense) or low (sleepiness) stress. The caregiver's words, tone of voice and behaviour become the physiological source of calming the child. Gradually the child masters these skills and begins to maintain a comfortable state independently (Blaustein & Kinniburgh, 2019; see also Siegel & Bryson, 2012).

When the caregiver is unresponsive, inconsistent, or abusive, infants and young children rely on primitive modulation skills (e.g., rocking, thumb sucking, dissociation) to calm their affect. Children who have experienced trauma often feel shame, isolation, the need to hide and that they are somehow damaged. They may believe that there is something wrong with them, that they are different, and that strong emotions are a sign of *craziness*, of feeling bad or out of control (Blaustein & Kinniburgh, 2019).

The authors (e.g., Blaustein & Kinniburgh, 2019) also draw attention to the importance of letting it be known from the beginning that the caregiver is interested in the whole child. The adaptive nature of disturbing behaviour must be confirmed. It is necessary to identify the role these behaviours play in the child's life. For example, if a child is aggressive with peers we might say, "It seems important for you to show others how strong you are". The child needs to be taught what a trauma reaction is, the trigger and the links with past experience and the current reaction. Understanding a person's victim response and its current role in dysregulated or self-defensive behaviour is an important step in giving the child some control and reducing the child's sense of stigma. It is important to distinguish between past and present events and, by working with the child on protective and adaptive behaviours in the present, to signal that the behaviours of the past may no longer be as useful in the present (Blaustein & Kinniburgh, 2019).

Bad behaviour of children, and especially teenagers, such as offences, substance abuse, aggressive and violent behaviour, as a rule, provokes the perception in adults that if such a child is not punished, they will develop a feeling of impunity which will lead them down a criminal path. But this is a wrong reaction. Young offenders also need trauma-informed care, not punishment (Evans et al., 2020). Punishment only exacerbates the child's isolation and stigmatisation and does nothing to help them make sense of their own traumatic experience and link it to their problematic behaviour. So instead of punishment, the child's experience of trauma needs to be dealt with care as recommended by the world's leading psychologists and psychiatrists, to whom we refer repeatedly in this chapter.

10.4.1 Resilience

In parallel with the research on the harmful effects of childhood trauma, another branch of research on children developed which drew attention to the fact that children who grow up in very adverse circumstances do not always become ill or engage in criminal behaviour but do well and sometimes even do very well (Blaustein & Kinniburgh, 2019; Masten, 2014, 2015; Masten & Reed, 2002; NCTSN; Treisman, 2017; Ungar et al., 2013). That is, traumatic conditions do not always produce the expected results in terms of child development. Researchers explained this sort of development in terms of an individual's ability to cope. Experiments on animals show that the individual response to toxic stress may differ (Panksepp & Biven, 2012).

Resilience has been described as a successful adaptation despite harsh circumstances. The following two quotations from Ann Masten give a good overview of the notion of resilience, which we also share:

> Resilience can be broadly defined as the capacity of a dynamic system to adapt successfully to disturbances that threaten system function, viability, or development. (Masten 2014, p. 6)

> Human adaptation and development are shaped by many interactions across levels, ranging from the molecular level to social and ecological systems. Therefore, the development of a child or adult, including that person's potential or manifested resilience, will be influenced by many interactions within the individual (genetic, neural, immunological, cognitive, etc.) and also between the person and the environment, including interactions with family, peers, school, community, and the natural and built environment. (Masten, 2015, p. 187)

Successful adaptation is characterised as involving positive and successful learning, completion of secondary education, positive social integration, or good communication skills, making friends and intimate relationships, coping with work tasks, displaying law-abiding behaviour and being relatively healthy physically and mentally. But it is not enough to have had a difficult childhood to define resilience. The childhood must be highly traumatic—characterised by such things as an adverse pregnancy, motherhood too young, premature birth, parental divorce, abuse, poverty, and homelessness, and the experience of massive community-based trauma such as war or other disaster. Such a confluence of risks is called cumulative risk. These risk factors predict one or more risks to normal child development (Masten & Reed, 2002).

Masten (2015), in a short article, gives a comprehensive overview of developments in the science of resilience, pointing out a number of peculiarities and evidence between the theories and levels of research on resilience that have been done so far. She distinguishes between individual, family, community and societal levels of resilience to the consequences of traumatic events; considers resilience as interactions of systems; looks at different qualities of traumatic risks—wars, disasters, economic hazards and epidemics and their impact on individuals, families, communities and societies. She analyses the contributions of different scientific disciplines to the study of resilience—neurobiological or brain research; developmental research; psychological or life-course and longitudinal research; pathway research—and concludes that much is already known about how adverse childhood experiences affect the functioning of different systems, which she considers to be as individual, family, community and society. At the same time, there are still many questions and challenges that need to be explored in order to be certain about what actually contributes to overcoming the various adverse traumatic events and relationships that pose a range of risks to the functioning of systems, and which can also underpin resilience—positive adaptation.

Vulnerability and resilience are connected with each other and may be abstractly marked at the two ends of the same scale: vulnerability on the one end and resilience at the other (see Chap. 2). However, this relation is not linear, but can be influenced by time, situation, relations, and structural characteristics (Virokannas et al., 2018). Of these components, we emphasise the central role of relations. The quality of relations between people is influenced by the structural quality of the actors participating in interactions, the timing, and the context.

Llistosella et al. (2022) conducted an integrative systematic review of literature to construct a conceptual model for building resilience in children and young people. They succeeded in creating a new dynamic and evidence-based model of resilience—the Individual and Environmental Resilience Model (IERM), which identifies environmental and individual protective factors. Among the individual domains, the authors consider biological, behavioural, communicative, cognitive, and emotional skills. Among the environmental factors, family, school, peers, culture, and community are highlighted. These domains contain protective mechanisms that prevent the negative impact of adverse situations; that is, they help build resilience in children and young people. On the one hand, it is an old truth that good relationships in the family and at school, with peers and adults in the community, and the culture of communication, in general, along with a high level of individual cognitive ability, good communication skills, and emotional self-regulation, have a significant impact on a child's well-being. So, support for the development of resilience must also build on this old knowledge which is now finding new evidence (Llistosella et al., 2022).

In the next part of the chapter, we summarise the insights that have emerged from the theoretical review into the risk factors of trauma as realised vulnerability, on the one hand, and protective factors as the basis for building resilience, on the other. We will look at how all these risk and protective factors appear in the different areas of children's lives presented in the different chapters of the current book.

10.5 Discussion and Conclusion

The previous chapters of this book show how relations with children in different areas of children's lives affect their vulnerability and well-being. How children interact within their families (Chap. 5), at school (Chap. 6), with doctors in the health system (Chap. 7), in the digital environment (Chap. 8), in the legal system (Chap. 9), and in substitute care (Chap. 13) also determines how their agency, positive identity, and autonomy develop. Interactions in which subjectivity and intersubjectivity are expressed (see the book's introduction) determine how children cope with the stresses of childhood, which certainly exist and, as we know from studies, are necessary for healthy human development. The kind of relationships we as adults develop with children in different areas of their/our common lives has a great effect on children's development, and their current and future well-being.

For example, in the family (Chap. 5), the source of trauma for children can be the separation of parents if the child is not spoken to, the situation is not explained, and decisions are made without taking into account the child's opinion, and the trauma can be compounded if the parents cannot resolve their problems with each other when the child would like to restore the wholeness of their biological family. Trauma can be mitigated by taking the child's feelings into account, even if the child is always caught in the middle of the problem (to not leave the child alone). School trauma can be prevented by teachers' good life skills and by not personalising difficult situations in the classroom, by treating pupils ethically and equally, by paying attention to pupils' needs, by listening to and respecting them, by creating friendship and a sense of belonging in the classroom (Chap. 6). In different settings such as education, healthcare, justice, or the welfare system, children must be treated holistically as an individual, a subject who is competent according to their current capabilities. By competence, we mean the ability to communicate information about one's condition, either verbally or non-verbally. It is the responsibility of adults to be able to read this information and, in turn, to inform the child about what is happening in child-friendly language. This ensures that the child's participation in the relationship is realised, which is crucial for both reducing childhood vulnerability and building resilience.

At the time of our studies, there were two phenomena taking place around the world that also affected children. We are talking about the COVID-19 pandemic and the war launched by Russia against neighbouring Ukraine. While the pandemic locked families in their homes, the war, on the contrary, drove them out—Ukrainian refugees appeared in other European countries, including Estonia. Here we can talk about situational and temporal aspects of vulnerability and resilience. Chapters 11 and 12 of the book deal with how children's lives changed in relation to these phenomena and how these difficult situations were resolved. Again, the relationship between the responsible adults and the children emerges, and again, as we can see in the above-mentioned chapters, children's well-being in these situations depended on the actions of the adults.

To some extent, this links with the research on ethics and methodology (Chap. 3). It is about how it could be the task of every adult, in dealing with every child, to be trauma-informed and to contribute to the child's development—to the development of agency and autonomy of any child. Child-friendly relationships include therapeutic effects for both the child and the adult. The researchers, especially the ones who conduct face-to-face data collection (Chap. 12, Chap. 13), but also those who give children structured questionnaires to fill in (e.g., Chap. 14), in the way that they interact with them and the way the topics under study are introduced and the way the questions are asked, have a certain influence on children as questionnaire fillers. This should be considered, and a trauma-informed approach should also be followed in the research.

And while we are talking about vulnerability and resilience being at two ends of the same scale (Chap. 2), we also must argue that life's hardships, those that have gone hand in hand with the pandemic and the hosting of refugees, make us vulnerable and at the same time enable development. Both phenomena (COVID and war), as well as an awareness of the risks associated with childhood trauma, guide us, as responsible adults, to develop trauma awareness in our interactions with children. Trauma awareness is not only useful as a way to understand the sources and signs of trauma in a child but also to be aware as an adult of how to avoid causing new trauma. One aspect of this is developing self-reflection skills of one's subjectivity towards the child and empathy towards the child's (un)expected reactions.

Acknowledgement Work on this chapter was supported by a grant from the Estonian Research Council (PRG700).

Competing Interests The authors have no conflicts of interest to declare that are relevant to the content of this chapter.

References

Akarsu, Ö., Budak, M. I., & Okanlı, A. (2022). The relationship of childhood trauma with cyberbulling and cyber victimization among university students. *Archives of Psychiatric Nursing, 41*, 181–187. https://doi.org/10.1016/j.apnu.2022.06.004

Asmussen, K., Fischer, F., Drayton, E., & McBride (2020). *Adverse childhood experiences. What we know, what we don't know, and what should happen next*. https://www.eif.org.uk/report/adverse-childhoodexperiences-what-we-know-what-we-dont-know-and-whatshould-happen-next; http://creativecommons.org/licenses/by-nc-nd/2.0/uk/

Blaustein, M., & Kinniburgh, K. (2019). *Treating traumatic stress in children and adolescents. How to foster resilience through attachment, self-regulation, and competency* (2nd ed.). The Guilford Press.

Bowlby, J. (1953). *Child care and growth of love*. Penguin.

Bowlby, J. (1988). *A secure base*. Routledge.

Briere, J. S., & Spinnazola, J. (2005). Phenomenology and psychological assessment of complex posttraumatic states. *Journal of Traumatic Stress, 18*, 401–412.

Burke Harris, N. (2020). *Toxic childhood stress. The legacy of early trauma and how to heal*. Bluebird.

Carliner, H., Keyes, K. H., McLaughlin, K. A., Meyers, J. L., Dunn, E. C., & Martins, S. S. (2016). Childhood trauma and illicit drug use in adolescence: A population-based national comorbidity survey replication – adolescent supplement study. *Journal of the American Academy of Child & Adolescent Psychiatry, 55*(8), 701–708. https://doi.org/10.1016/j.jaac.2016.05.010

Choi, A. (2018). *Emotional well-being of children and adolescents. Recent trends and relevant factors*. OECD Education Working Papers, No 169. Paris OECD Publishing. doi:https://doi.org/10.1787/41576fb2-en.

Choi, N. G., DiNitto, D. M., Marti, C. N., & Choi, B. Y. (2017). Association of adverse childhood experiences with lifetime mental and substance use disorders among men and women aged 50+ years. *International Psychogeriatrics, 29*(3), 359–372. https://doi.org/10.1017/S1041610216001800

Cook, A., Spinazzola, J., Ford, J. D., Lanktree, C., Blaustein, M., Cloitre, M., et al. (2005). Complex trauma in children and adolescents. *Psychiatric Annals, 35*(5), 390–398.

Courtois, C. A. (2004). Complex trauma reactions: Assessment and treatment. *Psychotherapy: Theory, Research, Practice, Training, 41*(4), 412–425.

D'Andrea, W., Stolbach, B., Ford, J., Spinazzola, J., & van der Kolk, B. (2012). Understanding interpersonal trauma in children: Why we need a developmentally apropriate trauma diagnosis. *American Journal of Orthopsychiatry, 82*(2), 187–200.

Danielson, C. K., Amstadter, A. B., Dangelmaier, R. E., Resnick, H. S., Saunders, B. E., & Kilpatrick, D. G. (2009). Trauma-related risk factors for substance abuse among male versus female young adults. *Addictive Behaviors, 34*(4), 395–399. https://doi.org/10.1016/j.addbeh.2008.11.009

de Koning, R. M., Kuzminskaite, E., Vinkers, C. H., Giltay, E. J., & Penninx, B. W. J. H. (2022). Childhood trauma and LPS-stimulated inflammation in adulthood: Results from the Netherlands study of depression and anxiety. *Brain, Behavior, and Immunity, 106*, 21–29.

Evans, J., Kennedy, D., Skuse, T., & Matthew, J. (2020). Trauma-informed practice and desistance theories. Competing or complementary approaches to working with children in conflict with the law. *Salus Journal, 8*(2), 55–75.

Fang, X., Wu, Z., Wen, L., Wang, D., Yu, L., Wang, Y., Chen, Y., Chen, L., Liu, H., Tang, W., & Zhang, C. (2022). Ruminiation mediates the relationship between childhood trauma and depressive symptoms in schizophrenia patients. *European Archives of Psychiatry and Clinical Neuroscience*. https://doi.org/10.1007/s00406-022-01525-2

Felitti, V. J., Anda, R. F., Nordebberg, D., Williamson, D. F., Spitz, A. M., Edwards, V., et al. (1998). Relationship of childhood abuse and household dysfunction to many of the leading causes of death in adults: The adverse childhood experiences (ACE) study. *American Journal of Preventive Medicine, 14*(4), 245–258.

Fereidooni, F., Daniels, J. K., & Lommen, M. J. J. (2023). Childhood maltreatment and revictimization: A systematic literature review. *Trauma, Violence, and Abuse*. https://doi.org/10.1177/15248380221150475

Groth, T., Hilsenroth, M., Boccio, D., & Gold, J. (2020). Relationship between trauma history and eating disorders in adolescence. *Journal of Child and Adolescent Trauma, 13*, 443–453. https://doi.org/10.1007/s40653-019-00275-z

Herman, J. (1992). Complex PTSD: A syndrome in survivors of prolonged and repeated trauma. *Journal of Traumatic Stress, 5*, 377–391.

Hong, A., Zhou, S., Yang, C., Liu, X., Su, S., & Wang, Z. (2023). Impact of childhood trauma on the abnormal functional connectivity of brain regions in the fear network model of panic disorder. *Journal of Affective Disorders, 329*, 500–510. https://doi.org/10.1016/j.jad.2023.02.128

Hoover, L. V., Yu, H. P., Duval, E. R., & Gearhardt, A. N. (2022). Childhood trauma and food addiction: The role of emotion regulation difficulties and gender differences. *Appetite, 177*. https://doi.org/10.1016/j.appet.2022.106137

Hughes, K., Bellis, M. A., Hardcastle, K. A., Sethi, D., Butchart, A., Mikton, C., Jones, L., & Dunne, M. P. (2017). The effect of multiple adverse childhood experiences on health: A systematic review and meta-analysis. *The Lancet Public Health, 2*(8), e356–e366. https://doi.org/10.1016/s2468-2667(17)30118-4

Kalmakis, K., & Chandel, G. (2015). Health consequences of adverse childhood experiences: A systematic review. *American Association of Nurse Practitioners, 27*(8), 457–465. https://doi.org/10.1002/2327-6924.12215

Kelleher, I., Keelay, H., Corcoran, P., Ramsay, H., Wasserman, C., Carli, V., Hoven, C., Wasserman, D., & Cannon, M. (2013). Childhood trauma and psychosis in a prospective cohort study: Cause, effect, and directionality. *The American Journal of Psychiatry*. https://doi.org/10.1176/appi.ajp.2012.12091169

LeMoult, J., Humphreys, K. L., Tracy, A., Hoffmeister, J. A., Ip, E., & Gotlib, I. H. (2020). Meta-analysis: Exposure to early life stress and risk for depression in childhood and adolescence. *Journal of the American Academy of Child and Adolescent Psychiatry, 59*(7), 842–855. https://doi.org/10.1016/j.jaac.2019.10.011

Lester, B. M., Marsit, C. J., & Bromer, C. (2014). Behavioral epigenetics and the developmental origins of child mental health disorders. In K. Brandt, B. Perry, S. Seligman, & E. Tronick (Eds.), *Infant and early childhood mental health. Core concepts and clinical practice* (pp. 161–174). American Psychiatric Publishing.

Liu, M., Loung, L., Lachaud, J., Edalati, H., Reeves, A., & Hwang, S. W. (2021). Adverse childhood experiences and related outcomes among adults experiencing homelessness: A systemic review and meta-analysis. *The LANCET Public Health, 6*, e836–e847. https://doi.org/10.1016/S2468-2667(21)00189-4

Llistosella, M., Casellvi, P., Limonero, J. T., Pérez-Ventana Ortiz, C., Baeza-Velasco, C., & Gutiérrez-Rosado, T. (2022). Development of the individual and environmental resilience model among children, adolescents and young adults using the empirical evidence: An integrative systematic review. *Health and Social Care in Community, 30*, e3277–e3299. https://doi.org/10.1111/hsc.13899

Lucero, M., Satz, S., Miceli, R., Swartz, H., & Manelis, A. (2022). The effects of mood disorders and childhood trauma on fear of positive and negative evaluation. *Acta Psychologica, 227*. https://doi.org/10.1016/j.actpsy.2022.103603

Masten, A. S. (2014). Global perspectives on resilience in children and youth. *Child Development, 85*(1), 6–20. https://doi.org/10.1111/cdev.12205

Masten, A. (2015). Pathways to integrated resilience schiene. *Psychological Inquiry, 26*, 187–196. https://doi.org/10.1080/1047840X.2015.1012041

Masten, A., & Reed, M.-G. (2002). Resilience in development, Ch. 6. In C. R. Snyder & S. J. Lopez (Eds.), *Handbook of positive psychology* (pp. 74–88). Oxford University Press.

Maté, G. (2003). *When the body says no. Understanding the stress-disease connection*. Wiley.

Maté, G. & Maté, D. (2022). *The myth of normal – trauma, illness and healing in a toxic culture*. Penguin Publishing Group.

Mayer, S. E., Surachman, A., Prather, A. A., Puterman, E., Delucchi, K. L., Irwin, M. R., Danese, A., Almeida, D. M., & Epel, E. S. (2021). The long shadow of childhood trauma for depression in midlife: Examining daily psychological stress processes as a persistent risk pathway. *Psychological Medicine, 52*, 4029–4038. https://doi.org/10.1017/S0033291721000921

Morelli, N. M., & Villodas, M. (2022). A systematic review of the validity, reliability, and clinical utility of developmental trauma disordes (DTD) symptom criteria. *Clinical Child and Family Psychology Review, 25*, 376–394.

NCTSN – The National Child Traumatic Stress Network. www.NCTSN.org

Panksepp, J. (1998). *Affective neuroscience. The foundations of human and animal emotions*. Oxford University Press.

Panksepp, J., & Biven, L. (2012). *Neuroevolutionary origins of human emotions*. W.W. Norton & Company.

Panlilio, C. C. (Ed.). (2019). *Trauma-informed schools. Integrating child maltreatment prevention, detection, and intervention*. Springer.

Perry, B. P. (2008). Child maltreatment: A neurodevelopmental perceptive on the role of trauma and neglect in psychopathology. In T. P. Beauchine & S. P. Hinshaw (Eds.), *Child and adolescent psychopathology* (pp. 93–128). Wiley.

Perry, B. D. (2009). Examining child maltreatment through a neurodevelopmental lens: Clinical applications of the neurosequential model of therapeutics. *Journal of Loss and Trauma, 14*, 240–255.

Perry, B. D., & Szalavitz, M. (2006/2017). *The boy who was raised as a dog and other stories from a child psychiatrist's notebook*. Basic Books.

Perry, B. D., & Winfrey, O. (2021). *What happened to you? Conversations on Trauma, Resilisence and Healing*. Flatiron Books.

SAMHSA (Substance Abuse and Mental Health Services Administration) Substance Abuse and Mental Health Services Administration. *SAMHSA's Concept of Trauma and Guidance for a Trauma-Informed Approach. HHS Publication No. (SMA) 14-4884*. Substance Abuse and Mental Health Services Administration; 2014. https://ncsacw.samhsa.gov/userfiles/files/SAMHSA_Trauma

Santo, T., Jr., Gisev, N., Campbell, G., Nelson, E., & Degenhardt, L. (2023). The effects of childhood trauma and mental disorders on treatment engagement, contact with the criminal justice system, and mortality among people with opioid dependence. *Drug and Alcohol Dependence, 243*. https://doi.org/10.1016/j.drugalcdep.2022.109734

Scott, A. & Anglin, J. P. (2015). *"We don't feel that love": Retrospective reflections on the experiences of removal, transitions and trauma from former youth in care report for the ministry of children and family development*. British Columbia.

Siegel, D. J. (2012). *The developing mind: How relationships and the brain interact to shape who we are* (2nd ed.). Guilford Press.

Siegel, D. J., & Bryson, T. P. (2012). *The whole-brain child: 12 proven strategies to nurture your child's developing mind*. Constable and Robinson.

Spinazzola, J., van der Kolk, B., & Ford, J. (2018). When nowhere is safe: Interpersonal trauma and attachment adversity as antecedents of posttraumatic stress disorder and developmental trauma disorder. *Journal of Traumatic Stress, 31*, 631–642.

Spinazzola, J., van der Kolk, B., & Ford, J. (2021). Developmental trauma disorder: A legacy of attachment trauma in victimized children. *Journal of Traumatic Stress, 34*, 711–720.

Strand, V. C., & Sprang, G. (Eds.). (2018). *Trauma responsive child welfare systems*. Springer.

Tomlinson, P. (2004). *Therapeutic approaches in work with traumatized children and young people. Theory and practice*. Jessica Kingsley Publishers.

Treisman, K. (2017). *Working with relational and developmental trauma in children and adolescents*. Routledge.

Ungar, M., Ghazinour, M., & Richter, J. (2013). Annual research review: What is resilience within the social ecology of human development? *The Journal of Child Psychology and Psychiatry, 54*(4), 348–366. https://doi.org/10.1111/jcpp.12025

van der Kolk, B. (2005). Developmental trauma disorder: Toward a rational diagnosis for children with complex trauma histories. *Psychiatric Annals, 35*(5), 401–408.

van der Kolk, B. (2015). *Body keeps the score: Brain, mind, and body in the healing of trauma*. Penguin Books.

van der Kolk, B., & Courtois, C. (2005). Editorial comments: Complex developmental trauma. *Journal of Traumatic Stress, 18*(5), 385–388.

van der Kolk, B. A., & d'Andrea, W. (2010). Towards a developmental trauma disorder diagnosis for childhood interpersonal trauma. In R. A. Lanius, E. Vermetten, & C. Pain (Eds.), *The impact of early life trauma on health and disease: The hidden epidemic* (pp. 57–68). Cambridge University Press.

Virokannas, E., Liuski, S., & Kuronen, M. (2018). The contested concept of vulnerability – a literature review. *European Journal of Social Work*. https://doi.org/10.1080/13691457.2018.1508001

Wang, X., Liu, Q., Fan, J., Gao, F., Xia, J., Liu, X., Du, H., Liao, H., Tan, C., & Zhu, X. (2022). Decreased functional coupling within default mode network in major depressive disorder with childhood trauma. *Journal of Psychiatric Research, 154*, 61–70. https://doi.org/10.1016/j.jpsychires.2022.07.051

Wiss, D. A., & Brewerton, T. D. (2020). Adverse childhood experiences and adult obesity: A systematic review of plausible mechanisms and meta-analysis of cross-sectional studies. *Physiology and Behavior, 223*, 112964. https://doi.org/10.1016/j.physbeh.2020.11296

Yang, C., Wang, J., Shiu, Y., Liu, M., & Geng, F. (2022). Antisocial and borderline personality traits and childhood trauma in male prisoners. *Child Abuse and Neglect*. https://doi.org/10.1016/j.chiabu.2022.105822

Judit Strömpl is Associate Professor of Social Work Research at the University of Tartu. Her main areas of research are childhood and youth vulnerability, child protection, especially substitute care, and juvenile justice. In her research, she is guided by a child rights and well-being perspective. She has researched sensitive topics such as violence, discrimination, and trauma. More recently, she has been focusing on the implementation of support measures for traumatised children in substitute care in Estonia. In her research, she prefers qualitative engaging methods such as ethnography, participatory action research, and playful techniques when interacting with children and their caregivers. She also believes in the transformative power of social work research; that is, while studying vulnerability, she seeks not only to understand the situation but to improve it.

Beata Žarkovski has graduated from the University of Debrecen (Hungary) with a master's degree in social policy, specialising in child protection. In the course of her work, she has been involved in various projects, all related to sensitive topics related to children and young people, such as juvenile delinquency, violence from children's perspective, children's rights, and trauma-informed approaches in professional work with children. She is currently working as an analyst at the Department of Criminal Law, School of Law, University of Tartu.

Part III
Child Vulnerability in Times of Crisis

Chapter 11
Subjective Well-Being and Vulnerability of Children During the Covid-19 Pandemic

Kadri Soo and Oliver Nahkur

11.1 Introduction

The vulnerability of the child, defined in terms of the risk of harm (Giesinger, 2019), is universal, and its level depends on the conditions in the child's immediate environments, including home and school, but also on general developments and events in society. One such example was the SARS-CoV-2 Coronavirus (Covid-19), which made people of all ages vulnerable in physical, social and psychological terms. Covid-19 turned out to be a serious public health concern with more than 772 million confirmed infections and 6.99 million confirmed deaths by December 2023 (WHO Covid-19 Dashboard—processed by Our World in Data). Although children were mostly not at high risk of severe illness, the spread of the virus influenced them in many ways. For example, as a response to the pandemic, most countries in the world implemented social distancing measures and ordered the lockdown of all residents, including school closures in approximately 114 countries affecting more than 1.2 billion children (Zhu et al., 2021). These measures aimed to slow the rate of transmission, protect at-risk populations, and ease the pressure on the healthcare system (Armitage & Nellums, 2020). In some countries, children could leave home for sports or walks with their parents or guardians, while in other countries, these activities were prohibited. Distancing rules, fear of infection and changed living and learning arrangements were a source of stress, fear and uncertainty. The World Health Organization (WHO, 2022) reported an increase in mental health problems (e.g., anxiety and symptoms of depression) in the general population, but especially among young people.

K. Soo (✉) · O. Nahkur
Institute of Social Studies, University of Tartu, Tartu, Estonia
e-mail: kadri.soo@ut.ee; oliver.nahkur@ut.ee

D. Kutsar et al. (eds.), *Child Vulnerability and Vulnerable Subjectivity*, Children's Well-Being: Indicators and Research 27,
https://doi.org/10.1007/978-3-031-61333-3_11

Such abrupt changes in society had worrying implications for children's development and well-being. Although vulnerability carries a reducing effect of subjective well-being, the presence of risks of harm does not always lead to a decline in well-being. The WHO survey, European Region Health Behaviour in School-aged Children, conducted in 2021–2022 in 22 countries displayed that 13% of children aged 11–15 reported negative and 31% positive impacts of the Covid-19 pandemic in most areas of their lives (Residori et al., 2023). Consequently, some children may have experienced conditions of support or altered social situations that underpin their well-being during the Covid-19 pandemic. In this chapter, we aim to examine how the Covid-19 pandemic has increased children's vulnerability and affected their subjective well-being. The chapter provides a brief overview of the changes in evaluations of overall subjective well-being of European children stemming from the pandemic, while the in-depth focus is on aspects that enhance or threaten well-being at home and school from the perspective of Estonian children.

To better describe children's vulnerability and subjective well-being in the context of the pandemic, we apply data from one quantitative and two qualitative studies. We use data from 25,865 children from the International Children's Worlds Covid-19 Supplement Survey (ISCWeB) collected in 2021 mostly between the peaks of the second and third waves, primarily from children aged 9–13 years (Savahl et al., 2022). Data was analysed from the following European countries: Belgium, Estonia, Finland, Germany, Italy, Spain, Albania, Romania, Wales, and Russia. In some cases, only regions within countries were captured. In addition, sample sizes vary broadly from 590 in Germany to 2422 in Belgium. Due to the difficulties in collecting data from children during the Covid-19 pandemic (and during the (semi) lockdown in many countries), representative samples were mostly not achieved. Different sampling and data-collection methods were used, varying from country to country between pencil and/or web survey methods. In Estonia, where the survey took place during the distance learning period, children completed the online questionnaire mainly during an online lesson. In addition, two Estonian qualitative studies are used. The first qualitative dataset stems from Kutsar and Kurvet-Käosaar (2021) and consists of 39 diaries and personal narratives by 12–13 and 17–18-year-olds written in spring 2020, and 24 semi-structured interviews with children aged 8–15 carried out during the lockdown in spring 2021. Lelov-Aasmaa (2022), the author of the second dataset, conducted three semi-structured qualitative focus group interviews among 5–7th graders (12–14-year-olds) in rural schools in winter 2022, examining children's retrospective interpretations of the period of distance learning.

11.2 Children's Overall Subjective Well-Being Before and During the Covid-19 Pandemic

Subjective well-being is understood as the judgements "people make regarding their lives, the events happening to them, their bodies and minds, and the circumstances in which they live" (Diener, 2006, p. 153). It mostly comprises cognitive and emotional dimensions (we will introduce the latter in the second half of the chapter). The cognitive part of subjective well-being—people's assessments of their lives as a whole—is a complex process combining perceived discrepancies between present and past experiences, comparisons of oneself with others, and the comparison of the circumstances of one's real life with a self-constructed standard (Davern et al., 2007; Pavot & Diener, 2009). Although subjective well-being is usually stable and positive, various positive and negative events can destabilise it. According to the theory of subjective well-being homeostasis, neurological and psychological processes control and maintain our level of well-being; therefore, as circumstances normalise, the baseline level of subjective well-being will be restored (Cummins, 2010, 2014). However, in the presence of persistent stressful life events, such as poverty, neglect, conflictual family relationships or social isolation, the homeostatic system cannot maintain the baseline and may lead to a substantial decline in well-being and endanger mental health.

The numerous unexpected alterations in children's lives since the outbreak of the Covid-19 pandemic may have posed a challenge to children's subjective well-being. The changes in children's subjective well-being associated with the pandemic has been investigated using longitudinal or cross-sectional survey design. For example, children have been asked to rate their overall life satisfaction after a few months of the implementation of restrictive measures, and the findings have been compared with pre-pandemic results collected from the same children or with equivalent studies, demonstrating a decline in children's well-being (van der Laan et al., 2021; Soest et al., 2020) or no change (Choi et al., 2021). However, in the multi-national ISCWeB Supplement study (Savahl et al., 2022), changes in children's subjective well-being were measured in terms of their evaluations of their happiness about their lives as a whole in the second year of Covid-19 and retrospectively before the pandemic. As these two context-free single-item indicators reflect the respondent's satisfaction with their life more broadly, we will further refer to it as overall subjective well-being (SWB) for the sake of simplicity. In all twenty countries surveyed across four continents, a decrease in the mean SWB of children was observed (Savahl et al., 2022).

A closer inspection of selected European countries in the ISCWeB Supplement study shows that the aggregated mean overall subjective well-being declined from 8.6 (retrospectively) before the pandemic to 7.1 during it (Table 11.1). A large proportion of European children (53%) judged their overall subjective well-being before Covid-19 with maximum estimates on the scale 0 … 10, but only a fifth assessed their SWB as high during the pandemic. Casas (2019) states that children, as a rule, tend to assess their subjective well-being with points close to the

Table 11.1 Children's assessments of their overall subjective well-being before and during Covid-19 (all surveyed European countries aggregated)

Compared to the time before Covid-19, the SWB ...	When thinking about your life before the Coronavirus, how happy were you about your life as a whole? (SWB mean = 8.6; SD = 2.2)				When thinking about your life now during the Coronavirus, how happy are you about your life as a whole? (SWB mean = 7.1; SD = 2.8)				Changes in SWB mean values
	Max %	Low %	Mean	SD	Max %	Low %	Mean	SD	
Increased ("gainers", 13%)	.0	27.3	5.7	2.5	32.1	6.4	8.2	2.0	2.5
Remained the same ("no changers", 30%)	58.8	6.0	8.7	2.3	58.8	6.0	8.7	2.3	.0
Decreased a bit ("slight decliners"; (31%)	54.0	2.6	9.0	1.6	.0	6.0	7.6	1.6	−1.4
Decreased much ("great decliners; 27%)	69.1	0.8	9.4	1.2	.0	45.0	4.2	2.3	−5.2

Note: Children could assess their overall subjective well-being using an 11-point assessment scale, where 0 was "not happy at all" and 10 "completely happy." Maximum refers to children who chose the scale point 10, low percentage refers to children who marked scale points 0–4

maximum on the scale (scale points 8–10, a high level), which raises the need to identify the groups of children whose subjective well-being scores are lower than the average for a certain population. Scores below the mid-point of the scale (five) are often defined as a low score (OECD, 2019; Rees, 2017), which may indicate that the child is at a risk of experiencing harm and is in need of assistance. For example, the share of children in Europe with very low ratings (scale points 0–4) increased from 6% to 16% in comparisons of SWB before and during the pandemic. Guided by these ideas, we intended to determine the structure of the changes in children's SWB and find out the groups of children who may be more vulnerable due to the pandemic. We constructed an aggregate variable by subtracting children's assessments of SWB before Covid-19 from their assessments given about the period during Covid-19, and grouped the difference into four, depending on whether the ratings for the time during the pandemic were higher, equal, slightly lower (up to two scale points) or much lower (three or more points) than the retrospective ratings for the pre-pandemic time. In defining the last two groups, we were inspired the suggestion by Cummins (2010) that a decline in well-being of one standard deviation (here about two points) from the mean is the lowest value that is still within the boundaries of homeostatic maintenance, but more than one standard deviation may be out of control of the homeostatic system.

Thirteen per cent of children in Europe reported an improvement in their overall subjective well-being (Table 11.1). Referred to as "gainers", they rated, on average, their SWB before Covid-19 as significantly lower than children in other groups, while their average score during the pandemic was among the highest, although it remained below the overall average before the pandemic. Children whose SWB score did not change ("no changers"; 30%) had generally maintained a high level of overall well-being during the pandemic. On average, SWB decreased for 58% of children. Children experiencing a small decrease, "slight decliners", had a very high level of SWB before, but slightly above average during the pandemic. Children who perceived the largest decline ("great decliners") were characterised by the highest retrospective assessment of SWB before the pandemic, but with the onset of Covid-19 their average SWB score decreased more than twice, and the proportion of low scorers rose to 45%. This suggests that many in this group need attention from adults because of their increased risk of harm.

Comparing by country, it turns out that the decrease in overall subjective well-being was most evident in Germany, where approximately three out of four children experienced a decline in SWB, every second child to a great extent (Fig. 11.1). In Romania, Finland, Italy, and Croatia, around two children out of three experienced a decrease, but the proportion of children belonging to the group of "great decliners" was smaller than in Germany. The lowest share of children reporting a decline in SWB was in Spain, Albania and Russia. The highest proportion of children whose well-being increased was in Wales, Belgium, Estonia, Spain, and Russia. One explanation for these results can be how children perceived the pandemic restrictions in their country and how they adjusted to them. For example, children in

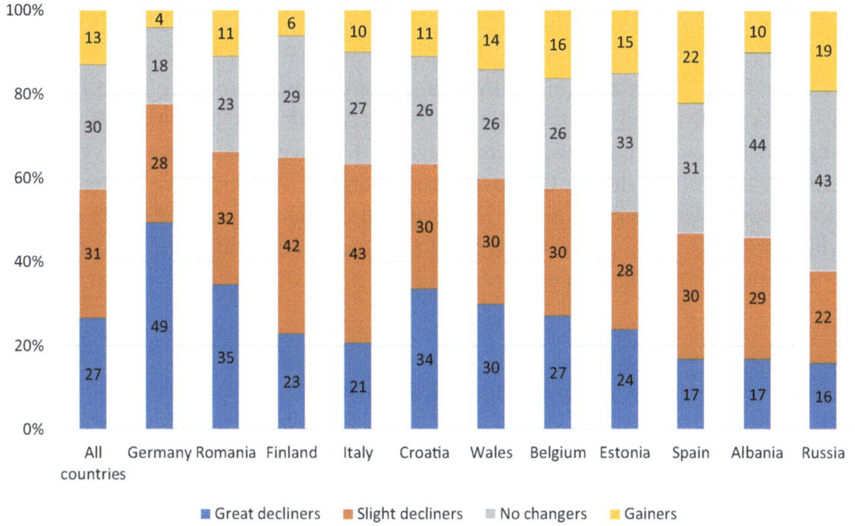

Fig. 11.1 Children's profiles of changes in overall subjective well-being during the Covid-19 pandemic by country

Germany reported most often that they could not attend school for many days during the pandemic and the decrease in satisfaction with relationships with family and friends during the pandemic were also steepest there (Nahkur & Kutsar, 2022).

11.3 Sources of Child Vulnerability in the Context of the Covid-19 Pandemic

Children's lives under pandemic-driven constraints carry a number of old and new risks that can endanger their overall subjective well-being. It can be assumed that children experiencing new risks, such as social isolation, overcrowding at home, poor educational attendance, and health problems (Public Health England, 2020), combined with previous risks (e.g., violence, lack of care and support, emotional problems, and poor school performance and connectedness; Arora et al., 2015), are especially vulnerable. In this section, we focus on Estonia—a country where new strict measures (i.e., semi-lockdown; distance learning, closures of shopping centres, theatres, cinemas, and all entertainment venues) were in place almost to the end of the 2020 and 2021 school years—and explore the formation of children's well-being and sources of vulnerability at home and school in the conditions of the pandemic. We take a closer look at the groups of SWB changes discussed above and try to find out which individual and relational characteristics can differentiate these groups (see variables used in the analysis in the Table 11.2).

As shown in Fig. 11.1, almost half of the children in Estonia experienced some decline in overall subjective well-being during the pandemic compared to the period before it. Girls and especially younger children were more vulnerable to the adverse effects of the pandemic. For instance, there were significantly more boys (38%) than girls (28%) who rated their SWB during Covid-19 at the same level as retrospectively before the pandemic. However, among girls, there were slightly more (26%) who considered their SWB greatly decreased than among boys (21%). Compared to 12–13-year-olds, children aged 10–11 were more likely to report a decline in their SWB during Covid-19 (percentages 28% and 20%, respectively). Older children were twice as likely to be "gainers" as younger children. In the following, we discuss how the children fared at home and at school and what feelings they experienced during the pandemic.

11.3.1 Turbulent Time in Family Life

The restrictive measures imposed after the Covid-19 outbreak affected the living arrangements of family members and was a source of stress, especially for families with children. For instance, nearly half of all parents of school-age children in Estonia found the reconciliation of work and family responsibilities during the

Table 11.2 Composite indicators related to home and school domains used in the analysis

Indices	Items	Scale (Cronbach's alpha)
Home-related indicators		
Family social climate	I feel safe at home During the Coronavirus, I felt well-supported by some people I live with There are people in my family who care about me My parent(s) listen to me and take what I say into account My parents and I make decisions about my life together	0—I do not agree, 1—I agree a little, 2—I agree somewhat, 3—I agree a lot, and 4—I totally agree (Cronbach's alpha .81)
Changes in satisfaction with relationships with family members	(A) Satisfaction with the relationships I had with the people I live with before Covid-19 (B) Satisfaction with the relationships I have with the people I live with now during Covid-19	0—not at all satisfied … 10—totally satisfied New scale: 1—decreased (A > B); 2— remain the same (A = B); 3—increased (A < B)
Concern about getting infected	During the last month, I have been worried that … … I may get infected by the Coronavirus … people I know may get infected by the Coronavirus … I may infect other people with the Coronavirus	0—not at all … 10—very much (Cronbach's alpha .84)
School-related indicators		
School social climate	I feel safe at school During the Coronavirus, I felt well-supported by some of my teachers My teachers care about me My teachers listen to me and take what I say into account At school I have opportunities to make decisions about things that are important to me	0—I do not agree, 1—I agree a little, 2—I agree somewhat, 3—I agree a lot, and 4—I totally agree (Cronbach's alpha .82)
Missing school	During Coronavirus… … how often did you miss your teacher's advice? … how often did you miss your classmates? … how often did you wish that you could go back to school?	0—never, 1—sometimes, 2—often, and 3—always (Cronbach's alpha .69)

(continued)

Table 11.2 (continued)

Indices	Items	Scale (Cronbach's alpha)
Concern about the impact of Covid-19 on learning	During the last month, I have been worried … … that I may get bad school marks because of the Coronavirus situation … about the changes in my life as a student because of the Coronavirus situation	0—not at all … 10—very much (Cronbach's alpha .70)
Effective coping with learning during Covid-19	Since the Coronavirus … … I can make my own schedule … I have learned new methods of doing schoolwork over the web	0—I do not agree, 1—I agree a little, 2—I agree somewhat, 3—I agree a lot, and 4—I totally agree (Cronbach's alpha .52)

Note: All composite indicators were computed by averaging the corresponding items, exceptions include the changes in satisfaction with relationships that were computed by subtracting the "before" value from the "during the Covid-19 pandemic" value and grouping these into three categories

crisis stressful and burdensome (Viira et al., 2020). A third of parents in this study worked from home, some parents had a reduced and some an increased workload, 5% became unemployed. The stay-at-home order led to a greater crowding of family members throughout the day, putting them under pressure to manage work and study commitments and privacy needs. According to the qualitative data collected from Estonian children in 2020–2021 (Kutsar & Kurvet-Käosaar, 2021), such new circumstances challenged coping skills, diminished opportunities for face-to-face sharing of personal issues and caused anxiety and tension at home. Children described increased conflicts with siblings and parents, even experiencing the atmosphere at home as unbearable: "I cannot stand my mother and brother alone anymore. Hell." (a girl) (Kutsar & Kurvet-Käosaar, 2021). Living in closer proximity tended to reduce the personal freedom and autonomy of children, being a risk factor of emotional well-being (Stoecklin et al., 2021). However, some children in the study by Kutsar and Kurvet-Käosaar (2021) mentioned that they enjoyed being at home with their family members. Lockdown allowed them to develop more (new) ways to spend time together, such as doing gardening or renovating the home, going for a walk, playing games, or cooking together. Togetherness and shared experiences strengthened ties between family members.

The data from the ISCWeB Supplement survey confirms the differential impact of Covid-19 on the quality of family relationships. The comparison of children's estimates of satisfaction with their relationships with family members before and during the pandemic revealed that almost two-thirds of children maintained stable and very good relationships at home as their average score of satisfaction during the pandemic was 9.3 on the scale 0 … 10. However, there were more children whose relationships with family members deteriorated (i.e., they were less satisfied; average score 6.4) than those who considered relations improved (average score 8.6).

Table 11.3 Children's home-related evaluations in general and by groups in terms of changes in SWB

	Total mean/%	"Gainers" (A)	"No changers" (B)	"Slight decliners" (C)	"Great decliners" (D)	Differences between groups based on the Scheffé test
(Positive) family social climate (scale 0–4) (mean)	3.3	3.1	3.5	3.4	3.1	D, A < C, B*
Satisfaction with the relationships with family members during Covid-19 (scale 0–10) (mean)	8.5	8.1	8.9	8.7	7.7	D, A < C, B*
Concern about getting infected (scale 0–10) (mean)	3.9	3.4	3.7	4.5	4.0	A, B < D < C*
Change in satisfaction with relationships with family members (%) *						
Decreased	24.6	23.3	14.5	26.5	39.1	
Remained the same	64.2	59.1	76.8	63.7	49.3	
Increased	11.2	17.6	8.7	9.8	11.6	

*p < .05
Note: For the first three composite indicators, we tested for the differences between groups of SWB using the one-way analysis of variance and the Scheffé *post-hoc* test. In the last column, the groups that statistically significantly differ from each other are marked with "<", indicating that some groups have a significantly lower mean value than others. For the change in satisfaction with relationships, that is a categorical variable, we employed Cramér's V

Children's ability to adapt to new situations like the pandemic depends on the quality and stability of family relationships, which in turn plays a crucial role in children's sense of well-being (Choi et al., 2021; Wang et al., 2021). Looking at the groups in terms of changes in SWB, it appears that "no changers" and "slight decliners" evaluated their family social climate,[1] an indicator of the quality of relationships, most positively (Table 11.3). They described their home as a very safe place where they are cared for and supported, involved in decision-making and

[1] In this chapter, we use the concepts *family social climate* and *school social climate* following previous definitions and classifications. Kurock et al. (2022) in their review article describe family (social) climate in terms of cohesion, expressiveness, acceptance, support, and conflict referring to relationships between family members. School social climate denotes the quality of interaction among and between students and teachers, including components like trust, caring, support, fairness, and shared decision-making (Kutsyuruba et al., 2015).

taken seriously. Both groups were generally very satisfied with their relationships within the family during the pandemic. In particular "no changers" said there was stability in family relationships—about three-quarters reported a similar (mostly high) level of satisfaction with their relationships both before and during Covid-19.

"Gainers" and "great decliners" were distinct from the two previous groups as they both experienced slightly less closeness and support at home and significantly fewer opportunities to participate in decision-making. For instance, among "great decliners" there was a high share (22%) of those who never or very rarely make decisions about their lives with their parents. The ratings of satisfaction with family relationships during the Coronavirus among "gainers" and especially "great decliners" are significantly lower than the average for all children. However, the assessment of change in satisfaction with relationships distinguishes these two groups from each other. Among "gainers" there were more who reported no change or even an improvement in the quality of the relationships at home, while "great decliners" were more likely to perceive a decrease in satisfaction compared to other groups.

Family life was also influenced by infection anxiety, especially if a family member belonged to a risk group. Children's diaries and interviews (Kutsar & Kurvet-Käosaar, 2021) revealed children's feelings of fear and anxiety about the spread of the virus in Estonia and worldwide, as well as their concern about family members becoming ill. In order to prevent grandparents from getting infected, children eschewed visiting them. In cases where they lived with their grandparents, they followed strict rules on movement and meeting friends, as one girl reflected in the following quote: "My mother has established a rule that no one can visit us right now. I respect my mother's rule and my grandmother's health" (Kutsar & Kurvet-Käosaar, 2021). The precautionary measures disrupted the children's normal social life, separating them from friends, relatives and family members that they did not live with. According to the children, a source of additional tension was when family members reproached each other for creating a heightened risk of infection by moving more in public (Kutsar & Kurvet-Käosaar, 2021).

According to the ISCWeB Supplement survey, the majority of children, more girls than boys, were concerned that they or their family members would become infected with Covid-19, while 16% of children mentioned themselves or their family members being infected. Complementary analysis showed that worrying about disease was not linked to actual infection, but rather to talking a lot about the pandemic at home and the need to be very careful because of a family member has a high risk of getting seriously ill if infected with the Coronavirus. In terms of changes in SWB, "slight decliners" were concerned about getting infected the most—44% of them were worried to a moderate or greater extent (scores 5–10) about infection, while about a third of the other groups felt the same. "Slight decliners" were more likely to report frequent conversations about the pandemic at home than did children from the other groups.

In conclusion, the vulnerability of some family members (e.g., parent's difficulties in reconciling work and family life, risk of serious illness due to poor health condition) may contribute to the vulnerability of other members, including children. In addition, personal vulnerabilities mingled with shared vulnerabilities (e.g., isolation, overcrowding and lack of privacy) may lead to the amplification of risks and negative outcomes. For instance, parental stress can result in poor parenting (Brown et al., 2020; Wang et al., 2021), creating tensions and conflicts between family members and making children feel insecure and unloved. The Covid-19 crisis tested family relationships and members' ability to resolve problems without harming each other. Children whose families were able to maintain the same level of closeness or even increase it and find the ways to support each other adapted better and perceived their well-being as stable or even improved. Open communication between parents and children, including about the Coronavirus, acts as a protective factor in mitigating the negative impact of the pandemic on children's mental health and life satisfaction (Tang et al., 2021). However, a worsening of the quality of family relationships during the turbulent times of Covid-19 could have been detrimental to children's sense of subjective well-being and make them vulnerable.

11.3.2 Challenges of Novel Learning Forms

To prevent the spread of the virus, schools switched to distance learning overnight. In Estonia, all schools were closed for about 2 months both during the first and second waves in 2020 and 2021. Outside the lockdown, certain schools or regions implemented temporary home learning rules. Although some schools provided children virtual classes via video platforms or communication through text messaging or email, the responsibility for teaching fell largely on parents. In Estonia, schools implemented different methods for distance learning and various forms of instructional support for children. A survey carried out during the first wave of the pandemic showed that about half of the teachers conducted video classes daily or at least once a week (Tammets et al., 2021). The remaining teachers did not conduct any lessons, and students had to learn on their own, doing assignments from a textbook or online. Teachers used the e-School or Stuudium environment to share information. Feedback from the students revealed that they needed virtual classes, in particular, when covering new topics (Tammets et al., 2021). The children complained about the excessive workload of independent learning, which was perceived as ineffective. The National Satisfaction and School Environment Survey conducted in Estonia partly at the beginning of the third wave displayed an increase in video classes (Lutsoja et al., 2022). About half of primary school students did not experience any difficulties in understanding what they were learning, but one in five agreed that they had such problems.

Distance learning had both positive and negative features which children actively described in the interviews conducted by Lelov-Aasmaa (2022) after the restriction measures were terminated. It turned out that children overwhelmingly preferred contact learning to distance learning because "everything was more free before" and they could ask for help from the teachers immediately. During remote learning, teachers took a long time to answer students' questions, or they did not answer at all. Some children in this study relied more on the assistance of their friends when doing schoolwork, or they gave up seeking help. “Previously, you could always ask the teacher [for advice]. Now it’s bad because when there is a difficult problem in maths, it’s so hard, you can’t even consult your mum and dad, they don’t remember anything [about maths]” (a boy). Children who managed to arrange a consultation with the teacher or get help from family members (e.g., an older sibling) did better: “When I was in [online] class with the teacher, or with a couple of other children, I felt much more courageous and wise … And then I also felt that I would try harder afterwards” (a girl) (Lelov-Aasmaa, 2022).

The ISCWeB Supplement survey highlighted that one in five children often missed their teachers’ advice and nearly half longed for their classmates a lot. Girls and younger children missed the advice from teachers and wanted to return to school more than boys and older children. The children whose SWB declined little or notably missed the traditional schooling the most (Table 11.4). They needed socialising with their peers, instructional guidance from teachers and the classroom context for supporting their learning. In contrast, the “gainers” can be characterised by an almost non-existent desire for the teachers’ advice and communication with classmates (64–82% never or sometimes missed it), reflected in their overwhelming preference for distance learning (Fig. 11.2). This group may include “self-omitters” from peer relationships—children who are likely to be victims of bullying and feel little connection to school (see Hall et al., 2021). This assumption is confirmed by

Table 11.4 Children’s school-related evaluations in general and by groups in terms of changes in SWB (mean values)

	Total mean	“Gainers” (A)	“No changers” (B)	“Slight decliners” (C)	“Great decliners” (D)	Differences between groups based on the Scheffé test
Missing school (scale 0–3)	1.3	1.0	1.2	1.4	1.4	A < B < C, D*
(Positive) school social climate (scale 0–4)	2.5	2.3	2.7	2.6	2.3	A, D < C, B*
Concern about the impact of corona on learning (scale 0–10)	3.8	3.1	3.2	4.3	4.5	A, B < C, D*
Effective coping with learning during COVID-19 (scale 0–4)	2.8	2.8	3.1	2.8	2.6	D < A, C < B*

*p < .05

Note: We tested the differences between groups based on SWB using one-way analysis of variance and the Scheffé *post-hoc* test. In the last column, the groups that statistically significantly differed from each other are marked with “<“, indicating that some groups have a significantly lower mean value than others

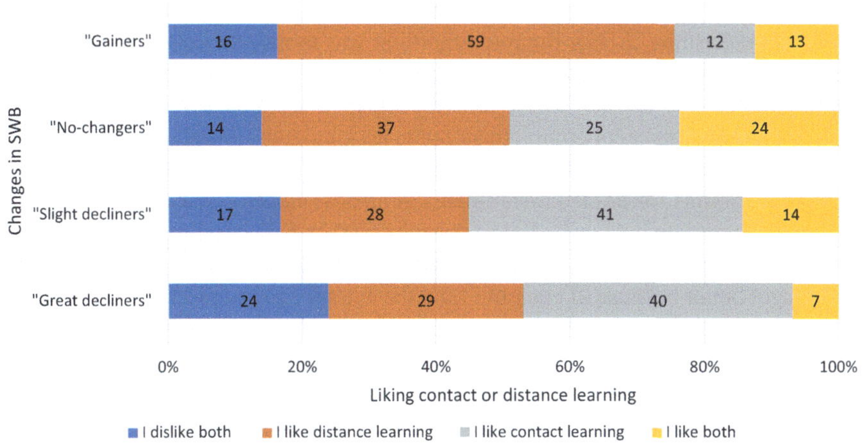

Fig. 11.2 Liking contact or distance learning during the pandemic by group in terms of changes in SWB (children in Estonia)
Note: The preference of learning form was measured by two items: "I like distance learning" and "I like going to school", using the scale 0—I do not agree, 1—I agree a little, 2—I agree somewhat, 3—I agree a lot, and 4—I totally agree. We combined the items so that children who totally agreed or agreed a lot with both belonged to a group "I like both". Those who chose options 0–2 for both items form the group who do not like either form of learning much ("I dislike both"). The remaining combinations constitute the groups "I like distance learning" and "I like contact learning"

the lowest rating of the school social climate in "gainers", who evaluated school as modestly safe and teachers as less caring and inclusive. Distance education prevented children from the possibility of face-to-face bullying and offered them an opportunity to avoid an environment perceived as unwelcoming and learn on their own (Nahkur & Kutsar, 2022).

The adjustment to distance learning requires a large amount of self-regulation; that is, the individual's ability to manage his or her cognitions, emotions and behaviour in a way that supports the planning of time and learning activities, self-motivation and self-monitoring, setting learning goals and the pursuit of them (Berger et al., 2021; Schunk & Greene, 2018). Self-regulation develops in interaction between the children's personal (e.g., reactivity to stimuli) and environmental characteristics (e.g., availability of support and close relationships), and has a significant effect on their academic performance (McClelland & Cameron, 2011). Focus group interviews with children (Lelov-Aasmaa, 2022) revealed that some students experienced difficulties in concentration and maintaining motivation during online classes or when studying on their own during lockdown. Their learning was challenging due to the distracting circumstances, such as sharing a room with other family members or pets, or their poor self-regulation and independent learning skills. They needed more social control, support and external motivation, as the following quote illustrates: "I played in the morning. At around 12 o'clock I started studying, but then I thought I would still play until 3 o'clock. But then it turned out that my mum would come home at 3 o'clock and see that I hadn't studied. My mum called and said she was going to drive home. Then I started studying quickly." (a boy) (Lelov-Aasmaa, 2022). Remote schooling was more praised by children who seemed to be self-efficient or who needed privacy and the absence of classroom competition to concentrate. These children liked to set their own time schedule, study at their own pace, or complete all home assignments several days in advance.

In addition to the flexibility of time and place, students considered the use of auxiliary materials for graded assignments as an advantage of distance learning. In the focus groups carried out by Lelov-Aasmaa (2022), a discussion emerged on the impact of home learning on educational outcomes. Some students stated that their "grades got better because of cheating" and the extra time they received to complete the assignments. The others felt that their academic performance had deteriorated because, when studying independently at home, they did not put in enough effort and performed superficially. Some children worried about the weak social support network that resulted in their incorrectly or undone homework and lower marks on the certificate: "I used to get all fives, but then [during Covid-19] I got all threes"[2] (a boy).

The ISCWeB Supplement survey also showed differences in the extent to which children worried about their learning and grades and in their ability to plan time and study online (as indications of self-regulation). Compared to boys, girls expressed more concern about the impact of the pandemic on learning, which may also be due to their higher perceived social pressure to perform better in school. When analysing the groups in terms of changes in SWB, it is evident that some groups had performed better during the remote learning, while some were more vulnerable. "No changers", having caring, supportive and inclusive relationships at school (the highest score of school social climate compared to the other three groups), worried rather less about the negative impact on their progress at school (Table 11.4). It is likely that their higher perceived support from family members and teachers, and capacity for online learning and time planning could facilitate their resilience in new circumstances and coping (independently) with different learning forms. "Slight decliners" with relatively good time planning and online learning skills predominantly preferred traditional schooling (they had the highest proportion in favouring contact learning, see Fig. 11.2). The absence of conventional education due to confinement measures has made them vulnerable—the reduced opportunities to rely on the teacher's instruction and support produced uncertainty and concern about their academic performance.

Both "gainers" and "great decliners" perceived their school environment to be not very caring, supportive and inclusive; however, worry about learning seems to differentiate them. More than a third of the children belonging to the "gainers" reported no concern about the impact of the pandemic on their achievements at school. Although the ISCWeB Supplement study did not measure children's academic performance, it can be assumed that some of these children are self-efficient enough (18% scored the maximum on the index for "effective coping with learning

[2] Five indicates the best grade, three means the lowest positive grade.

during Covid-19", see Table 11.4) in learning and do not need a classroom environment to maintain their motivation to learn. However, there may be children who are educationally disengaged (or with special educational needs), performing at a satisfactory level under distance learning conditions with little social support. Therefore, the improvement of SWB among "gainers" may carry risks in terms of declining learning motivation and connectedness to school, making it difficult to return to school at the end of the social distancing measures.

Compared to the other groups, "great decliners" were most concerned about the negative impact of the pandemic on school attendance and their grades. They preferred in-person learning (40%) to remote learning (29%), but one in four did not like learning in either way at all (Fig. 11.2). A survey conducted among schoolchildren in Estonia about the period of distance learning (Lauristin et al., 2020) showed that the most vulnerable were students with low self-regulation skills and negative attitudes towards school, who could easily become discouraged by difficulties and failures and *disappear* from the school radar during the remote education. Without external pressure and (professional) support, they struggle to cope with learning. "Great decliners" in the ISCWeB Supplement survey also appear to need assistance. Experiencing little support from home and school and lower self-regulation capacity, they may face difficulties in handling novel and complex learning situations. Being deprived of adult attention and contact with peers can put them at risk of unperforming at school, feeling alienation and, experiencing dissatisfaction with the way their lives are going.

11.3.3 Tension and Stress Overshadowing Happiness

Crises evoke a range of strong emotions. The interviews with the children and their diaries (Kutsar & Kurvet-Käosaar, 2021; Lelov-Aasmaa, 2022) indicated that being with family and doing (new) activities together made them happy, but physical distance from friends or losing them caused sadness and a sense of loneliness. Continuously staying at home and insufficient movement were a source of boredom and anxiety. Although some children enjoyed the quiet and independent learning during the remote education, many complained of uncertainty and anger because of this. For example, one sixth-grade boy explained his feelings this way: "I am so tired of distance learning, since I couldn't get out of the house and meet up with my friends. This routine is getting on my nerves." (Kutsar & Kurvet-Käosaar, 2021). The duration of the pandemic and the repeated imposition and cancellation of restriction measures seemed to increase the children's frustration with the situation, affecting their emotional well-being and mental health (Racine et al., 2021), especially if parents were not available during the day and the relationships with them were not warm (Wang et al., 2021). However, children having discussions (about the pandemic) with and being listened to by parents reported better emotional well-being and fewer symptoms of stress and anxiety (de Abreu et al., 2021; Tang et al., 2021).

Emotional well-being refers to feelings or emotional states that people experience during a certain period concerning their life, events or other people (Diener, 2006). In the ISCWeB Supplement study, emotional well-being was measured by using a short version of Russell's Core Affect scale (Russell, 2003). Children were asked to evaluate their experience of three positive (happy, calm and full of energy) and three negative (sad, stressed and bored) emotions over the past 2 weeks—a period during the second lockdown—on an 11-point scale (0—"not at all" … 10—"extremely"). Considering the evidence that positive and negative affect are negatively interrelated but do not constitute the endpoints of the continuum (Suar et al., 2019), we employed the cluster analysis method to determine the patterns of feeling different emotions. Three meaningful groups were formed. The largest share of children (40%) had a high level of positive and a low level of negative feelings (so called *very happy*). A third of the children felt happy and energetic, but also substantially stressed and bored (*happy but stressed*). More than a quarter of the children said they felt sad and stressed rather than happy and energetic (shortly *sad and stressed*). Boys and younger children expressed more positive emotions than did girls and older children. For example, the share of boys and girls who felt overwhelmingly positive emotions was 48% and 35% respectively; for 10–11-year-olds it was 45% and for 12–13-year-olds 37%. These findings reflect the vulnerability of girls and older children to stress and anxiety in pandemic conditions (WHO, 2022).

A comparison of these results with the responses of 12-year-olds in the ISCWeB survey conducted in Estonia in 2018 (Soo & Kutsar, 2020) reveals a decline in emotional well-being over time. The proportion of very happy children has remained stable, but the share of children who were both happy and stressed has decreased (from 44% in 2018 to 33%), while the proportion of children who were sad and stressed has increased (from 15% in 2018 to 27%). Although these are two separate surveys and samples, it can be assumed that children who were somewhat vulnerable (i.e., experiencing some degree of negative emotions) before Covid-19 were more susceptible to new risks and were more likely to perceive a worsening in their emotional well-being. Positive emotions promote building resilience to handle stressful events (Tugade & Fredrickson, 2007), but the more pre-pandemic anxiety and pandemic-related stress children have, the lower they rate their life satisfaction (Blackwell et al., 2022).

Looking at the groups in terms of changes in SWB in the ISCWeB Supplement survey, it emerges that the most vulnerable were the "great decliners" having the highest proportion of children (43%) experiencing predominantly negative emotions (Fig. 11.3). Nearly a third of "great decliners" were children who were both happy and stressed, and only a quarter experienced overwhelmingly positive emotions. Among the "gainers", there was a balance between very happy children and sad and stressed children, reflecting the high heterogeneity of this group. While "gainers" rated their overall subjective well-being as improved, many of the children in this group still found aspects of their lives that made them sad and anxious. Compared to the previous two groups, there were more children among the "slight decliners", who felt very happy or happy and stressed, and fewer children experiencing sadness, indicating their lower level of emotional vulnerability. However,

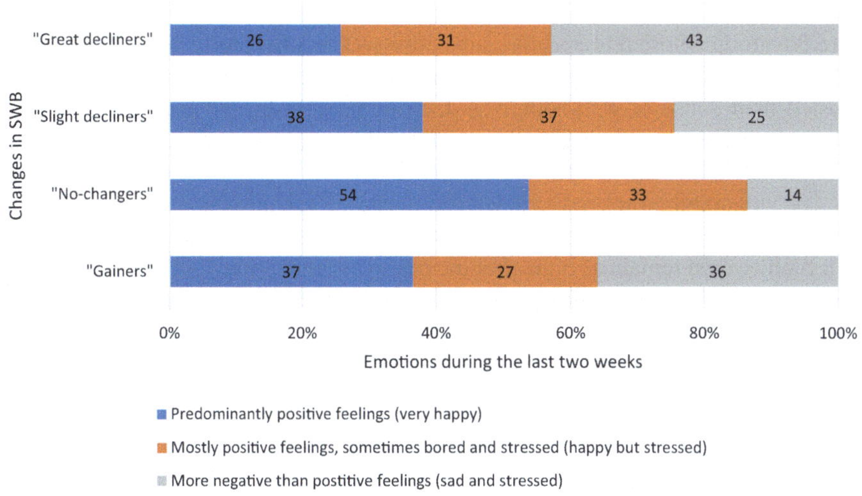

Fig. 11.3 Children's experiences of positive and negative affect over the last 2 weeks by groups in terms of changes in SWB (children in Estonia)-

"no changers" appear to be children who were least vulnerable. The vast majority of them were either happy or happy with moments of stress and boredom. Therefore, children whose perceived social climate at home and school was poor with lower levels of being heard were less happy with their lives and more burdened with negative emotions than those with good quality relationships and opportunities to participate.

11.4 Conclusion

This chapter highlighted how crises such as the Covid-19 pandemic and strict infection control measures were prone to increase the vulnerability of children, compounding pre-existing and new physical, social and emotional risks. Nonetheless, not all children were equally vulnerable, and their subjective well-being was not similarly threatened. The least vulnerable were children whose well-being in home and at school remained stable and who were able to maintain the same (high) level of overall life satisfaction compared to the pre-pandemic period. These children, "no changers", seemed to move smoothly and flexibly through the jungle of the pandemic-driven complexities. Their internal and external resources helped them to ensure stability. That is, their good self-regulation skills and supportive and caring relationships facilitated their resilience in handling distance learning or other changes without experiencing significant concern and stress.

The qualitative and quantitative data showed that pandemic situations can also lead to positive changes in children's lives, where a development perceived as positive can be the absence of some unpleasant situations or activities. "Gainers" were the group whose retrospective subjective well-being before the pandemic was average or low, but learning at their own pace in the safe environment of home boosted their sense of well-being. On the one hand, a longer period of distance learning may be appropriate for them, but on the other hand, it may contribute to their alienation from school and classmates. Therefore, it cannot be claimed that the risks of vulnerability are reduced for this group. Their modest assessment of the school social climate and low liking of going to school raises the question of whether their SWB would remain as high after the return to conventional schooling arrangements. Therefore, they would need attention from adults (e.g., teachers) and support to avoid a possible (re)increase in vulnerability.

Positive aspects children experienced during the pandemic period (e.g., caring and closeness from family members) may have neutralised to some extent the negative ones (e.g., separation from friends, problems with distance learning, risk of illness) and compensate for the deeper decline in well-being. "Slight decliners" were an example of such a case. Their baseline level of overall subjective well-being before Covid-19 was quite high, but the stress and anxiety caused by the spread of the virus, the restriction measures and the changes in daily life had a harmful influence on this. Considering the small magnitude of the decline in their SWB and the presence of a supportive social network, they have, according to Cummins' (2010) theory, a high likelihood of reaching the baseline level of SWB.

However, the most vulnerable were children whose SWB fell greatly, even dangerously, if we rely on Cummins (2010). "Great decliners" seemed to experience an accumulation of risks both at home and at school, struggling to cope in unstable circumstances. Challenging family relationships, learning on their own without the support of teachers, poor ability to study online, and concerns about educational performance contributed to their negative emotions and dissatisfaction with their lives. The persistence of adverse conditions and the lack or delay of support in their lives can complicate the improvement of SWB. They have a risk of continuing harm after the pandemic.

In conclusion, the chapter demonstrates the subjective and relational nature of vulnerability. The subjectivity of vulnerability in the context of Covid-19 stemmed from the way children perceived new life events (e.g., distance learning, isolation) and their effects on their lives. Relationality was reflected in the quality of the relationship network in which the child (as well as parents and teachers) was embedded, and which contributed to (joint) coping with the complexities of the pandemic. Intertwining subjectivity and relationality reveals the nuanced effects of the pandemic on children's sense of subjective well-being, highlighting children who benefited as well as those who experienced loss and harm. The chapter emphasises that in situations of crisis, children's well-being needs to come under special attention because of the elevated risk of vulnerability. The vulnerability of children has a tendency to accumulate and, thus, to undermine how well they function in their childhood and adulthood, but also the sustainability of society more broadly.

Acknowledgement Work on this chapter was supported by a grant from the Estonian Research Council (PRG700).

Competing Interests The authors have no conflicts of interest to declare that are relevant to the content of this chapter.

Ethics Approval This study was performed in line with the principles of the Declaration of Helsinki. Approval was granted by the Ethics Committee of the University of Tartu (18.05.2020/ No. 315/T-10).

References

Armitage, R., & Nellums, L. B. (2020). Considering inequalities in the school closure response to Covid—19. *The Lancet Global Health, 8*, E644. https://doi.org/10.1016/S2214-109X(20)30116-9

Arora, S. K., Shah, D., Chaturvedi, S., & Gupta, P. (2015). Defining and measuring vulnerability in young people. *Indian Journal of Community Medicine: Official Publication of Indian Association of Preventive & Social Medicine, 40*(3), 193–197. https://doi.org/10.4103/0970-0218.158868

Berger, F., Schreiner, C., Hagleitner, W., Jesacher-Rößler, L., Roßnagl, S., & Kraler, C. (2021). Predicting coping with self-regulated distance learning in times of COVID-19: Evidence from a longitudinal study. *Frontiers in Psychology, 12*, 701255. https://doi.org/10.3389/fpsyg.2021.701255

Blackwell, C. K., Mansolf, M., Sherlock, P., et al. (2022). Youth well-being during the COVID-19 pandemic. *Pediatrics, 149*(4), e2021054754. https://doi.org/10.1542/peds.2021-054754

Brown, S. M., Doom, J. R., Lechuga-Peña, S., Watamura, S. E., & Koppels, T. (2020). Stress and parenting during the global COVID-19 pandemic. *Child Abuse and Neglect, 110*(2), 104699. https://doi.org/10.1016/j.chiabu.2020.104699

Casas, F. (2019). Are all children very happy? An introduction to children's subjective well-being in international perspective. In D. Kutsar & K. Raid (Eds.), *Children's subjective well-being in local and international perspectives* (pp. 6–17). Statistics Estonia.

Choi, J., Park, Y., Kim, H.-E., Song, J., Lee, D., Lee, E., Kang, H., Lee, J., Park, J., Lee, J.-W., et al. (2021). Daily life changes and life satisfaction among Korean school-aged children in the COVID-19 pandemic. *International Journal of Environmental Research and Public Health, 18*, 3324. https://doi.org/10.3390/ijerph18063324

Cummins, R. A. (2010). Subjective wellbeing, homeostatically protected mood and depression: A synthesis. *Journal of Happiness Studies, 11*, 1–17. https://doi.org/10.1007/s10902-009-9167-0

Cummins, R. A. (2014). Understanding the well-being of children and adolescents through homeostatic theory. In A. Ben-Arieh, F. Casas, I. Frønes, & J. Korbin (Eds.), *Handbook of child well-being* (pp. 635–662). Springer.

Davern, M. T., Cummins, R. A., & Stokes, M. A. (2007). Subjective wellbeing as an affective-cognitive construct. *Journal of Happiness Studies, 8*, 429–449. https://doi.org/10.1007/s10902-007-9066-1

de Abreu, P. M. J. E., Neumann, S., Wealer, C., Abreu, N., Macedo, E. C., & Kirsch, C. (2021). Subjective well-being of adolescents in Luxembourg, Germany, and Brazil during the COVID-19 pandemic. *Journal of Adolescent Health, 69*, 211–218. https://doi.org/10.1016/j.jadohealth.2021.04.028

Diener, E. (2006). Guidelines for national indicators of subjective well-being and ill-being. *Applied Research in Quality of Life, 1*, 151–157. https://doi.org/10.1007/s11482-006-9007-x

Giesinger, J. (2019). Vulnerability and autonomy – children and adults. *Ethics and Social Welfare, 13*(3), 216–229. https://doi.org/10.1080/17496535.2019.1647262

Hall, C. M., Dawes, M., & Farmer, T. W. (2021). Social networks in fifth grade classrooms: Who reports being in a group and who does not? *Journal of Child and Family Studies, 30*, 808–823. https://doi.org/10.1007/s10826-020-01886-z

Kurock, R., Gruchel, N., Bonanati, S., & Buhl, H. M. (2022). Family climate and social adaptation of adolescents in community samples: A systematic review. *Adolescent Research Review, 7*, 551–563. https://doi.org/10.1007/s40894-022-00189-2

Kutsar, D., & Kurvet-Käosaar, L. (2021). The impact of the COVID-19 pandemic on families: Young people's experiences in Estonia. *Frontiers in Sociology, 6*, 732984. https://doi.org/10.3389/fsoc.2021.732984

Kutsyuruba, B., Klinger, D. A., & Hussain, A. (2015). Relationships among school climate, school safety, and student achievement and well-being: a review of the literature. *Review of Education, 3*(2), 103–135. https://doi.org/10.1002/rev3.3043

Lauristin, M., Loogma, K., Erss, M., Vernik-Tuubel, E.-M., & Sarv, E.-S. (2020). *Õpilaste, õpetajate ja lastevanemate toimetulek koroonakriisi aegses kaugõppes*. Eesti Haridusfoorum. Retrieved 24 Oct 2023 from https://haridusfoorum.ee/images/2020/Distantsppe_uuring_EHF_250720.pdf

Lelov-Aasmaa, L. (2022). *Laste suhtumine kontakt- ja distantsõppesse ning subjektiivne heaolu pandeemia tingimustes*. Magistritöö. Tartu Ülikool.

Lutsoja, K., Matina, J. Rebane, M. (2022). *Üldhariduskoolide 2021. aasta rahuloluküsitluse tulemused.* Aruanne. Retrieved 12 Oct 2023 from https://harno.ee/sites/default/files/documents/2022-01/%C3%9Cldhariduskoolide%20rahulolu-%20ja%20koolikeskkonna%20k%C3%BCsitluste%20riiklik%20aruanne%202021.pdf

McClelland, M. M., & Cameron, C. E. (2011). Self-regulation and academic achievement in elementary school children. *New Directions for Child and Adolescent Development, 133*, 29–44. https://doi.org/10.1002/cd.302

Nahkur, O., & Kutsar, D. (2022). The change in children's subjective relational social cohesion with family and friends during the COVID-19 pandemic: A multinational analysis. *Frontiers in Sociology, 7*, 974543. https://doi.org/10.3389/fsoc.2022.974543

OECD. (2019). *PISA 2018 results (Volume III): What school life means for students' lives*. PISA, OECD Publishing, Paris. Retrieved 12 Dec 2022 from doi:https://doi.org/10.1787/acd78851-en.

Our World in Data. (2023). *COVID-19 data explorer*. Retrieved 8 Nov 2023 from https://ourworldindata.org/explorers/coronavirus-data-explorer?zoomToSelection=true&country=USA~GBR~CAN~DEU~ITA~IND&pickerSort=asc&pickerMetric=location&Interval=Cumulative&Relative+to+Population=true&Color+by+test+positivity=false&Metric=Excess+mortality+%28estimates%29

Pavot, W., & Diener, E. (2009). Review of the satisfaction with life scale. In E. Diener (Ed.), *Assessing well-being the collected works of Ed Diener. Social indicators research series 39* (pp. 101–118). Springer.

Public Health England. (2020). No child left behind. Understanding and quantifying vulnerability. London, Public Health England. Retrieved 20 May 2023 from https://assets.publishing.service.gov.uk/media/5f4f72c68fa8f523f4c3c0ed/Understanding_and_quantifying_vulnerability_in_childhood.pdf

Racine, N., McArthur, B. A., Cooke, J. E., Eirich, R., Zhu, J., & Madigan, S. (2021). Global prevalence of depressive and anxiety symptoms in children and adolescents during COVID-19: A meta-analysis. *JAMA Pediatrics, 175*(11), 1142–1150. https://doi.org/10.1001/jamapediatrics.2021.2482

Rees, G. (2017). *Children's views on their lives and well-being. Findings from the children's worlds project*. Springer.

Residori, C., Költő, A., Várnai, D. E., & Nic Gabhainn, S. (2023). *Age, gender and class: How the COVID-19 pandemic affected school-aged children in the WHO European Region. Impact of the COVID-19 pandemic on young people's health and well-being from the findings of the HBSC survey round 2021/2022*. Copenhagen: WHO Regional Office for Europe; Licence: CC BY-NC-SA 3.0 IGO.

Russell, J. A. (2003). Core affect and the psychological construction of emotion. *Psychological Review, 110*(1), 145–172. https://doi.org/10.1037/0033-295X.110.1.145
Savahl, S., Lee, B. J., & Casas, F. (Eds.). (2022). *Children's views on their lives and well-being during Covid-19: A report on the Children's Worlds Project, 2020–2022*. Children's Worlds Project (ISCWeB).
Schunk, D. H., & Greene, J. A. (2018). Historical, contemporary, and future perspectives on self-regulated learning and performance. In D. H. Schunk & J. A. Greene (Eds.), *Handbook of self-regulation of learning and performance* (pp. 1–15). Routledge/Taylor & Francis Group.
Soo, K., & Kutsar, D. (2020). *Kuidas elad, Eestimaa laps? Ülevaade 8–12-aastaste laste subjektiivsest heaolust*. Tartu Ülikool.
Stoecklin, D., Gervais, C., Kutsar, D., & Heite, C. (2021). Lockdown and children's well-being: Experiences of children in Switzerland, Canada and Estonia. *Childhood Vulnerability Journal, 3*, 41–59. https://doi.org/10.1007/s41255-021-00015-2
Suar, D., Jha, A.K., Das, S.S., Alat, P., & Tommasi, M. (Reviewing editor) (2019). The structure and predictors of subjective well-being among millennials in India. *Cogent Psychology, 6*, 2–18.
Tammets, K., Ley, T., Eisenschmidt, E., Soodla, P., Sillat, P. J., Kollom, K., Väljataga, T., Loogma, K., & Sirk, M. (2021). *Eriolukorrast tingitud distantsõppe kogemused ja mõju Eesti üldharidussüsteemile Vahearuanne*. Tallinna Ülikool.
Tang, S., Xiang, M., Cheung, T., & Xiang, Y.-T. (2021). Mental health and its correlates among children and adolescents during COVID-19 school closure: The importance of parent-child discussion. *Journal of Affective Disorders, 279*, 353–360. https://doi.org/10.1016/j.jad.2020.10.016
Tugade, M. M., & Fredrickson, B. L. (2007). Regulation of positive emotions: Emotion regulation strategies that promote resilience. *Journal of Happiness Studies, 8*(3), 311–333.
van der Laan, S. E. I., Finkenauer, C., Lenters, V. C., van Harmelen, A.-L., van der Ent, C. K., & Nijhof, S. L. (2021). Gender-specific changes in life satisfaction after the COVID-19-related lockdown in Dutch adolescents: A longitudinal study. *Journal of Adolescent Health, 69*, 737–745. https://doi.org/10.1016/j.jadohealth.2021.07.013
Viira, A., Ilisson, K., & Turk, P. (2020). *Lapsevanemate töötamine ja perede toimetulek eriolukorras. Eelkoolieealiste ja põhikoolieealiste lastega elanike küsitlus*. Turu-uuringute AS, Sotsiaalministeerium.
von Soest, T., Bakken, A., Pedersen, W., & Sletten, M. A. (2020). Life satisfaction among adolescents before and during the COVID—19 pandemic. *Tidsskrift for den Norske Lægeforening, 140*. https://doi.org/10.4045/tidsskr.20.0437
Wang, M.-T., Henry, D. A., Del Toro, J., Scanlon, C. L., & Schall, J. D. (2021). COVID-19 employment status, dyadic family relationships, and child psychological well-being. *Journal of Adolescent Health, 69*(5), 705–712. https://doi.org/10.1016/j.jadohealth.2021.07.016
WHO. (2022). *Mental health and COVID-19: Early evidence of the pandemic's impact*. Scientific brief. World Health Organization Retrieved 1 Nov 2023 from https://iris.who.int/bitstream/handle/10665/352189/WHO-2019-nCoV-Sci-Brief-Mental-health-2022.1-eng.pdf?sequence=1
Zhu, S., Zhuang, Y., & Ip, P. (2021). Impacts on children and adolescents' lifestyle, social support and their association with negative impacts of the COVID-19 pandemic. *Public Health, 18*(9), 4780. https://doi.org/10.3390/ijerph18094780

Kadri Soo is a lecturer of social welfare at the Institute of Social Studies, University of Tartu, Estonia. Her research interests include child well-being, children's rights, child abuse, and domestic violence. She has also studied reconciliation of work and family life and family policies in local governments. Kadri has long-term experience in researching children using both quantitative and qualitative survey methods. She is a member of the International Society for Child Indicators and has conducted Children's Worlds surveys (ISCWeB, International Survey on Children's Well-Being) in Estonia.

Oliver Nahkur is a research fellow of Research of Social Wellbeing at the University of Tartu, Institute of Social Studies, Estonia. He is a member of the International Society for Child Indicators (ISCI) and the Estonian team of the International Survey of Children's Well-Being (ISCWeB) and secretary-treasurer of the International Sociological Association, Research Committee No 55—Social Indicators. He actively contributes to the development of child well-being data in Estonia. His research interests include child well-being and vulnerability research and social indicators research, including from a cross-national comparative studies perspective. In one of his latest research publications, he studied the change in children's subjective relational social cohesion with family and friends during the COVID-19 pandemic in 18 countries across the globe.

Chapter 12
Ukrainian Refugee Children in the Estonian Education System During the Russian Invasion of Ukraine: Vulnerable, Traumatised and Displaced

Yuliia Kravchenko and Judit Strömpl

12.1 Introduction: Yuliia's Story

We start our chapter with the first author's (Yuliia) story. Yuliia was a practicing psychologist in Kyiv but had to escape with her 6-year-old daughter because of the war. Her personal story provides an authentic insight into the experiences of a woman and mother, who had to leave her home, her grown-up son and other family members, her job, and her friends behind—her whole life as she knew it.

> **First Shocking Days of the War**
>
> On the eve of 24 February 2022 [when Russia attacked Ukraine and the war started], the feeling was twofold—a sense of inevitability in the impending and disbelief that it would happen. It seemed that even the air had become rigid from the general tension.
>
> [On February 24] I found out about 6:00 a.m. that "it had actually started". It was not the gunshots that woke me up, but the incessant glow of my phone from the pop-up messages. All the chats exploded. I opened one after another, and only one thing pounded in my temples: it had begun! I heard distant booming noises—explosions. I listened: it was quiet in the next room … my 6-year-old daughter was sleeping. I thought, I will let the little one sleep, let there still be peace for her. I needed to figure out what to do next.
>
> I went to the kitchen, with a familiar gesture, took the distiller, poured coffee into it, poured water, and brewed coffee. At that moment, it seemed that nothing would remain of my usual life except this coffee. I drank my coffee while looking out the window, it was almost dawn. Neighbours loaded their cars, put their children in them, and drove away. I did not have a car, and I had nowhere to go. How small and helpless I seemed to myself at the time. Smaller than the smallest grain of sand. And that damned war, like a desert storm,

Y. Kravchenko (✉)
Rajaleidja, The Education and Youth Board, Tartu, Estonia
e-mail: yuliia.kravchenko@harno.ee

J. Strömpl
Institute of Social Studies, University of Tartu, Tartu, Estonia
e-mail: judit.strompl@ut.ee

D. Kutsar et al. (eds.), *Child Vulnerability and Vulnerable Subjectivity*, Children's Well-Being: Indicators and Research 27,
https://doi.org/10.1007/978-3-031-61333-3_12

threatened to blow everything to smithereens. The invigorating coffee brought my thoughts back to reality and gave me hope again. We can handle it. However, I could not find a solution about what to do next. My daughter woke up, and I was distracted from my difficult thoughts. I helped her as always to wash her face and served her breakfast. I explained very calmly, but seriously that the situation we had been preparing for had happened and mom was still deciding how to proceed, and she needed to be prepared to pack. At that moment a client called me and asked for an online consultation; I could hear it in her voice, she was on the verge of a nervous breakdown. I felt I could not help, as I did not have a plan of action even for myself. I turned on a cartoon for my daughter, went into the other room, and started the video chat with my client. This counselling helped to clarify my mind and I decided to go to my mother's house to wait and see how events would develop. The only thing I knew was that being alone in the apartment with a child in this situation was dangerous.

My daughter surprised me by being so focused and remembering everything I had taught to her before the Russians' attack. I commanded her to get ready! And in a matter of minutes, she got dressed in the prepared clothes and put her backpack on her shoulders. The city was half-empty, which was creepy, but at the same time gave us a chance to get quickly to my parents' house. We were not alone anymore. It seemed like we just had to wait. Everyone believed it would be over soon.

We spent the next night in the basement, hoping to survive, to protect ourselves from air strikes. It was scary, stuffy, there were many people and little air. My daughter was not comfortable sleeping, and my sleep was out of the question. In the morning my parents tried to buy bread. There were huge queues everywhere—in stores, in pharmacies.

Everything that was happening seemed unrealistic, but it was the reality that had to be coped with. We stood in lines. We went down to the basement during the alarm. Listened to the explosions, trying to figure out where they were shooting. Watching the news, reading chat rooms. We called many times to friends and family, just to know whether they were alive.

From the first days of the war, I submitted my contacts to a psychological volunteer centre and provided online and telephone consultations.

The Decision to Escape

The turning point, which gave the impetus to move on, was the fighting in Bucha, Irpin and Gostomel. They tried to encircle Kyiv. Eyewitnesses and acquaintances spoke of Russian atrocities in the occupied territories, and it was terrifying. Looking at my daughter, I suddenly recognised that to save her we had to leave Kyiv. I received information about an evacuation train for mothers with children from the field kitchen that was prepared for the soldiers of the territorial defence, where my mom was volunteering. It was very difficult to leave Kyiv at that time. But we were lucky, our application was accepted, and we went to Helm.[1] Volunteers met us in Poland, gave us warm food, support, and a temporary shelter. We had to move on.

Life in Estonia

After consulting with friends, analysing the pros and cons, my daughter and I headed to Estonia. In Tallinn, we were hosted by a wonderful Estonian family who not only gave us shelter, but they also took us into their family. They warmed us up and helped us in any way they could. It was thanks to these people that I found the strength to move on and start a new chapter of mine and my daughter's life.

Very soon we moved to the beautiful city of Tartu. Here, I got a job counselling for Ukrainian children and families who had fled the war. We could talk about the events of the war, about the hard experience of evacuation, about the abandoned life with my clients. There is something common in all of us. I say "us" because I am also part of this community of forced emigrants, war refugees who reluctantly left home and left everything they had behind. Our souls are waiting for us back in our homeland.

---

[1] Town in Poland near the Ukrainian border.

Yuliia's story of escaping the war and adapting to life in Estonia, however, is more of a success story, if success can be considered at all in this terrible situation. She managed to protect her child from the trauma of the war in the best possible way, explaining the situation calmly and with the professionalism of a psychologist, thus minimising the damage caused by the escape. Yuliia was also supported by the opportunity to professionally help other war refugees as an insider. However, not all refugees were so aware and ready for change, not to mention children whose vulnerability was deepened by having to leave behind not only their homes and families, but also school, friends, and a familiar social culture, and having to enter a new environment where even the language of communication was unknown. In this we ask: How is the adaptation of Ukrainian war refugee schoolchildren taking place in Estonian schools? What do Estonian children and Ukrainian refugee children speak about at school? In what ways does the education and integration system help children to adapt or, on the contrary, increase their vulnerability?

To find answers to these questions, we conducted a small-scale qualitative study in the first half of 2023 in two Estonian schools attended by Ukrainian war refugee students and their Estonian classmates. We chose to study teenagers—students in grades 6–8 of basic school—because of the particularities of this transitional age, which is already in itself full of different challenges (Abrams, 2004; Vygotsky, 1984). However, before presenting the study's results, we will provide a brief overview of the situation of Ukrainian war refugees in Estonia, and introduce the Estonian education system, including its potential to adapt in order to aid the integration of Ukrainian war refugee students.

12.2 Ukrainian Refugees in Estonia

The first displaced people within and from Ukraine emerged in 2014, when Crimea was occupied by Russia and the People's Republic of Donetsk and the People's Republic of Luhansk were declared (Jauhiainen et al., 2022, p. 24). However, the first Ukrainian refugees appeared in Estonia soon after 24 February 2022, when Russia started the extensive war against Ukraine. The first refugees arrived already on 26 February 2022. In the first months of the war, immigration was particularly intense. Some of the refugees moved on to other European countries, where they had relatives, others stayed in Estonia. It is difficult to know the exact number of Ukrainian refugees, as people move without registering their movements. In September 2023, the official statistics put the number of beneficiaries of temporary protection at 50,450; the number of war refugees from Ukraine globally is 6,203,600, of which 5,834,400 are in European countries (UNHCR, 2023).

For Estonia as a host country, such a large volume of migrants was a shock; since the adoption of the Refugee Act and ratification of the Geneva Convention in 1997 by Estonia, the number of yearly asylum seekers had only ever been extremely small—less than 50 applications per year on average (Jauhiainen et al., 2022, p. 31). Between 2014 and 2022, there had only been 93 asylum seekers from Ukraine.

Despite the very small numbers of asylum seekers and new immigrants, Estonia has had to work on the topic of integration since regaining independence from the Soviet Union in 1991 because of the large Russophone population that migrated here during the Soviet period (Jauhiainen et al., 2022, p. 32). Several integration and development programmes and strategies had been adopted by the Estonian state, aimed at the integration of the Russian-speaking population already living in Estonia as well as the adaptation of new immigrants (Ministry of Culture, 2018, 2022). Nevertheless, the problem of integrating the Russian-speaking community has not yet been resolved.

The Ukrainian minority is the second largest ethnic minority in Estonia. At the beginning of 2022, there were 27,828 Ukrainians living in Estonia, many of them working in Estonia as migrant workers (Statistics of Estonia, 2022). The first refugees were the wives and children of these migrant workers. According to the results of a survey of Ukrainian refugees conducted in the summer of 2022, 92% of Ukrainian refugees felt comfortable in Estonia and perceived that Estonians were friendly towards them. On staying in Estonia or returning home, the majority (66%) of the refugees wanted to return to Ukraine, 2% wanted to move on to third countries and 12% thought they would stay in Estonia. Of the refugees, 60% are adults and 40% are children under the age of 18 years. As children of compulsory school age (7–17) have the right to education, the host country must respect this right. The first Ukrainian children of compulsory school age arrived in the spring of 2022, when the school year was nearing its end. This immediately created a series of urgent and difficult problems for the Estonian education system to solve (Jauhiainen et al., 2022).

It is worth mentioning that Estonians and Ukrainians share the historical memory of being part of the Soviet Union. Shortly after the collapse of the Soviet Union, Estonia became integrated with the Western world and today is a member of both NATO and the EU. Ukraine, on the other hand, developed in a completely different direction and has remained under the influence of the power of the Kremlin all this time. At the outbreak of the war in 2022, the Estonian state and the wider public took an active role on the Ukrainian side, and various measures to support the Ukrainians became available.

No one was prepared for war or for so many refugees. For Estonia, this was a particular challenge, as there was no previous experience of hosting unexpectedly large numbers of war refugees. However, it must be acknowledged that action was taken very quickly and quite successfully despite the fact that all these people needed a lot of help. People were in a difficult emotional state, they had had the ground pulled out from under their feet and many of them had no understanding of how to cope in the new conditions. It was not only psychological help that was required, but also various kinds of assistance in interacting with state bodies and medical institutions. By receiving the necessary information, explanations, and assistance in drawing up a plan of further steps to take, refugees gained at least a minimum of confidence, their anxiety levels decreased, and they were able to take further steps in settling into their new home. The successful integration of war refugees in the host country depends on the host country's regulations and hospitality, as well as on the refugees themselves. War refugees differ from voluntary migrants in the sense that they were forced to leave their homes. Ukrainian refugees often repeat: “We did not ask for this.” Because they had to face a direct threat to their lives, they are all traumatised. Traumatic events evoke a range of negative and difficult feelings that need to be considered when helping them (for more on this, see Chap. 10). Altinay et al. (2023) have examined the impact of host country hospitality on Ukrainian war refugees in Slovakia and found that hospitality in the host country has a direct impact on the psychological well-being of war refugees.

Returning to the question of our chapter—how Ukrainian war refugee schoolchildren have adapted to Estonian schools—we now turn to the analysis of the integration capacity of the Estonian education system and its hospitality towards students with a different mother tongue.

12.3 The Estonian School System as the Context of Integration and Adaptation of Refugees from Ukraine

To better understand the situation at the time the Ukrainian refugees arrived in Estonia, it is necessary to know more about the Estonian education system.

Since the middle of the twentieth century, education has been declared a basic social right and basis for citizenship (Marshall, 1950). Estonia, as an EU Member State that has ratified the UN Convention of the Rights of the Child (CRC), must guarantee the right to education for every child of compulsory school age residing permanently or temporarily in its territory. This also directly concerns the children of Ukrainian war refugees who have arrived in Estonia and who are of compulsory school age. The Children’s Ombudsman also addressed the issue in the Estonian media (Postimees, 2022).

It is important to examine how the state and the education system have been prepared for new immigrants in the context of Ukrainian children adapting to Estonian schools. There are several recommendations to consider when integrating students with other cultural backgrounds into a host country. At the national level, it is important to avoid educational segregation; that is, the concentration of a large proportion of immigrants in the same school, which can jeopardise social cohesion. To avoid segregation, migrant children should be randomly placed in different schools (Nusche, 2009). Preparing teachers to teach students with different cultures and language backgrounds and strong support systems in schools also play a major role. It is also important to increase the involvement of new immigrant parents in the school community, to keep them in a diversified information field. Authors (Gay, 2010; Kirss et al., 2020; Nusche, 2009;) warn that financial resources alone are not enough, care must be taken to ensure that these resources are used in a targeted way; for example, to improve the teachers’ competence in working with new immigrant students, class sizes, group methods and collaborative skills.

Former research shows that the development of a student's first language (referred to as the mother tongue) has a lasting positive effect on children's emotional well-being and academic development (Murillo & Smith, 2011), and also supports the acquisition of further languages (Kim & Pyun, 2014; May, 2017). However, this knowledge may not be present in Estonian schools—indeed, on the contrary, educators may recommend abandoning the use of the first language, believing that it will help to learn Estonian more quickly (Kaldur et al., 2021, p. 15).

Learning and teaching are always interactive, which means that the student is personally involved in the learning process. Studies (Järv & Kirss, 2019; Kirss et al., 2020; Kitsnik et al., 2019; Gay, 2010; Taylor & Sobel, 2011; Kaldur et al., 2019, 2021) point out that student participation in the learning process as well as the meaningfulness and cultural sensitivity of learning are important for the effectiveness of learning and the achievement of long-term educational goals. Teaching students with a migrant background can also be more effective if their experiences and cultural background are taken into account. In this context, it is also important not to forget learning success, which is one of the pillars of learning effectiveness (Ladson-Billings, 1995).

A study conducted in 2021 (Kaldur et al., 2021) provides a comprehensive overview of how Estonian schools were prepared to integrate new immigrants. The study identifies the following shortcomings in the Estonian education system that make it difficult for new immigrant students to adapt to Estonia. First, staff shortages, particularly of teachers and teaching assistants of Estonian as a second language for the child. Second, school staff sometimes lacking competence or being uncertain about existing knowledge and skills on how to integrate children from a different cultural background. Third, there is a need for a much more systematic approach than hitherto in shaping the learning experience of a child with a new migrant background. And fourth, the promotion of support for children and families with a migrant background. In addition, there were problems with communication and information—different kinds of financing and support services were not applied because schools and local governments did not know about their existence.

12.3.1 Transition to Estonian Language Instruction in Schools

As the mother tongue of nearly one third of the Estonian population is Russian, the Estonian school system is still divided into schools where teaching is either in Estonian or Russian. In recent years, however, efforts have been and are being made to convert Russian-language schools to Estonian-language ones. It is important to mention here that students from Ukrainian refugee families can choose to study in either the Estonian or Russian language. In making this choice, various circumstances must be considered. First, many Ukrainian refugees are proficient in Russian, and the choice of a school with a Russian language of instruction would be more comfortable for their studies. However, Estonia's general education policy does not support an increase in the number of students attending schools with

Russian as the language of instruction, as these schools are being smoothly converted to Estonian-language learning (Ministry of Education and Science, 2022).

On the other hand, ethnic Russians attending Russian schools do not all share Estonia's pro-Ukrainian sentiment, in other words, there are many pro-Kremlin people among local Russians whose children attend Russian-language schools (Astapova, 2023). The Estonian media has reported on conflicts in Russian-language schools following the arrival of Ukrainian war refugees (Astapova, 2023).

Choosing an Estonian-language school for Ukrainian students means that they have to learn in a new language that is very different from Ukrainian. At the same time, Estonian language teaching and the integration of a large group of non-native speakers into the classroom is still underdeveloped. Not all schools have special introductory Estonian language courses for new students. The knowledge of Russian language among teachers is also rather poor. The choice of school also depends on where Ukrainian refugees have been directed for accommodation. In Tallinn—the capital of Estonia—where there are many Ukrainian refugees, a school for Ukrainian students has been opened, where Estonian language teaching is well organised (see Ukraina Vabaduse Kool, 2023). However, refugees from Ukraine are placed across Estonia. This is also linked to the fact that, in an attempt not to overcrowd the schools, Ukrainian students are distributed to different schools. Teaching one or two students in the same class seemed to be easier than teaching a larger group. At the same time, in larger cities, where there are more refugees from Ukraine in general, there are also schools that take not only Ukrainian students, but also hire teachers, psychologists, and other support staff from amongst Ukrainian war refugees.

12.3.2 Ukrainian Children in Estonian School

From March 2022, the proportion of Ukrainian students in Estonian and Russian-language schools has changed. According to the results of the survey mentioned above (Jauhiainen et al., 2022), of the 13,000 Ukrainian children registered in Estonia, 36% were registered in the Estonian Education Information System. The language of instruction was Estonian for 80% of students, Russian for 20% and English for nearly 1% (Jauhiainen et al., 2022). In June 2023, 63% of Ukrainian students studied in Estonian-language schools; 24% in Russian-language and 13% in Russian schools with Estonian language immersion.[2] Thirty-eight students were studying in international schools with English as the language of instruction. (EHIS, 2023; Kendrali et al., 2023). Of all Ukrainian school-age children, 65% were enrolled in basic education. (Arenguseire Keskus, 2023). Of them 55% are in Harju County and Tallinn,12% in Tartu and 8% in Ida-Viru County. The rest are distributed across Estonia.

[2]This is one of the ways in which Estonian education can be transferred to teaching in Estonian. Some Russian-language schools are switching to 'hotchpotch' learning, which means that both teachers and students must use Estonian.

To facilitate communication with teachers, many schools assigned a Russian- or Ukrainian-speaking mentor to Ukrainian children, and this has greatly facilitated the situation, provided the children a sense of support, they understood more and became used to the new school more easily. Unfortunately, some schools plan to abandon such mentoring in the second year of studying, and having notified the parents about this received the opposite result to what they were expecting—the children are afraid of the beginning of the new school year, and parents have started thinking about transferring their children to other schools. Such a decision does not help the integration of Ukrainian children into the Estonian school system, on the contrary suspends this process. An important factor of successful adaptation and increased learning productivity was the availability of subject teachers and class teachers who speak Russian (Ukrainian) and are open to communicating with students from Ukraine.

A survey on school satisfaction among Ukrainian refugee students was recently published (Peetsalu, 2023). The data suggests that Ukrainian children's satisfaction with school is higher (3.7 out of total 5) than that of Estonian students (3.3); however, the longer Ukrainian refugees are in school, the less they are satisfied with it. Satisfaction was lowest among eighth graders (3.5 out of 5), with girls' satisfaction lower (3.3) than boys' (3.7). Ukrainian war refugees can attend only Estonian or Russian language schools or the combined study at an Estonian school with distance learning in their Ukrainian home school. Satisfaction with these learning options was divided as follows: satisfaction with studying in a purely Estonian-language school 3.3; satisfaction with studying only in Russian 3.4; and satisfaction with blended learning 3.8. Particularly noteworthy is the rating of students on how much teachers care: 70% of Ukrainian students reported that they sense the caring attitudes of their teachers, while only 51% of Estonian students reported the same.

12.4 Voices From the Field: A Small-Scale Study in Two Estonian Schools

In the spring of 2023, we, the authors of this chapter conducted a small-scale study in two schools with Estonian as the language of instruction attended by Ukrainian war refugee students. The aim was to get an insight into what Ukrainian children experience in Estonian schools and how Estonian students perceive the presence of new students in their classes.

Two basic schools were selected for the study. They differ from each other in terms of the linguistic skills of the students. One of the schools is located in an area with a large Russian-speaking population, and the school has a relatively large number of Russian-speaking, practically bilingual, children. The school is therefore accustomed to coping with a multilingual student contingent. The other school is in a district with a predominantly Estonian population, and the non-Estonian student population there are exceptions.

We conducted a total of four focus groups with students in grades 6, 7, and 8, two in each class—one with Ukrainian students and one with their Estonian classmates. A total of 8 Ukrainian students—6 from the first and 2 from the second school—and 11 of their Estonian classmates—6 from the first and 5 from the second school—participated in the focus groups.

The focus of the group conversations with Ukrainian students was on how they themselves feel at school, what challenges they have with their studies, and how the school and their fellow students support them. The Estonian children could discuss how Ukrainian students affect their school life, and what they think about the need to better integrate Ukrainian children?

The focus groups lasted over one hour each, were recorded and transcribed, coded, and analysed using thematic analysis.

All the students who participated in our study were teenagers, which adds an additional specificity that we need to take into account. According to Vygotsky, adolescence is associated with the crises of this transitional age, which is fraught with all sorts of challenges, but which is an indispensable and natural phase in the child's development (Vygotsky, 1984). The regular adaptation process in adolescence can be turbulent and not always easy. In the context of working with refugees (children and families), we can note that this is the most difficult age group and the most in need of support. Adolescence is not an easy age even without aggravating circumstances, and given the circumstances of Ukrainian refugees, a teenager could become really *problematic*. For teenagers in general, peers and friends are very important in shaping their personal identity. Being forced to move to a different cultural environment because of war leaves them without the opportunity to feel at one with their peers. This alone provokes protest in the protest-minded teenager (Abrams & Brown, 1989; Baumeister & Leary, 1995; Nesdale & Flesser 2001).

It was from teenagers in counselling sessions that the first author (Yuliia) heard: "better under fire, but with friends". Many teenagers said that they were ready to leave everything here and return home to Ukraine on their own. Establishing new contacts in a new school is no longer playful for an adolescent, as it is in the younger grades (Bahmutova & Neska, 2022; Maksimenko & Morozova-Johannessen, 2022). There is a lot of pressure on the teenager—an inner lament for the past and fear and uncertainty in the present. After all, given their status as a refugee, they feel acutely that they are strangers here, different from the others (Maksimenko & Morozova-Johannessen, 2022). Conformism, as one of the peculiarities of this age, can also make it hard for them to understand the uniqueness of their situation—yes complexity, but also uniqueness (Nesdale 2004; Nesdale & Brown, 2004)—or at least prevents them from treating their otherness neutrally and calmly. All these internal conflicts very often have negative behavioural manifestations. In addition, the potential trauma of students fleeing war zones must be considered, which can also result in troubled behaviour. They are the category of students for whom systematic psychological support throughout the adaptation process is vital.

12.4.1 Perception of Estonian Schools by Ukrainian Students

The analysis of the focus groups revealed the key difficulties faced by Ukrainian children upon entering an Estonian school. These are unfamiliarity with the language, lack of comfortable communication, changes in the times that school is on, and age and class mismatches compared to the Ukrainian educational system. In the children's view of, these problems are interrelated, but at the same time each of them has its own peculiarities and consequences. Of course, suddenly finding oneself in a foreign country where everyone speaks an incomprehensible language is very difficult in itself, and it is even more difficult to acquire new knowledge in an unknown language. Several children complained: "I don't understand anything and that's why it's not interesting to be in lessons", "I don't understand anything, and I feel alien and unnecessary", "I don't do anything in the lesson because I don't understand anything". The children also highlighted the changes over time: "When we first came here, everything was great. We felt that we were welcomed in a friendly way, but over time friendships didn't develop. My friends are still Ukrainian children and some Russians who study in this school." Here, too, language skills play a crucial role in forming friendships.

In the first school under our observation, many children are fluent in Russian and can easily interact with Ukrainian students. This school has also accepted more Ukrainian students, who stated that "we [Ukrainian refugees] are like a family, we communicate and support each other". In the other school, there were fewer Ukrainians, and they did not become friends, either. "We do talk to each other, but we are so different that we cannot be friends."

Due to their lack of proficiency in Estonian, Ukrainian children are placed in Estonian-language schools one grade lower, assuming that the study material is already familiar, and more time can be dedicated to language learning. This has a particularly negative impact on ninth graders, who would be finishing basic school in a Ukrainian school but in an Estonian school have to study in eighth grade again. Understandably, they prefer to focus on the distance learning offered by their home school and finish basic school in Ukraine. Studying at the same time in the eighth grade seems to them a pointless waste of time even when they were allowed to skip some lessons in the Estonian school and focus on distance learning at their home school. However, this was not always welcomed by their Estonian classmates. Both Ukrainian girls claimed that the boys in their class were teasing them.

When assessing children's perceptions, it is important to take into account their family's attitudes and plans to stay in Estonia or move on or return. Those children whose parents planned to stay in Estonia for a longer period or permanently took learning Estonian more seriously. They were also more motivated to make friends with Estonians and were more successful in doing so than those who considered living in Estonia only a temporary solution. Both families of the two eighth graders from the second school mentioned above planned to return to their home country as soon as possible.

Ukrainian children think that Estonian teachers are friendlier compared to Ukrainian teachers: "We have more vicious teachers [in Ukraine]". They highly appreciated those teachers who were able to occasionally translate incomprehensible words or sentences into Russian for them. The students appreciated the printouts of translated materials on the topic of the lesson, brief explanations for Ukrainians during the lesson, and additional explanations on homework. In this way the children felt like participants in the process and were interested. However, the students would have preferred to have more of such helpers among their classmates or tutors from other classes.

No less important a component of the communicative issue is communication with classmates and other peers outside school. The Ukrainian students told us that they went on several excursions—to the Tallinn Zoo, to the theatre, or to the cinema with their classmates. At the same time, they particularly enjoyed talking about the sights of their own country and expressed concern about the beautiful places that could be destroyed by bombing there.

12.4.2 Perception of Ukrainian Classmates by Estonian Students

The integration of children with a different mother tongue and little or no Estonian is a process that cannot be expressed simply. It was interesting to listen and talk to students about how they were prepared to welcome new students. In both schools from our study, students and teachers were open to accepting and helping Ukrainian war refugees in any way they could. All the Estonian students talked about how they knew what was happening in Ukraine and wanted to support the new arrivals. Estonian children also shared that their parents encouraged them to support and assist Ukrainian children in every way that they could.

The Estonian students have good proficiency in English, they have been learning English since kindergarten and initially, they tried to communicate with the Ukrainian students in English, but the latter found it difficult and preferred Russian, which is not the preference of Estonian students. This created a barrier to free communication with the newcomers. Unfortunately, initial enthusiasm and interest in the new students waned over time. "We used the Google Translate app, but how long do you bother translating back and forth?"—one girl told us.

According to Estonian students from the first school, Ukrainian students receive intensive teaching in Estonian separately from the class, but in some subjects, they go along with Estonian students (e.g., physical education, vocational education, music, art lessons, history). They reported that the teachers help and explain the topics of learning to them separately in Russian. Some Ukrainian children do not want this, they ask the teachers to speak only Estonian with them, so they can learn Estonian faster. "The teacher's attention is more on Ukrainian children, but it doesn't bother us because the teacher can cope with different tasks."—one Estonian boy explained. If there are some Russian-speaking students in the class, they prefer to speak Russian with the Ukrainian students, but that does not suit Estonian children, who are not good at the Russian language. At the same time, Estonian students understood that Ukrainian classmates find it difficult to learn in Estonian and that sometimes they do not understand anything in class.

According to the Estonian students, the school tries to involve Ukrainian children in extra-curricular activities. They go on excursions and attend other activities organised by the school. Some participants told us that they have invited newcomers from Ukraine to join them when they go out on their own (e.g., to the cinema or for a walk) or they invite them to visit their home. Communication also takes place on social media. But Ukrainian students still stick together more or interact with Russians from other grades.

Describing their Ukrainian classmates, the Estonian children claimed that the Ukrainian war refugees were not sad, as they would have expected, but that they are very close to each other. At the same time, they do not really let anyone into their circle: "We don't even know where they live, and we can't ask them. If we were friends we would visit each other at home." This kind of keeping at a distance is particularly characteristic of Ukrainian students in eighth grade. If we compare the experiences of Ukrainian and Estonian students studying in the eighth grade, we can understand what is behind this. Undoubtedly, the Ukrainian students want to finish basic school as soon as possible, which is made possible for them via distance learning in Ukraine at their home school, but their Estonian classmates feel this as an exclusion.

12.5 Discussion, Conclusion and Recommendations

The survey of the satisfaction of Ukrainian refugee students with Estonian schools, carried out by Peetsalu (2023), provides a good insight into what is happening in Estonian schools. In light of this data, it is easier to understand what the students who participated in the focus groups talked about in our research. The data from both studies are consistent and show that Ukrainian students rate Estonian schools higher than Estonian students. Especially noteworthy is the assessment of how caring the teachers were towards Ukrainian refugee students. The main findings of Peetsalu's survey show that blended learning, where Estonian language learning takes place through a gradual immersion into language learning, was the most highly rated option (Peetsalu, 2023). The students in our study did not have such an option, but this knowledge is significant and deserves further study. The most interesting theme of our study was the students' assessment of the relationship between language skills and communication when adapting to a new school.

12.5.1 Making Contacts First, Language Learning After

When comparing young children's adaptation to a new language context and a new school environment, it seems that verbal fluency does not play such a big role compared to communication—for young children learning a language is aided by the fact they also interact with each other through non-verbal means (Vygotsky, 1984). In adolescence, language skills play a more important role in communication, but the desire to communicate in itself is also important. If children are motivated and interested in communicating with speakers of a foreign language, language learning will go more smoothly than if language learning is seen as just a learning goal in itself.

It is interesting that the Estonian students, when meeting the Ukrainian refugees for the first time at school, started to look for a common language for communication and decided to go for English. This shows that a language that is not one's mother tongue is the most suitable for communication between students with different mother tongues. This suggests a desire on the part of Estonian students to be on an equal footing with their new classmates and not to dominate in terms of language skills. When smaller children with different mother tongues meet each other, they start playing and during play find a common language. In adolescence, the desire to communicate with speakers of another language also plays an essential role. Estonian students feel this perfectly, unfortunately, teachers do not always. Saar (2023, p. 19) describes a similar situation in her study. Her research shows that teachers do not support the use of a third language because they think it is important for Ukrainians to learn Estonian as quickly as possible and therefore recommend not communicating with Ukrainians in English.

Previous studies (Kaldur et al., 2019, 2021; Saar, 2023) and our study confirmed that students put communication (i.e. making contact) first, rather than communication in Estonian. Regarding the teaching of Estonian, students expect teachers and schools to use teaching methods and activities that support communication between Ukrainian and Estonian students (e.g., group work exercises, and other common activities in and out of class). Language learning comes next. While parallel learning of Estonian does not have to be completely ruled out, students need to feel that their mother tongue is not being neglected.

12.5.2 The Integrative Capacity of Estonian School

As mentioned above, there are two types of schools in Estonia—schools with Estonian language of instruction and schools with Russian language of instruction—and in recent years, the intensive reformation of the school system has begun, which means a transition to general education in Estonian as the language of instruction. Over the last 30 years, various efforts to switch to Estonian-language education has been met with resistance from both Estonian and Russian-language schools.

Proponents of schools with Estonian as the language of instruction, from education policymakers to teachers, were worried that too many Russian-speaking children in school would put the survival of the Estonian language in doubt. At the same time, proponents of schools with Russian as the language of instruction were worried that in Estonian language schools Russian children would lose out compared to their Estonian students and that they would lose connection to their culture of origin. The problem was, and still is, that a change to Estonian as the language of instruction means first of all assimilation, not integration. Refugees from Ukraine added an even greater challenge to this process. Ukrainian refugees do not want to lose their mother tongue or their culture—the war is about preserving their own language and culture. The transition to Estonian-language education does not have to take place by excluding the mother tongue of students with other mother tongues, as this will provoke resistance. Today, we know that different languages do not inhibit one another in the human brain, in fact, knowing more languages supports brain flexibility. The Estonian education system must move towards true integration, which does not seek to assimilate students from other languages or segregate them into separate schools, but to create a school community where non-native speakers of different cultures feel a sense of belonging and different languages are valued. The biggest challenge in the transition to Estonian-language education is the question of how to provide Estonian-language education in such a way that it does not displace and replace children's mother tongues but offers additional value to the school community.

The Estonian state must allow Ukrainian school-age children to attend school. The state fulfils this task in different ways. One positive example is the Ukrainian Freedom School, which is a school for Ukrainian students. Here refugees learn the Estonian language, but it can hardly be called an integration school, as Estonians practically do not study there at all. It is more reminiscent of a school with Russian language immersion, where students with a Russian mother tongue learn Estonian mainly under the guidance of Russian mother tongue teachers. We can see clear signs of segregation in these schools. The second option is to choose a school with Estonian as the language of instruction, which is the most supported by the state and the best version for integration. However, statistics from the last 2 years show that some Ukrainian refugees change schools and go on to study in Russian-language schools (EHIS). Why is this happening? This is the big question, which points to the lack of integration potential of Estonian-language schools. Taking the example of the two schools in our study, we can say that one school solves the problem better than the other. In the first school, emphasis is placed on ensuring that students who join the school have sufficient opportunities to socialise with their class and schoolmates. Fulfilling school obligations can mean different things.

12.5.3 Readiness of Estonian Education System to Cope with Students Traumatised by the War

Ukrainian war refugees are not just students who do not know the Estonian language. They are survivors of war trauma that must be considered in the host countries. The Estonian state reacted very quickly, and several psychologists and other specialists were also hired to help Ukrainian children and families. However, psychologists cannot solve the problem of the adaptation of Ukrainian students in Estonian schools alone. There is a need to create a generally safe and friendly school context for all children, both Estonian and non-Estonian.

A safe environment is the basis for integration. Where students feel safe, where there is support for those who need it, and where conflicts between students are prevented and resolved in a child-centred way, the adaptation of new students also works better. Where students see each other as a source of danger, new students, let alone refugees who have already experienced trauma, do not feel comfortable.

There is a need to develop a trauma sensitive school where the teachers and other staff members are aware of the marks of trauma and can deal with them (more about this in Chap. 10).

12.5.4 Recommendations

Ukrainian students recommend: Estonian schools could be more open to students with other mother tongues, which means more opportunities to interact with Estonian children both at school and outside the classroom. The school could organise more introductory events where both Estonian and Ukrainian children could do something together in a free form; for example, so both sides could introduce their school life and youth activities. This would be especially important for Ukrainian children to orient and adapt to new life circumstances.

Teaching and learning methodologies need to be rethought, involving much more collaborative activities between students, where Estonian and Ukrainian students are required to work together to solve some kinds of tasks, activating them to interact with each other. The role and actions of the teacher are also very important, as it is the teacher who is responsible for safety. Safety also means that children's interactions with each other are guided and directed by the teachers.

Trauma-informed pedagogy means more accentuation and a calm mind when things do not go right. Ukrainian students appreciate the caring attitude of Estonian teachers. This is an important quality, to which one could hope to add a sense of Estonian schools and classes being more like communities, where it is nicer for Ukrainian students to integrate. There is a lot of stress in schools, which negatively affects all students and teachers. By providing a safe learning environment, teachers can also take care of their own well-being. One cannot exist without the other.

More case-by-case solutions are needed in the Estonian education system to avoid exacerbating Ukrainian refugee children's vulnerability. For instance, ninth graders in the eighth grade could be supported more; for example, grouped together in the same room or in the same city or county, find a common room for them and hire an assistant teacher or use a volunteer to supervise their learning in their Ukrainian home school. This should be centrally co-ordinated and need not be the responsibility of each child and their parent. In this way, school attendance can be fulfilled. The same children could learn Estonian in an Estonian school where their compulsory education could be limited to physical education, art, music, and vocational education. There they would meet Estonian students, learn Estonian in a non-formal environment and feel a sense of belonging to the school and class community.

Volunteers could be recruited to provide discussion groups for Ukrainian students. At the moment, only Estonian teachers can teach Estonian. However, a child learns practical Estonian much faster in the context of free conversation. Conversation groups could focus on communication, and not so much on the *grammatically correct* use of the language. One should not be afraid of making mistakes, and it is not always necessary to correct language learners if they make mistakes. The ability of refugee children to make themselves understood and making friends in school should be prioritised over avoiding grammatical errors.

Acknowledgement Work on this chapter was supported by a grant from the Estonian Research Council (PRG700) and a special PRG700 Support Grant for Including Ukrainian War Refugee Researchers.

Competing Interests The authors have no conflicts of interest to declare that are relevant to the content of this chapter.

Ethics Approval This study was performed in line with the principles of the Declaration of Helsinki. Approval was granted by the Ethics Committee of the University of Tartu (18.05.2020/No. 315/T-10).

References

Abrams, D. (2004). The development of social identity: What develops? In M. Bennett & F. Sani (Eds.), *The development of the social self* (pp. 291–312). Psychology Press.

Abrams, D., & Brown, R. J. (1989). Self-consciousness and social identity: Self-regulation as a group member. *Social Psychology Quarterly, 52*, 311–318.

Altinay, L., Alrawadieh, Z., Hudec, O., Urbančíkova, N., & Arici, H. E. (2023). Modelling social inclusion, self-esteem, loneliness, psychological distress, and psychological resilience of refugees: Does hospitableness matter? *Journal of Business Research, 162*, 113901.

Arenguseire Keskus. (2023). *Ukraina lapsed Eesti hariduses*. Lühiraport. www.arenguseire.ee. Retrieved October 22, 2023.

Astapova, A. (2023). Russophones' attitudes towards Ukrainian refugees in Estonia. In *Forum: Russia's invasion of Ukraine*, pp 148–150. chrome-extension://efaidnbmnnnibpcajpcglclefindmkaj/https://uu.diva-portal.org/smash/get/diva2:1777043/FULLTEXT01.pdf

Bahmutova, L. M. & Neska, A. (2022). Особливості Психологічних Порушень Серед Українських Біженців у Польщі. *Актуальні проблеми психології: Збірник наукових праць Інституту психології імені Г.С. Костюка НАПН України.* Том. V: Психофізіологія. Психологія праці. Експериментальна психологія. Випуск 22. 177.

Baumeister, R. F., & Leary, M. R. (1995). The need to belong: Desire for interpersonal attachments as a fundamental human motivation. *Psychological Bulletin, 117*(3), 497–529.

EHIS [Estonian education information system]. https://www.haridussilm.ee/ee/valdkonnaraportid/ukraina-oppijad-eesti-hariduses. December 07, 2023.

Gay, G. (2010). *Culturally responsive teaching: Theory, research, and practice* (2nd ed.). Teachers College Press.

Järv, S., & Kirss, L. (2019). *Kultuuritundlikku õpetamist toetav materjal õpetajale. RITA-RÄNNE tööpaketi 7 teemakokkuvõte.* https://sisu.ut.ee/sites/default/files/ranne/files/rita_teemakokkuvote_8.pdf. Retrieved October 07, 2023.

Jauhiainen, J. S., Erbsen, H. A., Lysa, O. & Espenberg, K. (2022). *Temporary protected Ukrainans and other Ukrainians in Estonia, 2022.* Publications of the Department of Geography and Geology of University of Turku, 18. University of Truku.

Kaldur, K., Kivistik, K., Pohla, T., Välista, M., Käger, M., & Pertsjonok, N. (2019). *Uussisserändajast lapse kohanemine Eesti üldhariduskoolis: olukord, tugisüsteem ja valmisolek mitmekultuuriliseks õpikeskkonnaks.* https://www.ibs.ee/publikatsioonid/uussisserandajate-kohanemine-eestis/. Retrieved September 22, 2023.

Kaldur, K., Pertsjonok, N., Mäe, K., Adamson, A-K., Khrapunenko, M., Jurkov, K., & Kivistik, K. (2021). *Uussisserändajast lapse kohanemine Eesti üldhariduskoolis: olukord, tugisüsteem ja valmisolek mitmekultuuriliseks õpikeskkonnaks. Uuringuaruanne.* Balti Uuringute Instituut. doi: https://doi.org/10.23657/IBS.2021.8.

Kendrali, E., Allemann, M., & Kletter, T. (2023). *Ukraina sõjapõgenikud Eestis. Teemapaber nr 3: Haridus.* Poliitikauuringute Keskus Praxis.

Kim, C. E., & Pyun, D. O. (2014). Heritage language literacy maintenance: A study of Korean-American heritage learners. *Language, Culture and Curriculum, 27*(3), 294–315. doi:https://doi.org/10.1080/07908318.2014.970192. Retrieved October 25, 2023.

Kirss, L., Säälik, Ü., Pedaste, M., & Leijen, Ä. (2020). A synthesis of theoretical frameworks on multilingual education for school leaders. *Trames, 24*((74/69), 1), 27–51. https://doi.org/10.3176/tr.2020.1.02

Kitsnik, M., Kirss, L., & Pedaste, M. (2019). *Ühtne Eesti kool – visioon tuleviku Eesti koolist. RITA-RÄNNE tööpaketi 7 teemakokkuvõte.* Kasutatud 07.10.2023. https://sisu.ut.ee/sites/default/files/ranne/files/rita_teemakokkuvote_uhtnekool_28_03_2019.pdf. Retrieved October 07, 2023.

Ladson-Billings, G. (1995). But that's just good teaching! The case for culturally relevant pedagogy. *Theory Into Practice, 43*, 159–165.

Maksimenko, J., & Morozova-Johannessen, O. (2022). Психологічні особливості особистісних змін переселенців в умовах іншої країни (на прикладі Норвегії). *Вісник Національного університету оборони України, 69*(5), 90–97. https://doi.org/10.33099/2617-6858-2022-69-5-90-97

Marshall, T. H. (1950). *Citizenship and social class and other essays.* Cambridge University Press.

May, S. (2017). Bilingual education: What the research tells us. Bilingual and multilingual education. In *Encyclopedia of language and education* (3rd ed., pp. 81–100). Springer.

Ministry of Culture. (2018). *Strategy of integration and social cohesion in Estonia 2020.* https://www.kul.ee/kultuuriline-mitmekesisus-ja-loimumine/strateegilised-dokumendid/loimuv-eesti-2020. Retrieved October 15, 2023.

Ministry of Culture. (2022). *Cohesive Estonia strategy 2030.* Ministry of Culture.

Ministry of Education and Science. (2022). *Eestikeelsele haridusele üleminek* [Transition to Estonian language education]. https://www.hm.ee/uleminek. Retrieved October 07, 2023.

Murillo, L., & Smith, P. H. (2011). *"I will Never Forget That"*: Lasting effects of language discrimination on language-minority children in Colombia and on the U.S.-Mexico Border. *Childhood Education, 87*(3), 147–153. https://doi.org/10.1080/00094056.2011.10521714
Nesdale, D. (2004). Social identity processes and children's ethnic prejudice. In M. Bennet & F. Sani (Eds.), *The development of the social self* (pp. 219–245). Psychology Press.
Nesdale, D., & Brown, K. (2004). Children's attitudes towards an atypical member of an ethnic in-group. *International Journal of Behavioral Development, 28*(4), 328–335. https://doi.org/10.1080/01650250444000018
Nesdale, D., & Flesser, D. (2001). Social identity and the development of children's group attitudes. *Child Development, 72*, 506–517.
Nusche, D. (2009). *What works in migrant education? A review of evidence and policy options.* OECD Education Working Papers No. 22 doi:https://doi.org/10.1787/227131784531. Retrieved September 14, 2023.
Peetsalu, E. (2023). *Ukraina õpilased Eesti koolis. Õpilaste rahuloluküsitluse analüüs. Haridus- ja Teadusministeerium.*
Postimees. (2022). *Estonian children's Ombudsman: Ukrainian children must attend Estonian school.* https://haridus.postimees.ee/7635167/oiguskantsler-ukraina-lapsed-peavad-kaima-eesti-koolis. Retrieved September 28, 2023.
Saar, K. (2023). *Estonian and Ukrainian students in shared school environment during the Ukraine–Russian war crisis: From Estonian children's point of view.* Bachelor's Thesis. University of Tartu.
Statistics Estonia. (2022). Ukrainians in the Estonian labour market 24 July 2022. https://www.stat.ee/en/findstatistics/short-term-statistics/ukrainians-estonian-labour-market
Taylor, S.V. & Sobel, D. M. (2011). Culturally responsible pedagogy: Teaching like our students' *Lives Matter*. Brill.
Ukraina Vabaduse Kool [School of Ukraine Freedom] https://vabaduse.edu.ee/. Retrieved September 28, 2023.
UNHCR The UN Refugee Agency. (2023). *Ukraine Refugee Situation*. Selected location. Situation Ukraine Refugee Situation (unhcr.org). Retrieved December 22, 2023.
Vygotsky, L. (1984). Педология подростка. [Pedology of the adolescent] *Собрание сочинений* [*Collected Works*], Vol. 4. Москва, "Педагогика", 6–242.

Yuliia Kravchenko is a psychologist and lecturer. She graduated from the University of Education Management of the National Academy of Pedagogical Sciences of Ukraine in 2014 with a master's degree in psychology and is now a PhD student at her home university. Before the war, she worked as a lecturer at the National Aviation University, Department of Aviation Psychology, and as a psychologist at the psychological centre in Kiev (Ukraine). She currently lives in Tartu (Estonia) and works as a psychologist in the Out-of-School Counselling Department Rajaleidja of the Education and Youth Board.

Judit Strömpl is Associate Professor of Social Work Research at the University of Tartu. Her main areas of research are childhood and youth vulnerability, child protection, especially substitute care, and juvenile justice. In her research, she is guided by a child rights and well-being perspective. She has researched sensitive topics such as violence, discrimination, and trauma. More recently, she has been focusing on the implementation of support measures for traumatised children in substitute care in Estonia. In her research, she prefers qualitative engaging methods such as ethnography, participatory action research, and playful techniques when interacting with children and their caregivers. She also believes in the transformative power of social work research; that is, while studying vulnerability, she seeks not only to understand the situation but to improve it.

Part IV
Building Resilience in Children: Looking Forward

Chapter 13
Life Story Work: A Good Method to Reduce Child Vulnerability in Substitute Care

Judit Strömpl

13.1 Introduction

Childhood is fraught with various risks of harm, which national child protection systems have been set up to prevent and resolve. If we look at child protection systems worldwide, countries have different ways of addressing childhood vulnerability (Berrick et al., 2023). National child protection systems fall into four categories. First, developing countries focus on protecting children from poverty as the most serious threat to the well-being of children when the child's basic needs are not met. The second group is formed by countries whose child protection systems seek to protect children from maltreatment. The third group of countries seeks to protect the well-being of children based on universal standards. The fourth group is made up of countries that focus on protecting the rights of children (Berrick et al., 2023). However, in each country, there is at least one measure that requires the child to be separated from their birth family, either temporarily or for a longer period, and placed in substitute care.[1] This is undoubtedly a complex measure, which entails several contradictions and risks of harm for both the child, the birth family, the substitute carers and foster parents.

The Estonian child protection system is in between—on the one hand, it belongs to the risk-oriented countries which aim is to protect children from maltreatment by their birth family. At the same time, the rhetoric of the child protection policy is

[1] Various terms are used internationally for this phenomenon, e.g., out-of-home care, alternative care. In Estonia, the preferred term is *substitute care*, as it best conveys the concept – the birth family is replaced by care.

J. Strömpl (✉)
Institute of Social Studies, University of Tartu, Tartu, Estonia
e-mail: judit.strompl@ut.ee

D. Kutsar et al. (eds.), *Child Vulnerability and Vulnerable Subjectivity*, Children's Well-Being: Indicators and Research 27,
https://doi.org/10.1007/978-3-031-61333-3_13

increasingly dominated by the desire to protect the well-being of children according to universal standards. International experience shows that the best way to protect the well-being of children is through their rights. In Estonia, however, very few measures have been adopted until now to enable the child protection system to move towards the protection of children's rights (Linno & Strömpl, 2023).

In this chapter, I will briefly describe the current situation in Estonian substitute care, highlighting the risks of harm that manifest from residential substitute care services.[2] Recent studies in Estonia (Civitta, 2022; Osila et al., 2016) show that young people from residential substitute care face different problems in regard to coping during their independent life, many of them become clients of the social care system and repeat the life patterns of their parents (e.g., are unable to take responsibility for their lives, activities, and well-being, let alone for their own children). It is not enough to separate children from unsafe conditions, there is also a need to cautiously think about how to help them overcome the trauma they have experienced in their birth families in the process of the separation and during the placement. Relying solely on the diligence of the people working in substitute care is not enough either. Protecting children can put their welfare at risk if the protection is provided in an inappropriate manner. The central question of this chapter is: How to reduce the risks of harm that could turn substitute care—a measure designed to protect maltreated children—into an institution that exacerbates child vulnerability?

International studies provide evidence that untreated childhood trauma causes vulnerability in later life (for more on this, see Chap. 10). At the same time, international practice offers solutions to help minimise threats to children separated from their birth families (Bruskas, 2008; Habermas & Bluck, 2000). One such solution among others is life story work (LSW), which is a trauma sensitive method to support the holistic development of children in care (Atwool, 2017; Kontomichalos-Eyre et al., 2023; Rose, 2012; Rose & Philpot, 2005).

After becoming acquainted with the LSW methodology and being fascinated by it, I decided to translate some important materials and to pilot LSW activities in Estonian substitute care. In cooperation with Oma Pere NGO (*Own Family* in English) we developed an Estonian version of the life story book (LSB) for children living in substitute care and for those who have been adopted. The LSB includes materials for child protection workers with theoretical explanations of LSW and examples and recommendations for compiling a child's personal story in a child-friendly language. In this chapter, I present the findings of this work.

The chapter consists of five sub-chapters. The first is devoted to an introduction to substitute care in Estonia. In Sect. 13.2, I present the main ideas, aims, and activities of LSW as a good measure to prevent systemic risks of harm. Section 13.3 introduces the methodology of piloting LSW and the initial findings, and in Sect. 13.4 I discuss the issues related to the possible implementation of LSW in the

[2] Comprehensive studies on the outcomes of family-based substitute care in Estonia are unfortunately lacking.

Estonian child protection system. The chapter ends with a conclusion and recommendations for the development of substitute care in Estonia.

13.2 Estonian Substitute Care as Part of the Child Protection System

The reform of substitute care in Estonia has been going on for over 30 years since Estonia gained independence from the Soviet Union in 1991. In the Soviet Union, children without parental care were placed into large residential institutions—children's homes (Linno & Strömpl, 2023; Sindi, 2015). The state even supported state care for those children whose mothers were not able to combine work and childrearing (Luhamaa & Strömpl, 2021). Since regaining independence, the large children's homes from the Soviet era were reorganised into small family-like institutions, and the international SOS Children's Village was established in 1995 (Sindi, 2015). These reorganisations followed the requirements of the UN Convention of the Rights of the Child (CRC) signed by Estonia in 1991.

However, for a long time, Estonia has had difficulty responding to the requirements of the CRC. The UN CRC Committee and Council of Europe recommendations and guidelines for substitute care are followed more closely every year; however, many important standards are still waiting their time. For example, too many children remain in institutions, including shelters.[3] There is a lack of services targeted at birth families, which means that children tend to remain in care for long periods.

Today, Estonian substitute care is divided into family-based and institution-based substitute care (Nuiamäe et al., 2020; Ministry of Social Affairs, 2013, 2014). There are two types of family-based substitute care: one is a foster family, and the other is a guardianship family. Foster families are specially prepared for this work—they are obligated to undergo PRIDE[4] training. The local authority (LA) signs a contract with them, and the LA remains the guardian of the child in foster care. Foster families receive financial support. This is the best way to help children who are separated from their families, but unfortunately, the number of children living in foster care in Estonia is very small compared to children living in guardianship and institutional care. At the end of 2021, for example, the number of children in foster care was only 139 (Ministry of Social Affairs, 2023).

A guardianship family (in Estonian, *eestkoste pere*) means that the child is being raised by a guardianship family who is fully responsible for them (Leosk, 2021). The guardianship family does not have to undergo any special training, receives

[3] Shelters are not formally part of substitute care and provide a short-term service for children in need, but even small children can stay there for very long periods, up to a year (Ministry of Social Affairs, 2023).

[4] PRIDE – Parent Resources for Information, Development, and Education – a training programme for foster parents.

child benefits and a minimum allowance for bringing up the child, and must report on their financial resources. There is no compulsory regular support from the local authority (e.g., training, supervision), like there is for foster families. If problems arise, they can turn to the LA, but in this case, they may be concerned that their suitability as a guardianship family may be called into question (Leosk, 2021). A large proportion of guardians are relatives of the child, in particular, grandparents. At the end of 2021, the number of children in guardianship care was 1157 (Ministry of Social Affairs, 2023).

Institution-based substitute care is also divided into different types. One type is the traditional residential substitute home, which can be a large institution but where children live in smaller groups (maximum of six). Siblings can live together, except in cases where they pose a threat to each other. Substitute homes are staffed by caregivers who work 12 h a day. Each child has their own trusted caregiver who deals with the child's affairs more confidentially. At the same time, all carers also carry out routine tasks. This means that the trustee is not available for the child all the time because they are not at work 24/7. However, if necessary, the child can call them or ask for help from someone else who is at work. The second type of institution is the SOS Children's Village with a traditional structure. Here, the children have an SOS mother[5] who is always with her children (maximum of six). She has a week's holiday once a month, during which time the children have an *auntie* looking after them. Between the traditional substitute home and the SOS Children's Village, there is another type of institution known as a family home. Family homes were created to be more like foster families. Children live in small houses and are cared for by a *family parent* who works for at least 5 consecutive days followed by 15 rest days.

At the end of 2021, 735 children aged 0–17 were in institution-based substitute care. At the same time, it must be considered that many children are in a shelter awaiting a court decision on their separation from their family (in 2021, 660 children were in shelters). Data shows that many children separated from their families are in institutional care—in 2021 this number totalled 1395. Some children spend their whole childhood in an institution (Ministry of Social Affairs, 2023).

Although adoption is not a form of substitute care, it is one way for many children separated from their birth families to find a suitable environment to grow up. Estonia is not one of the countries with a high adoption rate. At the end of 2021, it had 585 adopted children (Ministry of Social Affairs, 2023).

At present, Estonian child protection protects children from maltreating families and provides them with a structured environment where their basic needs are met, but the special needs of traumatised children are not systematically addressed. This important work is left to caregivers who, as a rule, lack specific training. There are no adapted measures to support the complex development of traumatised children.

Trauma sensitive life story work (LSW) for children in substitute care, used in many countries around the world, is virtually unknown in Estonia. This short-fall

[5] More recently, some SOS families also employ married couples, called SOS family parents.

has led to the idea of introducing LSW activities to those involved in Estonian substitute care. The introduction of LSW as a good measure to help traumatised children will hopefully contribute to a more child-centred child protection system in Estonia, which supports the child's positive identity and autonomy rather than treating the child as an object of care.

13.3 Life Story Work as a Trauma Sensitive Measure to Support the Child's Identity and Autonomy During Substitute Care

Life story work (LSW) is an essential measure in substitute care (Atwool, 2017; Booth, 2022; Cook-Cottone & Beck, 2007; Hooley et al., 2016; Kontomichalos-Eyre et al., 2023; McGill et al., 2018; Pughe & Philpot, 2007; Rose, 2017; Watts, 2021; Willis & Holland, 2009), especially when we consider that those children have experienced traumatic relations and events in their childhood, including the process of removal and placement (Bruskas, 2008; Herrenkohl et al., 2003; Scott & Anglin, 2015).

In the beginning, the primary aim of LSW was to fill in the gaps in knowledge about a child's past (Besson, 2007; Habermas & Bluck, 2000; Rose, 2012). Children who are separated from their families in early childhood do not remember the events of their early life, and this causes a void in their memories. Especially when we consider that the beginning of their lives may have been full of traumatic events and relationships, which in turn damage both the development of the child's brain and their memory. On the other hand, children who are separated from their families may move from one place to another before reaching their permanent home. This, in turn, means that different people and places disappear from their memory, leaving incomprehensible signs. However, every child has the right under the law to know their past and what happened to them when they were young (Besson, 2007). All children have the right to know their origins (CRC, Art. 8 and 29), to communicate with their biological parents if they wish to and this does not disturb the child's best interests (CRC, Art. 9)—to be informed (CRC Art. 13) and take part in decisions affecting their life (CRC, Art.12), at least to know why they are in care (Staines & Selwyn, 2020). To realise these rights, children need information about the life events that they may not remember, the knowledge and skills to cope with unpleasant knowledge, and the support of trusted adults (Booth, 2022). Children need to have the conditions and opportunities to exercise their rights daily.

When the LSW was first introduced, the emphasis was on gathering information, so that children got to know where they came from, what happened to them and why they are in care—the events of the child's early years were recorded (Habermas & Bluck, 2000). For children separated from their families, a life story book (LSB) was compiled. The child's LSB had to include facts about the child's origin, placements, and other important information (Rees, 2009, 2018; Reimer & Schäfer,

2015; Rose, 2012, 2017; Ryan & Walker, 2007). The LSB started to accompany the child and provided answers to the child when they asked questions about their past (Habermas & Bluck, 2000). It is also an important source of information for carers.

Yet trauma sensitive LSW also has other objectives. One is linked to attachment theory on which LSW is based (Ainsworth et al., 1978; Bowlby, 1969/1982; Rose, 2012). Since children separated from their families lack trust in the world around them because of the traumatic relationships in their birth families or because of traumatic events during the separation and placement, one of the biggest challenges is to build a trusting and stable relationship with their caregivers (Cook-Cottone & Beck, 2007; Rose, 2012; Pughe & Philpot, 2007).

The third objective of LSW is to empower children through developing their self-awareness, self-confidence, and self-esteem, which together form the basis for a positive identity and autonomy (Gharabaghi, 2009). Drawing on narrative theory, the focus is on personhood, as the ability to make sense and interpret the person's own experience and the central actor within (Bamberg, 2011; Bruner, 1991, 2004; Polkinghorn, 1988). According to narrative theory:

> … we achieve our personal identities and self-concept through the use of the narrative configuration and make our existence into a whole by understanding it as an expression of a single unfolding and developing story. We are in the middle of our stories /…/. Self, then, is not a static thing nor a substance, but a configuring of personal events into a historical unity which includes not only what one has been but also anticipations of what one will be. (Polkinghorn, 1988, p. 150)

Bruner (2004) defines life story as a perpetual interpretation and reinterpretation of human experience. He writes:

> … eventually the culturally shaped cognitive and linguistic process that guides the self-telling of life narratives achieves the power to structure perceptual experience, to organise memory, to segment and purpose-build the very "events" of a life. In the end, we become the autobiographical narratives by which we "tell about" our lives. (Bruner, 2004, p. 694)

Children who grow up in their birth family get the foundation of their identity automatically, without any special effort. They have enough information about who they are and who their family members are, and by interpreting everyday activities, their identity is gradually being shaped. If something is not clear, they can ask questions because there are enough family members around them who can answer.

When a child is separated from their birth family, they are deprived of this natural environment for communication and family stories. Abused children, meanwhile, have a variety of unexplained negative experiences that need making sense of. If left unexplained, they can lead to self-blame, blaming others and anger. None of these feelings are good for developing a positive identity. If these children are surrounded by people who cannot answer their questions because they lack the information, or because the answers are emotionally too hard, there will be a lot of white holes in the child's story that will undermine the child's ability to create a complete autobiographical narrative. These children need special support to fill the gap in their life narrative and daily practice of making sense of and interpreting their life events. This daily practice could support developing a positive identity (Reimer

& Schäfer, 2015). Identity and self-awareness are essential for a child's participation in the development of relational agency and autonomy (Watts, 2021).

To reach all these objectives, LSW includes several playful exercises and activities that deal with relations and is directed to understanding of the role of people around the child and understanding who the child him/herself is (Besson, 2007; Cook-Cottone & Beck, 2007; McGill et al., 2018; Rose & Philpot, 2005; Wrench & Naylor, 2013). Therefore, LSW is directly aimed at developing the child's own positive identity.

13.4 Piloting LSW Through Participatory Action Research

As mentioned in the introduction, LSW inspired me to translate it for use in Estonia and test it among children and caregivers. In this subchapter, I will present the process and some findings from the participatory action research (PAR).

PAR is a good method for conducting research in social work, where the aim is not only to understand some social phenomena, but initiate changes in social life with the appropriate people (Bortoletto, 2017). However, this does not mean that PAR in any way limits the researcher's task of analysing, reflecting and understanding the phenomenon under study. PAR allows flexibility for the ongoing evaluation of data collection and analytical activities, for development (i.e., extending or narrowing the study design), for the use of new analytical methods where necessary, or for the use of new activities to better understand the phenomenon and improve the situation of the people participating in the process (van Bijleveld et al., 2020). PAR also provides the flexibility to involve different relevant actors in the study. Everyone can contribute to the process according to their competence. The researcher can expand their role and become an enabler for the research participants, empowering them to seek solutions to their problems. Research participants can provide the interpretations needed for the analysis by presenting an *insider's view*. Other contributors to the topic, such as NGOs, can become more involved in developing the field. More importantly, and more useful, is the dialogue between the different actors, joint planning, and the evaluation of the results.

Piloting LSW started with seminars organised by the NGO Oma Pere (which means Own Family in Estonian), where I introduced the basic ideas of LSW. In total, there were two seminars for staff members from substitute homes, foster parents, and adopters in Tartu and Tallinn—the two biggest cities of Estonia. During these seminars, a group of interested people emerged who were willing to participate in piloting LSW. PAR was planned in three phases. In the first phase of the study, the LSW methodology was translated and adapted for use in the Estonian context and the activities were tested. Testing was carried out in two different ways. First, I visited and met with children living in two residential care institutions face-to-face; and second, through the foster parents. During the second phase of PAR, an Estonian version of the life story book (LSB) was developed, tested, and published. In the third phase of the PAR, a training programme was developed, and training was provided to foster parents, residential care staff, and LA child protection workers to assist children in filling in the LSB.

13.4.1 Findings from Piloting LSW

The face-to-face meetings with children took place in two types of institutions—one traditional substitute home and one family home. The volunteer children were selected by the residential home staff. Before the first meeting, I wrote a letter to the children briefly introducing myself and inviting them to help me evaluate LSW activities. I also briefly introduced the issues these activities would address. I attached my photo to the letter so that the children would have an idea of who I am before the first meeting. At the first meeting, the children received a more detailed oral introduction to LSW, and they could ask questions. I also presented them with a written agreement, which they were given 2 weeks to think about before signing. I also explained the basic ethics, that their confidentiality and privacy would remain guaranteed, and that they had the right to stop participation at any time. Each meeting lasted about one hour. The meetings took place in their substitute home, but the children were free to choose the exact room they wanted to meet in. They also had the choice of meeting me one-on-one or to have a trusted carer present. My request was to perform LSW activities together and evaluate them. The participants had to evaluate the activities twice: first, immediately after they took place, and second, at the beginning of the next meeting. The process took almost a year instead of the 4 months initially planned, as several meetings were postponed due to the Covid-19 pandemic.

In total, I worked face-to-face with five young participants, three 15-year-olds and two 13-year-olds, three of whom were girls and two boys. Two of them had been in foster care for practically their entire lives, one since she was a 4-month-old baby, the other since he was a one-and-half-year-old small child. In both cases, the problem was child neglect. One of these children had lived in the same foster home for their whole life, while the other had to experience different placements in both family and residential care, as well as brutal abuse in both types of care.

The other three participants had lived in a substitute home for 3–5 years. One of the participants initiated the separation from his birth family due to the brutal violence of his stepfather, while the other was separated because of a disadvantaged family background including sexual abuse. The third child was separated based on suspected rather than proven abuse. This child had good relations with her biological family, and she once told me that she did not really know why she had to live in a substitute home. I promised I would find out if she wishes but then she drew back and said that she knew it was because of the bad conditions at home, and her father was not able to provide help in her school tasks.

I chose the specific activities according to who the participant was, what I learned about their past, and what form of activity they preferred—either with an immediate caregiver or alone. Information about the child's past was essential for me to be able to answer possible questions the child might have or to avoid certain sensitive topics. The most important criterion for my choice was sensitivity and avoidance of any risk of harm. Therefore, I focused my choice of activities first on the child in the present, leaving past events and family issues for later and leaving the choice of topics for the children.

The other way I piloted LSW was through the foster parents; in other words, I met with them, introduced them to the LSW activities, and asked them to perform and evaluate the exercises and activities. I asked the foster parents to write all their thoughts and feelings about the LSW activities. We discussed our experiences during the meetings and prepared for the next activities. The meetings were held twice a month with the parents of three different families. As they knew each other, they wanted to discuss testing the LSW activities together. Each meeting lasted more than an hour and due to the limitations of Covid-19 were moved to an online environment. There was a total of 9 children aged 4–10 living in these families, 4 boys and 5 girls.

13.4.2 Face-to-Face Testing of LSW Activities with Children in Substitute Homes

The most remarkable thing about LSW activities is that they offer topics that allow caregivers and parents to deal with issues that are not usually dealt with in the everyday life of a substitute home. For example, the child's thoughts and feelings about what is going on in their life, who they are, what they like, what they do not like, and why. All these activities allow for storytelling on seemingly simple topics. Talking about these topics does not make the child feel incompetent.

In the first meetings with the children and their caregivers/guardians, we had to get to know each other, and therefore the activities were chosen to allow the participants to tell their stories. A card game developed in Estonia called *This is My Story* was well suited for this purpose. There are simple and sometimes funny questions on the cards, and all participants must answer to them. Everyone draws a card, reads out the question and all participants have to answer the question. This activity helped to see how ready and used to talking about themselves the children are. At the same time, such games allow children to practice telling stories about themselves and small events in their lives. It was interesting to see how the children listened to what their carers had to say when answering these questions. In some cases, the child even asked additional questions, which I thought was very positive, as it shows that the child wants to know more about their caregiver outside of the work tasks.

In general, all the participants enjoyed the game, and the answers, which started as one-word answers, became longer. However, there was one participant for whom this simple game proved to be visibly distracting. Behind this little break from routine, he suspected something else, something devious that he could not see through.

All the other activities provoked a similar reaction in him. I had to ask repeatedly for him to explain what was bothering him or what he did not like about these activities, but I did not get any verbal feedback. At the same time, he did not make any independent decision either. When I asked him if he wanted to stop participating, he replied "You decide". I realised that his trust in everyone and everything had been destroyed and he needed serious professional help. I realised that he was struggling to understand his role in the pilot, and I ended the meeting with him, thanking him for his contribution. At the same time, he was directed by the institution to psychiatric help.

The other participants showed interest in the LSW activities and rated them as enjoyable activities that they would like to engage in more. With such a small sample, it is not possible to draw any conclusions, but the girls adopted the habit of noticing and verbalising even the smallest events in their lives particularly well. The other boy who took part tended to act as my helper in saying: "I don't need it myself, but I am ready to help you and evaluate these exercises."

Some participants showed me their photo albums with pictures of their birth family and other people from their childhood. However, they could not talk much about the people and events captured in the photos. Writing short explanations to the photos became the next task in our joint activity. The children had to find someone from among the adults who could explain the people in the photos and their role in the child's life. This task was also meant to stimulate communication between the child and the people around them.

Each meeting started with me asking what had happened in the meantime and if there was anything they would like to share with me since the previous meeting. The answers were pretty tongue-in-cheek, especially if the carer was not present. These children are used to being guided by adult teachers and carers and rarely asked to express their own views. When asked for their own views, the children will either want to guess the adult's expectations and give the *right* answer, or, on the contrary, be confrontational and avoid contact altogether. I experienced both reactions to my questions to share their own opinion. It is hard to judge which one would be preferred. Children who look an adult in the eye and try to be as good as possible are more *comfortable* from the adult's point of view, but not from the child's own. The second reaction provokes the adult's discontent, but at the same time forces the adult to act. Unfortunately, this action translates more into the punishment of the child, which only deepens the gap and mistrust between the child and the adult. These reactions show that the child is not very self-aware, and the development of this self-awareness is the objective of LSW activities. During the time that I was piloting LSW, I could see the subtle changes that occurred when children were able to practice telling stories about themselves and the small everyday events in their lives. The development of storytelling skills was visible. The stories became longer and more detailed over time, and the children became more assertive in the telling themselves. It is difficult to draw far-reaching conclusions from such a small-scale pilot study, but I am confident that if such a practice were to be introduced in every substitute home with every child, and for more than 8 times (twice a month), many more self-aware and confident young adults would leave the substitute homes.

13.4.3 The Different Objectives of LSW

When comparing the three objectives of LSW—(1) fill in the gaps in the child's life; (2) develop trusting relationships between the child and their carer, and (3) raise the child's self-awareness and self-esteem—the choice must be child-centred and case-based. If the child knows their family history, there is no need to deal with it separately as long as the child does not want to clarify anything themself, or if they have questions that need to be answered by referring to the family history. The children in our study were least willing to talk about their past and their biological family. This is understandable because they are used to their parents either being blamed for all sorts of troubles or, to avoid blaming the birth family, ignoring the subject. In any case, they are ashamed of their origins. If there was a question, it was more of a neutral curiosity to clarify an innocent question about their birth. For example, one participant asked me to find out the exact time of her birth. She has a twin sibling, and they would like to know which one is older. This seemingly simple request was not so simple because, in the view of personal data protection, sharing such information with the child would violate the protection of her mother's personal data. I had to seek advice from the Children's Ombudsman, who confirmed that a child has the right to know their exact date and time of birth. Fortunately, I was able to grant the child's wish, but this case illustrates how a child's right to information can be violated because of bureaucracy.

All the child participants told me that they know their family stories and do not want to deal with this issue. They were obviously uncomfortable and embarrassed to touch on family matters with me as a stranger. However, almost all of them had a relative they wanted to talk about. For example, one of the girls talked about how she used to visit her grandmother during the holidays and how they had a nice time together. Another talked about her older sister who she spent her summer holidays with in the countryside, helping her with the children and the household animals. The third also had a good relationship with her birth family, whom she met regularly. But knowing about family does not mean making peace with a parent. Abandoned by their parents at an early age, they carry with them resentment and anger towards their parents. This situation needs to be dealt with because getting free from negative emotions supports the child's development. This is a long and time-consuming process, during which the child can make sense of what has happened to them, perhaps also of what happened in their parent's life; that is, dealing with a trans-generational trauma. I did not have the opportunity to delve into this issue, but I forwarded the observation to the authorities.

When meeting children, I took every opportunity to reiterate that a child is never to blame for what has happened to them. At the same time, I did not want to create a situation where there was a possibility of blaming the parents. In any case, there must be some way for a parent to apologise for not being a good enough parent for their child. Perhaps some method of restorative justice could be considered to address the problem.

However, this work should remain the responsibility of the LA child protection worker to create a story for the child about their separation that explains what happened in child-friendly language and in a sensitive way for the child. They, as the most trusted professionals, can contribute a lot to the child's understanding and healing past hurts. They also have the most contact with the birth family, which also provides an opportunity to think about how in a particular case to arrange for the birth family to repair the damage caused to the child.

The second objective—improving the relationship between the child and their direct carer—was only observed where both parties were involved and where it was also reported by the foster parents. Foster parents were particularly satisfied with being able to talk with the children about topics they would not have been able to raise themselves, without LSW activities. Although even when carers were not personally present, their involvement was possible through various tasks. For example, if a child lacked information when completing an activity, they could be offered the opportunity to ask their carer for information or to discuss with them where they could find out about something important for the child. Similarly, during the child's self-evaluation activities, the child could be encouraged to ask the carer what she values most in the child, etc. This is a great opportunity to let children be aware that there are people around them who play positive roles in their lives.

Faced with a situation where the children were reluctant to deal with their biological family, and there was no opportunity to focus on developing the relationship between the child and their immediate caregiver, as some preferred not to be involved in the process, I focused on the third goal of LSW—the development of the child's self-awareness and self-confidence.

This turned out to be the right choice and it worked very well. The children were keen to engage in these activities and exercises and their enthusiasm grew with each session. Soon they started to offer exercises where they could engage themselves. The foster parents also talked about the same situation. They liked to engage in self-characterisation and to look for a hero in themselves. Soon they also started to tell quite long stories about how they could help their schoolmates in an activity they were not very good at before. For example, one participant told a story about teaching a classmate to ski during the sports day. I was amazed by the courage of the children to characterise themselves adequately. For example, one participant did an exercise where she had to place character traits about herself into three categories: *like me*, *a bit like me*, *not like me*. The sticker with the word *honest* was put in the third category (not like me). I was surprised and asked for an explanation. "Yes, I'm not very honest, I don't always tell the truth." she said with a smile. "Is it true now too?", I asked. Then she started to laugh herself and moved the sticker into the medium category (*a bit like me*). This case presented a good opportunity to talk at length about the fact that we ourselves are changing and that our self-esteem can change too. The same girl told me in the first meetings that she had no sense of humour at all. She does not understand why others laugh and what situations can be funny. This same girl still laughed about her own choices of whether she was being honest.

I handed children some nice notebooks and suggested they write down briefly or draw the most important events that happen to them during the day.

Of course, I cannot say with certainty that the children became more aware only because of these exercises. In any case, there was a certain increase in their autonomy. For example, one young participant, who was described as a very good child who obeyed wordlessly all orders, at one point gave up on the support family who wanted to take her to their home. The child felt that this would be a betrayal of her family and made a choice in favour of her own not very coping biological family. This was the first decision she had made that contradicted that of the carers. We can consider whether or not this decision was in the best interests of the child. In any case, it was her own decision, in which I see a clear expression of autonomy and I am pleased about that. It is also noteworthy that the support family was offended by the girl's decision and did not want to have any further contact with her.

LSW activities evoke the need to reflect on past events and on oneself. It is a difficult activity that evokes different feelings. The child needs special understanding and support in this process. The more aware the children are, the more uncomfortable they become for the caregivers. But there is no way to escape it.

13.4.4 Comparing Residential and Family-Based Substitute Care

Comparing the evaluations of LSW activities by foster parents and adopters with the perception of residential staff shows a big difference. Foster parents noted that the LSW activities allowed them to step outside their routine and talk to the children in a different way. This was evaluated by them as of great benefit for improving relations with the children. Parents began to understand their feelings better while playing with the children and doing different exercises. For example, one mother found that by completing the "Finish the sentence" exercise, she got information about her daughter that she would never have got by simply asking, "How are you?" or "How are you feeling?". Their mutual relationships became deeper. Another foster parent commented that without these activities she would not have been able to learn about a lot of very important events, experiences, and dilemmas her children were facing.

There was a big difference in attitudes towards the topic of children's feelings. While the residential staff were hesitant to touch upon the children's feelings, the foster parents were keen to understand and deal with the children's feelings.

Residential staff prefer to act in an unemotional and stable organised way. Indeed, a stable daily routine and regularity is an essential requirement in the care of traumatised children, whose lives before separation were usually characterised by total chaos. This is why some residential caregivers are not very enthusiastic about LSW-type activities, which can disrupt the peaceful life of the institution and cause too much emotion in the children. Going back to the example mentioned above, where a girl refused to communicate with a support family, the staff were of course upset with the girl's choice. Their lives would be a lot more peaceful if the girl continued in the same way to listen to what they said and obey the orders they felt were in the best interests of the child. But what would happen to the child's soul if she had to go on living with the guilt feeling that she had betrayed her loved ones?

Based on this analysis, it cannot be concluded that family-centred substitute care is better than residential care. However, there are some indications, and international experience tends to confirm this. Children, especially teenagers, who suffered abuse in their home prefer residential care because they are afraid to remain within the walls of someone's home. Sadly, there are indeed examples of abuse in foster care. That is why we must work on the basis of what is best for the individual child and improve the effectiveness of control through better training and professional support for staff, including measures such as LSW.

13.4.5 Drafting and Publishing the Life Story Book

Based on positive experiences, we started to draft a sample life story book (LSB) with the children. The drafting of the LSB also involved the working group of the NGO Oma Pere. Currently, a training curriculum is being developed and training is being provided for the staff members of those substitute homes, foster parents and adopters who wish to use the LSB. A special training course is also being developed for child protection workers in the local authorities. They have a special role in working with the removal of children.

LSB (Fig. 13.1) is a support tool for LSW. It is a quick binder folder filled by the child, providing topics relevant to the child's life. There is plenty of space for the child to draw or write, according to their age, information about themselves that is relevant to them. The themes are inspired by LSW activities. The LSB starts from the present and moves smoothly towards the past and the future. This means that the child can explore their past as much as they are ready to at the time. By exploring their own past, they should have a guide to whom they can turn. There is also room for *dreaming*; that is, planning one's future. It is very important that the child knows that they have a key role to play in planning their future. As the LSB is a binder, with the possibility of taking out some pages and adding others, it is possible to come back to the same topic over time and make changes to one's entries. This possibility is particularly important for reviews of favourites and relationship profiles. The LSB is accompanied by a separate booklet with a theoretical explanation of LSW and recommendations for the immediate carer of the child, who can, if necessary, assist the child in completing the book, and for the LA child protection worker. For the latter, some examples are given of how to write in child-friendly language about difficult family situations.

A special role in the LSW methodology is played by the local child protection worker. Their role is to assess the child's needs and provide services to families at risk. They are also responsible for initiating the separation of a child from their family when other means of support cannot ensure the child's well-being in their birth

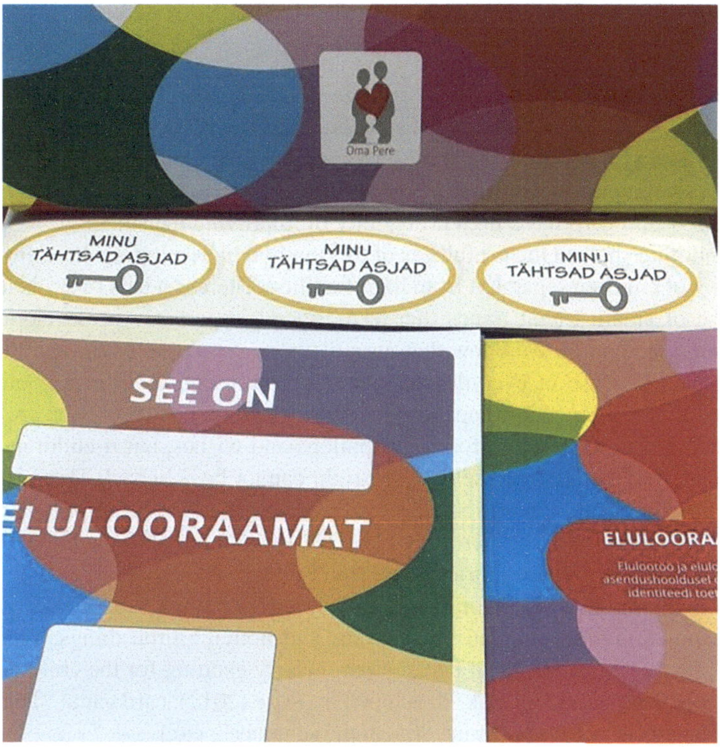

Fig. 13.1 LSB Estonian version

family. The child protection worker is responsible for preparing all the documents necessary for the separation and, together with the child's lawyer, for representing the child in court. As the representative of the local authority after the child has been separated, they also act as the child's guardian. From the LSW point of view, she is the person who knows most about the story of the child and her family. It is the child protection worker's task to draw up a case plan and an action plan for every child separated from their birth family. However, the case plan is not a life storybook. It is a document for the adult professionals who will be dealing with the child. Regardless of the age of the child, they are not involved in the preparation of the case plan. Otherwise, the information could be the basis for a child's life story book, but since their target audience is adults, it is written in language that the child may not understand.

The children I met know about who their child protection worker is but have no idea how to contact them directly if they need some help. They were contacted by the staff of the residential home and the foster parents. However, this means that if a child needs help, for example, because of abuse in substitute care, they would not have this option to contact the child protection worker directly.

13.5 Conclusion

The piloting of LSW highlighted the risks in the child protection system of exacerbating child vulnerability. This is not someone's deliberate desire to harm children, but rather that policymakers are failing to consider all the methods necessary for a child's development and well-being. However, it is good to see that the implementation of LSW and LSB has a high probability of improving the situation.

The piloting showed the usefulness of this method in developing the identity and autonomy of children separated from their families. There is a lack of skills in making sense of small, trivial issues that have crucial importance in developing the child's unique identity. We know that narrative memory develops through the process of making sense of everyday happenings—the telling of stories about what happened. As mentioned in Chap. 9, Estonian child protection legislation prescribes that children should be asked for their opinions and wishes, but if children do not have the skill to express themselves, this right cannot be achieved. There is ample evidence of this from previous studies (Falch-Eriksen, 2022; Strömpl et al., 2017; Strömpl & Luhamaa, 2020; Toros, 2021). That is why one of the activities turned out to be the telling of little stories about small things.

LSW activities provide opportunities for telling these small stories, asking someone questions, giving someone suggestions, and noticing little things. When this activity was linked to games, it became particularly exciting for the children (e.g., Jenga game with additional tasks developed by Rose (2012); card game "This is my story" developed in Estonia; game "finish the sentence", etc.).

In both child-related research and child protection practice, it is of particular importance to adopt more child-centred methods. The possibility of making choices for children supports the development of the child's autonomy. One important experience of the LSW pilot is the way in which these activities were chosen by the children. It was precisely the activity that was used at the time that was most appropriate for the child. The adult's task is to provide options, the child's task is to choose what is most appropriate for them at that moment.

In Estonia, the child-centred approach is often understood in a very adult way—children are offered to participate in the adults' world; for example, to take part in local elections, to have a say in local decisions, and so on, which is great; however, these activities are not equally available to all children (Allaste et al., 2022). Children vary in terms of age, stage of development, structural and family status, cognitive ability, and the different negative and positive experiences they have had in their lives, but at the same time, they have equal rights to participate prescribed by law (CRC, Art.12). This chapter involved children in extremely vulnerable situations, who had to experience a severe disadvantage early in their lives due to having an insecure relationship with their birth family. Unfortunately, some of them also experienced abuse when removed—they experienced complex trauma (for more about this see Chap. 10). But all children need to participate in every area of their lives, even those who have lost trust in the world and adults because of the hardships in their lives. Their childhood lost the most enjoyable and developmentally important activity of this time of life—playing. LSW brings childhood playfulness back into relationships with traumatised children in child protection. It equates children with adults as social partners, allowing the children to play a leading role in this interaction, as games are their domain. Here, their competence is paramount, and it certainly empowers the child. It takes away the adult's dominant position in the relationship with the child, but at the same time allows the adult to have an enjoyable time.

Specialists working with children need the kind of methodology that LSW offers. The experience presented here shows its great potential for children. The pilot project demonstrates its suitability for improving the child protection system in general and substitute care in particular.

Acknowledgement Work on this chapter was supported by a grant from the Estonian Research Council (PRG700).

Competing Interests The author has no conflicts of interest to declare that are relevant to the content of this chapter.

Ethics Approval This study was performed in line with the principles of the Declaration of Helsinki. Approval was granted by the Ethics Committee of the University of Tartu (18.05.2020/No. 315/T-10).

References

Ainsworth, M. D. S., Blehar, M. C., Waters, E., & Wall, S. (1978). *Patterns of attachment*. Erlbaum.

Allaste, A.-A., Beilmann, M., & Pirk, R. (2022). Non-formal and informal learning as citizenship education: The views of young people and youth policymakers. *Journal of Applied Youth Studies, 5*(1), 19–35. https://doi.org/10.1007/s43151-021-00059-z

Atwool, N. (2017). Life story work: Optional extra or fundamental entitlement? *Child Care in Practice, 23*(1), 64–76.

Bamberg, M. (2011). Who am I? Narration and its contribution to self and identity. *Theory and Psychology, 21*, 3–24.

Berrick, J. D., Gilbert, N., & Skivenes, M. (2023). Child protection systems: A global typology. In J. D. Berrick, N. Gilbert, & M. Skivenes (Eds.), *The Oxford handbook of child protection systems* (pp. 943–969). Oxford University Press.

Besson, S. (2007). Enforcing the child's right to know her origins: Contrasting the convention on the rights of the child and the European convention on human rights. *International Journal of Law, Policy and the Family, 21*, 137–159. https://doi.org/10.1093/lawfam/

Booth, R. (2022). Helping us heal; how creative life story work supports individuals and organisations to recover from trauma. *Journal of Social Work Practice, 36*(1), 119–127.

Bortoletto, N. (2017). Participatory action research in local development: An opportunity for social work. *European Journal of Social Work, 20*(4), 484–496.

Bowlby, J. (1969/1982). *Attachment and loss: Vol. 1. Attachment* (2nd ed.). Basic Books. (Orig. ed. published in 1969).

Bruner, J. (1991). Self-making and world-making. *Journal of Aesthetic Education, 25*(1), 67–78. https://doi.org/10.2307/3333092

Bruner, J. (2004). Life as narratiive. *Social Research, 71*(3), 691–710.

Bruskas, D. (2008). Children in foster care: A vulnerable population at risk. *Journal of Child and Adolescent Psychiatric Nursing, 21*(2), 70–77.

Civitta & Ministry of Social Affairs. (2022). Asendushoolduselt iseseisvasse ellu astuvate noorte *uuring [Survey of young people transitioning from institutional care to independent life].* Sotsiaalministeerium.

Cook-Cottone, C., & Beck, M. (2007). A model for life-story work: Facilitating the construction of personal narrative for foster children. *Child and Adolescent Mental Health, 12*(4), 193–195.

Falch-Eriksen, A. (2022). Professional child protection and the child's freedom of expression. In A. Falch-Eriksen & K. Toros (Eds.), *Professional practice in child protection and the child's right to participate* (pp. 31–46). Routledge. https://doi.org/10.4324/9781003150688-3

Gharabaghi, K. (2009). Boundaries and the exploration of self. *Child and Youth Services, 3*(3–4), 165–184. https://doi.org/10.1080/01459350903107327

Habermas, T., & Bluck, S. (2000). Getting a life: The emergence of the life story in adolescence. *Psychological Bulletin, 126*(5), 748–769.

Herrenkohl, E. C., Herrenkohl, R. C., & Egolf, B. P. (2003). The psychosocial consequences of living environment instability on maltreated children. *American Journal of Orthopsychiatry, 73*(4), 367–380.

Hooley, K., Stokes, L., & Combes, H. (2016). Life story work with looked after and adopted children: How professional training and experience determine perceptions of its value. *Adoption and Fostering, 40*(3), 219–233.

Kontomichalos-Eyre, S. A., Lake, A. J., & McGillivray, J. A. (2023). Life story work for children and youth in out of home care: A systematic review and synthesis of qualitative studies. *Children and Youth Services Review, 144*(2023), 106697.

Leosk, N. (2021). *Eestkoste laste eestkostjate narratiivides* [Guardianship in children's guardians' narratives]. Tartu Ülikool Magistritöö. https://dspace.ut.ee/handle/10062/73644

Linno, M., & Strömpl, J. (2023). Child protection systems in Estonia and Latvia. In J. D. Berrick, N. Gilbert, & M. Skivenes (Eds.), *The Oxford handbook of child protection systems* (pp. 444–467). Oxford University Press. https://doi.org/10.1093/oxfordhb/9780197503546.013.15

Luhamaa, K., & Strömpl, J. (2021). Overcoming the Soviet legacy? Adoption from care in Estonia. In T. Pösö, M. Skivenes, & J. Thoburn (Eds.), *Adoption from care. International perspectives on children's rights, family preservation and state intervention* (pp. 33–48). Policy Press. https://doi.org/10.51952/9781447351054.ch003

McGill, L., Coman, W., McWhirter, J., & O'Sullivan, C. (2018). Social workers' experiences of using the narrative model to talk to children about why they are in care and other sensitive issues. *Adoption and Fostering, 42*(1), 49–57. https://doi.org/10.1177/0308575917751999

Ministry of Social Affairs (2013). *Asendushoolduse kontseptsiooni alusanalüüs* [Basic analysis of the concept of substitute care]. Sotsiaalministeerium.

Ministry of Social Affairs (2014). *Asendushoolduse roheline raamat* : Sotsiaalministeerium.

Ministry of Social Affairs. (2023). *Statistics.* https://www.oiguskantsler.ee/et/statistika-ja-uuringud#1.%20LAPS%20JA%20PERE

Nuiamäe, M., Murasov, M., Masso, M. (2020). *Lapsendamise ja hooldusperre paigutamise järgne seiresüsteem* [Post-adoption and post-placement monitoring system]. Poliitikauuringute Keskus Praxis. https://www.praxis.ee/wp-content/uploads/2020/12/Lopparuanne-2.pdf

Osila, L., Turk, P., Piirits, M., Biin, H., Anniste, K., & Masso, M. (2016). *Asendushoolduselt elluastuvate noorte uuring* [Survey on young people leaving care]. Poliitikauuringute Keskus Praxis.

Polkinghorn, D. (1988). *Narrative knowing and the human sciences.* SUNY Press.

Pughe, B., & Philpot, T. (2007). *Living alongside a child's recovery. Therapeutic parenting with traumatized children.* Jessica Kingsley Publisher.

Rees, J. (2009). *Life story books for adopted children: A family friendly approach.* Jessica Kingsley Publisher.

Rees, J. (2018). *Life story work with children who are fostered or adopted: Using diverse techniques in a coordinated approach.* Jessica Kingsley Publisher.

Reimer, D., & Schäfer, D. (2015). The use of biographical narratives to explain favourable and unfavourable outcomes for children in foster care. *Adoption and Fostering, 39*(1), 5–20. https://doi.org/10.1177/0308575914565084

Rose, R. (2012). *Life story therapy with traumatized children. A model for practice*. Jessica Kingsley Publishers.

Rose, R. (Ed.). (2017). *Innovative therapeutic life story work. Developing trauma-informed practice for working with children, adolescents and young adults*. Jessica Kingsley Publisher.

Rose, R., & Philpot, T. (2005). *The child's own story: Life story work with traumatized children*. Jessica Kingsley Publishers.

Ryan, T., & Walker, R. (2007). *Life story work* (2nd ed.). BAAF.

Scott, A., & Anglin, J. P. (2015). *"We don't feel that love": Retrospective reflections on the experiences of removal, transitions and trauma from former youth in care report for the ministry of children and family development*. British Columbia.

Sindi, I. (2015). Changing discourse and changing institutional child substitute care: new terms and processes toward family-like and family-based care. *Child Care in Practice, 22*(1), 50–63. https://doi.org/10.1080/13575279.2015.1054785

Staines, J., & Selwyn, J. (2020). "I wish someone would explain why I am in care": The impact of children and young people's lack of understanding of why they are in out-of-home care on their well-being and felt security. *Child and Family Social Work, 25*(S1), 97–106. https://doi.org/10.1111/cfs.12721

Strömpl, J., & Luhamaa, K. (2020). Child participation in child welfare removals through the looking glass: Estonian children's and professionals' perspectives compared. *Children and Youth Services Review, 118*, 105421. https://doi.org/10.1016/j.childyouth.2020.105421

Strömpl, J., Kaldur, K., & Karu, M. (2017). *Child-friendly justice: Perspectives and experiences of children involved in judicial proceedings as victims, witnesses or parties*. Institute of Baltic Studies. https://www.ibs.ee/wp-content/uploads/Child-friendly-justice-Estonia-II-phase-report.pdf

Toros, K. (2021). A systemic review of children's participation in child protection decision-making: Tokenistic presence or not? *Children and Society, 35*, 395–441.

van Bijleveld, G. G., de Vetten, M., & Ja Dedding, C. (2020). Co-creating participation tools with children within child protection services: What lessons we can learn from the children. *Action Research, 19*(4), 693–709. https://doi.org/10.1177/1476750319899715

Watts, R. (2021). Relationships, reviews and recording: Development practice for children in care. *Practice: Social Work in Action, 33*(3), 207–222. https://doi.org/10.1080/09503153.2021.1889488

Willis, R., & Holland, S. (2009). Life story work: Reflections on the experience by looked after young people. *Adoption and Fostering, 33*(4), 44–52.

Wrench, K., & Naylor, L. (2013). *Life story work with children who are fostered or adopted. Creative ideas and activities*. Jessica Kingsley Publishers.

Judit Strömpl is Associate Professor of Social Work Research at the University of Tartu. Her main areas of research are childhood and youth vulnerability, child protection, especially substitute care, and juvenile justice. In her research, she is guided by a child rights and well-being perspective. She has researched sensitive topics such as violence, discrimination, and trauma. More recently, she has been focusing on the implementation of support measures for traumatised children in substitute care in Estonia. In her research, she prefers qualitative engaging methods such as ethnography, participatory action research, and playful techniques when interacting with children and their caregivers. She also believes in the transformative power of social work research; that is, while studying vulnerability, she seeks not only to understand the situation but to improve it.

Chapter 14
Building Resilience: Innovation in Research and Practice

Laura Palling and Triin Noorkõiv

14.1 Introduction

A large number of mental health disorders begin in childhood and adolescence. According to the WHO collaborative cross-national study *Health Behaviour in School-aged Children* (HBSC) in Estonia in 2018 and 2022, one in three 11 to 15-year-olds reported experiencing depressive episodes throughout the school year. Based on data from the HBSC survey in 2022, mental well-being was higher among boys than girls across all age groups (Pikksööt & Oja, 2023). According to the 2022 survey, three quarters of the children in Estonia were satisfied with their health and lives, but the level of satisfaction had decreased since the last survey in 2018 (Piksööt & Oja, 2023). Moreover, there were significantly more girls and boys in Estonia who had felt sad and depressed more than once a week compared to their peers in neighbouring countries (Vorobjov et al., 2023).

Unresolved mental health problems may have a negative impact on a child's development and learning outcomes, as well as significant lifelong consequences. It is costly for the individual and the society to allow problems to develop to the extent that requires professional intervention. Therefore, it is reasonable to prevent and solve as many mental health issues as early as possible. Systematic improvement of the situation must begin with promotion and prevention.

In recent decades, there has been a shift in the focus of mental health research from risk and psychopathology to the promotion of positive outcomes, such as resilience. Resilience is a dynamic and multi-factor construct that involves the maintenance or restoration of positive mental health following adversity by using internal (personal characteristics or strengths) and external (qualities of the wider family,

L. Palling (✉) · T. Noorkõiv
Clanbeat, Tallinn, Estonia
e-mail: laura@clanbeat.com; triin@clanbeat.com

D. Kutsar et al. (eds.), *Child Vulnerability and Vulnerable Subjectivity*, Children's Well-Being: Indicators and Research 27,
https://doi.org/10.1007/978-3-031-61333-3_14

social, and community environments) protective factors (assets and resources) that enable an individual to thrive and to overcome disadvantage or adversity (Dray et al., 2014). Studies have shown that higher levels of resilience are associated with lower levels of depression and better mental well-being (Imran et al., 2024). Resilience acts as a protective factor against negative mental health outcomes, such as anxiety, loneliness, and stress (Yang, 2023). It is generally accepted that one of the most potent factors in the development of resilience among children and adolescents is having relational support, including close and ongoing contact and interaction with a caring adult (Flett, 2018). Additionally, among others, promoting positive emotions, reducing negative emotions, developing high self-esteem, and improving coping styles are important in enhancing resilience and mental health in children (Li, 2022).

A person's awareness of their mental health, as well as their self-care and self-help skills are the foundation of the mental health services pyramid (World Health Organisation, 2023). Schools play a significant role in supporting the mental well-being of children and reducing the stigma attached to mental illness (Danby & Hamilton, 2016). There is evidence that the school environment makes a major contribution to the development of psychological resilience in children (Stewart et al., 2004). Schools can help students by providing close and ongoing contact and interaction with caring adults, such as teachers, who take a special interest in them. According to Flett (2018), developing the feeling that they matter to others can protect children and adolescents from psychological distress, so schools should foster an environment where students feel valued and supported. Schools can play a key role in building resilience among students by addressing interpersonal vulnerability factors and promoting positive relationships. A systematic review (Fenwick-Smith et al., 2018) found that school-based mental health promotion programmes which focus on resilience and coping skills have positive impacts on the ability of students to manage daily stressors.

On the other hand, there is a need for a stronger and broader evidence base in the field of mental health promotion in schools to inform interventions (O'Reilly et al., 2018). Data on children's perceptions and experiences of completing mental health and well-being measures in the school context is needed to support mental well-being in schools (Demkowicz et al., 2020). Mental well-being data can provide insights into the emotional experiences of students, inform interventions, and support the development of ethical and robust data collection procedures in school-based research. Such data can support children in schools to help themselves by providing insights into their perceptions and experiences of their mental health and well-being (Demkowicz et al., 2020). In addition, understanding the perspectives of students on well-being and how it can be facilitated is crucial, while mental well-being data can also contribute to the development of educational policy by providing important information about school satisfaction and subjective well-being in students (Hoover & Bostic, 2021).

In Estonia, the Accelerate Estonia programme has been founded to encourage innovation to tackle society's wicked issues, including mental health. It is a governmental innovation lab for the development of ideas that could generate systemic change via collaboration between the public and private sector (www.accelerateestonia.ee). As part of the Accelerate Estonia programme, in 2022, an Estonian education technology start-up called Clanbeat with experience working with the topics of student self-directed learning and well-being, committed to the mission of developing a novel solution that would help to improve mental well-being and prevent mental health issues among children. Clanbeat's team had shared the understanding that in Estonia, children's mental health had so far not been adequately supported (Ministry of Social Affairs, 2020), and was ready to contribute to addressing the issue.

The original conceptualisation of the solution and its pilots took place in the Estonian context, but the solution can provide several learning and implementation opportunities internationally to develop the connection and synergy between research and practice to build resilience among children. The next chapters introduce the solution design and the results of two pilots, and finally, ideas for the way forward.

14.2 The Pursuit of Two-in-One: Developing a Practice and a Research Solution to Support Resilience Among Children

The aim of the project initiated by Clanbeat was to prepare for a qualitative leap in promoting mental health and preventing mental health issues among children. The team set out to create a systemic practice for self-assessment that would assist in building greater awareness of the well-being states that are experienced by children and support their becoming more resilient via promoting their meaning-making and reactions to these states, including reaching out to their community and appropriate services as needed. Simultaneously, recognising the lack of operational data and insights into children's well-being, which would provide an overview of the context at school and classroom level, the team also aimed to create a solution that would be a vehicle for research into children's well-being and how to better support it—a solution which would better help understand the situation and the trends, and produce relevant insights for stakeholders around children for more timely and better targeted action. In the following paragraphs, the design decisions behind the solution are described in eight key steps.

14.2.1 Step 1. The Design of the Self-assessment

Experts in the field of psychology (including educational psychology) and social studies were engaged to develop a self-assessment solution to map children's mental health status effectively and on a regular basis without burdening the target group—students between 11 and 16 years old (grades 5 to 9), who are particularly vulnerable with regards to mental health. At the same time, the expectation was set that the results had to be meaningful and actionable for the children themselves and the stakeholders around them (school staff, local municipalities and the state) to facilitate (more) informed decisions, implementing needs-based and preventive interventions and measuring their impact.

Furthermore, it was anticipated that the self-assessment would not take more than a few minutes, yet provide quality results. Acknowledging the fact that the lives of children are undergoing rapid change, the team was also to identify a tool that could be implemented relatively frequently. Finally, it was important to find a tool that would easily provide prompt feedback in order to maintain relevance and provide empowerment for the children as well as the other stakeholders.

The expert group consisted of practitioners and researchers from Tallinn University, the University of Tartu and the National Institute for Health Development of Estonia. This group was facilitated by the Clanbeat team. As a result of the meetings, a consensus was reached that it would be appropriate to use a well-established instrument—the WHO-5 Well-Being Index (World Health Organisation, 1998).

The WHO-5 is a short questionnaire that helps to measure psychological and emotional well-being using five positively charged statements that are easy to understand. The WHO-5 instructions, statements and scoring are shown in Table 14.1.

Table 14.1 The WHO-5 questionnaire (Psychiatric Research Unit, n.d.). Instructions: Please indicate for each of the five statements which is closest to how you have been feeling over the last 2 weeks

Over the past 2 weeks …	All of the time	Most of the time	More than half the time	Less than half the time	Some of the time	At no time
1 … I have felt cheerful and in good spirits	5	4	3	2	1	0
2 … I have felt calm and relaxed	5	4	3	2	1	0
3 … I have felt active and vigorous	5	4	3	2	1	0
4 … I woke up feeling fresh and rested	5	4	3	2	1	0
5 … my daily life has been filled with things that interest me	5	4	3	2	1	0

Scoring. The raw score is calculated by totalling the figures of the five answers. The raw score ranges from 0 to 25, 0 representing the worst possible and 25 representing the best possible quality of life

To obtain a percentage score ranging from 0 to 100, the raw score is multiplied by 4. A percentage score of 0 represents the worst possible, whereas a score of 100 represents the best possible quality of life

According to the methodology, a percentage score below or equal to 50 can indicate poor mental well-being, and could be a basis for further evaluation of the risk of depression.

The WHO-5 assessment tool has been shown to be suitable for the target group of children aged 9–16 (Allgaier et al., 2012), and across cultural contexts; however, it has been recommended to translate the scale into local languages (Low et al., 2021). In addition, the WHO-5 assessment tool has been widely used and has significant associations with mental health conditions, such as depression and anxiety. Moreover, the use of WHO-5 as a universal assessment tool had also been proposed in the mental health strategy of the Estonian Mental Health and Well-Being Coalition (VATEK, 2016).

Next to the WHO-5 as a core tool, it was decided that the self-assessment could also involve a few additional questions that would provide further insight and feedback from the children on self-assessment and its surrounding experience. These questions would vary and could be based on input of various stakeholders, including the research community. The Clanbeat team has maintained that the total time of the self-assessment would be around 5 min on average.

14.2.2 Step 2. The Design of the Feedback Notes at the Completion of the Self-assessment

From the very beginning of this project, to create value for the children and contribute to their resilience, undertaking the self-assessment would need to go beyond filling in a questionnaire and receiving a "thank you" as the reply. To that end, the Clanbeat team worked with experts from nationally recognised mental health and well-being organisations in order to create empathetic feedback notes that would correspond to the state of the mental well-being experienced by the user, providing appreciation, normalisation and input for the next steps, which the children themselves can take. The notes would be visible to the children right after assessing their well-being: after they save their responses.

Based on the WHO-5 Well-Being Index methodology, two types of feedback notes were developed. The first type of note was for those whose score was below or equal to 50 indicating poor mental well-being, and the other was for those whose score was above 50. A more detailed overview of the feedback notes is provided in Table 14.2.

In the later self-assessments, the children were also asked whether they had used any resources or links and which ones. Early on during the first pilot, the Clanbeat team also received information that based on the input from the feedback notes, some children who had had suicidal intentions had contacted the help services and had reconsidered their intentions for the time being.

It should be noted that the process of compiling the links to age-appropriate resources and services had its own value. Several gaps were identified together with

Table 14.2 Structure of the feedback note for children following their self-assessment

Section of the feedback note	WHO-5 Well-Being Index value	
	>50	≤50 (low mental well-being)
1. Appreciation	**Example** [*here and below: free translation from Estonian to English*] Thank you for taking the time to think about yourself.	
2. Normalisation	Your evaluations indicate that lately you have been generally feeling good and comfortable. That's wonderful!	Your evaluations indicate that lately you have been feeling less cheerful, calm, active, rested or interested. Please know that you are not alone in these feelings.
3. Input for next steps	Be sure to continue with activities that nurture your well-being. Here you will find some additional ideas to support yourself, your friends and close ones. */Introduction and links to selected age-appropriate resources and services to follow/*	Please be sure to talk about your thoughts and feelings with an adult you trust—for example with someone from your family, school, hobby activities, Peaasi.ee (www.bit.ly/vt-peaasi) (Peaasi.ee is a nationwide non-government organisation for the promotion of people's mental health, the prevention of problems, early intervention, and the reduction of stigmatisation in society.) or one of the counsellors at Estonian Children's Help (24/7 phone 116111 and chat www.lasteabi.ee). (Estonian Children's Help is a 24/7 phone line, chat and email service for children needing help and adults needing help in supporting children. It is run by the Social Insurance Board of Estonia.) You can also support your own well-being. Here you will find some ideas for this. */Introduction and links to selected age-appropriate resources and services to follow/*
4. The ending	We would like to wish you all the best!	

shortcomings in some of the resources and services. This information has been and will be used by the Clanbeat team to do advocacy work for the improvement of the resources and services on mental health and well-being for children.

14.2.3 Step 3. The Choice of Software to be Used for the Self-assessment

In deciding which software was to be used and the experience created through it, user and child friendliness was an important criterion, in addition to its flexible usage on any device—computer, laptop, tablet and smartphone. In the current stage of the solution, it was decided to use the Typeform survey platform to administer the process, which allows enough customisation. In the future, there is the potential to explore integrating the self-assessment tool into school learning management systems.

14.2.4 Step 4. The Design of the Implementation of the Self-assessment

During the discussions on the self-assessment solution with the expert group of practitioners and researchers from Tallinn University, the University of Tartu and the National Institute for Health Development of Estonia, input was also gathered for its practical implementation. Most notably, the group suggested that the assessment be carried out in school environments in order to prepare the conditions for the assessments to be used with more children, especially those who might not have a conducive environment at home or who might not have the capacity to carry out the assessment on their own. After engaging the schools, in most cases the assessments have taken place in homeroom teacher lessons (sometimes also in subject lessons that are related to personal, social and health education, or IT lessons). The students have largely used their own smartphones for the assessments, and the schools have provided devices as needed.

Once it was decided to administer the self-assessments in the school setting, the Clanbeat team developed support processes and materials for the school staff to help them implement the self-assessment solution. In particular, the following materials were created with the goal of providing as much support for the schools as possible so that the implementation would go as smoothly as possible, taking up as little of the school's resources as possible.

- General information and process description for the school leadership and the assigned contact person.
- Information letter and materials template for parents—to provide information and ask for their consent for the participation of their children.
- Information letter and step-by-step guidelines for teachers/staff members who help to carry out the self-assessments with the children.
- Short videos for the children, to be shown before each assessment. These are easy to watch together in class in order to set the tone and promote unified key messages, as well as to minimise the task load for the school staff. The videos included various spokespeople from different organisations (e.g., the Estonian Students' Society, Estonian Mental Health and Well-Being Coalition, the President of Estonia, Clanbeat team members) in order to familiarise the children with different stakeholders and the mental health and well-being topic in general.

Along the way, the materials have been improved through feedback from the school leadership teams and staff. In addition, the school leadership and staff are always encouraged to personalise the letters they send to their stakeholders, knowing and sensing their local contexts the best.

14.2.5 Step 5. The Design of Frequency of Use for the Self-assessment

How frequently the self-assessment should be used was determined with the users—the children themselves. The first pilot took place with the self-assessments happening every 2 weeks for a total of three times. Based on the feedback, the second pilot had self-assessments once a month (preferred by 31% of the child respondents) and once more the children were asked for feedback on the frequency. Once again, the children confirmed that once a month was the most-favoured option. It might also be interesting to note that in a later pilot where school staff members were involved in the self-assessment, the most-favoured option was once a month also among adults.

14.2.6 Step 6. The Design of the Work with the School Leadership (and Support Staff)

After introducing the solution to the school leadership and them agreeing to participate, the Clanbeat team continues to work closely with each school. So far, the standard process steps include (1) sending the school leadership monthly overviews of the mental well-being of the children in their school based on the WHO-5 questionnaires within a week after the self-assessments having taken place, (2) having online meetings twice every half a year to discuss the data with the school leader and the staff members the leader has decided to involve (average length: 1 h).

The overview templates continue to evolve, as does the content and format of the meetings. Here the Clanbeat team works with the goal of providing the schools with helpful data-based input that could inform their next steps and to be available for discussion and consultation. During the meetings, the data is discussed and clarified and, as appropriate, the Clanbeat team also makes connections with other resources and services that might be helpful for the schools. With some of the schools, it has been decided as relevant that the Clanbeat team would also meet directly with the teachers and/or the students, and in some of the recent communications, meetings with parents have also been brought up. During the current stage, the Clanbeat team finds it important to be flexible and learn more about the ways that are important to provide support.

Among the several ideas that have been raised through the pilot processes, there has been one task in particular the Clanbeat team decided to execute immediately. Based on the input from the school meetings, the team together with its expert partners compiled info sheets for parents and teachers on how to support children. These materials were distributed to the target groups through the school leadership team and contact persons.

14.2.7 Step 7. The Design of the Work with Policymakers and Providers of Well-Being Resources and Services

The Clanbeat team provides general data overviews on the well-being of children to the Ministry of Education and Research and the Ministry of Social Affairs as well as other interested parties involved in policy and solutions development. This has currently been on a non-systemic level—based on opportunities and needs. The team sees the opportunities for it to become more systematic and strategic; however, the mechanisms and incentives for it are yet to be laid out. On a national level, the monthly well-being data acquired through the solution could be part of a system for monitoring the well-being of children.

More in-depth cooperation has so far emerged with some of the providers of resources and services for the well-being of children—most notably through Peaasi.ee, the nationwide non-government organisation for people's mental health. Peaasi.ee increasingly offers support to schools specifically, and cooperation with them and using their services is often the next step for schools and school owners.

14.2.8 Step 8. The Design of the Work with Researchers

The researchers have been and are directly engaged in the following:

- Design of the self-assessment methodology for the children, the choice of instruments and questions that are asked (University of Tartu, Tallinn University, Estonian National Health Foundation).
- The methods and approach used in the solution were validated by the Research Ethics Committee of the National Institute for Health Development to make sure that these were in line with ethical standards and could be put into practice in a school setting.
- Data analysis and insights (University of Tartu).
- Advocacy work (University of Tartu, Estonian National Health Foundation).

Cooperation with researchers is a constant process as the solution itself is developing, expanding and maturing. Different needs and opportunities surface as the partners get to know and engage with each other. In addition, research interest has been growing with the accumulation of data and the awareness of the solution—various stakeholders in the research field have started to reach out more to the Clanbeat team.

14.3 Mapping Children's Mental Well-Being in Estonia: What the First Results Have Shown

14.3.1 Pilot 1, Spring 2022

From May to June 2022, students from grades 5 to 9 assessed their state of mental well-being three times, once every 2 weeks. In total, 4430 students aged 11–16 from 54 schools took part in the first pilot. The invitation to participate had been sent to all general education schools in Estonia (505), and the share of schools who agreed was 11%. It is important to note that student participation depended on receiving informed consent from their parents.

The average WHO-5 Well-Being Index score for 11–16-year-old students was 58 (on a scale from 0 to 100). The proportion of students with low well-being was more than a third at 35%. These numbers remained similar throughout the three assessments. Table 14.3 provides a more detailed overview of the results.

The well-being of girls was consistently lower than the well-being of boys. The differences were particularly notable in grades 7–9 (13–16-year-olds), where the share of girls with low well-being peaked at 57% in grade 9 during the first assessment; at the same time the share of grade 9 boys with low well-being was 23%. In grade 5, the difference between the share of girls and the share boys with low well-being did not exceed 10%. In grade 6, the difference between the share of girls and boys with low well-being was the most at 19%.

The students with unknown gender (8% of the respondents throughout the three assessments) had lower levels of well-being among all. The unknown gender category includes students who marked their gender as *other*, those who indicated that they did not want to share information about their gender, and those who left the question unanswered.

Table 14.3 The self-reported mental well-being of 11–16-year-old students based on the WHO-5 scores collected in Pilot 1 (average scores and % of students with low mental well-being by gender)

	1st time	2nd time	3rd time
Time of assessment, 2022	May 2–13	May 16–27	May 30–June 10
Number of participants	3438	3037	2316
Average well-being score (scale 0 … 100)	**58.0**	**57.5**	**59.2**
Girls	54.4	54.0	56.2
Boys	63.9	63.6	64.8
Gender unknown	48.0	46.2	46.1
% of students with low well-being (WHO-5 score ≤ 50)	**35.1**	**36.1**	**33.5**
Girls	42.6	42.6	38.8
Boys	23.7	25.0	23.0
Gender unknown	52.7	55.3	60.0

Table 14.4 Answers to the question "*How important is it for you that you yourself are able to support your well-being?" (Pilot 1; %)*

	Grade 5	Grade 6	Grade 7	Grade 8	Grade 9
Very important	34.4	28.7	28.2	28.2	31.3
Rather important	52.2	54.4	51.6	52.0	50.5
Rather unimportant	9.7	12.7	15.3	16.2	13.3
Not at all important	2.1	2.7	3.7	2.5	4.3

Girls and students with unknown gender should be paid more attention. In addition, more is to be done to understand the differences in the experience of mental well-being among boys and girls.

Approximately a third of the students (37%) participated on all three occasions.[1] On the first self-assessment, students indicated their demographic information (i.e., school name, grade, gender, age) and assessed their well-being using the WHO-5 instrument. On the second time, students were asked, in addition to the demographic information and the WHO-5 assessment, how important mental health self-help is for them, and which topics related to mental well-being were important for them. On the third time, students were asked who they would be willing to share their mental well-being status with, how often they prefer assessing their mental well-being, and how the assessment made them feel. On the second and third assessment, the students were also asked to indicate whether they used any of the recommendations given to them the previous time, and which, if any, had been useful to them.

Based on the responses to the additional questions in Pilot 1, most students considered the capacity to support their own mental well-being rather important (52%), while less students considered it very important (30%) or rather unimportant (13%). These results emphasise the importance of mental health promotion and prevention work among children (as well as adults) (Table 14.4).

As to the design of the solution, at the end of each self-assessment, the potentially useful links and suggestions were displayed to the children. The most popular mental well-being resource with the students was an article *10 Tips for Supporting Mental Health* by Teeviit,[2] and talking to a trustworthy adult—11% of the respondents indicated they read the article after seeing it promoted at the end of the questionnaire, and the same proportion of students indicated having talked to an adult whom they trusted. A Peaasi.ee adviser was contacted on 100 occasions, Lasteabi was contacted on 87 occasions and the SOVA chat[3] on 69 occasions, as indicated by the students assessing their mental well-being for the second and third time. One

[1] This indicator was influenced by the fact that there were schools (and certain grades within schools) that did not join from the first assessment; and some of the schools also did not want certain grade students to participate on all three occasions (commonly excluding grade 9 students from the third assessment due to the exam period).

[2] Teeviit (www.teeviit.ee) is a national level youth info portal run by the Education and Youth Board of Estonia.

[3] SOVA (www.sova.ee) is a chat dedicated to supporting children. It is run by the SOS Children's Village in Estonia.

third of the students (33% both times the question was asked) confirmed that they had used at least one of the recommendations given to them at the end of the self-assessment.

When asked what kinds of resources would be most useful for children, they indicated the practical tips for taking care of themselves, and face-to-face discussions with adults who are knowledgeable about mental health topics. Interestingly, 29% of students indicated that they do not need anyone's help to take care of their mental well-being.

When asked about the most relevant topics related to mental well-being, the students highlighted free time, relationships with friends, and sleep. In the open-ended answers, students added playing with pets and spending time outside/in nature.

14.3.2 Pilot 2, Autumn 2022

From the start of the school year in September till November 2022, students assessed their state of mental well-being three times, once per month, and received feedback with resources and services they could use to support their own well-being. Students were again asked for feedback on the procedure as well as the recommendations and references they were given.

A total of 3450 students from grade 5 to 9, aged 11–16 from 40 Estonian general education schools took part in Pilot 2. Half of the schools were those who had also participated in Pilot 1. As shown by the data collected in Pilot 2 (Table 14.5), the average well-being score of 11–16-year-old students was 57 (compared to the average of 58 in Pilot 1). The average proportion of students with low well-being increased to 37% (compared to 35% in Pilot 1). While the average well-being index throughout the three assessments in Pilot 2 remained similar, the increase in the share of students with low well-being has become steep. Similar to the results in Pilot 1 in spring, the self-assessed mental well-being of girls was consistently lower

Table 14.5 The self-reported mental well-being of 11–16-year-old students based on the WHO-5 scores collected in Pilot 2 (average scores and % of students with low mental well-being by gender)

	1st time	2nd time	3rd time
Time of assessment, 2022	Sept 26-30	Oct 17-21	Nov 14-18
Number of participants	2670	2095	2006
Average well-being score (scale 0 … 100)	**58.0**	**57.3**	**55.7**
Girls	55.6	54.2	52.6
Boys	62.9	63.2	61.2
Gender unknown	42.9	46.3	44.2
% of students with low well-being (WHO-5 score $\leq$ 50)	**33.7**	**36.7**	**38.8**
Girls	39.4	43.3	44.5
Boys	24.1	24.8	28.7
Gender unknown	58.6	57.9	59.1

than for boys, and the students with unknown gender had the lowest levels of mental well-being.

In Pilot 2, teachers and other school staff (management, support specialists, *etc.*) were also provided an opportunity to map their mental well-being—37 out of the 40 participating schools used this opportunity, with eight schools only mapping the well-being of staff and not engaging their students (the decision of those eight schools to not map the well-being of students was mainly due to the view that asking and managing informed consent from all the parents would bring too much extra workload). As can be seen from the results in Table 14.6, the average well-being scores of school staff were rather similar to the average scores of students. When we compare the share of those with low well-being among school staff, the percentage remained lower than that of the students.

In all of the months, the mental well-being of men was lower than that of women among school staff. This requires further attention. It should be noted that in Estonia, the vast majority of school staff is female (in the 2022/23 school year among general education teachers 13% of teachers were male). As expected, the share of men among the school staff respondents during the pilot was low (between 7–9%). More data would be needed to draw more reliable conclusions.

Additional analyses of school staff demographics and low well-being showed that through the months of the pilot, the increase in the proportion of school staff with low well-being is steeper among those who are younger, and those with less working experience as a teacher. With higher numbers of staff participants, more insights could be gathered about particular groups of staff. This is particularly important as teacher shortage is an urgent issue in Estonia, and the data shows that leaving the profession is especially significant in the first 2–5 years of working (Taimalu, 2020).

Table 14.6 The self-assessed mental well-being of school staff based on the WHO-5 scores collected in Pilot 2 (average scores and % of staff with low well-being by gender)

	1st time	2nd time	3rd time
Time of assessment, 2022	Sept 26–30	Oct 17–21	Nov 14–18
Number of participants	436	502	454
Average well-being score (scale 0 … 100)	**60.0**	**59.1**	**58.2**
Women	60.5	59.1	58.7
Men	56.8	58.1	56.4
% of school staff with low well-being (WHO-5 score ≤ 50)	**25.5**	**31.9**	**31.3**
Women	24.6	31.7	30.1
Men	29.0	32.6	33.3

14.4 Concluding Insights from the Two Pilots

The pilots confirmed that as a rule of thumb, at least one in three teenagers in Estonia are experiencing low mental well-being as also revealed through the HBSC survey. The situation is most critical among girls in grades 7–9 as well as among students of unknown gender. The differences between boys and girls in the experience of mental well-being also requires special attention. While most students considered the skills to support their own mental well-being rather important, nearly a third indicated that they do not need any help from others in relation to their well-being. This may indicate that more information and skills are needed for students to be ready to ask for help for themselves (and others) if needed.

When looking at the data month after month, more detailed hypotheses and patterns begin to emerge, which are yet to be confirmed in the next well-being self-assessment rounds and other sources of data. One of the insights that has come up from the pilots so far about the youth mental well-being surveys (as well as those for school staff) is that the timing of the survey matters, is likely affected by the season as well as the course of the school year.

Mapping the well-being of school staff revealed that approximately every third school staff member was experiencing low well-being, similar to the statistics for the students. It is important to know the situation for school staff in order to better understand their needs and to take steps to support them. Moreover, it helps to direct attention to groups that have very low well-being, who are often younger teachers and teachers with less teaching experience. The well-being of teachers and other school staff is a prerequisite for enabling them to support the well-being of students.

It is important to indicate that when looking at the data at school level and class level, the differences in children's mental well-being become more explicit and some of them also break general patterns. These examples give clear hope: there are things we can do and there are environments that we can create which promote mental well-being. Through direct work with the schools, it is possible to understand more about the conditions that shape the mental well-being in particular groups, and learn from them.

Working with and within each school for positive change takes time, but having the data to support it is a powerful foundation and enabler. The Clanbeat team has experienced that the presence of data supports positive change in the tone of conversations, making discussions more humble and open, and helping schools to prioritise and work on this topic.

14.5 The Way Forward

As the Clanbeat project strides forward, its vision for the future is driven by a commitment to fostering the mental well-being of children through innovative solutions and comprehensive support systems. The team envisions a multifaceted approach that encompasses technical developments, but also a deeper understanding of individual experiences of mental well-being as well as organisational culture and processes around them.

The project will continue to include the mental well-being assessment of both the children and school staff, recognising the importance of staff in the overall well-being ecosystem of the children, and providing them also with support tools and resources to better manage their own well-being. This approach creates a more supportive and mentally healthy environment for the children, reinforcing the goal of promoting mental health and preventing mental health issues among children.

Moving forward, the Clanbeat team foresees a shift towards the collection of personal histories of the mental well-being scores and providing more adaptive responses. This is expected to further empower children and school staff to map their own mental well-being over time, promoting self-awareness and calling for more proactive interventions when needed. To support the relevance of the practice over time, the user experience of both the children and the staff is also to be studied more closely.

Clanbeat strives to develop a model for supporting mental well-being in schools in Estonia. By collaborating with partners from mental health and well-being organisations at the national level, the team contributes to establishing a comprehensive model that would also include school processes and organisation, and ways for stakeholders within schools to work together throughout the school year, keeping in mind the changing situation over different months of the school year. The mental well-being of individuals depends on their ability to act both independently and together as a group—everyone's open and active participation and mutually respectful communication is crucial for their well-being (Kutsar, 2023).

Another intention is to keep looking into ethical and inclusivity considerations. Recognising the importance of ethics and the privacy and autonomy of both children and parents, the Clanbeat team is willing to contribute to the discussion on how we can make the voices of more vulnerable children heard, while their parents may not be the ones giving the explicit consent for their children to participate.

Integration with information platforms within the education system is another potential future step: for more seamless and efficient processes, the team would like to look into the option of connecting the self-assessment solution with learning management systems, such as eKool and Stuudium in Estonia. Integrations of this kind would facilitate easy access for students, teachers, and other relevant stakeholders, and enable more efficient and meaningful processes.

Children's mental health and well-being continues to be a central challenge in our societies. The Clanbeat team is committed to advancing innovative solutions to tackle this challenge, ensuring that it becomes embedded in the educational landscape, respects individual privacy, and involves all the relevant stakeholders, with a constant commitment to ethical and responsible practices. The idea that practical value creation can go together with research continues to inspire the work.

Acknowledgements Authors are grateful to the the expert group of practitioners and researchers from Tallinn University, the National Institute for Health Development of Estonia, and from the

Institute of Social Studies at the University of Tartu. Work on this chapter was supported by a grant from the Estonian Research Council (PRG700).

Competing Interests The authors have no conflicts of interest to declare that are relevant to the content of this chapter.

Ethics Approval This study was performed in line with the principles of the Declaration of Helsinki. Approval was granted by the Ethics Committee of the Estonian National Institute for Health Development (10.03.2022/No. 1052; 25.04.2022/No. 1066; 16.09.2022/No. 1114).

References

Allgaier, A. K., Pietsch, K., Frühe, B., Prast, E., Sigl-Glöckner, J., & Schulte-Körne, G. (2012). Depression in pediatric care: Is the WHO-Five Well-Being Index a valid screening instrument for children and adolescents? *General hospital psychiatry, 34*(3), 234–241.

Danby, G., & Hamilton, P. (2016). Addressing the 'elephant in the room'. The role of the primary school practitioner in supporting children's mental well-being. *Pastoral Care in Education, 34*, 103–190. https://doi.org/10.1080/02643944.2016.1167110

Demkowicz, O., Ashworth, E., Mansfield, R., Stapley, E., Miles, H., Hayes, D., et al. (2020). Children and young people's experiences of completing mental health and wellbeing measures for research: Learning from two school-based pilot projects. *Child and Adolescent Psychiatry and Mental Health, 14*, 1–18.

Dray, J., Bowman, J., Freund, M., Campbell, E., Wolfenden, L., Hodder, R., & Wiggers, J. (2014). Improving adolescent mental health and resilience through a resilience-based intervention in schools: Study protocol for a randomised controlled trial. *Trials, 15*, 289–289. https://doi.org/10.1186/1745-6215-15-289

Fenwick-Smith, A., Dahlberg, E. E., & Thompson, S. C. (2018). Systematic review of resilience-enhancing, universal, primary school-based mental health promotion programs. *BMC psychology, 6*, 1–17.

Flett, G. L. (2018). Resilience to interpersonal stress: Why mattering matters when building the foundation of mentally healthy schools. *Handbook of school-based mental health promotion: An evidence-informed framework for implementation* (pp. 383–410).

Hoover, S., & Bostic, J. (2021). Schools as a vital component of the child and adolescent mental health system. *Psychiatric Services, 72*(1), 37–48.

Imran, A., Tariq, S., Kapczinski, F., & de Azevedo Cardoso, T. (2024). Psychological resilience and mood disorders: A systematic review and meta-analysis. *Trends in Psychiatry and Psychotherapy, 46*, e20220524.

Kutsar, D. (2023). Psychosocial environments and mental well-being. *Estonian Human Development Report, 2023*, 165–172.

Li, C. R. (2022). Promoting positive mental health in children through the empowerment of teachers in delivery and resilience. *Perspectives in Public Health, 142*(5), 251–252.

Low, K. Y., Pheh, K. S., & Tan, C. S. (2021). Validation and optimal cut-off score of the WHO-5 as a screening tool for depression among young adults in Malaysia

Ministry of Social Affairs. (2020). *Green paper on mental health.* Retrieved from https://www.sm.ee/sites/default/files/news-related-files/vaimse_tervise_roheline_raamat_0.pdf

O'Reilly, M., Svirydzenka, N., Adams, S., & Dogra, N. (2018). Review of mental health promotion interventions in schools. *Social Psychiatry and Psychiatric Epidemiology, 53*, 647–662.

Piksööt, J., & Oja, L. (2023). *Eesti kooliõpilaste tervisekäitumise uuring: 2021/2022. õppeaasta tabelid.* Tervise Arengu Instituut. https://www.tai.ee/sites/default/files/2023-03/HBSC_Tabeliraamat_2022.pdf

Psychiatric Research Unit. (n.d.). *WHO (Five) well-being index (1998 version).* Retrieved December 7, 2023, from http://www.who-5.org

Stewart, D., Sun, J., Patterson, C., Lemerle, K., & Hardie, M. (2004). Promoting and building resilience in primary school communities: Evidence from a comprehensive 'health promoting school' approach. *International Journal of Mental Health Promotion, 6*(3), 26–33.

Taimalu, M. (2020). Mida räägib meile TALIS 2018 uuring õpetaja ja koolijuhi karjääriteest? *Eesti Haridusteaduste Ajakiri, 8*(1), 217–220.

VATEK. (2016). Vaimse tervise strateegia 2016-2025. https://vatek.ee/wp-content/uploads/2016/04/Vaimse_tervise_heaolu_strateegia_2016-2025_30.03.2016.pdf

Vorobjov, S., Oja, L., & Piksööt, J. (2023). Young people's mental health and well-being and its relationship with lifestyle. *Estonian Human Development Report, 2023*, 123–134.

World Health Organisation. (1998). *Wellbeing measures in primary health care/the depcare project.* WHO Regional Office for Europe.

World Health Organisation. (2023). *The optimal mix of services for mental health. Organization of services for mental health: Mental health policy and service guidance package.* WHO. https://www.mhinnovation.net/sites/default/files/files/2_Optimal%20Mix%20of%20Services_Infosheet%5B1%5D.pdf

Yang, Z. (2023). Review of resilience conceptual, assessment and intervention. *Pacific International Journal, 6*(1), 110–115.

Laura Palling holds a master's degree in psychology from Maastricht University and in digital health from Tallinn University of Technology. She has led an experiment to map the mental well-being status and concerns of school children using technology. This was a collaboration between Clanbeat and Accelerate Estonia with the aim of creating a model that enables the efficient, easy, and low-cost measurement of well-being as well as data-driven insights to relevant stakeholders.

Triin Noorkõiv is a graduate of the University of Tartu—with a BA equivalent to a master's degree in economic policy and international management. Triin's career has evolved in the field of education, bringing together experience from all three sectors. She has set up NGOs to contribute to the development of a new generation of teachers and leaders in education and the learning of life skills in general education. She has also worked as a teacher herself and as a civil servant in Estonia's Ministry of Education and Research. In the past few years, Triin has been committed to supporting mental well-being in education as a partner in Clanbeat, an educational technology start-up. In collaboration between Clanbeat and Accelerate Estonia, she has been iterating the development of a solution that enables the efficient, easy, and low-cost measurement of well-being as well as data-driven insights to relevant stakeholders. She is often a speaker and facilitator at various programmes and events and collaborates widely with different counterparts across society.

Chapter 15
Public Policies to Overcome the Vulnerability of Children

Graciela H. Tonon

15.1 Introduction: Children's Vulnerability

Vulnerability is situational, for it is conditioned by the context in which it develops, and can be caused or exacerbated by personal, social, political, economic, environmental, and situational circumstances (Mackenzie et al., 2013). Furthermore, if we regard vulnerability as situational, we may also be able to identify the different contexts in which this concept is applied and consider that it is not the same to refer to economic vulnerability as to refer to social or political vulnerability (Tonon, 2022c). In the case of children, vulnerability is considered a multidimensional and multi-causal process, in which children may be injured or damaged in the face of changes or the permanence of external and/or internal situations that affect their level of well-being and the exercise of their rights (Tonon, 2022c).

Boys and girls form part of a peculiar population group that presents certain characteristics according to the historical moment they are living in and in which they show their perceptions and opinions about their own reality (Tonon et al., 2021). The social context in which children's lives currently develop in each society is not only configured by material elements but also by the attitudinal and psycho-social elements they perceive from adults (Tonon, 2001). Children's social vulnerability is defined as the insecurity, precariousness and defencelessness in which children are immersed, being a product of asymmetric social relations with adults, which continue to exist in the actions of families and organisations (Tonon, 2022c). Children's political vulnerability is related to the fact that they cannot organise themselves in a way that may generate a political influence that may change their lives (Schweiger & Graf, 2015).

G. H. Tonon (✉)
Research Center in Social Sciences, Universidad de Palermo, Buenos Aires, Argentina
e-mail: gtonon1@palermo.edu

D. Kutsar et al. (eds.), *Child Vulnerability and Vulnerable Subjectivity*, Children's Well-Being: Indicators and Research 27,
https://doi.org/10.1007/978-3-031-61333-3_15

Nearly a decade ago the Human Development Report 2014 had already referred to children as one of the most intrinsically vulnerable groups compared to others. The contexts of vulnerability in which children live require the creation of new public policies dedicated to solve this social problem, particularly considering that the twenty-first century has witnessed innovative proposals for public policies based on human rights, which allow the possibility of permanent interaction and adjustment, according to the contexts in which children live (Tonon, 2012).

15.2 Public Policies and Their Actors

Public policies may be defined as the response governments give to arising problems. The conception of public policies has witnessed an evolution in the past few years, from the traditional perspective, according to which decisions flowed from the top downwards (i.e., the designs dominating and determining the results), to the inclusion of the influence of other actors apart from the government in the definition of problems and the formulation of alternatives (Iguiñiz Echeverría & Tonon de Toscano, 2014).

In the public policy circuit, the state has traditionally been an agent of organisation and institutionalisation, based on the establishment of rules and decisions originated in the public debate between the different agents and their demands or interests (Bonetti, 2017). But public policies are not merely the objects of choice for a policymaker who attempts to maximise the well-being of the population; they emerge from a decision-making process involving a multiplicity of political actors that interact in a variety of scenarios (Scartascini et al., 2011). The traditional actors in the public policy cycle are the different government agencies, but in the twenty-first century other actors have been included; namely, citizens' social movements, social groups, and NGOs. Back in 1986, Mayntz pointed out the importance of the role played by actors in the public policy circuit and highlighted the significance of considering their ideological orientation and their social origin.

In the case of political decision-makers, they will require the information provided by the systems of quantitative and qualitative indicators if they intend to generate public policies which not only respond to the external conditions of people's lives but also to their quality of life in multidimensional terms. In this sense, we coincide with Veenhoven (2000) regarding the fact that public policies are not merely restricted to material issues, but also embrace situations related to people's mentality.

Regonini (1989) identified five analytical categories to explain the processes of public policy formulation and implementation; namely, the characteristics of the most influential and recurrent actors, the style of decision-making processes, the dynamics of the stages in the life cycle of public policy, the structure of the policy problem, and the rules of the game. Therefore, an analysis of public policy ought to consider—within a space-time dimension—the conditions of its emergence, the dynamics of its development, and the tendencies and contradictions of its political-institutional unfolding (Fleury, 1997).

Our proposal does not imply failing to consider the actions of the different government agencies for the generation of public policies; that is, we do not propose to overlook the role of the institutions, but we wish to highlight a change in the theoretical proposal and the importance of considering the actions of people; in other words, moving from an institutionalist view to a subject-centred view. Furthermore, if we consider people as the fundamental actors in the process of generating public policies, we must highlight the importance of sustained dialogue between actors. In this respect, Iguiñiz Echeverría and Tonon de Toscano (2014) have previously pointed out that the continuous dialogue between actors was the factor that tended to ensure sustainability in the achievement of results—public deliberation thus being considered an essential part of the public policy process.

The policy formulation process is a dynamic game between actors who interact in different scenarios and the policymakers are the ones in charge of carrying out this process. Policymakers are devoted to finding solutions that can be generally applied to a wide variety of problems (Tonon, 2022b). According to Bauman (2006), a characteristic of the political class is that it has a natural tendency to seek explanations and remedies to everyday experiences which explains why, before discussing the possibilities of policymakers deciding and designing public policies, we must first remember that politics is a continuous process. Policymakers tend to rely on their own previous experiences when making decisions and, since they generally do not have all the resources or power to carry out such decisions, they resort to formulas that have given them good results in the past (Tonon, 2022a). Resources is the other important issue to consider when referring to the policy formulation process, since economic restrictions function as another important impediment, which acts as a barrier to change (Trostle et al., 1999).

Public policies are not independent of the place and circumstances in which they are formulated, it all depends on the characteristics of the historical moment in which they are carried out (Tonon, 2022b). This implies that a policy that may be successful at a given place and time, may not be successful at another place and time. Hence, the importance of considering the characteristics of context at the time of the decision, and taking the precaution to avoid transferring policies that arose in one context directly to another since, in those cases, it is imperative to make the necessary adaptations that the new application context calls for.

We therefore propose the existence of a social protection system that contemplates the individuals' biographical trajectory in order to prevent the incidents they are exposed to, on a daily basis, from becoming social determinants (Fitoussi & Rosanvallon, 2006). It is at this point in our reflection that we wonder if it is possible to include children as new actors in the public policy cycle, in addition to the well-known traditional ones. In order to answer this question, we will have to delve into the topic of childhood citizenship.

15.3 Children as Citizens

Nowadays, citizenship cannot merely be considered a legal status associated with rights and responsibilities; it should further be regarded in terms of identity and belonging to a certain political community (Tonon, 2021). Citizenship is categorised as a concept based on meanings, narratives, and discourse. It is also categorised as historical, since its empirical contents are in a constant process of transformation, for its significance in each historical stage has depended on the political and cultural conditions in which it was developed (Sandoval Moya, 2003). In this respect Somers (1997) argued that citizenship cannot be considered a natural category as it depends on public and intersubjective relationships.

Different theoretical conceptions of citizenship were identified by several authors during the 1990s; namely, Rawls (1996) based on the achievement of a social agreement on distributive justice regarding minimum wages to safeguard individual rights; thus, aiming at equality; and Walzer (1993) and Taylor (1993), among others, based on communitarianism which, not only involves equality but also respect for ethnic, religious, and cultural differences (Seibold, 1999). With reference to citizenship, Kymlicka (1996) pointed out that, in the definition of this concept, its legal condition; that is, full membership of a political community, must not be confused with the definition of citizenship as concrete community participation.

This process of the expansion of the concept of citizenship has elicited the recognition of different subjects allowed to acquire the status of citizen in current societies (Sandoval Moya, 2003). Therefore, the so-called integration discourse is centred on an effort to define citizenship by following the logics of the redistribution of wealth and social protection services, as well as a system of public policies aimed at tackling structural inequality. On the other hand, the diversity discourse focuses on the task of defining citizenship on the basis of the theory of the recognition of identities, languages, and the cultural products of minority groups. Hence, the logics of redistribution and the logics of recognition focus on different dimensions of citizenship—neither of which is, at first sight, more important than the other (Sandoval Moya, 2003).

The evolution of citizenship rights has turned out to be the result of a threefold process; namely, socio-political (citizen mobilisation), cultural (legitimation of achievements), and political-legal or institutional processes (concerning legalisation and new public policies). In other words, the notion of citizenship goes far beyond the right to vote (Tonon, 2021). The citizen configuration processes derive from the ways in which people relate and the ways in which they build their lives in a community (Castillo García, 2007).

At this point it is important to reflect on the role of citizens in the public policy cycle. Traditionally, citizens were conceived as beneficiaries or users of policies. Under the conception of citizens as beneficiaries, citizens are viewed as individuals with needs that must be satisfied by the state or by private charity—in the latter case, citizens have a passive role and are deprived of any action and involvement in public policy design processes. On the other hand, under the conception of citizens as users, citizens are regarded as users of the services they receive because they need them, but without any engagement in the relevant decision-making process (Tonon, 2022b). Today the emerging idea is the consideration of citizens as actors and protagonists in the public policy cycle of a democratic system.

If we specifically refer to the relationship between the concept of citizenship and the concept of democracy, Przeworski (1998) comes to mind, when he expressed that citizenship can be fully exercised if the regulatory system is guided by universal criteria, the rule of law prevails, public powers effectively protect rights, and citizens enjoy certain social and economic prerequisites, adding that only an effective state can generate the conditions for citizenship to be effective in a democratic system. Przeworski (1998) further argued that the difficulty faced by democracy is that, while it is a system of positive rights, the conditions required for the effective exercise of those rights and obligations are not created automatically. In other words, for all citizens to be able to exercise their rights and for citizenship to be effective, it is vital to generate the necessary social conditions (Tonon, 2022b).

In the concrete case of child citizenship, we follow Liebel (2008), who states that the use of the concept citizenship is closely connected with notions of democracy and participation. And since we recognise children as subjects of law, we therefore consider it necessary to further our studies on the concept of child citizenship.

There are different conceptualisations related to the notion of children being regarded as citizens. Lister (2008) explains that children's claim to citizenship lies in their acceptance as members of the citizenship community. The author marks the difference between being a citizen and acting as one: "Being a citizen, in the legal and sociological sense, means enjoying the rights of citizenship necessary for agency, and social and political participation. Acting as a citizen involves fulfilling the full potential of the status" (Lister, 2008, p.11). Also the Inter-Agency Working Group on Children's Participation (IAWGCP, 2008) considers that citizenship represents the collection of rights and obligations that define the members of a community, considering that these rights and obligations encompass legal empowerment and justice, political participation and decision-making, social engagement, economic rights, and access to resources.

Liebel (2008) expressed that an equal citizenship for children considers the differences between children and adults and the lower social status of children, considering citizenship not only as a set of rights, but also as a social relationship, in which norms, institutional practices, meanings, cultural assumptions, and the sense of belonging are combined (Isin & Turner, 2003). The notion of citizenship as a practice articulates the inclusive and the relational dimensions, encompassing, not only problems and issues of culture and identity, but also bringing together these different dynamic aspects in a world of constantly changing differences (Lawy & Biesta, 2006).

The IAWGCP (2008) pointed out that all children are born with civil, political, social, and economic rights and that these rights allow them to exercise their citizenship, at least to some extent. And that is why it is necessary to remember that the right of children to be citizens does not solely depend on their future contributions to society. Children's ability to exercise their civic rights and responsibilities evolves as they grow up and learn because, as competent social actors, children are already making important contributions to society. In addition, children are persons in constant evolution and development, so they do not become citizens simply because they come of age, particularly considering that the definitions of legal age do not reflect the range of children's abilities, for they vary from one child to another and depend on the contexts in which they grow up. Citizenship must be learned through daily experiences of family and community life, education, and civic and political awareness.

The new ideas regarding child citizenship include children's participation as performing a central role. Tonon (2022b) points out that in order to be effective participation needs to go beyond the individual act and develop a collective and organised action taking the form of a collective decision. For this reason, citizen information and consultation concerning previously established programmes cannot be regarded as participation. Previously, in the 1990s, Sirvent (1994) had made a distinction between real and symbolic participation. The author argued that participation is real when the members of an institution or group carry out actions that have an effective influence on all the processes of institutional life and on the nature of decisions, leading to changes in the existing power structures. She expressed that, on the other hand, participation is symbolic when actions have little or no influence on institutional policies and management (2010). According to Sirvent (1994), symbolic participation creates, in both individuals and groups, the illusion of exercising a non-existent power—it is the "as if" of participation. Also, Liebel and Saadi (2012) expressed that participation is a possibility or opportunity to have a wider scope of action, power, and influence in an unequal society, as well as a possibility or opportunity to escape from a marginal position and achieve social recognition and a sense of belonging in society.

In the case of children's participation, Malone and Hartung (2010, p. 26) forewarn that "children's participation is often defined in terms of the roles that adults ascribe to children, as though children were unable to participate in decision-making or contribute to society unless they were formally engaged through adult-initiated projects." Moses (2008) pointed out that children's participation takes place in two dimensions: the private or personal dimension, focused on the household and family; and the public dimension, which comprises the community, school, and government.

Children's participation must be analysed taking into consideration the time and space in which it is developed, as each society constructs its notion of childhood in social and historical terms (Tonon, 2022a). "From our point of view, the essential concept of participation lies in joint decision-making, which implies distribution of power, rather than simply acting together" (Tonon, 2020, p. 411). Liebel (2008) also proposes citizenship from below, which is different from participatory approaches in which children are offered participation in adult decision-making, since he considers that in these approaches the possibilities of children's action are limited within a space predefined by adults. Citizenship from below is expressed when children themselves establish the goals that they wish to achieve and choose the way they want to act.

15.4 Public Policies to Overcome Children's Vulnerability

The role of children as protagonists and the development of their freedom are not only related to the autonomy or independence they may enjoy but are also based on an active relationship with the world around them. This relationship is closely connected with the social structure in which their lives unfold, and it provides them with an opportunity to play an active role in society (Liebel, 2008).

The consolidation of universal social protection systems, sensitive to children's rights and which guarantee child allowance, is essential (Tonon, 2022c). At this point, we ought to define the concept of the social protection system, and in this process we follow Sen (2000), who defines it as a stable social protection network and further makes reference to extraordinary aid that the citizens receive from the state in emergencies, such as floods or wildfires. According to Sen (2000), the improvement of a population's living conditions responds to two possible models: first, economic growth, which implies base broadening; that is, a general expansion of social welfare, and second, social policies generated by the government, founded on health, education, and social welfare. This scenario calls for citizen participation, regarded as a policy cycle process which consists of civic organising strategies, in order to defend their rights and satisfy their needs, thus exerting an influence on the public policy making process, and furthermore, bridging the gap between state and society. In this sense, these two poles—the state and the society—would be regarded as complementary rather than antagonistic (Espinoza, 2009).

Linares Ponton and Velez (2007) state that promoting children's participation in concrete actions that improve their lives and those of the members of their communities is a strategy aimed at transforming the democratic culture not only of children but also of their community, situating them as social subjects capable of contributing to the transformation of their environment. Therefore, to decrease children's vulnerability, it is necessary to promote the inclusion of the child's voice in decision-making bodies, encourage community participation in relation to the problems that concern children, and generate learning spaces in which both children and adults may acquire the skills for the necessary competencies for responsible participation (Linares Ponton & Velez, 2007).

15.5 Conclusion

Constructing knowledge regarding quality of life and well-being, and understanding the sources of the vulnerability of children facilitates a closer inspection of a group of peculiar characteristics, special outlooks on the dimensions and variables contemplated in research studies on child well-being, and therefore children as subjects of law as established in the Convention on the Rights of the Child (Tonon, 2016). We need to remember that three decades ago Quotrup (1990) already expressed that childhood was a particular and distinct form of the social structure, a permanent social category, which was exposed to the same forces as adulthood but in a particular way, being in turn subjected to tendencies of parentification and marginalisation. Considering this, when making reference to childhood, it is vital to regard this stage of life as a present state, in which multiple factors converge allowing peculiarities in a boy or girl to emerge, with their own problems and expectations derived from the social, cultural, and economic context in which they build their biographies (Mieles Barrera & Tonon, 2015).

It is imperative to overcome the stereotyped views and deep-rooted beliefs of adults, which set up barriers that hinder the various ways of approaching different situations, often unexpected, that might be valued positively or negatively by children (Mieles Barrera & Tonon, 2015). This is because being aware of the real situation of childhood—from its own perspective—will allow us to better understand the type of society in which we live, as well as the particular way in which each society values the life experience of childhood. It is clear that active child participation is required in public policy making processes in order to tackle children's needs and problems—for it is the children themselves who can best express their thoughts and feelings, because "child participation is part of a movement towards the construction of a fair, democratic, and inclusive culture" (Corona Caraveo & Linares Pontón, 2007, p. 14).

Moreover, the production of knowledge and methodologies that integrate children makes visible the need to develop the interdisciplinary work that delves into the complexity of childhood and generates their empowerment and public recognition as protagonists of the entire research process (Mieles Barrera & Tonon, 2015). If we merely continue to consider the opinions of adults, no matter how well-intentioned they may be, the task of policymaking to tackle child vulnerability will remain incomplete, as the true protagonists—children—lack a leading role in that process and their vulnerability in terms of personal, social, political, economic, environmental, and situational circumstances remains unresolved. In other words, if our intention is to build a democratic society, we need children's participation as active citizens. That is our challenge.

Acknowledgement Work on this chapter was supported by a grant from the Estonian Research Council (PRG700).

Competing Interests The author has no conflicts of interest to declare that are relevant to the content of this chapter.

References

Bauman, Z. (2006). *En busca de la política*. Fondo de Cultura Económica.

Bonetti, L. (2017). *Políticas públicas por dentro*. CLACSO.

Castillo García, J. (2007). La configuración de las ciudadanías en estudiantes universitarios y universitarias de pregrado en Manizales, Colombia. *En Revista Latinoamericana de Ciencias Sociales, Niñez y Juventud, Manizales, 5*(2), 755–809.

Corona Caraveo, Y., & Linares Pontón, M. E. (2007). Promoviendo la participación infantil y juvenil en el marco de la construcción de ciudadanía. In Y. Corona Caraveo & M. E. Linares Pontón (Eds.), *Participación infantil y juvenil en América Latina* (pp. 1–16). Universidad Autónoma Metropolitana-México.
Espinoza, M. (2009). La participación ciudadana como una relación socio-estatal acotada por la concepción de democracia y ciudadanía. *Andamios, 4*(10), 71–109. https://andamios.uacm.edu.mx/index.php/andamios/article/view/169/154
Fitoussi, J., & Rosanvallon, P. (2006). *La nueva era de las desigualdades*. Manantial.
Fleury, S. (1997). *Estado sin ciudadanos*. Lugar Editorial.
IAWGCP. (2008). *Children as active citizens*. ECPAT international, knowing children, plan international, save the children sweden, save the children UK, UNICEF and World Vision.
Iguiñiz Echeverrìa, J., & Tonon de Toscano, G. (2014). Políticas públicas y libertad. In M. Nebel, P. Flores-Crespo, & M. T. Herra (Eds.), *Desarrollo como libertad en Amèrica Latina. Fudamentos y aplicaciones* (pp. 297–305). Universidad Iberoamericana.
Isin, E. F., & Turner, B. (Eds.). (2003). *Handbook of citizenship studies*. Sage.
Kymlicka, W. (1996). *Ciudadanía multicultural*. Paidós.
Lawy, R., & Biesta, G. (2006). Citizenship-as-practice: The educational implications of an inclusive and relational understanding of citizenship. *British Journal of Educational Studies, 54*(1), 34–50. https://doi.org/10.1111/j.1467-8527.2006.00335.x
Liebel, M. (2008). Citizenship from below: Children's rights and social movements. In A. Invernizzi & J. William (Eds.), *Children and citizenship* (pp. 32–43). Sage.
Liebel, M., & Saadi, I. (2012). La participación infantil ante el desafío de la diversidad cultural. *Desacatos, 39*, 123–140.
Linares Ponton, M. E., & Velez, H. (2007). Las niñas y los niños como agentes de cambio social. In Y. Corona Caraveo & M. E. Linares Pontón (Eds.), *Participación infantil y juvenil en América Latina* (pp. 217–255). Universidad Autònoma Metropolitana-Mèxico.
Lister, R. (2008). Unpacking children's citizenship. In A. Inernizzi & J. Williams (Eds.), *Children and citizenship* (pp. 9–19). Sage.
Mackenzie, C., Rogers, W., & Dodds, S. (2013). *Vulnerability. New essays in ethics and feminist philosophy*. Oxford University Press.
Malone, K., & Hartung, C. (2010). Challenges of participatory practice with children. In B. Percy-Smith & N. Thomas (Eds.), *A handbook of children and young people's participation. Perspectives from theory and practice* (pp. 24–38). Taylor and Francis Group.
Mayntz, R. (1986). Corporate actors in public policy: Changing perspectives in policy analysis. *Norsk Statsvitenskapelig Tidsskrift, 2*(3), 7–25.
Mieles Barrera, M. D., & Tonon, G. (2015). *Calidad de vida y niñez, perspectivas desde la investigación cualitativa*. Universidad del Magdalena.
Moses, S. (2008). Children and participation in South Africa: An overview. *International Journal of Children's Rights, 16*, 327–342.
Przeworski, A. (1998). *Democracia sustentable*. Paidos.
Quotrup, J. (1990). *Childhood as a social phenomenon. An introduction to a series of National reports. Eurosocial Report 36*. European Center.
Rawls, J. (1996). *El liberalismo político*. CRITICA.
Regonini, G. (1989). *El estudio de las políticas públicas. Documentación Administrativa /n.u 224–225* (octubre 1990 – marzo 1991) (pp. 59–87). https://revistasonline.inap.es/index.php/DA/article/view/5206/5260
Sandoval Moya, J. (2003). Ciudadanía y juventud: el dilema entre la integración social y la diversidad cultural. *Última Década, 19*. https://doi.org/10.4067/S0718-22362003000200003
Scartascini, C., Spiller, P., Stein, E., & Tommasi, M. (2011). *El juego político en América Latina: ¿Cómo se deciden las políticas públicas?* BID.
Schweiger, G., & Graf, G. (2015). *A philosophical examination of social justice and child poverty*. Palgrave Macmillan. https://doi.org/10.1057/9781137426024

Seibold, J. (1999). Ciudadanía, transformación educativa e imaginario social urbano. In J. Scanonne & V. Santuc (Eds.), *Lo político en América Latina* (pp. 463–511). Editorial Bonum.
Sen, A. (2000). *Desarrollo y libertad*. Editorial Planeta.
Sirvent, M. T. (1994). *Educación de adultos: Investigación y participación*. Desafíos y contradicciones.
Sirvent, M. T. (2010). La investigación acción participativa y la animación socio-cultural. Su papel en la participación ciudadana. *ATPS, 1*, 61–74. https://edition.uqam.ca/atps/article/view/84/8
Somers, M. (1997). ¿Qué hay de político o de cultural en la cultura política y en la esfera pública? Hacia una sociología histórica de la formación de conceptos. *Zona Abierta, 77*(78), 31–94. https://dialnet.unirioja.es/ejemplar/5061
Taylor, C. (1993). *El multiculturalismo y la política del reconocimiento*. Fondo de Cultura Económica.
Tonon, G. (2001). *Maltrato Infantil intrafamiliar: una propuesta de intervención*. Espacio Editorial.
Tonon, G. (2012). *Young people's quality of life and construction of citizenship*. Springer briefs in well-being and quality of life research. Springer.
Tonon, G. (2016). Introducción: UNICOM y la historia del proyecto. In G. Tonon, C. Mikkelsen, L. R. de la Vega, & W. Toscano (Eds.), *Investigar la calidad de vida con niños y niñas* (Vol. 8, pp. 6–10). Colección Científica UNICOM.
Tonon, G. (2020). The new role of the university in community development. In R. Phillips (Ed.), *The research handbook on community development* (pp. 407–415). Edward Elgar Publishing.
Tonon, G. (2021). El rol de la ciudadanía en los sistemas de protección social: una mirada desde el enfoque de capacidades de Amartya Sen. In N. Zambam, J. Kraemer Bortoloti, & Z. Pierdoná (Eds.), *Estudos sobre Amartya Sen. Volumen 10. Protecao Social e Debate Público* (pp. 310–319). IMED.
Tonon, G. (2022a). Children's participation in South America: A proposal based in the capability approach. In G. Tonon (Ed.), *Redefining children's participation in the countries of the South* (pp. 1–14). Kindheit – Bildung – Erziehung. Philosophische Perspektiven Series. Metzler- Springer.
Tonon, G. (Ed.) (2022b). Key actors in public policy makers for quality of life. *Facilitators and obstacles*. Human well-being research and policy making series. Springer.
Tonon, G. (2022c). Children social vulnerability and social justice in the South. In G. Tonon (Ed.), *Social justice for children in the South* (pp. 1–23). Evidence-based approaches to peace and conflict studies series. Springer.
Tonon, G., Molgaray, D., & Laurito, M. (2021). El bienestar de niños y niñas durante el confinamiento de la pandemia por COVID-19. *Revista Ciudadanías: de políticas urbanas, 9*. http://revistas.untref.edu.ar/index.php/ciudadanias/article/view/1280/1047
Trostle, J., Bronfman, M., & Langer, A. (1999). How do researchers influence decision-makers? Case studies of Mexican policies. *Health Policy and Planning, 14*(2), 103–114. https://doi.org/10.1093/heapol/14.2.103
Veenhoven, R. (2000). Why social policy needs subjective indicators? In F. Casas & C. Saurina (Eds.), *Proceedings of the Third Conference of the ISQOLS* (pp. 807–817). Universidad de Girona.
Walzer, M. (1993). *Esferas de la justicia*. Fondo de Cultura Económica.

Graciela H. Tonon is Full Professor and Director of the Research Center in Social Sciences of Universidad de Palermo and Director of UNICOM, Universidad Nacional de Lomas de Zamora, Argentina. However, she is also a social worker. She is editor of the *International Handbooks of Quality of Life Series* (Springer), Associate Editor of *Applied Research in Quality of Life* (ISQOLS-Springer), Vice-president of Publications of ISQOLS and Fellow of HDCA, and Director of the *Journal of Social Sciences*, UP. She is a member of CUWB, and she received the ISQOLS Distinguished Service Award in 2016. She is also a member of the Argentina National Olympic Committee.

GPSR Compliance

The European Union's (EU) General Product Safety Regulation (GPSR) is a set of rules that requires consumer products to be safe and our obligations to ensure this.

If you have any concerns about our products, you can contact us on ProductSafety@springernature.com

In case Publisher is established outside the EU, the EU authorized representative is:

Springer Nature Customer Service Center GmbH
Europaplatz 3
69115 Heidelberg, Germany

The manufacturer's authorised representative in the EU is Springer Nature Customer Service Centre GmbH, Europaplatz 3, 69115 Heidelberg, Germany. If you have any concerns regarding our products, please contact ProductSafety@springernature.com

Printed and bound by CPI Group (UK) Ltd, Croydon, CR0 4YY
01/10/2026
02225863-0005